Contemporary Cases in U.S. Foreign Policy

From Terrorism to Trade

Ralph G. Carter, *Editor*
Texas Christian University

CQ PRESS

A Division of Congressional Quarterly Inc.
Washington, D.C.

CQ Press
A Division of Congressional Quarterly Inc.
1255 22nd Street, N.W., Suite 400
Washington, D.C. 20037

202-729-1800; 800-638-1710

www.cqpress.com

Cover Design: Ed Atkeson

Printed and bound in the United States of America

05 04 03 02 01   5 4 3 2 1

PHOTO AND ILLUSTRATION CREDITS: Cover (top), aftermath of the U.S. embassy bombing in Nairobi, Kenya, August 10, 1998, Agence France-Presse; (bottom) street advertisement, Beijing, May 25, 2000, Andrew Wong, Reuters; p. 222, the V-22 Osprey, Petty Officer 3rd Class Jason A. Pylarinos, U.S. Navy. Maps, p. 63, Gerry Quinn; p. 135, Debra Naylor.

Library of Congress Cataloging-in-Publication Data
Contemporary cases in U.S. foreign policy : from terrorism to trade / Ralph G. Carter, editor.
    p. cm.
  Includes bibliographical references and index.
  ISBN 1-56802-646-3 (alk. paper)
    1. United States—Foreign relations—1989—Case studies. I. Carter, Ralph G.

E840 .C66 2001
327.73—dc21   2001037361

Contents

Preface

The fall of the Berlin Wall in 1989 and the collapse of the Soviet Union a few years later ushered in an exciting, turbulent, and often puzzling time for U.S. foreign policy. Although expectations for a more peaceful world built on a foundation of liberal democracies have not been fulfilled, the international system has not descended into a violent "clash of civilizations" either. Instead, the post–cold war era has been marked by a wide range of new and traditional foreign policy challenges. Military conflicts and national security issues continue to occupy the spotlight, and less traditional foreign policy concerns have emerged. Human rights, trade matters, and the broader U.S. role in the international community moved to the front burner, as foreign policy making became a much more complex and crowded affair than it had been during the cold war.

Major foreign policy issues are no longer confined to national security concerns and cold war competition, and White House and top administrative officials are not the only policy makers. Although at times a president still can act more or less unilaterally in making policy—as in the case of the air strikes on Afghanistan, Sudan, and Iraq during the Clinton administration—presidential preeminence has diminished. Domestic and international interest groups, nongovernmental organizations, and members of Congress are actively challenging the executive branch's ability to direct foreign policy. In the post–cold war period, public opinion also seems to play a greater role in policy makers' decisions.

This historic shift in the policy process raises new questions. Can international institutions contain ethnic violence? Will disgruntled U.S. domestic actors create a new cold war with China? Will the international economy be marked by trade wars between regions and free trade within them? Will terrorist activity lead to more intrusive internal security efforts? What is more important to U.S. foreign policy: human rights or corporate profits and market share? These questions and similar concerns prompted the conception of this book.

Each of the fifteen case studies speaks to a foreign policy process that has become more open, pluralistic, and deeply partisan. With the dramatic increase in the number of congressional subcommittees in the 1970s, followed by the explosive growth of the electronic media in the 1980s and 1990s, individuals and groups now have more points of access through which to participate in policy making. These new actors have their own needs, interests, and agendas. They are more partisan as well, with Democrats and Republicans vying to put *their* foreign policy agenda or policy alternatives forward. In short, U.S. foreign policy making now resembles U.S. domestic policy making—it has become political.

Jurisdictional competition between the president and Congress over the control and direction of foreign policy marks most of the cases presented here. Even members of the president's own party resist executive leadership when they think the White House has trampled on the legitimate jurisdictional responsibilities of Congress. Another theme is that the opposition party regularly challenges the executive office. Such actions have led to "bad blood" between the branches, a situation that cannot help but strain the policy-making process. Finally, White House scandals—like the Monica Lewinsky affair and allegations of illegal campaign contributions from Indonesian and Chinese sources—have further weakened presidential power. These themes combine to reveal the chinks in the armor of the presidential preeminence model of policy making.

Using Case Studies in the Classroom

Although many excellent U.S. foreign policy texts exist, most fall short in their coverage of more recent events and debates. This volume aims to cover contemporary incidents so that instructors can raise issues confronting today's policy makers. Each case study is an original work written expressly for this volume and is organized in a format that places emphasis on the substance of the situations. A general description of the foreign policy–making process simply cannot capture all of the intricacies, nuances, and subtleties involved in the events chronicled here. The cases starkly reveal the human dimension of policy making in the 1990s and also help instructors show how a sitting administration in Washington often takes pains to attempt to do things differently from its predecessor, thereby extending the value of such a context well into the twenty-first century. In addition to showing students the human, political, and organizational faces of policy making, these case studies introduce them to the wide variety of issues and actors of the post–cold war period.

Students are presented with a "good story," filled with compelling characters and daunting challenges, along with a sense of why the issues are important and why particular policy choices were made.

A variety of pedagogical advantages have spurred interest in the case study approach within the international studies community. It is for good reason that military, business, public policy, and public administration schools have long employed this approach. For graduates to compete and perform effectively in the real world, they must first see the world as it is. Simplified models of reality may be necessary, but they are rarely sufficient by themselves. In the realm of foreign policy, theoretical models alone do not capture the messy nature of policy making. If instructors are to facilitate an understanding of the political arena, in which everything seemingly affects everything else, they must confront students with the policy-making dynamics illustrated by real world cases. Were policy makers consciously trying to make rational choices? Were they trying to balance power concerns on a regional or global basis? Were they more responsive to external threats or opportunities or to internal political pressures at home? Were they reacting to widely shared perceptions of reality? Did analogies mold their decisions, or were they just used to convey decisions to the public? These and other theoretical concerns are addressed through the case study method.

Case studies also promote critical thinking and encourage active intellectual engagement. None of the advantages noted earlier can be realized unless students ask themselves why things occurred as they did. Requiring students to reason, to consider alternatives, to decide on one alternative rather than another, and to communicate the reasoning behind that choice are skills integral to lifelong learning and success in any professional career.

Because different educational environments—seminars or large lecture courses, upper-level courses or introductory classes—require different teaching approaches, this collection includes a number of aids to help students and instructors get the most out of each case study. A series of critical questions at the beginning of each case ("Before You Begin") serves as a touchstone, giving students ideas to consider and later to review. Each case includes a brief chronology, noting the important events covered. A list of key figures appears as an appendix, which students can turn to as a reference tool and study aid. Collectively, our goal is to encourage students to think without crossing the threshold of telling them what to think. Finally, we provide instructors with guidance in using the studies. The instructor's manual includes a section on the nuts and bolts of case-based teaching as well as separate entries for analyzing

and discussing each case study. The manual can be found at http://college.
cqpress.com/ccusfp.

The Cases

The case studies in this book were selected to illustrate two important realities of the post–cold war period: the range and diversity of the old and new
issues facing U.S. foreign policy makers and the variety of participants in the
current policy-making process. The first set of cases is concerned with the ongoing questions of when and how the United States should intervene militarily. Interventions had always been considered "high politics," but in the
post–cold war period this situation has changed. Decision-making influence
now extends beyond the White House and top administration officials. The
story of U.S. policy toward East Timor is incomplete without acknowledging
the roles of interest groups—multinational corporations and human rights
organizations—and members of Congress. The Clinton administration's
decisions to intervene in the wars in Bosnia and Kosovo and to assist the
Colombian government in its fight against insurgents and drug traffickers were
significantly shaped by the administration's anticipation of how Congress and
the public would react; key members of Congress made their preferences clear
in these cases.

Changing military demands prompted another set of cases. Three of these
cases involve important challenges to presidential preferences. The Comprehensive Test Ban Treaty of 1996 is the most high-profile rejection of a treaty
since the Treaty of Versailles in 1919. Partisan pressures in Congress brought
about its demise, despite the president's advocacy for its passage. The story
of the V-22 Osprey reveals the determined inner workings of a strong sub-
government—comprising key members of Congress, the Marine Corps, defense contractors, and labor unions—to keep funds available for the aircraft in
the face of numerous attempts by the Bush administration to kill it. Critics,
particularly those in Congress, thought the Arms Control and Disarmament
Agency's time had passed and it therefore should be dismantled. The president
opposed the idea, but his hand was forced in a budget-cutting compromise.
Conversely, U.S. decisions to apply sanctions against India and Pakistan, after
these two states carried out nuclear tests, and to conduct air strikes against targets associated with Usama Bin Laden, after the bombing of U.S. embassies in
Kenya and Tanzania, largely reflect executive branch decision making that
would not have seemed out of place during the cold war.

Many observers predicted that the hallmark of the post–cold war period would be a new emphasis on trade and more cooperative international initiatives. The trade cases here highlight a diverse group of issues. The case of hormone-injected beef exports to the European Community shows the policy-making dynamics of a low-visibility issue, with major roles being played by trade industry representatives and administrative actors below the level of the president as they try to open the European market to American beef producers. The Helms-Burton Act highlights the influence of Cuban-American groups and members of Congress on U.S. Cuba policy as they struggled to maintain the U.S. embargo of Cuba while the Clinton administration attempted to loosen it. Finally, the case of the Clinton administration's engagement policy toward China is an illustration of a variety of domestic groups (and their congressional advocates) pitted against each other; business interests prevailed over human rights, labor, and environmental groups that were lobbying to deny China permanent normal trade relations with the United States.

The difficulties the United States currently faces in its relations with a range of international organizations are demonstrated in the final group of cases. Pressure from interest groups and Congress prevented the Kyoto Protocol on global warming from being submitted to the Senate for ratification. To gain approval of desperately needed additional loan capital for the International Monetary Fund following the 1997–1998 Asian financial crisis, the Clinton administration had to agree to congressional opponents' demands to seek reform in how the IMF conducted business. Finally, congressional pressures and Defense Department concerns forced the Clinton administration to attempt to weaken the authority of the new International Criminal Court against the wishes of more than 100 other nations. These are a few examples of the wide range and diversity of U.S. foreign policy making in the post–cold war era.

Acknowledgments

This book, as is always the case, has benefited from the efforts of many individuals. First, my thanks to the authors of the case studies. They volunteered to write the cases that interested them, but then they were willing to make all the changes that the CQ editors, a number of referees and reviewers, and I requested. I also appreciate the degree to which they produced their chapters in a timely fashion. Second, a number of colleagues and friends have provided valuable assistance at various stages of this process. I must thank Jim Scott, Heidi Hobbs, Steve Hook, Doug Van Belle, Pat Haney, Jeff Lantis, and Dave Waselkow for all their advice and assistance. Getting good help when you need it is a treasure, and this volume is better as a result of their respective contributions.

I also want to thank Lynn Kuzma at the University of Southern Maine, James Lindsay at the Brookings Institution, Brandon Prins at the University of New Orleans, Helen Purkitt at the U.S. Naval Academy, and Michael Sullivan at the University of Arizona for their careful review of the initial book proposal. Their suggestions improved the resulting volume. Jean Garrison at the University of Wyoming, Karen Rasler at Indiana University, and Brandon Prins reviewed the entire manuscript, and their constructive suggestions were deeply appreciated. This volume has benefited from their careful reading.

Luckily for me, the professionals at CQ Press have also been great to work with. First, I have been extremely fortunate to work with Charisse Kiino from the start of this project. Her early and consistent support is deeply appreciated, as are all the helpful suggestions she made along the way. She really guided this project, and I appreciate all of her help and counsel. Second, Amy Briggs helped to sharpen the case studies and to transform them from fifteen disparate cases into a more unified set. Her expertise and good judgment were invaluable as well. Robin Surratt's careful copy editing further improved the writing, and Elizabeth Jones added editorial assistance as well.

Finally, I must thank those closest to me. First, Nita has been wonderful throughout the long life of this project. Her understanding and encouragement, particularly on the many nights and weekends when I had to work, helped me keep my focus on the job at hand. Her consistent support has been instrumental to the successful completion of this project. Second, I also need to thank my extended family and friends. They too have been supportive and understanding when my work pulled me away at times. I am truly fortunate to be surrounded by caring individuals.

Contributors

UMA BALAKRISHNAN is associate professor of government and politics at St. John's University, Jamaica, New York. Her research interests include sustainable development, human rights, international law and regime creation, and gender issues. She is the author of the forthcoming *International Regimes and Global Warming* (2001). She holds a Ph.D. from the University of Notre Dame.

RALPH G. CARTER is professor of political science at Texas Christian University. His research interests are U.S. trade, defense, and foreign policies and the domestic sources of policy making, with particular attention on the role of Congress. He is the co-author of *Making American Foreign Policy* (1994, 1996). He is a past president of the Foreign Policy Analysis section of the International Studies Association and has served on ISA's executive committee and on the program committee of the American Political Science Association. His Ph.D. is from Ohio State University.

DOUGLAS C. FOYLE is assistant professor of government at Wesleyan University, where he specializes in international relations and U.S. foreign policy. His research focus is the connection between public opinion and foreign and national security policy and how impending elections affect the manner in which leaders confront international threats. He has a Ph.D. from Duke University and is the author of *Counting the Public In: Presidents, Public Opinion, and Foreign Policy* (1999).

GREGORY P. GRANGER is assistant professor of political science at Northwestern State University in Natchitoches, Louisiana. His teaching and research interests are in the areas of U.S. foreign policy and international institutions, with an emphasis on arms control and transatlantic relations. He is the co-author of *International Organizations: A Comparative Approach to the Management of Cooperation* (2001) and vice president of the Louisiana Political Science Association. He holds a Ph.D. from the University of New Orleans.

PATRICK J. HANEY is associate professor of political science at Miami University in Oxford, Ohio. His research interests are U.S. foreign policy, crisis decision making, and U.S. Cuba policy. He is the author of *Organizing for Foreign Policy* (1997) and co-author with Walt Vanderbush of articles on U.S. Cuba policy that have recently appeared in *Political Science Quarterly* and *International Studies Quarterly.* He is also a past president of the Active Learning in International Affairs section of the International Studies Association.

RYAN C. HENDRICKSON is assistant professor of political science at Eastern Illinois University. His research interests are the U.S. use of force abroad and NATO's evolution after the cold war. His research has been published in *European Security, Parameters, Political Science Quarterly, Presidential Studies Quarterly, Security Dialogue,* and *Studies in Conflict and Terrorism.*

JENNIFER S. HOLMES is assistant professor of government and politics and political economy at the University of Texas at Dallas. Her major area of research concerns democratic stability, which she examines in terms of regime change (with an emphasis on Latin America and southern Europe), the consequences of terrorism and state repression, and the effects of the drug trade and dollarization. She is the author of *Terrorism and Democratic Stability* (2001) and received her Ph.D. from the University of Minnesota.

STEVEN W. HOOK is associate professor of political science at Kent State University. He is author of *National Interest and Foreign Aid* (1995), co-author with John Spanier of *American Foreign Policy since World War II* (15th ed., 2000), and editor of *Foreign Aid toward the Millennium* (1996) and *Comparative Foreign Policy: Adaptation Strategies of the Great and Emerging Powers* (forthcoming). He currently chairs the foreign policy section of the American Political Science Association.

DONALD W. JACKSON is Herman Brown Professor of Political Science at Texas Christian University. His current research interests include methods of international human rights enforcement and democratic transitions in Central America, focusing on the rule of law, on which he has written a series of articles on El Salvador and Guatemala with Mike Dodson. He is the author of *Even the Children of Strangers: Equality under the U.S. Constitution* (1992) and *The United Kingdom Confronts the European Convention on Human Rights* (1997) and co-editor of *Presidential Leadership and Civil Rights Policy* (1995). His Ph.D. is from the University of Wisconsin, Madison.

CHRISTOPHER M. JONES is assistant professor of political science at Northern Illinois University. His research interests are U.S. foreign and defense policy, with an emphasis on the domestic determinants of such policies. He has published a number of studies on the foreign policy bureaucracy and is co-editor with Eugene R. Wittkopf of *The Future of American Foreign Policy* (1999). His Ph.D. is from the Maxwell School of Citizenship and Public Affairs at Syracuse University.

JEFFREY S. LANTIS is associate professor of political science and chair of the international relations program at the College of Wooster in Wooster, Ohio. His research interests include foreign policy decision making in democratic states, international cooperation and conflict, and European politics. He is the author of *Domestic Constraints and the Breakdown of International Agreements* (1997) and co-editor of *The New International Studies Classroom: Active Teaching, Active Learning* (2000) and *Foreign Policy in Comparative Perspective: Domestic and International Influences on State Behavior* (2001). His Ph.D. is from Ohio State University.

JEREMY LESH is pursuing an M.A. in public policy at Kent State University, focusing on the areas of globalization, Sino-U.S. relations, and technological development. He provided research and editorial assistance for Steven W. Hook and John Spanier, *American Foreign Policy since World War II* (15th ed., 2000).

CHRISTOPHER ALLAN McHORNEY is associate professor of political science at Southwest State University in Marshall, Minnesota. His Ph.D. is from the University of California, Riverside. His research interests include proliferation issues and voting behavior in eastern and central Europe. He is the co-author with Brian Bates of *Developing a Theoretical Model of Counterproliferation for the Twenty-first Century* (2000).

ERIC MOSKOWITZ is associate professor of political science and chair of the urban studies program at the College of Wooster in Wooster, Ohio. His research centers on presidential decision making, U.S. racial politics, and the public policy–making process. He has also published on housing and neighborhood policy and contemporary U.S. decision making on foreign policy. He received his Ph.D. from Indiana University.

CAROLYN RHODES is professor of political science and director of the Mountain West Center for Regional Studies at Utah State University. She is the author of *Reciprocity, U.S. Trade Policy and the GATT Regime* (1993), *The State of the European Union: Building a European Polity?* (1995), *The European Union in the World Community* (1998), and *Pivotal Decisions: Selected Cases in Twentieth Century International Politics* (2000).

JAMES M. SCOTT is associate professor of political science at the University of Nebraska at Kearney. His teaching and research focus on U.S. foreign policy. He is the author of *Deciding to Intervene: The Reagan Doctrine and American Foreign Policy* (1996) and numerous journal articles and book chapters, co-author with Eugene Wittkopf and Charles Kegley of *America Foreign Policy: Pattern and Process* (6th ed., forthcoming), and editor of *After the End: Making U.S. Foreign Policy in the Post–Cold War World* (1998).

BEN TERRALL is a San Francisco–based writer and activist who has worked for Global Exchange, the East Timor Action Network, and other non-governmental organizations addressing human rights concerns in Southeast Asia.

WALT VANDERBUSH is associate professor of political science at Miami University in Oxford, Ohio. His research interests are Latin American political economy and U.S.–Latin American relations. He has published articles on the Mexican political economy in the *Journal of Interamerican Studies and World Affairs* and *Economic Development Quarterly*. He is the co-author with Patrick Haney of papers on U.S. Cuba policy that have appeared in *Political Science Quarterly* and *International Studies Quarterly*.

STEPHEN ZUNES is associate professor of politics and chair of the peace and justice studies program at the University of San Francisco. He has written about U.S. policy on self-determination for East Timor, Western Sahara, and Palestine. He is a contributing editor to the Foreign Policy in Focus project on self-determination.

Introduction

Ralph G. Carter

The dawn of the twenty-first century presents the administration of George W. Bush with significant international challenges. Bush's generation learned about foreign policy during the "bad old days" of the cold war. Then, our attention was focused on the Soviet-U.S. relationship. The overriding goal was preventing nuclear war and possible global annihilation. Things are different now. In 1991 the Soviet Union broke into fifteen countries, and Russians and Americans are now trying to forge new cooperative relationships while still protecting their national interests. What should security arrangements entail? Should the United States offer aid to Russia and the other former Soviet republics? If so, how much and under what terms? How can trade be structured to benefit all parties? Can the United States and these new countries be friends and competitors at the same time?

Without the glue of anti-communism, the United States and its traditional allies and trading partners face the task of forging similar new cooperative relationships. Again, new questions have risen. Should NATO continue to expand? What should the United States' relationship be with the European Union? Are they friends or "friendly competitors"? What are the United States' interests in, and thus relationships to, Africa, Asia, and Latin America?

Global issues are also on the front burner. How should the United States react to regional conflicts, attempted genocides, terrorism, global poverty, and threats to the environment? How much should the United States depend on international organizations to pursue its goals? What place should international actors like NATO, the United Nations, the World Bank, the World Trade Organization, and the International Monetary Fund have in U.S. foreign policy? Should the United States lead these organizations, or should it act as a "first among equals" in a team-like environment? As the international arena has changed, so has the U.S. foreign policy process. Understanding the dynamics of this process is the goal of this volume.

Then and Now

U.S. foreign policy making has changed dramatically since the end of the cold war. These changes are evident in the external environment as well as the internal policy-making process.

The "Old" Foreign Policy System

With the exception of a few periods of "thaw," the cold war dominated U.S. foreign policy from 1947 until the demise of the Soviet Union in late 1991. The threat of nuclear war between the U.S.- and Soviet-led blocs put a premium on national security policy, and the U.S. foreign policy process evolved to meet that threat. As commander in chief, the president was at the heart of this process. Moreover, the National Security Act of 1947 gave him a lot of help—by creating a unified Department of Defense, the Central Intelligence Agency, the National Security Council, and the post of national security adviser.

Not surprisingly during this period, the focus of the policy-making process became the presidency and the executive branch. This process is well represented by the presidential preeminence model of foreign policy making, which views foreign policy as the result of decisions and actions by the president and his closest advisers and relevant other officials in the executive branch.[1] Other theoretical approaches were developed within the presidential preeminence model to reflect the processes by which presidential administrations made foreign policy. These included seeing their actions and decisions as

- optimal choices of a rational calculation of costs and benefits;
- choices between various bureaucratic routines appropriate to the situation; or
- the result of political processes played out within the administration by actors with differing degrees of power and interests in a particular issue.[2]

Members of Congress, interest groups, the media, and the public were seen as playing little or no role in the making of U.S. foreign policy.[3]

The "New" Foreign Policy System

Anecdotal evidence and the early results of scholarly studies suggest that with the threat of nuclear annihilation no longer an issue, the post–cold war era will trigger changes in the way in which U.S. foreign policy is made. The ability of the president to play a predominant role in shaping policy can be expected to diminish, and the roles played by a host of other actors should increase.[4] Two factors drive this expectation. First, the global economy has become more interdependent, and decisions made elsewhere now have greater influence on the United States. In short, intermestic issues—those that occur in the international environment but are reacted to as if they are domestic policy issues—are likely to be more common in the future than was previously the case. Take for example the possible ways of formulating policy toward China: Should U.S. policy be defined primarily as national security policy, thus mobilizing the State and Defense Departments to rein in China's ability to threaten U.S. security interests? Should it increasingly be defined as trade policy, mobilizing officials in the Department of Commerce, national and state chambers of commerce, trade groups, and U.S.-based multinational corporations that want to sell more to the enormous Chinese market? Should China policy be defined as "jobs policy," thus mobilizing members of the Labor Department and labor unions, whose members and leaders fear the loss of U.S. jobs to lower-paid Chinese workers? Or should it be defined as human rights policy, thus mobilizing the State Department's undersecretary for global affairs (under whose jurisdiction human rights issues fall) and interest groups like Amnesty International, Human Rights Watch, and Freedom House? In short, how an issue is defined determines who play active roles in the resolution of the matter.

Second, during the cold war, foreign and national security policies were deemed too important and too risky to let non-experts play an important role. Primary policy-making actors included the president, his closest White House advisers, and key officials from the foreign and defense bureaucracies—the National Security Council staff, State Department, Defense Department, and Central Intelligence Agency and other parts of the intelligence community. Congressional and public roles were generally relegated to supporting the actions of the White House, except in those instances of a major mistake in policy.

Now, however, there is no domestic political consensus regarding the central aims of U.S. foreign policy in the post–cold war era. Without widely shared norms that exclude their participation, more and more domestic actors can be expected to try to shape policy. Hence, we can expect more foreign policy activity by members of Congress through legislation (whether an administration likes it or not) and other actions that administrations often resent (such as holding critical committee hearings, using oversight rules to monitor the administration's foreign policy performance, requiring extensive briefings and reports by administration actors, and making speeches critical of administration policy). Members of the opposition party can be particularly expected to challenge the president's foreign policy in terms of ends pursued and means employed. Interest groups and other non-governmental organizations will get more involved also, lobbying government officials on behalf of their policy preferences, using the written and electronic media to get their positions before the public and government officials, engaging in letter-writing campaigns to influence officials, using campaign contributions to help friendly officials get elected, and so on. Members of the media and other pundits will use their access to editorial pages, television, and the expanding constellation of news and information outlets to influence foreign policy in their preferred direction. Finally, grassroots activists, public opinion pollsters, and others who claim to represent the public will get involved. Even the ability of the president to control his own administration may weaken, as bureaucratic actors become more active in policy making and become the targets of other actors.[5]

Thus, the unifying theme of this volume is that the U.S. foreign policy–making process is becoming more open, pluralistic, and partisan. It resembles more the decade leading up to World War II than the four decades that followed the war. One leading scholar summarizes the current period as follows:

> There now seems to be a *post–cold war dissensus* predicated on societal disagreement on the nature and extent of U.S. leadership, policy disagreement on the proper role, strategy, goals, and instruments of U.S. foreign policy, and procedural decentralization away from presidential leadership to more widely diffused involvement of actors from a wider circle of bureaucratic agencies, members of Congress, and non-governmental actors.[6]

In short, the foreign policy process is becoming more like the domestic policy process, and thus it is becoming more political. As President Bill Clinton said in 1995, "The more time I spend on foreign policy ... the more I become convinced that there is no longer a clear distinction between what is foreign and domestic."[7] More actors are involved, and they have their own foreign policy needs, interests, and agendas. Although the president still has impressive formal and informal foreign policy roles and powers, he is now less able to dominate foreign policy processes and outcomes than was the case during the cold war.[8] Presidential foreign policy "wins" may become less frequent than previously was the case, and they will most likely always represent hard-fought victories.

A number of other themes unify this volume. Jurisdictional competition between the president and Congress over control and direction of foreign policy is commonplace. Even members of the president's own party resist his policies if they think the White House is trampling on the legitimate jurisdictional responsibilities of Congress to legislate policy or appropriate funds. The opposition party can be expected to challenge the president's wishes and do so in a number of cases. For example, in what may be a worst-case scenario, congressional Republicans developed a visceral dislike for President Clinton. It seemed that Republican Party leaders Trent Lott, Dick Armey, and Tom DeLay and Republican committee leader Jesse Helms opposed anything Clinton supported. White House scandals like the Monica Lewinsky affair and allegations of illegal campaign contributions gave presidential critics another reason to oppose Clinton's desires. The high-water mark of their opposition was Clinton's impeachment. Such bad blood between the branches of government cannot help but strain the policy-making process. The themes discussed here reveal the chinks in the armor of the presidential preeminence model of U.S. foreign policy making.

The Case Study Approach

We often hear statements like "Today Washington announced ..." or "the United States responded by...." Such statements obscure the fact that it is specific individuals who "announce" or make the decisions to "respond." Saying "The United States decided to do X" is shorthand for the more accurate statement that a number of people acting in the name of the state decided to do X, usually for a variety of reasons. Case studies are perhaps the best way to illustrate how such individuals cooperate, conflict, and compromise to produce foreign policy.

The fifteen studies that comprise this volume are teaching cases. The definition of a teaching case is that it tells the story of what happened, "who was involved, what they contended with, and, sometimes, how it came out." [9] Rather than provide analysis of why things happened as they did, teaching cases rely on the reader to determine why individuals took the stances or engaged in the actions discussed. They vividly illustrate how policy making brings together individuals who see matters from different perspectives and who are motivated by an assortment of goals and objectives. Such cases also help show that these policy makers live in a political environment in which everything affects everything else; foreign policy decisions are not decided in a vacuum. They affect and are affected by other foreign and domestic issues at the time the policy is devised and into the unforeseeable future. Like the rest of the political process, foreign policy making can be a messy affair, and case studies help illustrate the process realistically.

One advantage of the cases in this volume is their contemporary nature. Textbooks usually cover the broad themes and theoretical issues involving foreign policy making, but often do not have many contemporary illustrations of what happens or how things happen in the policy-making process. These cases focus on issues and events that confronted U.S. policy makers in the late 1980s and throughout the 1990s. A second advantage of the studies here is their range. They were chosen to represent the array of external challenges and opportunities, substantive issues, internal political situations, and policy-making dynamics that seem likely to repeatedly confront U.S. foreign policy makers in the post–cold war world.

Each case study offers a unique perspective on the events, issues, and policy makers involved, but beyond their uniqueness are patterns in the influences at work. Where do the causal factors of U.S. foreign policy arise? According to realists and neo-realists, the answer lies beyond U.S. borders. These observers see foreign policy as a state's reaction to events arising in an international system based on anarchy and lacking a strong legal structure. In essence, states can be expected to pursue their self-defined interests in ways that are, at least at some level, rational.[10] On the other hand, advocates of liberalism argue that what happens within a state's borders also matters, often as much as (or maybe more than) external situations facing policy makers. Thus for liberals and neo-liberals, a central belief is "*state structures matter:* the structure of their domestic governments and the values and views of their citizens affect their behavior in international affairs."[11] According to this point of view, one cannot ignore who is in the government, what they think, and what motivates them. In short, different administrations and Congresses will react differently to similar external events. The cases in this volume illustrate the importance of external and internal factors and help us understand what U.S. officials have been dealing with in the post–cold war era. In this respect, they provide a realistic understanding of how policy is actually made. They remind us that people often have to make quick decisions based on less-than-complete information, and they help hone critical-thinking skills in preparation for real world situations.[12]

Each case opens with a section titled "Before You Begin," which poses questions about that particular case. These questions will help in organizing thoughts and directing attention to important issues. All the cases follow a similar internal organization. Each introduces the case, provides background information, relates events, and offers a conclusion that should help in identifying some of the broader issues or themes involved. Each study is accompanied by a chronology of events, and the major characters are listed in an appendix.

Case-based teaching requires class participation. Instructors ask questions, and students are expected to discuss what happened and, more important, determine why it happened as it did. Such active learning requires that students come to class prepared to contribute to an informed discussion of the day's case assignment, including putting themselves in the place of the major actors in the case in order to assess issues and events: Why did policy makers do what they did? What internal or external factors affected their decisions? Was that their only option? If not, why was that option chosen over others? What could be gained, and what could be lost? Students will get the most from this approach if they come to class having carefully thought about such things in addition to having reviewed the "Before You Begin" questions. Such preparation will make for a better understanding of the real world of foreign policy making.

As the cold war was ending, some observers of international politics began speculating about the nature of the post–cold war world. Many welcomed the optimistic assessment that international conflict would decline, and widely shared liberal values would become the new glue of international politics.[13] Unfortunately, violent conflict did not disappear, and not all people endorsed liberal values.[14] Consequently, U.S. foreign policy still deals with the difficult issues involving the use of military force and how to protect national interests in an uncertain environment. The first four cases in this volume focus on matters involving U.S. decisions on whether and how to participate in military interventions. In Chapter 1, Stephen Zunes and Ben Terrall illustrate the roles of governmental and non-governmental organizations in U.S. decisions regarding the territory of East Timor and the winning of its autonomy from Indonesia. In Chapter 2, Douglas Foyle examines the role of public opinion in the Clinton administration's consideration of what to do about the Bosnian civil war. In Chapter 3, Eric Moskowitz and Jeffrey Lantis examine President Clinton's responses to the humanitarian crisis in Kosovo, which ultimately resulted in a U.S.-led NATO bombing campaign against Yugoslavia. In Chapter 4, Jennifer Holmes examines the Clinton administration's efforts to slow the smuggling of illegal drugs into the United States by helping the Colombian government fight drug traffickers, a decision that many feel risked U.S. involvement in Colombia's long-standing civil war.

The next five case studies examine national security issues facing the United States. In Chapter 5, Gregory Granger looks at the dynamics that resulted in the abolition of the Arms Control and Disarmament Agency, a move predicated on the belief that nuclear weapons issues had receded in priority in the post-cold war period. Christopher McHorney revisits such nuclear concerns in Chapter 6, where he details the Clinton administration's reaction to the 1998 nuclear weapons tests conducted by Asian rivals India and Pakistan. The global effort to ban such weapons tests is the focus of Christopher Jones' examination in Chapter 7 of the Senate's 1999 rejection of the Comprehensive Test Ban Treaty. Beyond nuclear weapons issues, another national security threat facing the United States is terrorism. In Chapter 8, Ryan Hendrickson discusses the Clinton administration's air strikes on Sudan and Afghanistan in retaliation against suspected terrorist Usama Bin Laden following the bombing of two U.S. embassies in East Africa. Finally, in Chapter 9, Christopher Jones addresses the development of the controversial V-22 Osprey tilt-rotor aircraft by examining whether new threats should generate new military missions and whether new missions require new and expensive equipment.

Some observers thought the post–cold war world would be an era marked by international trade, so the next section of case studies focuses on trade issues. In Chapter 10, Carolyn Rhodes illustrates how differing politics and values can come between friends through an examination of the clash between the United States and the European Community over U.S. exports of beef injected with growth hormones. In Chapter 11, trade issues involving friends and enemies are examined by Patrick Haney and Walt Vanderbush in a discussion of the 1996 Helms-Burton Act. This controversial legislation upset U.S. allies and trading partners by imposing more unilateral sanctions on the Castro regime in Cuba. Finally, a wide range of trade-related issues come to the fore in Chapter 12, where Steven Hook and Jeremy Lesh look at the impact of an array of interest groups on the Clinton administration's decisions regarding trade with China.

A more liberal post–cold war world would be one marked by a greater reliance on international organizations, institutions, and law. The last section of this book examines how U.S. concerns mesh with the concerns of others in dealing with system-wide international issues. In Chapter 13, Uma Balakrishnan focuses on how the Bush and Clinton administrations dealt with the policy challenges represented by the global climate change convention signed in 1997 in Kyoto, Japan. In Chapter 14, Ralph Carter and James Scott review the political battle between President Clinton and the Republican Congress over the issue of providing more money to the International Monetary Fund following the Asian financial crisis of 1997–1998. In Chapter 15, Ralph Carter and Donald Jackson illustrate the Clinton administration's dilemma when faced with the question of whether the United States should sign the Rome statute creating a new International Criminal Court to try cases involving war crimes, crimes against humanity, and genocide. They do so with a focus on U.S. discomfort at possibly being subject to international law.

The cases here present the wide range of actors, interests, and issues in contemporary U.S. foreign policy. In the conclusion, we return to the book's primary unifying theme—that in the post–cold war period, U.S. foreign policy making is becoming increasingly open, pluralistic, and partisan. New issues are now found on the policy agenda, and many newcomers—agencies, interests, and constituencies—have involved themselves in addressing them. In short, U.S. foreign policy making looks increasingly like U.S. domestic policy making, and in a world marked by increasing interdependence between states, perhaps that is to be expected.

Notes

1. James M. Scott and A. Lane Crothers, "Out of the Cold: The Post–Cold War Context of U.S. Foreign Policy," in *After the End: Making U.S. Foreign Policy in the Post–Cold War World,* ed. James M. Scott (Durham, N.C.: Duke University Press, 1998), 1–25.

2. Graham Allison and Philip Zelikow, *Essence of Decision: Explaining the Cuban Missile Crisis,* 2d ed. (New York: Longman, 1999).

3. See, for example, Samuel P. Huntington, *The Common Defense: Strategic Programs in National Politics* (New York: Columbia University Press, 1961); Roger Hilsman, *To Move a Nation* (New York: Doubleday, 1967); Morton Halperin, *Bureaucratic Politics and Foreign Policy* (Washington, D.C.: Brookings Institution Press, 1974); John Steinbruner, *The Cybernetic Theory of Decision: New Dimensions of Political Analysis* (Princeton: Princeton University Press, 1974); Roger Hilsman, *The Politics of Policy Making in Defense and Foreign Affairs,* 2d ed. (Englewood Cliffs, N.J.: Prentice Hall, 1990); and Allison and Zelikow, *Essence of Decision.*

4. See James M. Lindsay and Randall B. Ripley, "How Congress Influences Foreign and Defense Policy," in *Congress Resurgent: Foreign and Defense Policy on Capitol Hill,* ed. Randall B. Ripley and James M. Lindsay (Ann Arbor: University of Michigan Press, 1993), 17–35; James M. Lindsay, *Congress and the Politics of U.S. Foreign Policy* (Baltimore: Johns Hopkins University Press, 1994); and virtually all of the selections in Scott, *After the End.*

5. Scott and Crothers, "Out of the Cold"; James M. Scott, "Interbranch Policy Making after the End," in Scott, *After the End,* 389–407.

6. Scott, "Interbranch Policy Making after the End," 405.

7. Quoted in Ralph G. Carter, "Congress and Post–Cold War U.S. Foreign Policy," in Scott, *After the End,* 129–130.

8. See Carter, "Congress and Post–Cold War U.S. Foreign Policy," 108–137; Jerel Rosati and Stephen Twing, "The Presidency and U.S. Foreign Policy after the Cold War," in Scott, *After the End,* 29–56.

9. John Boehrer, quoted in Vicki L. Golich, "The ABCs of Case Teaching," *International Studies Perspectives* 1 (2000): 12.

10. There are lots of sources on realism and neo-realism. For reasonably concise discussions of these topics, see David A. Lake, "Realism," in *The Oxford Companion to Politics of the World,* ed. Joel Krieger (Oxford: Oxford University Press, 1993), 771–773; and Allison and Zelikow, *Essence of Decision,* 30–33.

11. Allison and Zelikow, *Essence of Decision,* 39 (emphasis in original).

12. Laurence E. Lynn, Jr., *Teaching and Learning with Cases: A Guidebook* (New York: Chatham House Publishers/Seven Bridges Press, 1999), 2.

13. See Francis Fukuyama, "The End of History?" *National Interest* 16 (summer 1989) 3–16.

14. See Samuel P. Huntington, *The Clash of Civilizations and the Remaking of World Order* (New York: Simon and Schuster, 1996).

1 East Timor: Reluctant Support for Self-Determination

Stephen Zunes and Ben Terrall

Before You Begin

1. What was the basis of U.S. opposition to East Timorese independence in 1975? Why did the United States maintain this position until the 1990s?

2. Why was there not better knowledge of or opposition to U.S. policy toward Indonesia and East Timor prior to the 1990s?

3. Who were the major forces backing U.S. support for Indonesia? Who were the major forces backing U.S. support for East Timor?

4. Why were perceived U.S. economic and strategic interests initially seen as more important than concerns about human rights and international law?

5. How might the end of the cold war have affected U.S. policy toward Indonesia and East Timor?

6. What led to the growth in popular awareness of East Timor and opposition to the U.S. role in the ongoing Indonesian occupation?

7. How were grassroots human rights groups able to successfully challenge U.S. foreign policy toward Indonesia, an important ally?

8. Why did the media finally become interested in East Timor in the 1990s? What was the impact of increased media attention?

9. What are other foreign policy cases in which popular concerns regarding human rights and international law successfully reversed U.S. policy?

Introduction: The Conflict over Values and Power Politics

The United States has long prided itself on support of democracy and human rights, but Democratic and Republican administrations chose to ignore some of the most horrific human rights violations of the past half century by the government of Indonesia against the people of East Timor. A former Portuguese colony the size of Maryland, East Timor was invaded by its giant U.S.-backed neighbor just days after the Front for the Liberation of East Timor (Fretilin) declared independence in 1975. During a twenty-four-year occupation, Indonesian forces killed approximately one-third of East Timor's population. How could U.S. policy makers ignore or in numerous instances knowingly back such actions? What caused this policy to finally change?

The United States, reluctantly and gradually, began to acknowledge the injustice inflicted upon the East Timorese and eventually came out in support of East Timor's independence in 1999. The change in U.S. policy was brought about by the success of human rights groups and other non-governmental organizations in pressuring the Clinton administration to follow a policy more consistent with international law and universal standards of human rights.

Despite being couched in moralistic terms, most U.S. foreign policy decisions during the cold war were driven by concepts of power, influence, and geostrategic concerns, an approach known as *realpolitik,* or realism. Issues of human rights and international law were considered secondary. The rare triumph of popular moral outrage over realpolitik in this case followed Indonesia's 1997 financial collapse, which made the regime more dependent on others' goodwill and more vulnerable to international pressure. U.S. officials recognized that their ability to support Indonesia's economic recovery and to maintain a strategic relationship was threatened by growing popular concern over ongoing Indonesian atrocities in East Timor. In the spring of 1999, the Clinton administration backed Indonesia's decision to allow a popular referendum to determine the fate of the territory. In the wake of mass killings and destruction of property wrought by the Indonesian military and militias following the overwhelming vote for independence on August 30 of that year, the United States supported—albeit hesitantly and belatedly—an Australian-led United Nations–endorsed peacekeeping force to restore order and maintain stability during the transition to independence.

Background: Cold War Attitudes in the 1970s

In April 1974, the nonviolent Carnation Revolution overthrew the fascist dictatorship ruling Portugal. The new government began to ease out of its far-flung colonies, including East Timor, half of an island in a Southeast Asian archipelago that had been under Portuguese control for four hundred years (see map, p. 135). As political parties sprang up in East Timor, the Indonesian military launched an intelligence operation that backed the tiny pro-Indonesian Apodeti Party and encouraged divisions between Fretilin and the Union of Democratic Timorese, the two main pro-independence parties, resulting in a brief civil war in September 1975. The Indonesian army also

East Timor's Struggle for Self-Determination

April 1974   The nonviolent Carnation Revolution forces the overthrow of Portugal's fascist dictatorship. The new government begins to disengage from its far-flung colonies, including East Timor, which had been under Portuguese control for four hundred years.

September 1975   Indonesia provokes a civil war by supporting the pro-Indonesian Apodeti Party and encouraging division between two rival East Timorese pro-independence factions.

December 7, 1975   Indonesia launches an all-out invasion of East Timor hours after President Gerald R. Ford and Secretary of State Henry Kissinger meet with Indonesian president Suharto in Jakarta and give an apparent green light.

July 1976   Indonesia annexes East Timor.

1977   The Carter administration authorizes $112 million in military sales to Indonesia, including counterinsurgency aircraft. Widespread massacres and forced starvation of civilians ensue.

November 12, 1991   In the Santa Cruz cemetery in Dili, Indonesian troops gun down more than 270 unarmed civilians with U.S.-supplied M-16s. Western journalists film the killings.

December 1991   U.S. officials reassure top Indonesian military commanders of continued support in the face of international condemnation after the Santa Cruz massacre. The East Timor Action Network (ETAN) is formed.

October 1992   Congress votes to cut off aid to the Indonesian military, which was being provided through the International Military Education and Training program.

March 1994   ETAN, working with sympathetic U.S. legislators, successfully lobbies for a State Department ban on the sale of small and light arms to Indonesia.

November 1994   During the Asia-Pacific Economic Conference summit in Jakarta, 29 East Timorese students and workers jump the fence at the U.S. embassy and demand an opportunity to deliver a message of protest to President Bill Clinton regarding U.S. support of Indonesia's occupation of East Timor.

June 1995   Congress agrees to restore training assistance in ostensibly non-military subjects through Expanded International Military Education and Training, E-IMET.

continued on the next page

continued from the previous page

October 1995   President Clinton and other administration officials welcome President Suharto to the Oval Office and offer to sell Indonesia twenty F-16 fighters.

October 11, 1996   It is announced that the Nobel Peace Prize has been awarded to Bishop Carlos Belo and de facto East Timorese foreign minister-in-exile Jose Ramos-Horta.

June 1997   In the face of widespread opposition in Congress, President Suharto withdraws a request for aircraft and military training.

October 1997   An economic crisis sweeps across Asia.

November 1997   The White House offers to bail out Indonesia following the financial collapse in Asia. Congress votes to block the use of U.S. weapons in occupied East Timor.

May 21, 1998   President Suharto resigns in the face of mass demonstrations by pro-democracy students and others in Jakarta.

July 10, 1998   The U.S. Senate unanimously passes Resolution 237, expressing support for East Timorese self-determination. The House of Representatives follows soon afterward with passage of similar legislation.

January 1999   Indonesian president B. J. Habibie, Suharto's successor, offers the East Timorese a vote on independence.

May 5, 1999   Portugal and Indonesia sign an agreement in New York to send UN personnel into East Timor to prepare for a August 30 plebiscite on independence; Indonesia is granted responsibility for security arrangements on the ground.

August 30, 1999   The East Timorese vote on independence. Voter turnout is 98.5 percent, with 78 percent voting for independence.

September 1999   Indonesian troops and allied militia rampage in East Timor. An estimated fifteen hundred civilians are killed, several hundred thousand are displaced, and most buildings are destroyed.

September 12–14, 1999   The United States suspends all military relations with Indonesia and threatens to block multilateral monetary assistance. Indonesia halts military assaults in East Timor and allows Australian-led UN forces to enter.

October 1999   All Indonesian forces and allied militias withdraw from East Timor.

engaged in a series of cross-border attacks. Hard-line Indonesian officers were concerned about the prospects of a democratic and left-leaning government amid the archipelago and therefore wanted to annex the territory.

President Suharto, the Indonesian dictator who came to power in 1965, was reluctant to push the matter too quickly, despite being encouraged by Gen. Benny Murdani to launch a full-scale invasion of East Timor. An August 20, 1975, a Central Intelligence Agency (CIA) cable noted that "a major consideration on [Suharto's] part is that an invasion of Timor, if it comes, must be justified as an act of defense of Indonesian security. He is acutely aware that conditions of U.S. military assistance to Indonesia specifically limit the use of this equipment to defensive purposes."[1]

In December 1975, President Gerald R. Ford and Secretary of State Henry Kissinger visited Jakarta, the Indonesian capital. In meeting with President Suharto, Ford—who later referred to East Timor as a "lower-echelon priority" in U.S.-Indonesia relations[2]—gave what a CIA official stationed in Jakarta at the time called "the green light" for a full-scale invasion.[3] The invasion of East Timor was launched on December 7, sixteen hours after Ford and Kissinger left Indonesia. Kissinger publicly stated that the United States "understands Indonesia's position on East Timor," namely, that it not be allowed self-determination. Behind closed doors, Kissinger recommended that the United States suspend arms sales to Indonesia "for a few weeks and then open it up again." During discussions to arrive at a justification for continued U.S. military backing for Jakarta, he asked his staff, "Can't we construe a communist government in the middle of Asia as self-defense?" Kissinger also instructed U.S. ambassador to Indonesia David Newsom to avoid discussion of East Timor and limit embassy reporting, thus allowing "events to take their course."[4] The United States also stifled efforts by the United Nations in support of the East Timorese. Although the Security Council voted unanimously for Indonesia to halt its invasion and withdraw to within its internationally recognized borders, the United States blocked it from imposing economic sanctions or otherwise enforcing its mandate.[5]

Behind the U.S. Response

In the mid-1970s, the United States supported a series of right-wing military dictatorships in Asia, Latin America, and other parts of the Third World. During the cold war, the developing world was seen as a major battleground between the United States and its superpower rival, the Soviet Union. This period also saw an unprecedented expansion of U.S. business interests in the

Third World in mining, agriculture, and manufacturing. Rejecting Western military and economic dominance, nationalist and socialist Third World movements challenged what they saw as an attempt at U.S. hegemony. Some of these movements were communist led and allied with the Soviet Union, but others, such as the East Timorese movement against Portuguese colonialism, were not. Yet through the lens of realpolitik, virtually all such struggles were seen as zero-sum games, that is, a loss to U.S. interests meant a gain for the Soviet Union. Similarly, movements suspicious of foreign investment–driven models for economic development and advocating some form of socialism were often seen as communists and potential allies of the Soviet Union.

The rise of leftist movements throughout the Third World exacerbated this belief. The United States and its allied regimes had been defeated by communist-led movements in Vietnam, Laos, and Cambodia in the months leading up to East Timor's expected independence from Portugal. Some claimed a leftist government in East Timor would be another step in the spread of communism in Southeast Asia. The prospect of an independent East Timor, some feared, would provide the Soviet navy an additional base and threaten the ability of U.S. submarines to pass unimpeded through such deep-water corridors as the Ombai-Wetar Straits north of East Timor. Indeed, the adjacent sea lanes were among the most important in international trade.

In hindsight, these fears were greatly exaggerated. Fretilin, the dominant East Timorese nationalist movement, was social democratic in orientation and never received any support from the Soviet Union or any other communist country. It is extremely unlikely that it would have established an alliance with the Soviet Union; also, East Timor was far too small and poor to threaten any U.S. strategic or economic interests in the region. Yet, its being so "insignificant" in many ways allowed U.S. policy makers to overlook East Timor in the face of broader strategic interests. This small, remote island nation remained too far removed from the awareness of most people who might otherwise care about the humanitarian consequences of a U.S.-backed invasion.

The United States did not want to risk a confrontation with Indonesia, a staunchly pro-Western, pro-capitalist, and anti-communist country with the world's largest Muslim population and close ties to the Middle East. Following the energy crisis of 1973–1974, the United States felt a need to maintain a strong relationship with Indonesia, also one of the world's largest exporters of oil. Indonesia welcomed U.S. business interests. The fifth largest country in terms of population, Indonesia represented a huge potential market for U.S. goods. The United States also valued the strategic location of the islands, bridging the Asian mainland and Australia and linking the Pacific and Indian Oceans.

Continued Support for Indonesia, 1975–1991

From the beginning of the 1975 invasion, the scale of killing carried out by the invading Indonesian military was staggering. In the first few months of the occupation, the military, which faced unexpectedly tenacious resistance, killed more than 60,000 East Timorese. In one instance, hundreds of East Timorese were lined up on a dock in the capital of Dili and shot. President Jimmy Carter, in 1977, his first year in office, authorized $112 million in military sales to Indonesia, up from $13 million the year before. These sales included deliveries of counterinsurgency OV-10 Bronco aircraft, which allowed a dramatic expansion of the air war with devastating consequences.[6] When asked about U.S. law prohibiting arms transfers for anything other than self-defense, a State Department official asserted that because Indonesia had annexed East Timor, in July 1976, Jakarta's actions were a response to an internal rebellion, not an invasion. By the decade's end, as many as 200,000 East Timorese—more than one-third of the nation's pre-invasion population—were dead as a result of aerial bombing, massacres, forced starvation and preventable diseases, especially in the detention camps, where tens of thousands were eventually herded.[7]

Large-scale arms transfers continued to flow to Indonesia under the Reagan and Bush administrations. In the years subsequent to the 1975 invasion, the United States voted repeatedly with a minority of countries in the UN General Assembly opposed to East Timorese self-determination. As President Ford explained, given a choice between East Timor and Indonesia, the United States "had to be on the side of Indonesia."[8] The United States was one of the few countries to recognize Indonesian sovereignty over the territory, albeit with the acknowledgment that an act of self-determination had not taken place.

Despite a growing sensitivity about human rights issues among the American public and some liberal members of Congress, the U.S. role in East Timor was largely ignored during the first fifteen years of the Indonesian occupation. The geographic isolation and lack of media coverage, combined with the absence of direct involvement by U.S. personnel, led to the political opposition being slow to mobilize. What little public awareness did exist was a result of published research by academics, among them Ben Anderson of Cornell University (one of the country's leading scholars on Indonesia) and linguist and social critic Noam Chomsky of the Massachusetts Institute of Technology.[9] Political activism on the issue was limited to a tiny group of human rights advocates, church groups, leftists, and Portuguese Americans. Detailed journalistic accounts were largely limited to a few leftist and liberal public affairs magazines. On a practical level, East Timor remained a foreign policy item that could be pursued by successive administrations with little concern for public opinion or opposition from Congress.

Changing U.S. Policy toward East Timor

The movement opposing U.S. support for Indonesia's occupation of East Timor grew steadily after the November 12, 1991, massacre at the Santa Cruz cemetery in Dili, where Indonesian troops gunned down more than 270 unarmed East Timorese with U.S.-supplied M-16s. In contrast to many earlier such atrocities, Western journalists were present with cameras to record the killing of civilians taking part in a peaceful funeral procession for Sebastiao Gomes, a slain activist. Two of the reporters, Amy Goodman and Allan Nairn, who narrowly escaped a summary execution, became activists themselves, detailing their experience to members of Congress and at public presentations sponsored by churches and peace and human rights groups. Indonesia did not help its case when, following the massacre, its armed forces commander, Gen. Try Sutrisno, declared, "These ill-bred people have to be shot, and we will shoot them." Gen. Herman Mantiri later said that the massacre was "quite proper" because the East Timorese "were opposing us, demonstrating, even yelling things against the government."[10]

Internal State Department documents obtained by Nairn through the Freedom of Information Act show that in a December meeting in Surabaya, Indonesia, just four weeks after the Santa Cruz massacre, U.S. officials reassured Suharto's top officials that although Washington "understand[s] Indonesia is under considerable pressure from the world at large, we do not believe that friends should abandon friends in times of adversity."[11] Indeed, the State Department and Pentagon were so adamant about standing with Indonesia that they proposed doubling aid to the Suharto regime through the International Military Education and Training (IMET) program—designed to build relations with foreign militaries and train them in the use of U.S.-supplied weapons—and continuing to supply arms. A State Department spokesman explained that IMET would expose Indonesian officers to "democratic ideas and humanitarian standards."[12]

Growing Support for Independence

In response to the 1991 massacre and the failure of the U.S. government to respond, a small group of veteran human rights activists formed the East Timor Action Network (ETAN) in December of that year. Based in New York, the group during the next four years built on existing activist networks and through the Internet developed a nationwide presence, establishing a dozen local chapters with several thousand members. Although protests were held at Indonesian consulates, and educational events were organized all over the country, the group's main efforts focused on Washington, where ETAN challenged U.S. arms transfers and military training to Indonesian forces. The group organized phone banks and letter-writing campaigns, targeting key congressional committees and members at critical times in the legislative calendar. The new network developed its own base of supporters but also worked in coalitions with church and peace groups to reach larger numbers of people.

For the first time, U.S. aid to Indonesia became an issue for members of Congress. At a public event in Providence, Rhode Island, on March 13, 1992, Rep. Ron Machtley, R-R.I., condemned the Indonesian military killings in East Timor. Allan Nairn followed Machtley to the podium and asked him if he would commit to opposing IMET, which Machtley did in front of an audience of hundreds.[13] The result of the activists' sustained pressure was that Congress passed an amendment by Machtley and Rep. Tony Hall, D-Ohio, with assistance from Rep. David Obey, D-Wis., and Sen. Patrick Leahy, D-Vt., that cut off IMET funding for Indonesia.[14]

While running for president in 1992, Bill Clinton said that the United States had ignored East Timor in ways that were "unconscionable." During his first six years in office, however, Clinton's policy essentially mirrored that of his predecessors. Stapleton Roy, Clinton's ambassador to Indonesia, quite explicitly summarized the administration's policy when he said, "Indonesia matters, East Timor does not."[15] Richard Holbrooke, one of the principal architects of the Carter administration's policy, was appointed U.S. ambassador to the United Nations by Clinton. Holbrooke was not the only high-ranking Clinton official who supported the Jakarta regime. In the late 1970s, Stanley Roth, Clinton's second assistant secretary of state for Asia, had visited the country at the invitation of the Jakarta-based Center for Strategic and International Studies (CSIS) and had since maintained personal friendships with high-ranking Indonesian officials. He was particularly close with Yusuf Wanandi, a top official at CSIS who played a key role in secretly lining up U.S. and European support for the invasion of East Timor. Yet, the burgeoning human rights movement for East Timor provided a tough challenge to Clinton administration policies. During Clinton's first term, in addition to successfully lobbying to bar U.S. military training through IMET, ETAN's largely volunteer, grassroots campaigns blocked several weapons sales and raised the profile of East Timor in both the mainstream and alternative media. They also succeeded in reversing the United States' pro-Indonesia position on East Timor at the UN Human Rights Commission and pressuring Congress into imposing a State Department ban on the sale of small and light arms to Indonesia in March 1994. The grassroot opposition's victories and criticism from the halls of Congress built awareness of events in East Timor and the United States' role as Indonesia's chief arms supplier. A key element in the turning of the tide was the threat of floor debates in the Senate. Fearing that the administration's policy of supporting Indonesia's occupation of East Timor would be dragged before a national audience on C-SPAN, the Clinton administration was willing to accept the small-arms ban in order to avoid potentially embarrassing publicity.

U.S. support of Indonesia was made possible in part because most Americans, including members of Congress, were largely unaware of the situation in East Timor and U.S. complicity in it. As a result of increasing media attention, grassroots pressure, and congressional activity, the Clinton administration became the first U.S. government since the 1975 Indonesian takeover to face scrutiny of its policy on East Timor. The pressure had some effect on high-level communications between Washington and Jakarta. Though they did not argue openly for East Timorese self-determination, State Department and other administration officials did begin to express concern to Indonesian officials about human rights abuses in East Timor.

Despite these advances, however, the Clinton administration remained able to largely resist the growing pro-independence movement. Stanley Roth, then deputy assistant secretary of defense for East Asian and Pacific Affairs, strenuously opposed efforts to condition U.S. arms sales to Indonesia on human rights improvements in East Timor. In 1992 Roth had said that the United States would consider reducing arms sales only if the East Timorese suffered another massacre at the hands of the Indonesian military.[16]

Another important venue for organizing came with the release of the 1993 Canadian documentary *Manufacturing Consent: Noam Chomsky and the Media*, a biographical film about the linguist and his analysis of propaganda in contemporary U.S. society. The film, which was widely circulated in the United States, included a powerful section on the U.S. role in the East Timor tragedy. ETAN and other groups working on East Timor recruited hundreds of activists at movie screenings. Pressure on Congress and the administration increased.

During the November 1994 Asia-Pacific Economic Conference (APEC) summit in Jakarta, twenty-nine East Timorese students and workers jumped the fence at the U.S. embassy and demanded an opportunity to deliver a message to President Clinton. Simultaneously, uprisings organized by the un-armed clandestine front of the East Timorese resistance brought further media attention. Prior to the summit, Winston Lord, Clinton's assistant secretary of state for East Asia, declared that the president would only raise the issue of East Timor in private conversations and would restrict discussions to concerns about human rights. Because the East Timorese activists successfully grabbed the media's attention, Clinton was forced to respond to questions. Remarkably, he declared that the East Timorese should have more say in their own gover-nance, an unprecedented statement by a U.S. president.

In October 1995 prior to a presidental meeting with Suharto, legislators from both houses of Congress and both parties wrote Clinton regarding East Timor: "Violence in the territory has been on the increase, especially since the APEC in Jakarta last November. [D]uring the Summit, protestors were detained and, by most accounts, tortured at the hands of Indonesian soldiers. Other reports of deaths of protestors at the hands of Indonesian soldiers have continued all year."[17] That same month, Clinton—along with Vice President Al Gore, Secre-tary of Commerce Ron Brown, and U.S. Special Trade Representative Mickey Kantor—welcomed Suharto to the Oval Office, and during the meeting offered to sell Suharto twenty F-16 fighter jets. An administration official described Suharto to the *New York Times* as "our kind of guy."[18] The administration had earlier pushed for a resumption of unrestricted military training aid through IMET. Though Congress had suspended aid in 1992, the Clinton administra-tion evaded the restriction by *selling* the training. In June 1995, a new Republi-can Congress, despite opposition from many members, had restored training assistance in ostensibly non-military subjects through Expanded International Military Education and Training, or E-IMET.

Although the cold war had ended, U.S. policy continued to tilt strongly toward Indonesia. The vast archipelago, with its large cheap labor force and markets, was a model of the so-called Washington consensus for economic de-velopment based on foreign investment and an export-oriented economy. Though millions of Indonesians remained in dire poverty, the nation's econ-omy was booming, and enormous profits had created a wealthy elite and a comfortable middle class. Indonesia remained a country that the United States was unwilling to alienate over the fate of a small captive nation.

Increasing Pressure for Human Rights

Toward the close of the 1996 presidental campaign, the *New York Times* revealed that President Clinton's reelection efforts had been aided by legally questionable campaign contributions from wealthy Indonesian businessmen James and Mochtar Riady of the Lippo Group and their associates. Some of the subsequent media coverage made reference to the Clinton administration's support for Indonesia's occupation of East Timor. Although East Timor never became an election issue per se, the preelection scandal involving Indonesians with close ties to their government did allow for some rare open criticism of the Indonesian regime by leading politicians and an opportunity for critics of the occupation to receive some much-needed media attention.

Former Senate majority leader and Republican presidential nominee Bob Dole, R-Kan.—who only two years earlier had fought against the legislation restricting arms sales to Indonesia—dubbed the Suharto regime "a brutal military dictatorship."[19] Speaker of the House Newt Gingrich, R-Ga., called for a suspension of "any actions towards Indonesia until we've had a chance to review this," including a proposed sale of nine F-16 Falcon fighter planes to Jakarta.[20] Conservative columnists and pundits—including some who served in previous pro-Indonesian Republican administrations—began criticizing in print and other media the Clinton administration's support for the Indonesian occupation and serious ongoing human rights violations. East Timor had once primarily been the concern of a handful of liberal Democrats, but conservative Republicans had finally discovered it.

Opposition to U.S. policy toward Indonesia had never neatly followed party lines, however. Some Democratic representatives with close ties to U.S. corporations with investments in Indonesia—such as Rep. Lee Hamilton (Ind.) and Sen. John Breaux (La.)—were strong defenders of continued close U.S.-Indonesian ties. Similarly, even prior to the Lippo scandal, a number of Republicans had spoken out against Indonesia's occupation, including Sen. Malcolm Wallop (Wyo.) and Reps. Ben Gilman (N.Y.), Chris Smith (N.J.), John Porter (Ill.), and Frank Wolf (Va.).

One of the most significant developments occurred on October 11, when it was announced that the Nobel Peace Prize had been awarded to two East Timorese activists—Jose Ramos-Horta and Roman Catholic bishop Carlos Belo. Ramos-Horta, a bespectacled and soft-spoken former journalist, had been living in exile and working as East Timor's de facto foreign minister since 1975. Having previously spoken without honoraria to tiny audiences in the United States, this new Nobel laureate suddenly found himself in great demand as a speaker and talk show guest, explaining for the first time to millions of Americans the plight of his country and the complicity of the U.S. government in it. ETAN and other groups working on East Timor also received unprecedented media coverage and additional contributions, allowing for an expansion of their meager staffing and operations. At the same time, the Clinton administration and members of Congress faced pressure as never before to end U.S. support for the Indonesian military and to call openly for East Timorese self-determination.

The Nobel committee acknowledged that its intent in awarding the prize to Belo and Ramos-Horta was to mobilize international opinion on East Timor. The political impact in the United States soon became apparent. Throughout the first half of 1997, ETAN and other human rights groups campaigned against the planned sale of F-16s to Jakarta. Undaunted, the Clinton administration repeatedly announced plans to go forward with the sale. On May 20, a State Department official stated, "We remain committed to the sale of nine F-16s to Indonesia, but we don't plan to notify Congress formally at this time." Asked why formal notification had not yet been given, the official acknowledged that it was because the administration knew that Congress would likely block the sale.[21]

By late that spring, the Clinton administration informed President Suharto that while it could conceivably win a battle with Congress on the issue, it would not be easy and would likely result in a public airing of sharp criticisms of his military government. In June, Suharto wrote Clinton of his annoyance at the "wholly unjustified criticisms in the United States Congress against Indonesia which are linked to its participation in the [E-IMET] program and the planned purchase of the F-16 planes" and formally withdrew his request for the training and the planes.[22] Meanwhile, after years of silence, editorials in influential U.S. newspapers, including the *New York Times,* finally called for East Timorese self-determination. In addition, the Roman Catholic Church began taking an increasingly active role in supporting East Timor, a predominantly Catholic nation. The tide had finally turned in the public's perception of U.S. policy toward Indonesia and East Timor, as had the policy itself.

Still, there was considerable opposition to the growth of the East Timor support movement. A well-funded pro-Indonesia lobby had been in existence for some time. Coalescing in late 1994, the United States–Indonesia Society was backed by Indonesian intelligence operatives, Suharto's son-in-law General Prabowo, the Lippo Group, Chevron, Texaco, the mining giant Freeport McMoRan, and various former State Department, Pentagon, and CIA officials. Several oil companies and the Lippo Bank also funded an initiative to distribute educational materials to 10 million U.S. high school students "to increase understanding of a country that has long been a solid friend of the United States and a nation that offers a great number of opportunities for American business."[23] Although the United States–Indonesia Society was certainly influential, East Timorese activists were not up against a well-organized grassroots movement supporting a more hard-line U.S. policy like the pressure groups defending the government of Israel or opposing the Castro regime in Cuba. Indeed, the transparency of the powerful financial interests behind the pro-Indonesia lobby did little to enhance its credibility.

During the 1990s demonstrations, vigils and acts of civil disobedience organized by ETAN and other groups at the Indonesian embassy and various Indonesian consulates increased. The solidarity movement also infiltrated, distributed literature, and asked tough questions at pro-Suharto public events organized by the Indonesian government and U.S. corporations. It soon became difficult for Indonesian leaders to visit the United States without being dogged by pro–East Timorese demonstrators and reporters questioning Jakarta's East Timor policy. Support for Indonesian control of East Timor became an embarrassment for the Clinton administration. With the end of the cold war, backing for friendly dictators like Suharto was more and more difficult to justify to an increasingly skeptical public and Congress.

In October 1997 Indonesia was hit hard by the financial crisis sweeping across Asia. In November, as the White House was working on the financial bailout of Indonesia, Congress voted to block the use of U.S. weapons in occupied East Timor. A significant political milestone, this legislation implicitly recognized that despite claims of the Suharto regime, East Timor was distinct from Indonesia. As concern about human rights abuses in East Timor and in Indonesia itself continued to grow, Rep. Lane Evans, D-Ill., released documents in March 1998 detailing continued, illegal U.S. training of the Indonesian armed forces in urban guerrilla warfare, surveillance, counterintelligence, sniper marksmanship, and "psychological operations" tactics designed for military repression in East Timor and elsewhere.[24] The Joint Combined Exchange Training (JCET) involved at least thirty-six exercises in which fully armed U.S. combat troops worked with trainees consisting mainly of members of KOPASSUS, the elite Indonesian commando group notorious for torture, disappearances, and night raids on civilian homes in East Timor and Indonesia.[25] ETAN extracted maximum political capital from the release of JCET documents by holding a press conference in Washington at the same time that Allan Nairn, who had been banned from Indonesia as a "threat to national security" but nevertheless managed to slip back into the country, held a similar press conference in Jakarta. JCET training was strictly in violation of congressional intent, and the program was soon shut down over Pentagon objections.

ETAN's role was crucial in mobilizing public opinion and congressional action. Sen. Russell Feingold, D-Wis., the leading advocate for East Timor in Congress, acknowledged that he would have never embraced the issue were it not for the efforts of the Madison chapter of ETAN in his home state. Furthermore, Feingold noted, "The situation in East Timor, which was once unknown or ignored [in] the U.S., is today an important item on the foreign policy agenda. ETAN has been the driving force behind this sea change." He further noted ETAN's role in the series of legislative victories limiting military aid and training to the Indonesian dictatorship.[26]

By the spring of 1998, an unarmed popular uprising challenged President Suharto's rule. As repression continued in East Timor and the threat of mass killings of dissidents loomed over Jakarta, U.S. secretary of defense William Cohen stated, "I am not going to give [Suharto] any guidance in terms of what he should or should not do in maintaining control of his own country."[27] Cohen also pledged to restore funds for military training assistance to Indonesia and expand joint training.[28] Just ten hours before Suharto was driven from power, Secretary of State Madeleine Albright gave a speech in which she praised the Indonesian dictator for having given "much to his country over the past thirty years, raising Indonesia's standing in the world and hastening Indonesia's economic growth."[29] Suharto was forced to resign on May 21, 1998. B. J. Habibie, Suharto's handpicked successor, then became president of Indonesia.

Realizing that stability for Jakarta's elite required appeasement of a world community no longer tolerant of Indonesian brutality in East Timor, Habibie proposed general autonomy for the occupied territory. It soon became clear, however, that the East Timorese would not accept anything less than a valid act of self-determination, which would likely mean independence. On July 10, 1998, the U.S. Senate unanimously passed Resolution 237, expressing its support for East Timorese self-determination.[30] The House of Representatives incorporated language from that resolution into its fall 1998 appropriations bill. By January 1999 Habibie was willing to offer a vote on East Timorese independence. Portugal, Indonesia, and the United Nations soon began negotiating details of the referendum, though Jakarta would not allow direct participation of East Timorese leaders in the talks.

Meanwhile, the Indonesian armed forces increased their repression in East Timor, including the training and arming of pro-integration militias. These groupings were, at least publicly, led by long-time East Timorese collaborators. The real forces in charge, however, were Indonesian intelligence operatives. As violence escalated, the rank and file came to include increasing numbers of the

Indonesian military and police. Leaked documents indicate that while the Clinton administration was publicly pressuring Indonesia to sever its ties with the violent, pro-annexationist East Timorese militias, in an April 8 meeting, U.S. Pacific Fleet commander Admiral Dennis Blair privately reassured General Wiranto, the Indonesian armed forces commander, of continued strategic cooperation.[31] This vote of confidence came just days after a horrific massacre in Liquisa, East Timor, where Indonesian police backed up machete-wielding militia members as they slaughtered dozens of refugees in a church.

On May 5, 1999, Portugal and Indonesia signed an agreement in New York to send UN personnel into East Timor to prepare for a plebiscite in August. Despite warnings by the East Timorese and international observers, Indonesia was allowed to retain responsibility for security arrangements on the ground. As a direct result of this concession, more than 70,000 East Timorese were driven from their homes in the lead up to the vote, and untold numbers were killed or threatened with death if they voted for independence. Nevertheless, an impressive 98.5 percent of East Timorese voters went to the polls, and despite horrific levels of intimidation, more than 78 percent voted for independence.

Though they ultimately could not derail the process, in subsequent weeks Indonesian soldiers, police, and militias killed more than 1,500 civilians, demolished much of East Timor's infrastructure, and drove several hundred thousand Timorese into the mountains and into Indonesian-controlled West Timor. The occupation forces backed off on their campaign of destruction when the Clinton administration, under growing popular pressure at home, announced the severing of military cooperation and threatened the coordinated suspension of pending funds for Indonesia from the World Bank and International Monetary Fund. That it took the administration a full nine days into the post-referendum scorched-earth assault on East Timor to take decisive action showed that there was still a great reluctance to pressure its Indonesian ally. Widespread media coverage of the massacres—sorely missing during the massive bloodbaths of the 1970s—combined with intense activist organizing of popular outrage, made ongoing inaction by the administration impossible. On September 14, soon after the administration's announcement, the Indonesians and their allied militias reduced their attacks, began to withdraw, and were replaced by a UN-endorsed peacekeeping force led by Australia and with very limited U.S. participation. By the end of October, all Indonesian forces and their allies had withdrawn from East Timor. Democratic elections that month had brought forth Indonesia's first civilian president, Abdurrahman Wahid, though the role of the military remained strong. Suspension of military aid and training of the Indonesian military was upheld for the remainder of the Clinton administration though assistance through international financial institutions continued.

Conclusion: A Victory for Human Rights Advocates

A number of factors led the Clinton administration to reluctantly support East Timor's independence, reversing the policies of U.S. administrations going back nearly a quarter century. The end of the cold war and the increasing political moderation of Fretilin, which had previously identified with Third World leftist causes, undoubtedly eased U.S. concerns about an independent East Timor. Another factor may have been the enactment of the Law of the Sea Treaty, which lessened concerns about safe passage through the nearby straits. Profound dissatisfaction within the administration over the Indonesian regime's reluctance to abide by suggested International Monetary Fund reforms further weakened U.S. support for Indonesia. Although the United States did not link a bailout of Indonesia to the situation in East Timor, the perceived need to appease the Indonesian regime certainly lessened.

The Clinton administration did not want to see its ally weakened or distracted by East Timor in the wake of what was, to the United States, the far more significant problem of the economic crisis. As a result, the administration began throwing its weight behind more moderate elements within the Indonesian leadership, who hoped that a just solution would prove to be a relatively painless way of assuaging international criticisms of Indonesia's domestic political repression, its labor practices, environmental policies, and response to the economic crisis. The need to support Indonesia's stability and economic recovery was seen as more important than holding on to half of an island that Indonesian foreign minister Ali Alatas referred to as "a pebble in our shoe."[32]

One cannot ignore the effectiveness of the pressure applied by human rights activists. Their awareness raising and lobbying took a toll on foreign companies seeking investment opportunities in the archipelago, and on the regime itself, and helped create momentum for a diplomatic solution involving Indonesia simply wanting to wash its hands of the affair. The Clinton administration and members of Congress in both parties were clearly embarrassed about supporting a regime whose history of atrocities was finally noted by the mainstream media after decades of being ignored. Indeed, one of the factors that allowed U.S. support for Indonesia to continue unchallenged was the fact that prior to the late 1990s only a tiny percentage of the American people had even heard of East Timor or of the Indonesian military atrocities committed there. With increased public awareness through long-overdue media coverage and greater grassroots pressure on influential members of Congress—along with the post–cold war difficulty of making East Timor's independence movement appear a threat to U.S. interests—U.S. support of Indonesia's occupation became exceptionally difficult to defend.

The shift in U.S. policy toward East Timor is an important example of how U.S. foreign policy is becoming more pluralistic, more open to small but well-organized grassroots movements whose message includes a strong moral imperative that resonates with the majority of the public. These concerns, magnified by the news media, can influence elected representatives and thereby foreign policy. With a public less willing to tolerate support for regimes that violate human rights in the absence of an alleged communist threat, continued U.S. support for autocratic regimes and occupying armies such as Indonesia's has become increasingly problematic. Related to this is a growing skepticism among the public and the media toward political leaders who minimize the importance of such principles as human rights for narrow strategic or economic imperatives. With foreign policy becoming increasingly partisan in the post–cold war era, even politicians not known for their strong support of human rights and international law have found that they are able to capitalize on exposing an administration of the opposing party in league with a disreputable foreign government, as some Republicans did with the Clinton administration's pro-Indonesian tilt. For both principled and less-than-principled reasons, then, East Timor—long considered an irreversible victim of realpolitik—is now free, in part a product of the changing nature of the U.S. foreign policy process.

Notes

1. Cited by Allan Nairn in the foreword to Constancio Pinto and Matthew Jardine, *East Timor's Unfinished Struggle* (Cambridge, Mass.: South End Press, 1997), xii.

2. Ibid., xiii.

3. Cited in an interview of Philip Liechty by John Pilger in the documentary *Death of a Nation: The Timor Conspiracy,* directed by David Munro, Great Britain, 1994, 76 minutes.

4. Cited in Walter Isaacson, *Kissinger: A Biography* (New York: Simon and Schuster, 1992), 680.

5. Then-U.S. ambassador to the United Nations Daniel Patrick Moynihan later bragged in his memoirs how he had made the United Nations "utterly ineffective" in its

attempt to bring a halt to the invasion: "The United States wished things to turn out as they did, and I worked to bring this about. The Department of State desired that the United Nations prove utterly ineffective in whatever measures it undertook. This task was given me, and I carried it forward with no inconsiderable success." Daniel Patrick Moynihan, *A Dangerous Place* (Boston: Little, Brown and Company, 1980), 247.

6. Matthew Jardine, *East Timor: Genocide in Paradise*, 2d ed. (Tucson, Ariz.: Odonian Press, 1999), 42.

7. Asia Watch, *Human Rights in Indonesia and East Timor* (New York: Human Rights Watch, 1989), 253. Assistant Secretary of State for East Asian and Pacific Affairs Richard Holbrooke played a major role in formulating the Carter administration's pro-Indonesian tilt and the military aid package. Holbrooke would later downplay reports of Indonesian atrocities. In testimony before Congress on December 4, 1979, Holbrooke claimed that mass starvation in East Timor was simply a legacy of Portuguese neglect. "War Reduced E. Timor Population," *Facts on File World News Digest*, December 31, 1979, citing Holbrooke's written statement to the House Subcommittee on Asian and Pacific Affairs, December 4, 1979.

8. Jardine, *East Timor*, 38.

9. See, for example, "Ten Years after Integration," *Inside Indonesia*, December 1986; and Noam Chomsky and Edward Herman, *The Political Economy of Human Rights*, vol. 1, *The Washington Connection and Third World Fascism* (Cambridge, Mass.: South End Press, 1979).

10. Nairn, in Pinto and Jardine, *East Timor's Unfinished Struggle*, xx.

11. Allan Nairn, "Indonesia's Killers," *Nation*, March 30, 1998.

12. Nairn, in Pinto and Jardine, *East Timor's Unfinished Struggle*, xix.

13. Rebecca Hirschfield Brown, "Nairn Lauds Student Activism in E. Timor," *Daily Herald*, November 13, 1996.

14. Interview with Allan Nairn, San Francisco, December 1, 2000.

15. Cited in Noam Chomsky, "Comments on the Occasion of the Forthcoming APEC Summit," Znet Update, September 10, 1999, http://www.lbbs.org.

16. Conversation with Allan Nairn, San Francisco, December 1991. Roth laid out his position to Nairn and Amy Goodman at a meeting in Washington, D.C., December 1991.

17. East Timor Action Network, *Background on East Timor and U.S. Policy*, April 1998.

18. David E. Sanger, "Real Politics: Why Suharto Is In and Castro Is Out," *New York Times*, October 31, 1995.

19. Cited in Steven Thomma and Frank Greve, "Contributions to Clinton Challenged," *Post and Courier* (Charleston, S.C.), October 15, 1996.

20. Eyal Press, "The Right Discovers East Timor: Concern for Timorese People Used as Political Weapon," *Progressive*, May 1997.

21. Nicholas Burns, State Department spokesman, State Department press briefing, May 20, 1997.

22. Keith B. Richburg, "Indonesia Drops Plans to Buy U.S. F-16s," *Washington Post*, June 7, 1997, A1.

23. Eyal Press, "Lippo Goes to High School," *Progressive*, May 1997, 24.

24. "US Continues Training Indonesian Troops Despite Ban," *New York Times*, March 17, 1998.

25. Catholic church officials in East Timor noted that KOPASSUS was known to pick up young East Timorese, torture them to death and leave their bodies, sometimes

decapitated, in public as a warning to anyone sympathetic to the resistance. Lynn Fredricksson of ETAN, press conference, Washington, D.C., March 17, 1998.

26. Prepared remarks of Sen. Russell Feingold, "A New Currency of the Body Politic: Students Changing the Face of Political Involvement," Brown University, March 17, 2000, 3–4.

27. Reuters, "U.S. Pledges Support for Asia, Wants Reforms," January 11, 1998.

28. In response to a question about the message he conveyed by visiting Jakarta while the regime was being challenged by pro-democracy forces, Cohen replied, "It's simple. The United States is close to and loves the army." Nairn, "Indonesia's Killers."

29. Text of Albright's address at the Coast Guard Academy commencement, May 20, 1998, http://dns.usis-israel.org.il/publish/press/state/archive/1998/may/sd1521.htm.

30. U.S. Senate, "Regarding the Situation in Indonesia and East Timor," *Congressional Record,* July 10, 1998, S8015.

31. Allan Nairn, "U.S. Complicity in Timor," *Nation,* September 27, 1999.

32. Cited in Robert Kroon, "Jakarta Goal for East Timor: Autonomy," *International Herald Tribune,* February 3, 1999.

2 Public Opinion and Bosnia: Anticipating Disaster

Douglas C. Foyle

Before You Begin

1. How did pressures from the domestic and international arenas interact in the formulation of U.S. policy on Bosnia during 1993?

2. Why did the Clinton administration adopt the lift and strike policy in 1993? Why did lift and strike fail? What policy do you think should have been adopted?

3. Why did the Clinton administration believe that U.S policy toward Bosnia needed changing in the summer of 1995? Why did the administration choose to adopt a more active policy?

4. Why did the administration adopt a one-year deadline for an implementation military force (IFOR)? Were the maximalists or minimalists correct in crafting the IFOR mission?

5. How did public opinion affect decision making on Bosnia? How did its influence vary in the period 1992 to 1995? Why?

6. How did electoral calculations affect the foreign policy choices that were made? How were they similar or different during the 1992 campaign, in 1993 following the 1992 election, and in 1995 in the shadow of the 1996 election?

7. How did the United States' experience in Vietnam affect policy choices in the case of Bosnia?

Introduction: "What about Bosnia?"

President Bill Clinton and First Lady Hillary Rodham Clinton danced alone to the Marine Corps band after having dinner with visiting French president Jacques Chirac on June 14, 1995. Although the Clinton-Chirac summit was scheduled to deal with a range of international issues, Bosnia had dominated the meeting. At the end of the evening, the Clintons strolled over to a small group of the president's advisers that included Secretary of State Warren Christopher, Ambassador to the United Nations Madeleine Albright, and Assistant Secretary of State for European and Canadian Affairs Richard Holbrooke, who had gathered on the North Portico. The president asked abruptly, "What about Bosnia?"[1]

Although Clinton had made verbal commitments to send U.S. ground forces to Bosnia to enforce a possible peace agreement, implement a NATO plan to withdraw the United Nations Protection Force (UNPROFOR, composed largely of troops from European NATO nations) should that decision be made, or assist in the emergency extraction of exposed UNPROFOR units, he still believed that he could avoid sending troops. Holbrooke warned, "Hate to ruin a wonderful evening, Mr. President ... but we should clarify something that came up during the day. Under existing NATO plans, the United States is already committed to sending troops to Bosnia if the UN decides to withdraw. I'm afraid we may not have that much flexibility left." Taken aback that his previous commitments potentially locked him into sending troops, Clinton retorted, "What do you mean? ... I'll decide the troop issue if and when the time comes." An awkward silence followed. Holbrooke explained, "While you have the power to stop [the implementation of the NATO troop deployment plan], it has a high degree of automaticity built into it, especially since we have committed ourselves publicly to assisting NATO troops if the UN decides to withdraw." Christopher confirmed Holbrooke's assessment, "That's right.... This is serious stuff. We have to talk further about this." With that, the president and his wife strolled off.[2]

This conversation highlighted the dilemma Clinton faced: A peace agreement seemed a distant possibility, and UNPROFOR's withdrawal seemed the more likely prospect. Clinton knew that the insertion of American forces to protect UNPROFOR's removal would likely occur under hostile conditions and would surely result in casualties, possibly a large number of them. On the other hand, reversing his commitment could cause NATO's dissolution, thus gutting the foundation of the United States' policy for European stability in the post–cold war world. If he found no alternative, Clinton risked his worst nightmare—the involvement of American troops in potentially bloody combat as the 1996 presidential election campaign kicked off. For a president who came into office promising to focus on the economy like "a laser beam," how did he get himself into such a politically disastrous position?

Background: The Bosnian Crisis

For the Bush and Clinton administrations, Bosnia was the foreign policy problem that would not go away. Fighting in Bosnia, part of the former

Yugoslavia, began in early 1992 as Bosnian Serbs strove to include Bosnia in the new Federal Republic of Yugoslavia (consisting of Serbia and Montenegro) by attacking the multiethnic Bosnian government and non-Serbs (see map, p. 63). The republics of Croatia and Slovenia had declared their independence from Yugoslavia in 1991. Fearing domination by a Serbian majority in the reconstituted Yugoslavia, the Bosnian Muslims (44 percent of the population) sought to establish a united and independent Bosnia that would include the Bosnian Serbs (32 percent of the population) as well as Bosnian Croats (17 percent of the population). In hopes of containing the fighting, in September 1991 the United Nations imposed an arms embargo on all the territories of the former Yugoslavia. The embargo was followed in 1992 by UNPROFOR's arrival and international sanctions against Yugoslavia for aiding the Bosnian Serbs. In prewar Bosnia, the Muslim, Croat, and Serb populations were largely intermingled. As part of their war effort, Bosnian Serb forces drove non-Serbs, often in massive numbers, out of Serb-held areas in a policy that became known as ethnic cleansing.

At the outbreak of the war in March–April 1992, President George Bush concluded that Bosnia represented a regional problem unconnected to fundamental U.S. interests and decided to cede the problem to the Europeans. Despite reports of ethnic cleansing, on June 4, 1992, Bush observed, "Prudence and caution prevents military action."[3] Sensing an opportunity, Clinton's campaign team decided they needed to challenge Bush's foreign policy record and provide a more dynamic vision for U.S. foreign policy. Bosnia offered the opportunity to do both.[4] In early August, opinion polls seemed to indicate growing support for U.S. action to combat the growing humanitarian crisis brought on by forced migrations, ethnic cleansing, Serbian death camps, and attacks on civilians in Bosnia. When asked whether the United States had an "obligation to use military force in Bosnia" as a last resort to ensure the flow of aid and prevent atrocities, 54 percent of Americans surveyed favored the action, with 28 percent favoring it strongly. At the same time, the public split on Bush's Bosnia policy, with 38 percent equally approving and disapproving it.[5] As a result, Bosnia became the cornerstone positioning the Democratic challenger to the "right" of Bush on foreign policy. Clinton attacked, saying, "President Bush's policy toward former Yugoslavia mirrors his indifference to the massacre at Tiananmen Square [where the Chinese government put a bloody end to democracy demonstrations] and his coddling of [Iraqi leader] Saddam Hussein.... Once again, the administration is turning its back on violations of basic human rights and our own democratic values."[6] Some members of the administration

The Bosnian Crisis, 1991–1995

September 25, 1991 The UN Security Council imposes an arms embargo on all of the former Yugoslavia.

March–April 1992 War breaks out in Bosnia.

May 30, 1992 The UN Security Council imposes sanctions against Yugoslavia (Serbia and Montenegro).

September 14, 1992 UN peacekeepers are authorized for Bosnia by the UN Security Council.

February 5, 1993 The Clinton administration decides to deploy U.S. troops to enforce a peace agreement if one is reached.

May 1993 European leaders reject the proposed U.S. policy of lift and strike.

February 5, 1994 A Serb mortar attack hits Sarajevo's marketplace.

December 7, 1994 President Bill Clinton agrees to deploy U.S. troops to assist a possible withdrawal of the United Nations Protection Force (UNPROFOR).

May 1995 Bosnian Serbs attack Muslim safe areas. NATO launches limited air strikes against Serbian positions, and in retaliation the Serbs take peacekeepers as hostages.

May 30, 1995 Clinton agrees to use U.S. ground troops to help redeploy UNPROFOR within Bosnia if requested.

June 14, 1995 On the North Portico of the White House, Clinton's top foreign policy advisers contend that previous U.S. commitments virtually ensure the deployment of American forces.

June 21, 1995 U.S. ambassador to the United Nations Madeleine Albright submits "Elements of a New Strategy," a policy argument in favor of air strikes against Bosnian Serbs.

July 1995 Bosnian Serbs attack and occupy the safe areas of Srebrenica and Zepa.

July 17, 1995 Clinton administration senior foreign policy advisers discuss the endgame strategy devised by National Security Adviser Anthony Lake.

July 26, 1995 The Senate approves unilaterally lifting the arms embargo.

August 1, 1995 The House approves unilaterally lifting the arms embargo.

August 4, 1995 Croatians launch a major attack against Serb-held territories.

August 9, 1995 Clinton approves the endgame strategy, a series of threats and incentives to compel the Bosnian Muslims and Serbs to negotiate.

August 9–14, 1995 Lake successfully convinces NATO leaders to support the endgame strategy.

August 11, 1995 Clinton vetoes the bill lifting the arms embargo.

August 28, 1995 Bosnian Serbs shell Sarajevo.

August 30, 1995 NATO launches air strikes against Bosnian Serbs.

September 8, 1995 Bosnian, Croatian, and Serbian foreign ministers agree to principles for negotiation.

September 14, 1995 NATO air strikes are suspended.

October 10, 1995 A Bosnian cease-fire begins.

November 1, 1995 Peace talks open in Dayton, Ohio.

November 21, 1995 The Dayton Peace Accord is initialed, outlining a power-sharing arrangement for Bosnia and authorizing international forces to enforce it.

December 14, 1995 The Dayton Peace Accord is signed.

December 29–30, 1995 The U.S. implementation military force (IFOR) enters Bosnia.

would later come to regret Clinton's campaign rhetoric. White House communications director George Stephanopoulos recalled,

> Before [taking office], our foreign policy had been more a matter of words than deeds.... But winning the White House added retroactive weight to everything we had said before.... Besieged Bosnians heard that [Clinton] had vowed to bomb the Serbs, and they hunkered down with heightened expectations, waiting for the American cavalry. Promises that were briefly considered and barely noticed during a presidential campaign, we had learned, could set entire worlds in motion, proving again the poet's words: "In dreams begin responsibilities."[7]

After the election, the administration found itself moving quickly away from its campaign rhetoric. In response to criticism in early 1993 that the administration was not following through on its promises, Secretary of State Christopher observed, "I don't suppose you'd want anybody to keep a campaign promise if it was a very unsound policy."[8]

Opening Positions, 1993

Given the campaign's emphasis on the economy and other domestic issues, Clinton preferred to spend as little time as possible on foreign policy. The one foreign policy adviser he did see every day was National Security Adviser Anthony Lake. A former professor, Lake had previously served as a Foreign Service officer in Vietnam, on the National Security Council (NSC) staff under Richard Nixon (he resigned in 1970 to protest U.S. military action in Cambodia during the Vietnam War), and in the State Department under Jimmy Carter. Lake was an effective bureaucratic infighter who exhibited an idealistic streak and was described by one associate as a strong "moralist" on foreign policy.[9] Admittedly "emotional" over Bosnia, he defended its place in foreign policy decision making:

> [W]hen I resigned over Vietnam ... some said that I had been "emotional." I think those comments flow from a potential disease of people in my racket, because people are dying and we're deciding on whether to conduct air strikes. There's a tremendous comfort in not being emotional and numbing yourself—blinding yourself—to the human consequences of your decisions. ... I think you should be emotional, but I don't think you should let your emotions cloud your judgment.[10]

For Lake, Bosnia represented the danger of the potential spread of conflict to other countries in the Balkans, the question of ethnic cleansing, and the link between the fate of the Bosnian Muslims and support for U.S. policy in the Middle East by Islamic nations.[11] Consequently, Lake became a strong proponent of U.S. action on Bosnia. Others, particularly Joint Chiefs of Staff (JCS) chairman Colin Powell and many in the military, opposed intervention, because they saw Bosnia as another Vietnam—a quagmire, a long and indeterminate intervention in an internal conflict associated with increasing casualties and rising domestic opposition. The "lessons of Vietnam" would underlie much of the discussion on U.S. intervention. To varying degrees after Vietnam, most foreign policy observers shared the conviction that American forces should not intervene in civil wars in the developing world since intervention would not end them. Instead the inevitable result would be a prolonged, costly, and unsuccessful intervention regardless of the actor's intended purposes.

A consensus within the military drew several other lessons for how future U.S. interventions should be designed. In particular, these individuals, of whom Powell had become one of the most identifiable representatives, suggested that several factors had contributed to the debacle in Vietnam: a lack of clear objectives, the failure initially to define an "exit strategy" (when and how the U.S. commitment would end), and the slow, incremental increase of the military commitment's size and scope. In Powell's analysis, intervention in Bosnia would lead to the sort of failure that the United States had experienced in Vietnam. Powell insisted that U.S. military actions should be guided by a clear mission objective, which he found sorely lacking in any potential Bosnian intervention. Reminiscent of the internal conflict in Vietnam, he saw Bosnia as "an ethnic tangle with roots reaching back a thousand years."[12] In his memoirs, he recalled his reaction to the Clinton administration's approach:

> In response to constant calls by the new team to "do something" to punish the Bosnian Serbs from the air for shelling Sarajevo, I laid out the same military options that I had presented to President Bush. Our choices ranged from limited air strikes around Sarajevo to heavy bombing of the Serbs throughout the theater. I emphasized that none of these actions was guaranteed to change Serb behavior. Only troops on the ground could do that. Heavy bombing might persuade them to give in, but would not compel them to quit. And faced with limited air strikes, the Serbs would have little difficulty hiding tanks and artillery in the woods and fog of Bosnia or keeping them close to civilian populations. Furthermore, no matter what we did, it would be easy for the Serbs to respond by seizing U.N. humanitarian personnel as hostages.[13]

In the event that the administration was tempted to insert ground troops, Powell felt that "no American President could defend to the American people the heavy sacrifice of lives it would cost to resolve this baffling conflict. Nor could a President likely sustain the long-term involvement necessary to keep the protagonists from going at each other's throats all over again at the first opportunity."[14] In short, he felt potential military involvement in Bosnia lacked a clear political objective, public support, and the political will to take the steps necessary to resolve it.

Perhaps the most ardent advocate of American intervention in Bosnia was Ambassador Albright, who envisioned an extension of traditional UN peacekeeping operations in the post–cold war international system to confront issues such as ethnic conflict, state collapse, and humanitarian relief. She believed Bosnia provided a good opportunity to implement the policy she called "assertive multilateralism." As a staunch advocate of using U.S. forces to support diplomatic objectives, she often clashed with Powell over the use of the military. At one point, when Powell pressed the need to have a clear political objective before committing forces, Albright complained, "What's the point of having this superb military that you're always talking about if we can't use it." [15]

Lift and Strike

As an initial step and to address its campaign commitments on Bosnia, the Clinton administration decided to take several quick actions. In February 1993 it pressed the United Nations to authorize enforcement of a previously enacted no-fly zone and, most significant, committed to send American troops to implement a peace agreement if all the warring parties agreed, a commitment seen as a necessary step for establishing U.S credibility on Bosnian policy. Instead of agreeing to reach a negotiated settlement, however, the Serbs increased military activity against Bosnian Muslim towns. By March 25, the administration sensed that the Europeans might be more accepting of lifting the arms embargo because of the constant barrage of horrific pictures and reports of carnage from Bosnia. Lake concluded, "The old policy was running out." [16]

In the face of ongoing disturbing images coming out of Bosnia, Clinton, Vice President Al Gore, and Lake felt a strong ethical and moral compulsion to thwart Serbian aggression and halt their ethnic cleansing campaign. Yet, this desire conflicted with Clinton's preference to stop the bloodshed as quickly as possible, because any reaction to Serbian aggression would surely extend the length of the conflict. [17] Clinton's attendance at the dedication of the United States Holocaust Memorial Museum in Washington on April 21 seemed to bolster his determination. One adviser reported, "Clinton was very anguished about it. The decisive things were the dedication of the Holocaust Museum, with [Holocaust survivor] Elie Wiesel's lecture, and the bad pictures on television of Srebrenica. The pictures of Srebrenica brought ethnic cleansing home." [18]

Pressure from the public to "do something" mounted as well. Lobbying efforts on the part of the Bosnian government in Congress started to pay dividends as more interest developed around resolving the issue. Constant and critical media attention on the network news as well as in the print media continued to focus attention on Bosnia. Its effect was felt within the administration,[19] with Clinton concluding that public opinion was shifting in support of multilateral action. Stanley Greenberg, Clinton's pollster, informed the president that U.S. action as part of the United Nations was becoming increasingly popular, but the public opposed unilateral action. Greenberg also advised Clinton that public opinion on Bosnia would be particularly pliant to leadership efforts. As a result, Clinton remained determined that the United States should act in a multilateral context.[20]

Other polls reinforced Greenberg's basic conclusions, suggesting that the public would oppose unilateral intervention, especially with ground troops, but would support multilateral action. An early May poll found 12 percent of the public favored and 86 percent opposed the United States taking "military action alone to try to stop the fighting in Bosnia." Another poll found that 65 percent favored and 32 percent opposed "carrying out air strikes" along with the European allies against the Serbs. After Clinton announced in February his pledge to send troops to enforce a peace, 41 percent favored and 51 percent opposed "using American ground troops" as "part of a peacekeeping force if a peace agreement is reached between the warring factions." Support rose to 58 percent favoring and 32 percent opposing if the troops were part of an "international peacekeeping force." Little support existed for unilateral action by the United States to end the war. In an April 1993 poll, only 35 percent favored while 52 percent opposed the United States "sending troops to Yugoslavia to try to help stop the civil war there." Even so, reports indicated that the public was not following the issue closely, which made it susceptible to new information about the situation. For example, polls indicated that only around 15 percent of the public tracked news from Bosnia "very closely" in 1993. This figure would not change dramatically in 1994 or 1995.[21]

In response to changing domestic and international conditions, the administration began a process that would result in a new policy known as lift and strike. While Clinton favored "doing something" about the Bosnian conflict, the core problem remained what to do. For Clinton, public opinion was the concern that provided context for any action. He therefore ruled out two options: First, because he feared any unilateral action would erode domestic support, he rejected acting without allied support. Second, other than to enforce a peace, he removed ground troops from the table because of doubts about public support coupled with the military's fear of a quagmire and concerns that deploying ground troops would undermine the stability of Russia, a traditional Serb ally.[22]

Several options remained. First, the arms embargo could be lifted so that arms could flow to the Bosnian government. This might influence the situation while avoiding a serious commitment of U.S. resources. While the Bosnian government had reserve troops that it could call up, it lacked the equipment necessary to mount an effective resistance against the Bosnian Serbs. Assuming the embargo was lifted, while the Bosnians learned to use their new weapons, the Serbs might attempt a last-ditch offensive to win the war before an effective defense could be mounted. A flood of weapons might also increase danger to peacekeepers.[23]

Second, the United States could launch air strikes against Serb forces and their assets to reduce their capability to kill. Gen. Merrill A. McPeak, U.S. Air Force chief of staff, argued that bombing strikes would succeed in destroying the Serbian forces and that there would be "virtually no risk" to American planes and pilots.[24] Powell remained skeptical and asked, "What is the end point? ... If we bomb Serb military targets in Bosnia and that doesn't bring them to the conference table, then what?" The Serbs could also hide military hardware in the mountains and woods, create the potential for civilian casualties by placing targeted weapons next to schools and hospitals, or threaten peacekeepers.[25] Finally, "safe areas," where Muslim civilians could be protected from attack, could be created. While military planners thought this plan could largely be enforced from the air, they conceded that some ground forces would be needed. This option required that the United States' European allies increase their ground forces, an action they would probably oppose because it could drag them into a ground war with the Serbs.[26]

By the end of April, the choice had been narrowed to two options: lift and strike, that is, lifting the arms embargo and initiating air strikes to stop Serb aggression while the Muslims were being armed or mediating a cease-fire and establishing protection for Muslim enclaves.[27] The administration publicly emphasized several conditions on its use of force, all of which directly or indirectly reflected the need for public support. In congressional testimony, Christopher indicated that any military intervention would have to meet four conditions: (1) goals that the American public could understand; (2) a high probability of success; (3) public support for the action; and (4) an "exit strategy" to remove American forces if necessary.[28] Clinton met with a bipartisan group of congressional members on April 27 to ascertain their views before making a final decision. He wondered whether there would be a politically feasible way to extricate American forces from the situation if a limited intervention failed to produce decisive results. Rep. Lee H. Hamilton, D-Ind., chairman of the House Foreign Affairs Committee, reported,

> He asked us what if we do everything we can to lift the arms embargo and use air strikes and we lose, what then?... Several of us said that the republic will survive, but that his Presidency will be badly damaged, and the standing and credibility of the United States in the world will be damaged. If you decide to go, you have to prevail. And if the steps you take are insufficient to achieve your objectives, then you have to increase the steps you take.[29]

Sen. Richard G. Lugar, R-Ind., concurred, saying, "As Republicans our advice was that the President was going to suffer substantially if in fact this doesn't work out well, that people will not be generous and he ought to anticipate that."[30] After the meeting, a Democratic leader warned Clinton that any undesirable consequences, including civilian deaths, would be used by the Republicans politically.[31] The meeting seemed to suggest that the political consequences of a failed policy could be dramatic. Clinton chose the lift and strike alternative on May 1. According to one policy maker, "The basic strategy was, This thing is a no-winner, it's going to be a quagmire. Let's not make it our quagmire. That's what lift the arms embargo, and the limited air strikes, was about."[32] Another high-level official described the plan of action as "the least bad thing we could come up with in a situation where we think we have to do something."[33]

European Reaction

Lift and strike began to erode almost immediately. The British and French had previously warned the administration that the policy was a non-starter, primarily because they had troops exposed on the ground.[34] One administration official describing the predicament said, "If we'd bet the ranch, said to the French and English, 'This threatens a fundamental breach in our relationships,' we could perhaps have got the Europeans—kicking and screaming—involved. But this would have made it an American problem. We would have taken over. We have viewed it as a European problem where we'd help out."[35] Given Clinton's concerns about public opposition, the administration was not willing to press the Europeans at the risk of having to shoulder most of the responsibility. Despite the Europeans' opposition, Clinton still hoped for success.

While Christopher visited European capitals in May collecting negative responses—the British essentially said no, the French opposed lifting the embargo and favored air strikes *if* the United States sent in ground troops, the

Russians refused to discuss the plan—lift and strike lost its luster at home as well. Administration officials, meeting with Congress, found only tepid support for the proposal. Clinton, too, seemed to be having second thoughts. The president had been reading Robert Kaplan's *Balkan Ghosts*, which portrays the Balkans as a region seething with intractable historical hatreds that inevitably result in wars. Clinton's thinking might also have been influenced by a May 3 article in the *Wall Street Journal* by Arthur Schlesinger Jr., who suggested that Clinton's policy on Bosnia could subvert his domestic policy initiatives in a manner similar to what President Lyndon Johnson experienced during the Vietnam War.[36]

In a May 8 meeting with the president upon his return, Christopher reported staunch European opposition to lift and strike. One attendee reported, "[Christopher] made it clear that if we wanted to get this done, we'd have to push them very hard, and at the end of the day they might go along, but this would create strains." Someone else indicated, "We didn't want to stake the alliance on this, or totally Americanize the issue."[37] Fearing strains within the alliance if it pushed for a multilateral solution and domestic opposition if it moved unilaterally, the administration abandoned lift and strike.

The European trip changed Christopher's mind about U.S. intervention in the Bosnian conflict. He now saw the issue as one that could only damage Clinton's presidency and the domestic agenda he wanted to emphasize. One high-level official said, "I don't think it was until [Christopher] made the trip that [he] focused on what a loser this policy was." As a result, after his trip Christopher shifted his efforts to diverting attention from Bosnia.[38] In the attempt to "do something" about Bosnia, on May 22 the Europeans and Americans finally settled on a safe haven plan for six Muslim cities, pledging to protect them even if it entailed the use of force. With the agreement in place, which required the United States only to supply air support for the ground forces providing protection, Christopher concluded that he had successfully removed Bosnia from the foreign policy agenda and allowed Clinton to refocus on domestic issues.[39]

Preserving Credibility and NATO, 1994

When a mortar shell struck the marketplace in Sarajevo on February 5, 1994, the grizzly scenes of civilian deaths and injuries burst onto television screens around the globe. The shelling found the administration in the midst of reevaluating its policy because of concerns it was undermining U.S. credibility and NATO. The main effect of the shelling was to accelerate the pace of the policy shift already underway by changing the domestic context. The day before the Sarajevo attack, Christopher had proposed a new policy that emphasized the need for U.S. leadership and included using the threat of air power to persuade the Serbs to be more forthcoming in negotiations;[40] the shelling shifted public support in favor of air strikes. Although a January poll about U.S. participation in multilateral air strikes found only 35 percent of Americans favoring such action and 56 percent opposing it, polls shortly after the shelling found that the public now favored multilateral air strikes, 48 percent to 45 percent, while 65 percent said they would favor and 29 percent said they would oppose the strikes if the United States ordered them.[41] The administration seized the opportunity. Michael McCurry, the secretary of state's spokesman, said, "[The policy reevaluation] could have taken weeks or months.... The impact of the marketplace bombing ... was to force there to be a response much quicker than the U.S. government" usually would act.[42] White House spokeswoman Dee Dee Myers contends that the shelling changed the public opinion to the extent that it provided the administration the latitude it needed to shift its policy. She explained, "It was a short window. We took advantage of it. We moved the policy forward and it was successful."[43]

In contrast to his previous behavior, Clinton now took a more active interest in Bosnian policy and worked to convince European leaders to support the new approach. After intense deliberations, NATO demanded that the Serbs stop attacking Sarajevo and withdraw their heavy weapons from around the city or be subjected to NATO air strikes. At the same time, the Bosnians were warned not to use the Muslim safe havens as bases from which to attack the Serbs. After several days of intense negotiations, the Serbs backed down and agreed to NATO's terms.[44]

Throughout 1994, the United States pressed for a more assertive policy against the Bosnian Serbs. In November, with the safe haven of Bihac threatened by the Serbs, U.S. pressure for greater action to save the city—but Washington's unwillingness to send ground troops—caused a rift within NATO. The European allies with troops on the ground told the Clinton administration that it could either deploy ground troops to enable UNPROFOR to do as the United States wished, or UNPROFOR would pursue a more limited role of protecting humanitarian efforts.[45] As tensions rose, the administration, in order to preserve good relations in NATO, abandoned the proposed, more assertive policy that included air strikes. One official said that "the United States couldn't keep asking for things that weren't going to happen. The strains on the alliance, the credibility question, the futility of it all—it was better to be realistic." [46] Secretary of Defense William Perry explained the choice, saying, "We have rejected both walking away and an extensive use of military force." [47] Public opinion remained staunchly opposed to action to end the war, with 34 percent favoring and 58 percent opposing "the United States sending ground troops as part of the United Nations peace-keeping force." [48] In essence, one official noted, "The problem is that we have no maneuver room. This time we have no leverage with the Europeans unless we agree to put peacekeeping troops on the ground." [49] That option remained out of the question because of public opposition.

Although the United States had essentially decided to take the use of force off the table, Clinton almost immediately made a commitment guaranteeing that the United States would send ground troops to Bosnia. Clinton did not realize it until some time later, but for him the issue was no longer whether the United States would send ground troops to Bosnia, but when and why. In December 1994, the NATO nations with peacekeepers in Bosnia indicated that they might withdraw their troops. In order to counter their resolve to do so, on December 7, 1994, Clinton expanded his previous pledge to send 25,000 American troops to implement a peace treaty to include assisting with the evacuation of UNPROFOR if it became necessary. [50] Administration officials painted the decision as an effort to alleviate the friction that had developed within the Western alliance, in addition to it being a practical matter of helping facilitate a possible withdrawal. As a result, the European nations decided to continue their deployment.

In early 1995, NATO planners drafted OPPLAN 40104, a strategy for withdrawal. The plan envisioned an extensive commitment of NATO and U.S. resources, with some 82,000 troops to be used (including the 25,000 pledged by the United States) during a twenty-two-week operation. Public perceptions of the plan were positive, with 57 percent of the American public favoring it and 36 percent opposing Clinton's offer to send troops to assist with an UNPROFOR withdrawal. [51]

Bosnia Back on the Front Burner, Spring and Early Summer 1995

The next crisis emerged in May 1995. After the failure of another cease-fire and further Serb attacks on safe areas, NATO air forces bombed Serbian positions. In response, the Serbs took several hundred UNPROFOR troops hostage and chained them to potential targets. Although the peacekeepers were eventually released, the action provided the impetus for another rethinking of U.S. policy in the summer of 1995. Senior administration officials met several times in May and June to debate OPPLAN 40104. Along with logistical concerns about getting troops to the area, refugee issues, and the problem of withdrawing NATO troops once UNPROFOR left, administration officials also had to work on bolstering public and congressional support for a commitment that was controversial among policy elites when it was announced in December 1994.[52] Because of the seriousness of the issues needing to be addressed, top officials believed that UNPROFOR remained the best alternative. Lake concluded, "We all agreed that collapse would mean that American troops would have to go into Bosnia in order to rescue UNPROFOR, which meant that we were going in the context of a defeat. And nobody wanted that. It would have had huge consequences."[53]

The principals met amid these deliberations on May 28 to discuss U.S. policy options. Secretary of Defense Perry and JCS chairman John Shalikashvili (Powell's successor) proposed committing American forces to redeploying UNPROFOR troops to more defensible positions to reduce their exposure to Serb aggression and retribution. Over Christopher's objections that "no support in the Congress or among the public for deeper involvement" existed, the group agreed that the United States should extend such a promise, especially if it bolstered the Europeans' commitment to stay in Bosnia.[54] On May 30, Clinton approved the suggested policy change "that if requested by NATO, we should provide assistance to our allies to redeploy from the eastern enclaves, provided we get Congress to go along."[55]

When Clinton announced this decision on May 31 at the Air Force Academy graduation, the resulting uproar in the press and Congress required that he clarify the policy on June 3. In his weekly radio address, Clinton explained that American forces would be introduced into Bosnia under one of three conditions: to implement a peace agreement, to withdraw UNPROFOR, or to help in the emergency redeployment of an exposed force.[56] Dick Morris, a Clinton political consultant, was particularly concerned about the public opinion implications, exclaiming, "Eighty percent of the country is against sending ground troops to Bosnia!" He was able to convince Clinton to ad-lib in his address that the redeployment option was "highly unlikely."[57]

Polls from early June, after Clinton's clarification, indicate that, as Morris thought, the public overwhelmingly opposed sending troops to Bosnia to "try and end the fighting," with 21 percent in favor and 73 percent opposed.[58] At the same time, however, the public favored the policies the administration had selected. The public supported sending American troops to "maintain peace and protect relief operations" (61 percent to 32 percent),[59] favored "the use of U.S.

military forces to help U.N. peacekeepers move to safer places in Bosnia" (65 percent to 29 percent), approved of sending ground troops to "help U.N. forces to withdraw safely" (68 percent to 27 percent), and regarding more aggressive action, favored multilateral air strikes if the Serbs continued "to attack Bosnian cities or U.N. peacekeeping troops" (56 percent to 33 percent).[60] As it stood in early June, the public supported the commitments that Clinton had made and appeared to favor more aggressive action under limited conditions.

NATO's inability to respond effectively to the May Serb hostage taking spurred Clinton to search for alternatives to the UNPROFOR deployment. One adviser reported that Clinton complained, "I want for us to be more on top of this thing, more shaping of it. If we were going to be blamed for the failures, it should at least be for concrete decisions that we had taken." [61] Still, both the State and Defense Departments were hesitant to press for more aggressive action. Christopher remained wary of taking the lead on policy given the failure of lift and strike in 1993. At the Pentagon, fears of another Vietnam continued to perpetuate apprehension about possible long-term commitments.[62]

At a June 14 Oval Office meeting, Clinton expressed his frustration with the continuing problem of Bosnia and the threat to NATO created by the appearance of weakness in response to the May hostage taking. Clinton, exasperated, stated, "We need to get the policy straight ... or we're just going to be kicking the can down the road again. Right now we've got a situation, we've got no clear mission, no one's in control of events." Citing efforts by Republicans in Congress, led by 1996 Republican presidential candidate Senator Bob Dole, R-Kan., to lift the arms embargo against the Bosnian Muslims, Vice President Gore concluded that continued inaction was "driving us into a brick wall with Congress." [63] That evening top officials intimated, during the North Portico discussion after the Chirac dinner, that NATO commitments might restrict U.S. flexibility on ground troops.

Although he had previously allowed the Europeans to lead on Bosnia policy, Clinton concluded that only bold U.S. action would allow the allies to gain control of the situation. As one senior official put it, "The president wanted this dealt with. It was not acceptable to go into another winter as a hostage to fortune." While Clinton knew what he needed to avoid—an UNPROFOR pullout, humanitarian atrocities, an endless war, and congressional action to lift the arms embargo—he did not know what he wanted to achieve. One senior official recalled, "We sat and watched [the situation in Bosnia] drift slowly away and the debacle of the hostage-taking ... and Clinton got this sort of 'never-again' attitude and said to his guys, 'I need some options. I need a better way.' " [64]

On June 21 during a meeting of Clinton's foreign policy advisers, Ambassador Albright presented a memo to the president entitled "Elements of a New Strategy." Pointing to the harm the Bosnia issue was causing to U.S. credibility, she suggested that the way out of the dilemma was the withdrawal of UNPROFOR, whose presence prevented implementing what she believed was the best policy—lifting the arms embargo and using air strikes against the Bosnian Serbs. [65]

Spurred by Clinton's positive response to Albright's suggestion, National Security Adviser Lake and his staff developed an approach that eventually became known as the endgame strategy. When Lake preliminarily discussed it with Clinton in late June, he cautioned the president about the risks (damage to the United States' reputation) and possible success (enforcing a peace or assisting UNPROFOR pull out) of the new, proposed effort. As usual, public opinion weighed heavily on Clinton's mind. He likened a Balkan troop deployment to the beginning of Vietnam, and wondered whether the public or Congress would support such a risk. On balance, he viewed the status quo, which entailed the risk of a U.S.-supported UNPROFOR pullout under fire, as worse and approved examining Lake's approach. [66]

Lake's proposal ultimately suggested that he act as a messenger and communicate to Europe that the president had reached a final decision on Bosnian policy and was prepared to implement it unilaterally. The policy offered carrots and sticks to both combatants. The Bosnian Serbs would face extensive bombing if they refused to negotiate, but Western economic sanctions would be lifted against Yugoslavia if it recognized the independence of Bosnia, Croatia, and Macedonia. To entice the Bosnian Muslims, the United States would unilaterally lift the arms embargo but would then disengage from the region if they did not negotiate. [67]

On a separate track, Christopher sent to Clinton a summary of the State Department's thinking in early July. The memo expressed concern about the prospects of an UNPROFOR withdrawal and NATO's plan to insert troops to cover it. Christopher suggested developing options that would avoid troop commitments and place more emphasis on diplomatic initiatives (including an offer to lift sanctions on Yugoslavia if talks were successful), with the United States taking the lead. [68] If it worked, the policy promised the prospect of reducing the need for American ground troops and placing the United States in the lead.

The situation worsened on July 11, when the Srebrenica safe area fell to Serbian aggression. Because NATO and the United States had promised to protect the safe areas, the Serbs' attack seriously threatened U.S. and NATO credibility.[69] When the Serbs killed thousands of Muslims and forced many more to flee Srebrenica, one senior official recalled, "We were failing, the West was failing and the Bosnian Serbs were on the march." Clinton concluded that the feeble Western response had harmed the United States' prestige. He became increasingly frustrated by his lack of options and the worsening situation.[70] Following the fall of Srebrenica a senior official lamented, "[We were] faced with the worst possible outcome: we were going to have to initiate the evacuation of the United Nations forces in Bosnia—a move that would be very risky to American life, and expensive, and would lead to a wider war."[71]

On July 14, while putting on the White House green, Clinton's agitation rose as he contemplated a likely UNPROFOR withdrawal and the attendant American troop commitment. He concluded, "The status quo is not acceptable. We've got to really dig in and think about this."[72] Perhaps in reference to mounting congressional pressure for action, he insisted, "We have to seize control of this," and exclaimed, "I'm getting creamed!"[73] Although some of his domestic advisers suggested a clean break from Bosnia and a push for UNPROFOR's pullout, his foreign policy advisers pointed out that UNPROFOR's extraction under fire was much more dangerous than enforcing a peace plan. While neither alternative was appealing, Clinton feared the extraction to a greater extent because of its electoral implications. If he waited, he knew he would likely be forced to use troops to extract UNPROFOR either on the eve of or during the 1996 election.[74]

Gruesome images, like a front-page picture in the *Washington Post* of a female refugee from Srebrenica who had hanged herself rather than be captured or killed by the Serbs, touched the public as well as officials. On July 18 in an Oval Office meeting, Gore said, "My 21-year-old daughter asked about that picture.... What am I supposed to tell her? Why is this happening and we're not doing anything? ... My daughter is surprised the world is allowing this to happen.... I am too." Gore argued, "The cost of this is going to cascade over several decades. It goes to what kind of people we are. Acquiescence is the worst alternative." Clinton responded, "I've been thinking along similar lines. ... So we all agree the status quo is untenable."[75]

A Time for Decision, Midsummer 1995

On July 17, National Security Adviser Lake convened a meeting of Clinton's top foreign policy advisers to discuss Bosnia and to present the outline of his proposed strategy. He suggested that the United States embark on a diplomatic effort to end the war by the end of 1995 on the basis of a single Bosnia. If this failed, the United States would force UNPROFOR's withdrawal before the end of the year, thus avoiding action during an election year, which Lake reasoned was undesirable because some actors might attempt to take advantage of the U.S domestic situation. Following a discussion of Lake's proposal and other aspects of U.S. policy, Clinton stopped by the meeting by pre-arrangement to emphasize his desire to undertake a new policy direction.[76] Clinton complained, "I don't like where we are now....This policy is doing enormous damage to the United States and to our standing in the world. We look weak. ... And it can only get worse down the road. The only time we've ever made any progress is when we geared up NATO to pose a real threat to the Serbs." He concluded, "Our position is unsustainable, it's killing the U.S. position of strength in the world." The meeting ended with an agreement that each adviser would prepare a paper detailing suggestions for the future direction of U.S. policy.[77]

On July 26, the day after the Zepa safe area fell to the Serbs, the Senate passed Bob Dole's resolution to lift the arms embargo unilaterally, an action 61 percent of the American public supported and only 24 percent opposed.[78] On August 1, the House approved the Senate resolution by a veto-proof margin. If the administration failed to implement a solution that would head off the lifting of the embargo, Clinton faced the worst case scenario—UNPROFOR's collapse and its extraction by American troops under fire. While Clinton could veto the legislation, he felt Congress might override it. He, therefore, instructed Lake to move ahead briskly on the development of policy options. Lake warned that they were "rolling the dice." Clinton concluded, "I'm risking my presidency."[79] As Clinton and his staff worked on alternatives, he vetoed the bill on August 11.

Based on polling conducted by Dick Morris, Clinton thought the public would support military action if it was directed at halting the killing of women and children and stopping the Serbs' genocidal activities. While the public would support peacekeeping, it remained steadfastly opposed to the United States becoming involved in combat in Bosnia.[80] He thought that if the United States failed to act, UNPROFOR would most likely survive the winter only to ask for relief in the spring, which meant the issue would be "dropped in during the middle of the campaign."[81] This "political time bomb" would then become the primary case for the public's assessment of Clinton's foreign policy record. As one senior official put it, "I don't think the President relishes going into the 1996 election hostage to fortune in the Balkans, with the Bosnian Serbs able to bring us deeper into a war." [82] Fearing that the issue might be used in the election, Morris warned other officials "you guys ought to take care of Bosnia before 1996 so it does not screw us up." [83]

On August 4, the Croatians had launched a successful attack on the Croatian Serbs who held a portion of Croatia, which, by highlighting Serbian vulnerability and completing the almost total ethnic separation within Bosnia and Croatia, provided a window of opportunity for negotiations. [84] In this increasingly fluid situation, Clinton met with his top advisers to discuss the agency policy papers on August 7. Albright's paper largely supported Lake's proposed endgame strategy. She emphasized several factors from her "Elements of a New Strategy," including the damage to U.S. credibility created by inaction in Bosnia, the need to insert American troops under the most favorable conditions (since intervention now appeared inevitable), and the necessity of a credible military threat to force the Bosnian Serbs to respond. The NSC endgame strategy paper suggested a diplomatic initiative to reach a peace agreement in 1995 by offering an end to all sanctions and regional economic assistance. Failing an agreement, UNPROFOR should be withdrawn, the arms embargo lifted and the Bosnians armed, and airpower used to protect the remaining safe areas. If the Bosnians appeared obstructionist, the arms embargo would be lifted and the United States would disengage from the area.

The State Department paper also recommended undertaking a diplomatic initiative to foster negotiations between the parties and recognized the risks involved in deploying American troops, such as the lack of congressional and public support. Although it favored keeping UNPROFOR in Bosnia, if the Europeans decided to pull out State favored lifting the arms embargo and arming Bosnia while opposing air intervention. Finally, the Defense Department paper argued against a large military commitment because U.S. interests were not sufficient to support such action. Instead, it supported what boiled down to a partition of Bosnia along the prevailing battle line, the withdrawal of UNPROFOR, and an end to the fighting. [85]

After hearing all the views, Clinton supported Albright's argument. [86] Reflecting his desire to resolve the issue before the 1996 campaign, Clinton emphasized, "We should bust our ass to get a settlement within the next few months.... We've got to exhaust every alternative, roll every die, take risks." [87] Otherwise, Clinton feared, "If we let this moment slip away ... we are history." [88] After meetings on August 8 and 9 to work out the details, Clinton decided to implement the NSC endgame strategy and sent Lake to Europe to present the decision. [89]

Lake successfully convinced the Europeans to support the endgame strategy, so allied negotiators were dispatched to the Balkans. On August 28, in a direct challenge to the negotiation efforts, the Bosnian Serbs launched a mortar attack on Sarajevo, killing thirty-eight civilians. Negotiations between the United Nations and NATO in July had resulted in an agreement that committed them to responding with air strikes if the Serbs attacked more safe areas. With U.S. and NATO credibility on the line, NATO launched a massive air campaign on August 30 against the Bosnian Serbs that lasted until mid September and included more than thirty-five hundred sorties. American negotiators used the leverage of the attacks to convince the Bosnian, Croatian, and Yugoslav foreign ministers on September 8 to agree to principles for negotiation. NATO suspended the strikes on September 14. Negotiators achieved a cease-fire on October 5, it went into effect on October 10, and talks on a final settlement began on November 1 in Dayton, Ohio. An agreement on a power-sharing arrangement for Bosnia and international forces to enforce it, the Dayton Peace Accord, was initialed by the parties on November 21.[90]

As the negotiations progressed, the administration increasingly focused its attention on gaining domestic approval for the troop deployment to enforce the peace. Although Clinton found that public opinion disapproved of the planned deployment, 38 percent for to 55 percent against, he thought he had to follow through on his commitment and therefore sought to convince the public of the appropriateness of his approach. He concluded from White House polls that if he framed the issue in terms of peacekeeping as opposed to combat, he could build the support he needed. He concluded that if the public understood the limited risk and duration of the mission, he would gain "sufficient support" for the peace plan.[91]

Two implementation issues focused administration deliberations. First, how long would the implementation military force (IFOR) remain in Bosnia to enforce an agreement? After the U.S. experiences in Haiti, Somalia, and Vietnam, the need for an exit strategy remained unquestioned among the NSC staff, the military, and other senior members of the administration. Politically, it was assumed that neither Congress nor the public would support a commitment of American forces without a specified date for their withdrawal.[92] Pressed by skeptical senators during a Senate Armed Services Committee hearing on October 17, Secretary Perry and JCS chief of staff Shalikashvili promised that IFOR would "complete its mission in twelve months and [then] withdraw."[93]

Within the administration, officials planned on a six-to-eight-month mission that would allow troops to begin returning home in summer 1996 and Clinton to speak of troop departures during the election. In addition to the politics, it was thought that the military objectives could be achieved within that time frame.[94] Since this was, in the words of one senior official, "abundantly preferable" to moving slowly with negotiations, the administration pressed for an early conclusion to talks in order to get the deployment started and over as soon as possible. While officials publicly denied that their decisions were influenced in any way by the election, one official noted privately that they "are certainly aware of the election, and I don't think it has escaped the president's attention." [95] In the end, the one-year exit date was agreed to and publicly defended by administration officials.

Second, a debate emerged within the U.S. government about the scope of IFOR's mission. On the one side sat the "minimalists," led by the military, who believed IFOR should focus on a narrow range of tasks, such as separating the sides, enforcing the cease-fire, and monitoring compliance. Based on the experience of Vietnam, Somalia, and other events, the military feared "mission creep," in which it would slowly become engaged in tasks associated with nation building, such as assisting in the election process, facilitating the return of refugees, and ensuring freedom of movement. Mission creep held the potential to put American forces on a slippery slope, sliding toward another quagmire. In addition to nation-building activities being domestically unpopular, the military feared they would create security problems that would tie down its forces and create a need for more troops. These views resonated with Lake and others in the White House.[96]

On the other side, the "maximalists," who included Holbrooke and the civilian U.S. negotiating team, argued that IFOR should be used to enforce the agreement's civilian aspects, that is, the actions the military labeled nation-building activities. The maximalists saw the civilian elements of the mission as providing the backbone of a lasting peace. Without military backing, they argued, the civilian components would most likely not be implemented, which would make IFOR's ultimate extraction more difficult.[97]

Within the White House, Pentagon backing of the IFOR mission remained a central concern. Given the forthcoming election and public trepidation about troop deployment to Bosnia (at this point, 70 percent of Americans opposed deploying ground forces even to enforce the peace), military support of IFOR became a requirement. Later, even Holbrooke would concede, "We had to have [the military's] backing to get congressional and public support for the mission."[98] Given the domestically contentious nature of the IFOR deployment, White House officials found the thought of ordering a deployment that the military opposed politically untenable. In the end, a compromise was achieved that essentially granted the military its wishes: IFOR would only have the *obligation* of enforcing the more limited military aspects of the agreement, and it would have the *authority* to implement the more controversial ones, but it would not be required to do so. It was assumed that local commanders would consider implementing the civilian tasks as the successful completion of the military tasks allowed.[99] Following the signing of the Dayton accord on December 14, Clinton met with his top advisers. Concerned that Pentagon presentations to Congress were raising, instead of easing, discomfort on Capitol Hill, he stressed to the military,

> My sense ... is that the diplomatic breakthrough in Dayton has given us a chance to prevail in Congress and in the nation. People see the stakes and the big picture. But we can't get congressional support without Defense and the military fully behind this.... We have to convey a high level of confidence in our capacity to carry out the mission and to manage the gaps in the agreement.... We can't close the deal without the Pentagon's support.... I want everyone here to get behind the agreement.[100]

Subsequently, the military publicly supported IFOR's role. Although the Congress remained divided, it did not prevent the deployment, which occurred as planned after an intense lobbying effort by the administration. IFOR moved largely unchallenged into Bosnia in late December 1995. Shortly after the 1996 election, Clinton extended the term of IFOR's deployment as a smaller, renamed United States and NATO force (SFOR, for stabilization force) for another eighteen months.[101] When Clinton left office in January 2001, several thousand American troops remained on the ground in Bosnia enforcing the Dayton accord.

Conclusion: Public Opinion to the Fore?

Throughout the Bosnia crisis, the Clinton administration focused on domestic considerations during deliberations over policy goals and means. During the cold war, the policy consensus largely limited debates on intervention in places such as Lebanon, Nicaragua, and Vietnam to questions of whether a communist threat existed in the location, and if so, whether intervention was the most effective means to combat it. Throughout these debates, public opinion was an important constraining influence.[102] With the cold war over, if decisions on intervention in Bosnia are an accurate indicator, public opinion will play a role in an even wider range of calculations. Throughout the case of Bosnia, public opinion affected choices concerning foreign policy priorities, goals, and means. To be sure, international considerations continued to affect foreign policy deliberations, but at several points domestic pressures played an equal role with international developments. The challenge for decision makers in this environment was to balance the pressures of acting in a multilateral context with domestic concerns.

Public opinion throughout the Clinton administration's handling of the Bosnian problem acted as inducement and disincentive regarding policy options. Electoral promises chosen for political advantage to curry favor with voters became imperatives to "do something" once in office and were compounded by the international expectations they created. The electoral calendar created its own pressures, as the administration grappled with its policies. At the same time, the administration remained intimately familiar with just how far the public was willing to go to stop the bloodshed.

The dynamics of the Clinton administration's decisions illustrate larger trends in U.S. foreign policy in the post–cold war world. Most polls reveal that foreign policy holds little salience in the public's eye. Yet, since U.S. interests, as well as policy means, are now open to debate, public opinion has increased in significance to decision makers because they fear that public opinion can easily turn against any of their policies. As the Clinton administration deliberated on Bosnia, policy makers continually worked to anticipate how the public would eventually react, especially in the next election. In this way, the new international order has broadened the realm of decisions that the public has the power to influence.

The contentiousness of both policy goals and means in the current era suggests that future debates on intervention are likely to possess a similar dynamic. As policy makers consider intervention, they must again grapple with a number of issues: avoiding potential quagmires; deciding on humanitarian intervention; dealing with pressure and constraints from allies; formulating effective peacekeeping operations; and determining how the military should be employed. Intertwined in these perspectives will emerge a central issue for policy makers in the twenty-first century: What policies of intervention will the public support when U.S. interests themselves are open to debate? This uncertainty will undoubtedly compel future policy makers to place public opinion at the forefront of their intervention deliberations.

Notes

1. Richard Holbrooke, *To End a War* (New York: The Modern Library, 1999), 67–68.

2. Ibid.; Bob Woodward, *The Choice* (New York: Simon and Schuster, 1996), 256–257. For an account that disputes the accuracy of some of Holbrooke's assertions to Clinton and assessments of Clinton's attitude, but affirms the basic point that Clinton's decisions and commitment to NATO had nearly locked in U.S. policy, see Ivo H. Daalder, *Getting to Dayton: The Making of America's Bosnia Policy* (Washington, D.C.: Brookings Institution Press, 1999), 56–61.

3. Steven L. Burg and Paul S. Shoup, *The War in Bosnia-Herzegovina* (Armonk, N.Y.: M. E. Sharpe, 1999), 200–202, 206.

4. Holbrooke, *To End a War,* 41.

5. Questions USLAT.081792, R68, and USGALNEW.305023, R09, Roper Center, University of Connecticut, Public Opinion Online, Lexis-Nexis.

6. Elizabeth Drew, *On the Edge* (New York: Touchstone, 1994), 138.

7. George Stephanopoulos, *All Too Human* (Boston: Little, Brown and Company, 1999), 157.

8. Drew, *Edge,* 139.

9. Ibid., 138, 141, 144.

10. Ibid., 143–144.

11. Ibid., 144.

12. Colin Powell, *My American Journey* (New York: Random House, 1995), 558–559, 577.

13. Ibid., 576.

14. Ibid., 577–578.

15. Ibid., 576; Drew, *Edge,* 145.

16. Drew, *Edge,* 148.

17. Ibid., 151; James Gow, *Triumph of the Lack of Will* (New York: Columbia University Press, 1997), 214–215; Stephen Engelberg, "What to Do in Bosnia? Hard Choices for Clinton," *New York Times,* April 29, 1993, A6.

18. Drew, *Edge,* 153. Bosnian Serbs laid siege to Srebrenica in spring 1993, producing searing images of dead, wounded, and fleeing civilians.

19. Gow, *Triumph,* 215.

20. Drew, *Edge,* 150.

21. Richard Sobel, "The Polls—Trends: United States Intervention in Bosnia," *Public Opinion Quarterly* 62 (summer 1998): 258–259, 264, 267–268, 270–271.

22. Drew, *Edge,* 145, 150. The administration feared that U.S. ground forces would undermine Russian national prestige, and thus the internal credibility of Russian leader Boris Yeltsin's government.

23. Engelberg, "Bosnia."

24. Elaine Sciolino, "U.S. Military Split on Using Air Power against the Serbs," *New York Times,* April 29, 1993, A1.

25. Drew, *Edge,* 145, 149.

26. Ibid.

27. Ibid., 151.

28. Ann Devroy and Daniel Williams, "Clinton Backs Balkan Action," *Washington Post*, April 28, 1993, A6.

29. Elaine Sciolino, "Clinton on Serbs: Pacing Shaky Ground," *New York Times*, May 1, 1993, 16.

30. Ibid.

31. Burg and Shoup, *War*, 252.

32. Drew, *Edge*, 155.

33. Burg and Shoup, *War*, 252.

34. Drew, *Edge*, 155–156.

35. Ibid.

36. Arthur M. Schlesinger Jr., "How to Think about Bosnia," *Wall Street Journal*, May 3, 1993, A16.

37. Drew, *Edge*, 158.

38. Ibid., 159–160.

39. Ibid., 161–163.

40. Warren P. Strobel, *Late-Breaking Foreign Policy* (Washington, D.C.: United States Institute of Peace Press, 1997), 156; Daalder, *Dayton*, 24–25.

41. Questions USNBCWSJ.94JAN, R20B; USGALLUP.020894, R4; and USGALLUP. 020894, R8, Roper Center, University of Connecticut, Public Opinion Online, Lexis-Nexis.

42. Strobel, *Late-Breaking*, 157.

43. Ibid., 155.

44. Burg and Shoup, *War*, 287–288.

45. Daalder, *Dayton*, 33.

46. Ruth Marcus and John R. Harris, "Behind U.S. Policy Shift on Bosnia: Strains in NATO," *Washington Post*, December 5, 1994, A26.

47. Norman Kempster and Jim Mann, "U.S. Says Talks Remain Best Option in Bosnia," *Los Angeles Times*, November 30, 1994, A1.

48. Question USCBS.112994, R46, Roper Center, University of Connecticut, Public Opinion Online, Lexis-Nexis.

49. Michael Gordon, "U.S., In Shift, Gives Up Its Talk of Tough Action against Serbs," *New York Times*, November 29, 1994, A16.

50. Clinton's senior advisers had concluded that the United States' commitment to NATO required that it assist fellow NATO forces if necessary. Douglas Jehl, "25,000 U.S. Troops to Aid U.N. Force If It Quits Bosnia," *New York Times*, December 9, 1994, A1; Daalder, *Dayton*, 47.

51. Daalder, *Dayton*, 47; Sobel, "The Polls," 273.

52. Daalder, *Dayton*, 49.

53. Ibid., 50.

54. Ibid., 51.

55. Ibid., 53.

56. Ibid., 54–55.

57. Stephanopoulos, *All Too Human*, 355.

58. Sobel, "The Polls," 272.

59. Question USPSRNEW.95JUN1, R08A, Roper Center, University of Connecticut, Public Opinion Online, Lexis-Nexis.

60. Sobel, " The Polls," 267, 272–273.

61. Stephen Engelberg, "How Events Drew U.S. into Balkans," *New York Times*, August 19, 1995, A1, A4.

62. Woodward, *Choice*, 254.

63. Ibid., 255.

64. Thomas W. Lippman and Ann Devroy, "Clinton's Policy Evolution," *Washington Post*, September 11, 1995, A1, A16.

65. Daalder, *Dayton*, 93.

66. Daalder, *Dayton*, 93–95; Woodward, *Choice*, 258–259.

67. Daalder, *Dayton*, 93–95; Woodward, *Choice*, 258–259.

68. Daalder, *Dayton*, 97–98.

69. Michael Dobbs, "Bosnia Crystallizes U.S. Post–Cold War Role," *Washington Post*, December 3, 1995, A1, A34.

70. Lippman and Devroy, "Clinton's Policy."

71. Burg and Shoup, *War*, 325.

72. Engelberg, "Events."

73. Woodward, *Choice*, 260.

74. Dobbs, "Bosnia Crystallizes"; Burg and Shoup, *War*, 325; William J. Durch and James A. Schear, "Faultlines: U.N. Operations in the Former Yugoslavia," in *U.N. Peacekeeping, American Politics, and the Uncivil Wars of the 1990s*, ed. William J. Durch (New York: St. Martin's Press, 1996), 246; Alison Mitchell, "Clinton Lays Out His Case for U.S. Troops in Balkans," *New York Times*, November 28, 1995, A1, A15.

75. Woodward, *Choice*, 261–263.

76. Daalder, *Dayton*, 98–101.

77. Woodward, *Choice*, 261; Daalder, *Dayton*, 101.

78. Sobel, "The Polls," 276.

79. Woodward, *Choice*, 265.

80. Dick Morris, *Behind the Oval Office* (New York: Random House, 1997), 248–249.

81. Stephanopoulos, *All Too Human*, 383.

82. Ann Devroy, "Europeans Respond Favorably to Ideas for Bosnia Settlement, Clinton Is Told," *Washington Post*, August 16, 1995, A16; Engelberg, "Events."

83. Morris, *Behind*, 244–265; Lippman and Devroy, "Clinton's Policy."

84. Dobbs, "Bosnia Crystallizes"; Lippman and Devroy, "Clinton's Policy."

85. Daalder, *Dayton*, 102–106, 110–111.

86. Ibid., 108–109

87. Woodward, *Choice*, 265–266.

88. Stephanopoulos, *All Too Human*, 383.

89. Daalder, *Dayton*, 110–113.

90. Ibid., 73–79; Durch, "Faultlines," 246–247. On the negotiations, see Holbrooke, *To End a War*.

91. Morris, *Behind*, 255–256, 339; Dana Priest and Ann Devroy, "White House to Ask $1 Billion for Bosnia Troop Deployment," *Washington Post*, September 28, 1995, A24.

92. Daalder, *Dayton*, 149–150; Holbrooke, *To End a War*, 210–211.

93. Holbrooke, *To End a War*, 210–211.

94. Daalder, *Dayton*, 150–151.

95. Ann Devroy and Dana Priest, "Clinton Aides Debate Size of U.S. Peacekeeping Force for Bosnia," *Washington Post*, September 21, 1995, A24.

96. Daalder, *Dayton*, 145–147; Holbrooke, *To End a War*, 215–219.

97. Holbrooke, *To End a War*, 218–219.

98. Ibid., 219.

99. Daalder, *Dayton*, 147.

100. Holbrooke, *To End a War*, 316.

101. Ibid., 316–318; Daalder, *Dayton*, 148, 150, 176.

102. Douglas C. Foyle, *Counting the Public In: Presidents, Public Opinion, and Foreign Policy* (New York: Columbia University Press, 1999); Richard Sobel, *The Impact of Public Opinion on U.S. Foreign Policy since Vietnam* (New York: Oxford University Press, 2001).

3 The War in Kosovo: Coercive Diplomacy

Eric Moskowitz and Jeffrey S. Lantis

Before You Begin

1. What were the origins of conflict in Kosovo? Was conflict over autonomy for Kosovo inevitable given conditions in the 1990s?

2. What options were available to the United States and NATO to halt the conflict in Kosovo?

3. Why did the Clinton administration choose to conduct coercive diplomacy in 1998? What were the advantages and disadvantages of this strategy?

4. What were the key factors that led the Clinton administration to change its position on Kosovo in 1999?

5. Put yourself in the position of the president: Would you support military force or diplomacy to respond to the Kosovo crisis in 1999? Why?

6. Was the NATO air campaign against Serbia a victory in the Kosovo war? What are the lessons of the Kosovo crisis for the conduct of coercive diplomacy?

7. What criteria should the United States use when deciding whether to intervene in foreign conflicts? Should the United States regularly practice humanitarian intervention in global affairs? Why?

Introduction: The Challenge of Kosovo

The crisis in Kosovo represented a major challenge for U.S. foreign policy in the post–cold war era. The Clinton administration was faced with mounting evidence of systematic killings of ethnic Albanians in Kosovo at the hands of Serb paramilitary groups in 1998 and 1999. On the heels of the war in Bosnia, President Clinton and his advisers faced a brewing humanitarian tragedy in which ethnic Albanians sought independence from Serbia while the Serbs struggled to retain control of the province. Clinton administration officials could agree that Kosovo represented a special challenge for the United States and raised important questions about humanitarian intervention, but for almost a year the president's advisers could not agree on what to do.

After months of internal disagreements over the best course of action for the United States and its allies, the Clinton administration first chose to conduct coercive diplomacy in the fall of 1998—pressuring Serbian president Slobodan Milosevic to negotiate a limited autonomy deal for Kosovo while at the same time threatening the use of military force to stop the killings. In the face of Serb resistance to independence for Kosovo, Clinton then chose to pursue a temporary diplomatic solution in October 1998. Sadly, the situation in Kosovo rapidly deteriorated through the winter months that followed, as Serb paramilitary units and Kosovars stepped up their raids and reprisals against one another.

Media coverage of massacres in Kosovo in early 1999 brought the crisis into stark relief for western governments. The Clinton administration pursued several rounds of new diplomatic overtures, including the Rambouillet conference that began in February 1999, but Milosevic remained steadfast in his refusal to negotiate autonomy for Kosovo. U.S. officials finally felt compelled to act militarily. On March 24, 1999, Clinton announced his decision to launch massive air attacks against Serbia in cooperation with NATO allies. He claimed that ending the tragedy was "a moral imperative" and important to the U.S. national interest. Operation Allied Force was the largest military assault in Europe since World War II and led to the introduction of 50,000 NATO peacekeepers into Kosovo. This case study reviews these significant foreign policy decisions and considers the pressures and constraints faced by the Clinton administration in responding to a humanitarian tragedy.

Background: Crises in the Balkans

The Kosovo crisis of 1998–1999 was an extension of close to a century of upheaval in the Balkans. In 1914, the assassination of Archduke Franz Ferdinand of the Austro-Hungarian Empire by a Serbian nationalist in the streets of Sarajevo effectively ignited the fires of World War I. After the war, the Kingdom of the Serbs, Croats, and Slovenes was created from the remains of the Ottoman and Habsburg Empires. The first leader of the unified country, King Alexander, changed the name to Yugoslavia but was unable to resolve simmering rivalries among the three nationalities in the region. He, too, was killed by an assassin, in 1934.[1]

In 1945, Josip Broz Tito emerged as the victor of the communist partisan resistance against the Axis occupation in World War II, and he soon became the popular ruler of a liberated Yugoslavia.[2] Under the so-called Tito Constitution

The Kosovo Crisis

1389   Southern Slavs lose a major battle with the Ottoman Empire in Kosovo at the Field of Blackbirds, opening five centuries of Turkish rule of the Balkans.

1913   Serbs gain control over Kosovo and eliminate all vestiges of Ottoman rule.

1945   Yugoslavia is established under the leadership of Josip Broz Tito.

1974   The Tito Constitution formalizes the federal state arrangement in Yugoslavia, consisting of six republics—Bosnia-Herzegovina, Croatia, Macedonia, Montenegro, Serbia, and Slovenia—and regions with provincial autonomy, such as Kosovo and Vojvodina, to be governed by a collective presidency with rotating political authority.

1987   Slobodan Milosevic becomes president of Serbia and begins consolidating his power over Yugoslavia.

March 1989   Milosevic formally suspends Kosovo's provincial autonomy and rallies Serbian nationalist sentiment against ethnic Albanians.

June 25, 1991   Yugoslavia dissolves when Slovenia and Croatia declare their independence.

September 1991   The Kosovo political assembly votes in favor of independence and establishes a shadow government for the province.

1991–1992   Croatia and Slovenia declare independence from Yugoslavia and fight wars for independence against the Yugoslav National Army (JNA).

March 1992   Bosnia declares independence, leading to three years of conflict against Serb factions in Bosnia and the JNA.

December 1992   The U.S. embassy delivers the Christmas Warning to Milosevic, threatening U.S. military action if Serb repression in Kosovo continues.

1995   The Dayton Peace Accord is signed, ending the war in Bosnia and paving the way for the deployment of international peacekeeping forces there.

1996   The Kosovo Liberation Army (KLA) is established as a partisan movement that targets Serb police and paramilitary units in Kosovo.

February–October 1998   Milosevic responds to KLA attacks in Kosovo by intensifying the Serb military presence in the province.

continued on the next page

continued from the previous page

KLA and Serb paramilitary units skirmish during the spring. Throughout the spring and summer, the Clinton administration's Principals Committee deliberates intervening with NATO allies in Kosovo. Clashes between Serb forces and the KLA intensify. Western media report of massacres by paramilitary forces in Kosovo villages. More than 250,000 Kosovars become refugees.

September 23, 1998   The UN Security Council passes Resolution 1199 calling for a cease-fire in Kosovo, a Serb withdrawal of forces, and the return of refugees.

October 12, 1998   NATO issues an activation order authorizing preparations for the bombing of Serb forces in Kosovo.

October 15, 1998   U.S. envoy Richard Holbrooke brokers a deal with Milosevic to withdraw the majority of Serb forces from Kosovo and to permit 1,800 inspectors from the Organization for Security and Cooperation in Europe (OSCE) to monitor the peace in the region.

November 1998   OSCE observer groups begin patrolling Kosovo. Meanwhile warring factions in the region prepare for more fighting.

January 19, 1999   With news of a Serb massacre of Kosovar civilians in Racak, the Principals Committee agrees to issue an ultimatum to Milosevic threatening a NATO bombing campaign if he refuses to end attacks on Kosovars and negotiate a settlement. Clinton begins building a consensus in NATO for air strikes.

February 6, 1999   The Rambouillet conference opens in an attempt to reach a diplomatic settlement of the crisis in Kosovo. Milosevic refuses to attend, and the Serb and KLA delegations refuse to accept an agreement.

March 18, 1999   The Kosovar delegation signs the Rambouillet agreement, but the Serbs refuse.

March 24, 1999   NATO begins Operation Allied Force, a campaign of air strikes primarily targeted against Serbian military, paramilitary, and police units in Kosovo and in Serbia proper.

Late March 1999   Serb crackdowns in Kosovo intensify, creating a severe refugee crisis with more than 500,000 Kosovars crossing the border into Albania and Macedonia.

June 1999   The Kosovo war ends. Milosevic agrees to allow limited provincial autonomy for Kosovo, remove Serb security forces from the province, and allow the deployment of a 50,000-strong NATO peacekeeping force under UN auspices. Peacekeepers and non-governmental organizations in Kosovo discover that some 10,000 ethnic Albanian civilians were killed during the conflict.

Yugoslavia's Cold War Stability, 1945–1990

Yugoslavia's Disintegration, 1991 to the Present

In 1945 Yugoslavia was established under the leadership of Josip Brotz Tito. The country began to disintegrate in June 1991, when Slovenia and Croatia declared independence. In March 1989 Serbian president Slobodan Milosevic revoked Kosovo's provincial autonomy and rallied Serbian nationalist sentiment against ethnic Albanians in the province. The Kosovo assembly voted in favor of independence in September 1991, and the Serbian government launched crackdowns, massacres, and other measures to force ethnic Albanians from their homes. In March 1999 NATO began Operation Allied Force, a campaign of air strikes against Serbian forces, to stop Serbian repression in Kosovo.

of 1974, Yugoslavia was established as a federal state consisting of six republics—Bosnia-Herzegovina, Croatia, Macedonia, Montenegro, Serbia, and Slovenia—and regions with provincial autonomy, including Kosovo and Vojvodina, to be governed by a collective federal presidency with rotating political authority (see map).[3] Tito's approach to dealing with ethnic nationalist differences in the Balkans was heavy-handed; he stifled the expression of differences through determined support for federal unity. Tito's death in 1980 created an opening for a liberalization of the system, which would include free market economics, democratization, and a resurgence of ethnic nationalism.[4]

In 1987 Slobodan Milosevic became president of Serbia, the dominant national component within Yugoslavia. Milosevic interpreted the liberalization of politics in the region as a challenge to the power of the Yugoslav federal government and a threat to Yugoslavia's security.[5] He began to mobilize Serbian nationalist sentiment and stepped up rhetorical attacks against Albanians, Croats, Muslims, and Slovenes, all of whom he believed were threatening the centralization of Yugoslav political authority. At the same time, new leaders in Slovenia and Croatia opposed Milosevic's demands for a return to a centralized system, preferring instead a loose confederation of states.[6]

Yugoslavia dissolved on June 25, 1991, when the regional governments of Slovenia and Croatia declared their national independence. Milosevic declared war on the secessionist republics, demanded a return to federation, and sent the Serb-dominated Yugoslav National Army (JNA) to stop them.[7] The war pitted Slovenia against Yugoslavia. The conflict lasted only ten days, with the Slovenes quickly winning de facto independence. The war between Croatia and Serbia, however, was much more intense. After six months of fighting that claimed 10,000 lives, Croatian and Serbian negotiators agreed to a cease-fire and the positioning of United Nations peacekeeping troops in a buffer zone in the spring of 1992.

April 1992 marked the beginning of a third conflict: the war in Bosnia, which had declared its independence in March 1992. This war began when Serb soldiers from the JNA crossed the Drina River in eastern Bosnia and joined forces with Bosnian Serb irregulars. The Serbs pressed their attacks against towns and villages in eastern Bosnia and soon surrounded Sarajevo, the Bosnian capital.[8] Experts estimate that 250,000 people were killed during the war and 2 million more became refugees between 1992 and 1995. The conflict ended with a negotiated settlement, the Dayton Peace Accord, on November 21, 1995. Leaders of the warring groups agreed that Bosnia would remain intact and its 1992 international borders legitimized. All parties to the conflict would provide for the safe return of refugees to their home regions, and an international tribunal for the investigation and prosecution of war crimes would be established at The Hague.[9] This arrangement would be supported by an international peace enforcement operation of 60,000 troops from European countries, the United States, and even Russia.

History of the Kosovo Crisis

Most parties to the Dayton negotiations were aware that Kosovo represented another potential ethno-political battleground in the Balkans. Kosovo, a small southern province of Serbia in Yugoslavia, had a population of about 2 million in the early 1990s. Ninety percent of the population were ethnic Albanian Muslim, or Kosovars. The remaining 10 percent were Serbs, who adhere to Orthodox Christianity. The demographics of the province, however, belied the tremendous religious and historical significance of Kosovo to the Serbs. Kosovo was the site of several Serbian Orthodox shrines from the Dark and Middle Ages, and many Serbs viewed Kosovo as the heart of their centuries-old religious traditions. In 1389, southern Slavs lost a major battle with the Ottoman Empire in Kosovo at the Field of Blackbirds, opening five centuries of Turkish rule of the Balkans. The Serbs did not succeed in fully dominating Kosovo until the Balkan War of 1912, when they destroyed all vestiges of Ottoman rule and forcibly expelled tens of thousands of ethnic Albanians from the region.[10]

In the immediate aftermath of World War II, the Kosovars were ruled in "semicolonial fashion by the Serbian communists, whose discriminatory policies caused 250,000 ethnic Albanians to emigrate from Kosovo."[11] In the interest of ethnic harmony (and political stability), however, in 1974 Tito recognized limited autonomy for Kosovo and for Vojvodina as part of the new constitutional arrangement. After Tito's death in 1980, Kosovo slowly became engulfed by ethnopolitical struggles. On the surface, Yugoslavia remained a communist country with a centralized federal government in Belgrade, but behind the rhetoric of ideology, Serb officials were well aware of simmering ethnic tensions in Kosovo. Ethnic Albanians there remained largely impoverished and disempowered by the communist system, while Serbs controlled municipal governments, schools, and police forces, in spite of being a minority in the province.

In the late 1980s Milosevic decided to use Kosovo as a staging ground for his rise to power in Serbia. In a speech commemorating the 600-year anniversary of the Serbs' defeat at the Field of Blackbirds, Milosevic promised the Serb minority that he would never allow the "sacred ground" of Kosovo to be taken from Serb control.[12] In 1989 he revoked Kosovo's provincial autonomy and imposed direct rule from Belgrade. Ethnic Albanians in Kosovo were outraged and deeply resented the Serb crackdown. In September 1991, the Kosovo political assembly voted in favor of independence and established a shadow government. Groups who favored armed insurrection against Serb dominance formed the Kosovo Liberation Army (KLA) in 1996, a guerrilla force that rapidly gained support.[13]

In the early 1990s, the administration of George Bush believed that a conflict in Kosovo would have far more serious consequences for U.S. interests than had the wars in Bosnia, Croatia, or Slovenia. Bush's advisers feared that Kosovo could become a tinderbox igniting a broader war involving Bulgaria, Greece, Turkey, and the Former Yugoslav Republic of Macedonia because of its location on the Serbia-Kosovo border and the mix of ethnic groups in the region. Consequently, Secretary of State Lawrence Eagleburger sent a cable to the U.S. embassy in Belgrade on Christmas Eve 1992 with instructions to read verbatim a one-sentence message to Milosevic, in person: "In the event of conflict in Kosovo caused by Serbian action, the United States will be prepared to employ military force against Serbians in Kosovo and in Serbia proper."[14] The Clinton administration reiterated the so-called Christmas Warning to Milosevic in February and July 1993, as the conflict in Bosnia worsened. After the signing of the Dayton Peace Accord in 1995, Milosevic and his allies worked to establish political footholds in Serb-dominated areas of internally divided Bosnia. In Kosovo, Serb paramilitary units and police continued to control the province with a tight fist, which Western governments chose to interpret as "compliance" with the Christmas Warning.

The Diplomacy of Delay

Simmering tensions came to a boil on February 28, 1998, when two Serb policemen were killed by Kosovars, and Serb police units retaliated by killing dozens of Kosovars suspected of nationalist activities and their families in Drenica. A few weeks later, Serb police units rounded up suspected members of the KLA and destroyed several neighborhoods in Racak. KLA fighters were undeterred by Serb reprisals in early 1998, however, and they pressed ahead in attacks against the Serb police and paramilitary presence in the province. Milosevic responded with sweeps of key villages in the search for KLA fighters. Images of the slain were televised around the world.

President Clinton and his advisers began to consider ways to respond to what was clearly becoming another ethnic war in the Balkans. His key foreign policy advisers during the crisis included Secretary of Defense William Cohen, Secretary of State Madeleine Albright, National Security Adviser Samuel Berger, and Chairman of the Joint Chiefs of Staff General Henry Shelton, the core of the Principals Committee of the National Security Council.

The committee agreed in early 1998 that conditions in the Balkans had changed so significantly that they were no longer willing to follow through on the Christmas Warning. The rise of the KLA and its attacks on Serb police and civilians had complicated the situation. The Kosovars were no longer peaceful civilians, according to Western intelligence reports. Perhaps more important, U.S. freedom to respond militarily in Kosovo was now vastly limited by the introduction into Bosnia of troops from NATO nations as part of the Dayton Peace Accord. U.S. military action would place these peacekeepers in jeopardy from Serb retaliation.

In early 1998 Clinton's advisers disagreed on a number of issues related to Kosovo, divisions that would become apparent in subsequent high-level meetings. Secretary of State Albright was an outspoken advocate of coercive diplomacy to restore stability to the region. She compared the standoff with Milosevic to the appeasement at Munich that led to Adolf Hitler's aggression in Europe. She began describing the events unfolding in Kosovo as "ethnic cleansing" and warned that the United States had learned a hard lesson from Bosnia—diplomacy not backed by force is ineffective against tyrants like Milosevic. Albright argued that NATO should immediately threaten air strikes against Serb units and facilities in Kosovo to stop the killings. She later noted, "I felt that there was still time to do something about this, and that we should not wait as long as we did on Bosnia to have dreadful things happen; that we could get it ahead of the curve."[15] Other top administration officials disagreed with Albright, however. National Security Adviser Berger preferred diplomatic options, and Secretary Cohen and General Shelton argued against the deployment of U.S. troops.

Unfortunately, there was no sustained focus on the crisis in Kosovo in the early months of 1998 by the Principals Committee. Instead, the White House was dealing with the burgeoning Monica Lewinsky scandal, Russia's severe economic problems, and upcoming presidential trips to China and Africa. One adviser recalled, "I hardly remember Kosovo in political discussions. It was all impeachment, impeachment, impeachment. There was nothing else."[16] There was little consensus about how to deal with Kosovo throughout the spring of 1998, so U.S. officials explored diplomatic routes. Robert Gelbard, the administration's envoy to the Balkans, was sent to Belgrade to confront Milosevic about escalating violence in Kosovo, and he hinted that NATO was considering the use of military force against Serbia.[17] Milosevic was reportedly so offended by Gelbard's harsh criticisms of Serb actions that he refused further meetings with the envoy.

Meanwhile, Albright decided to use the bully pulpit of her position as secretary of state to push for a more rapid and aggressive response to Milosevic's crackdown in Kosovo. She hoped that if she made her case persistently, she could possibly "force the administration to come along, convince the public and the American Congress to come along, and in the end give the allies no choice but to join what the United States is about to embark upon."[18] At a hastily arranged news conference on her way to a March 1998 meeting of the Contact Group in London, Albright announced without an administration consensus, "We are not going to stand by and watch the Serbian authorities do in Kosovo what they can no longer get away with doing in Bosnia. We have a broad range of options available to us."[19] At the London meeting she aggressively pushed for the West to actively resist Serbian aggression in Kosovo. Back in Washington there was much concern about the tenor of Albright's statement. The Pentagon was not supportive of issuing threats without careful consideration of U.S. willingness and ability to carry them out. Berger was also said to be concerned that U.S. credibility could be damaged by threatening actions that the president was unwilling to undertake.[20] According to close observers, the White House saw the Kosovo situation very differently from Albright. The White House believed,

> Milosevic is a man who, however odious his behavior, however wrong his policies, if you deal with him with the right kind of carrots and the right kind of sticks, you get a deal. There's a strong belief in the White House, and in other parts of the administration, that forceful rhetoric—threats without really having a policy behind it, such as those coming from the State Department—was the wrong kind of policy at the wrong time.[21]

In a May 1998 meeting at the White House, Gelbard made the case for air strikes against Serbia. Berger challenged Gelbard's proposal, saying that he had doubts about how such actions would play on the domestic front: "Are we going to bomb on Kosovo? Can I explain that to Congress? They'll kill us."[22] Berger also argued that threats should not be made without specific actions in mind. Gelbard responded that he had already worked out some targets with NATO's supreme allied commander, General Wesley Clark. According to secondary accounts, "Berger rejected the plan and no one else in the room supported Mr. Gelbard."[23] Instead the administration turned to Richard

Holbrooke, negotiator of the Dayton accord, to convince Kosovar leader Ibrahim Rugova to meet with Milosevic.[24] In return, Rugova was granted a meeting with President Clinton in the Oval Office on May 27 in which he warned that Kosovo was headed for all-out war and pleaded the case for urgent Western intervention and an increased U.S. presence to halt the escalating violence. According to reports, Clinton told him, "We will not allow another Bosnia to happen in Kosovo," but the president made no specific guarantees.[25]

NATO Military Planning

The conflict in Kosovo continued to escalate during the summer. At a NATO summit of defense ministers in June, Secretary of Defense Cohen asked allied ministers to consider developing contingency plans for intervention in Kosovo, but the Europeans were skeptical about taking any action without explicit authority from the UN Security Council. Eventually NATO defense ministers agreed to authorize the military command to begin planning options. They also agreed to present a show of force on the Yugoslavian border to send a message of resolve to Milosevic. On June 15, eighty-five NATO warplanes flew over Albania and Macedonia, but Serb generals interpreted it as a sign of NATO's *lack* of military resolve and derogatorily referred to the operation as the "Balkan Air Show." Soon thereafter, Serb forces began to retake the initiative in clashes with the KLA. By midsummer, more than 250,000 Kosovars had been made homeless by the fighting.

NATO planners considered a range of possibilities, including a massive air campaign, a peacekeeping operation, and an all-out ground war against Serbia. Alliance planning, however, was confounded by mixed political signals from NATO governments. In July, U.S. officials reportedly told NATO planners that "there is no way we are ever going to consider the deployment of ground troops, NATO or U.S., in [Kosovo]. The only thing that we are willing to do, and even to look at seriously, is the question of air strikes."[26]

In September, NATO military planners reported to President Clinton a worst-case scenario: 200,000 troops would be required to stop the killings in Kosovo and to occupy Serbia in the event of a ground war. They estimated that 75,000 troops would be needed for a more narrowly defined mission to occupy Kosovo and create safe havens for the ethnic Albanians there. For the White House, a major military invasion and occupation was out of the question. In high-level deliberations, Clinton drew parallels between such an operation and the Vietnam War and the debacle in Somalia. Key advisers expressed similar skepticism, warning that the American public knew little about the region or its problems and probably could not locate Kosovo on a map. Secretary Cohen and General Shelton argued that the operational details for ground operations were not well developed and that such a mission would be too vague and open-ended.[27] In consultation with General Clark, Secretaries Albright and Cohen began to believe that a concentrated program of air strikes might achieve the same objective as an invasion. They reasoned that the air war against Bosnian Serb positions in 1995 had brought Milosevic to the negotiating table in Dayton, so perhaps it would work a second time.

The Clinton Administration Moves to Strike

Serious fighting between Serb forces and the KLA in September—and televised images of massacres—pushed the West into action. On September 16, Serb paramilitary units attacked a village in central Kosovo, killing twenty-two civilians, and on September 29 Western media reported a massacre in Donji Obrinje.

On September 23, the Security Council had passed Resolution 1199, which called for a cease-fire, a Serb withdrawal of forces, and the return of refugees. NATO defense ministers meeting in Vilamoura, Portugal, deliberated air strikes against Serbia. NATO secretary-general Javier Solana argued that the very credibility of the alliance was at stake and that the West could not stand by and allow a gradual takeover of the province by Serb forces. He was outraged by a Serb diplomat who had joked, "A village a day keeps NATO away." [28] On September 24, 1998, with the legitimation of Resolution 1199, NATO leaders agreed to warn Milosevic that an activation order for allied air strikes might be issued in the near future.

The president convened a meeting of the Principals Committee on September 30 to evaluate the U.S. response to the crisis. Sitting on the conference table in front of the participants that morning was a copy of the day's *New York Times,* with a front-page story and pictures of the massacre in Donji Obrinje. Secretary Albright reiterated her plea for air strikes to bring Milosevic to the bargaining table. Instead of their usual debates, however, members of the committee supported her recommendations. They decided to ask NATO ministers for an activation order authorizing General Clark to put alliance aircraft on ready alert.

The committee also agreed to send Holbrooke back to Belgrade with the threat of air strikes to win Milosevic's acceptance of Resolution 1199, but he was instructed that U.S. ground troops were not to be involved in any settlement he negotiated, including peacekeeping.[29] Ideally, the administration hoped to achieve peace in Kosovo, but more pragmatically it believed that a diplomatic settlement with a moderate level of commitment would at least stabilize the crisis in the short term. Holbrooke and Albright believed that a commitment of U.S. troops was necessary for a lasting settlement, but unfortunately, strained relations between the president and Congress made such a commitment politically impossible.

The White House decided to go on a domestic political offensive to build support for a possible NATO air war against Serbia. The president outlined the plan for air strikes in a letter to leading senators in early October. Clinton wrote that the air strikes "would start out strong and progressively expand in scale and scope" if Serbian forces remained in Kosovo. "There will be no pinprick strikes," the president promised.[30] The congressional response to Clinton's appeal was swift. On October 4, Senate majority leader Trent Lott, R-Miss., warned the president that Congress would not support military action.[31] Other Republican and Democratic leaders expressed their displeasure with the White House approach as well. Critics inside and outside the government warned of the "wag the dog" scenario—a reference to the 1998 film of the same name that portrayed a fictional president's decision to go to war against Albania to distract the public from a sex scandal in Washington.[32]

Early Attempts at Coercive Diplomacy

By mid-October, the White House recognized that there was little domestic consensus for military action in Kosovo, and the NATO alliance was also divided on the question. Furthermore, the pressures of congressional elections in November had diverted a great deal of Washington's attention inward. Clinton pinned his hopes on negotiations with Milosevic. Holbrooke and his diplomatic team traveled to Belgrade for nine days of talks. On October 15, Holbrooke announced a settlement. Milosevic agreed to withdraw the majority of Serb forces from Kosovo and ordered the end to paramilitary and police repression of Kosovars. Milosevic further agreed to permit 1,800 unarmed, international inspectors to monitor the peace in Kosovo and to allow overflights by NATO reconnaissance planes to complement verification of Serb compliance.[33] Clinton hailed the deal as a triumph of coercive diplomacy—a carrot-and-stick diplomatic approach backed by the threat of force. The president announced that Milosevic had "agreed to internationally supervised democratic elections in Kosovo, substantial self-government and a local police—in short, rights that the Kosovars have been demanding since Mr. Milosevic stripped their autonomy a decade ago."[34]

The Organization for Security and Cooperation in Europe (OSCE) sponsored the creation and deployment of the unarmed international observer force and selected veteran U.S. diplomat William Walker to head the operation. OSCE observer groups began patrolling Kosovo in November 1998. Although Americans participated as unarmed monitors, the United States refused to contribute combat troops to an extrication force stationed in Macedonia, to be mobilized if the monitors required emergency evacuation from the province.

Unfortunately, the warring factions in the region viewed the October agreement more as an opportunity to regroup and gain strategic advantage than a pledge for permanent peace. According to NATO officials, Serb forces began sending reinforcements and equipment to the region under cover of darkness in the late fall. At the same time, KLA forces took the opportunity to relocate troops and resupply. Ethnic Albanians living in other countries, including the United States, stepped up financial support of the KLA resupply effort in the winter of 1998–1999. Soon both sides were engaged in attacks and counterattacks, but this time OSCE observers were caught in the middle. Ambassador Walker was personally threatened at one point by a drunken belligerent Serb wielding a gun and a hand grenade, and OSCE representatives began to plead to their home governments for security.

The Road to Operation Allied Force

In December 1998—just weeks after OSCE representatives arrived and began monitoring operations—Serbian soldiers rounded up and killed thirty-six suspected KLA rebels. The Kosovars retaliated sporadically in the northern part of the province. Observers estimated that some 2,500 ethnic Albanian Kosovars had been killed in the struggle for autonomy by the end of 1998 and about 230,000 had fled their homes in the face of the violence and fear of Serb paramilitary killings.[35]

NATO and U.S. intelligence agencies began to detect signs of increased Serbian activity around Kosovo in January 1999 and learned that the Serbs were planning a massive encircling operation against the KLA after the spring thaw. The plan was to move tanks and artillery into Kosovo to attack KLA strongholds and drive hundreds of thousands of ethnic Albanians from key areas. Intercepted messages suggested that Serbian military leaders believed that the West would tolerate the operation if they "only attacked a village a week."[36]

Despite this deteriorating situation, there was little response from the Clinton administration. The White House was distracted by brinksmanship with Iraq over United Nations inspections of suspected nuclear, chemical, and biological weapons facilities. Saddam Hussein had once again chosen to challenge the UN inspection regime, and Western allies were confronted with a dilemma over the proper course of action to force compliance. Thus after consideration of problems in the Persian Gulf, the president approved four days of isolated bombings of Iraq.

October Plus

On January 15, the Principals Committee met to discuss the deteriorating situation in Kosovo. All agreed that Milosevic had reneged on the October agreement.[37] The most recent intelligence on Kosovo, completed in November, concluded that "the October agreement indicates that Milosevic is susceptible to outside pressure. He will eventually accept a number of outcomes, from autonomy to provisional status with final resolution to be determined, as long as he remains the undisputed leader in Belgrade." The report also concluded, however, that Milosevic would accept a change in the status of Kosovo "only when he believes his power is endangered" by "insurgents driving up the economic and military costs of holding onto the province, or the West threatening to use sustained and decisive military power against his forces."[38] Albright insisted that it was time to use threats of military intervention to force a comprehensive settlement. She argued that Milosevic "understands only the language of force."[39]

General Shelton continued to voice the Pentagon's strong opposition to using force in Kosovo.[40] First, the Joint Chiefs of Staff questioned whether the conflict in Kosovo significantly affected U.S. national interests. They doubted Albright's domino theory that the fall of Kosovo would inevitably cause the conflict to spread throughout the Balkans. It struck them as reminiscent of the flawed arguments that led to the ill-conceived U.S. participation in the Vietnam War. Second, Shelton argued that air strikes would not guarantee the political aims of the administration; they would neither inhibit the ethnic cleansing taking place on the ground nor force Milosevic to the negotiating table. Third, ground troops were out of the question, in part because the months it would take to build up the 100,000 to 200,000 troops needed to control Kosovo would provide Serbia with time to overrun the province and ethnically cleanse it. Given the lack of a clear vision for Balkan policy, the Pentagon feared that any use of ground troops would devolve into a long-term, open-ended commitment. The Pentagon therefore suggested the increased use of economic sanctions and other non-military forms of pressure, such as indicting Milosevic for war crimes in Bosnia.

Albright failed to carry the day at this meeting. Berger remained unconvinced that the threat of military intervention was a wise choice at this time.

On the political front, the Senate impeachment trial of Clinton over the Lewinsky matter had just begun. There was little sense that the American public would support a military escalation in an obscure part of Europe during a political crisis at home. Furthermore, there was no allied commitment for a more aggressive stance. National Security Council analysts believed that Albright underestimated the difficulties of using military forces to support diplomacy. Cohen, too, rejected Albright's recommendations and was generally supportive of the Pentagon position. Speaking about his position in January 1999, Cohen recollected,

> I felt that military force should be the absolute last resort. Everything else has to fail before you turn to the military. And if you turn to the military, you must be very clear on what the objectives are, measuring those political objectives, and how military action can be consistent with carrying out and furthering those goals. I want to be very clear that we have domestic support before we ever commit our forces to combat.... Also we must have the support of the allies.[41]

Albright, Berger, and Cohen could only agree on what was called the October Plus strategy, that is, bolstering the ongoing process constructed by Holbrooke the previous fall by renewing shuttle diplomacy between the warring sides in an effort to better protect the peace monitors, train a Kosovar police force, and prepare for elections. After the meeting, Albright was furious that the White House had made no progress toward constructing a more comprehensive, effective policy. "We're just gerbils running on a wheel," she said.[42]

The policy gerbils would soon break free from their cage, however. On the day of the disappointing Principals Committee meeting, Serb forces executed forty-five unarmed villagers in Racak. The bodies were discovered by OSCE monitors, and Ambassador Walker personally called the State Department with the news. Albright realized that with swift action, Racak could be the event to galvanize U.S. and NATO policy on Kosovo. One adviser reportedly told her, "Whatever threat of force you don't get in the next two weeks you're never getting ... at least until the next Racak."[43]

Berger reconvened the Principals Committee on the evening of January 19, a night of high drama. The Senate impeachment trial of President Clinton had begun days before, and that night the president was to deliver his State of the Union address to the very Congress that was seeking to remove him from office. It also became clear that Racak had changed the decision-making dynamics in the administration. One senior U.S. official observed, "Racak made clear that Milosevic was not going to live up to his commitments."[44] There was also growing evidence that a major escalation was planned for the spring. Above and beyond the humanitarian concern for the hundreds of thousands of refugees that would be generated by the fighting, the administration began to see the containment of this conflict as a vital interest to the United States. More decision makers seemed to accept Undersecretary of State Thomas Pickering's argument that "the conflict in Kosovo has no natural boundaries."[45] As fighting in the province intensified and huge numbers of refugees flooded across Kosovo's borders, the administration began to fear that the war would engulf large parts of southern and central Europe. A foreign policy official describing administration thinking at the time said, "In short, we're at the edge of a precipice. There's a reason why our central military alliance in the world is in Europe. It's the history of the 20th century."[46]

Albright opened the Principals meeting by once again presenting her strategy to issue an ultimatum to Milosevic and back it with the threat of NATO bombing. The ultimatum would require that Milosevic accept NATO troops in Kosovo to enforce the terms of a peace agreement and that Serbia withdraw almost all of its forces from the province and provide it with meaningful autonomy. Albright argued that the United States, in order to convince Milosevic and the allies of the seriousness of its commitment, had to be prepared to deploy ground troops as part of a peace deal. She added that after eight years of issuing ultimatums, U.S. and NATO credibility was at risk. One adviser commented at the time, "There are massive bloodbaths all over the world and we're not intervening in them ... [but] this one's in the heart of Europe. I'd argue that the alliance itself is at risk because if it's unable to address a major threat within Europe, it really loses its reason for being."[47]

Albright knew that to gain approval of her position she had to be sensitive to other political realities. The NATO allies would only accept ground troops as a peacekeeping operation for implementing a settlement, not as combat units invading Kosovo to impose a settlement. An aide to Albright who helped draft her position noted, "Our assumption was that we had to find ways to minimize the percentage of American troops and emphasize a 'permissive environment' if there was any hope of getting the Pentagon and the president and Congress to buy it."[48] Consequently, the issue of using combat ground troops to halt ethnic cleansing or to force Milosevic to negotiate was never seriously discussed.[49]

Until this meeting, Berger had opposed doing anything more than supplement the October agreement. Cohen and General Shelton had been even more adamant in their refusal to go beyond October Plus. Both sought to avoid strategies calling for the introduction of more U.S. troops to the Balkans in any role.[50] Berger and Cohen also realized, however, that "the politics [were] moving in the direction that Albright wants to go."[51] Berger therefore agreed to Albright's proposal. In the early stages of the discussion, Cohen continued to resist the use of ground troops even in a permissive environment. According to one participant, a two-part consensus evolved at the meeting: one was to make a credible threat of military force, and the other was to demand the attendance of Serb and Kosovar representatives for a meeting at which the basic principles of a settlement would be decided in advance by the Contact Group, including Russia. These basic principles would be non-negotiable, including a NATO implementation force.[52] The following day Berger informed President Clinton of the new consensus. Clinton agreed with it, though he made no formal decision about whether U.S. troops would participate in the implementation of a settlement.

Planning for Action

On January 21, Clinton phoned British prime minister Tony Blair to discuss the new U.S. direction in Kosovo strategy. Both agreed that there were two options available: reprisal bombings for Racak or a comprehensive diplomatic agreement enforced by NATO troops.[53] Even as the Clinton administration moved toward a more aggressive policy on Kosovo, however, it was troubled by the inability to agree on an analysis of Milosevic's motivation and likely reaction to the policy options being considered. One senior administration official, looking back, noted,

> As we contemplated the use of force over the past 14 months, we constructed four different models. One was that the whiff of gunpowder, just the threat of force would make [Milosevic] back down. Another was that he needed to take some hit to justify acquiescence. Another was that he was a playground bully who would fight but back off after a punch in the nose. And fourth was that he would react like Saddam Hussein. On any given day people would pick one or the other. We thought the Saddam Hussein option was always the least likely, but we knew it was out there and now we're looking at it.[54]

High-ranking officials at the State Department tended to view Milosevic as the schoolyard bully, based on his concession in Bosnia after NATO air strikes and a ground offensive by Croatian troops and on his willingness to bargain with Holbrooke in October 1998 under the threat of additional NATO air strikes. An Albright aide stated, "What happened in Bosnia and in October showed that the threat of force can work, not that it will work, and therefore it was worth trying." [55] On the other hand, most of the Pentagon and parts of the intelligence apparatus tended to see Milosevic as far more intransigent and dangerous. A late January intelligence report concluded, "Confronted with a take it or leave it deal, Milosevic may opt to risk a NATO bombing campaign rather than surrender control over Kosovo. He may assume he can absorb a limited attack and the allies will not support a long campaign." Another report filed just a week later contradictorily predicted, "Milosevic will seek to give just enough to avoid NATO bombing." [56]

Albright spent much of the rest of January negotiating the terms for NATO's threat of force. On January 30, after UN secretary-general Kofi Annan indicated that force would be justified to bring the Serbs to the bargaining table, the allies agreed that they had sufficient legal grounds to use force if Serbia refused to enter into negotiations. NATO ministers approved its second activation order in preparation for war. Clinton and his foreign policy advisers convened on February 1 for further consideration of the plan to threaten air strikes. Clinton recognized that because Kosovo was probably more important to Milosevic than was Bosnia, he "may be sorely tempted to take the first round of air strikes. I hope we don't have to bomb, but we may need to." [57] Though the administration was now committed to the use of air strikes as part of a strategy of coercive diplomacy, the Joint Chiefs of Staff continued to doubt its efficacy. Despite conflicting intelligence analyses of Milosevic's motivation and likely reaction to coercion, none of the participants at the meeting raised the issue of contingencies if the bombings failed. An administration official later observed, "Governments make the decisions that are necessary to make and they leave for another day decisions that are very hard, for eventualities that everybody hopes will never occur." [58]

Secretary of State Albright did order her department's Policy Planning director, Morton Halperin, to investigate the possible negative consequences of the threat of air strikes. Halperin later presented decision makers with a five-page memorandum titled "Surprises." The memo noted a number of problematic possibilities, including (1) that the Kosovars would renege on an agreement or initiate military operations; (2) that Milosevic would continue low-level fighting while offering a false peace; (3) that NATO would ultimately refuse to launch air strikes; or (4) that Russia would resist peace efforts, perhaps by offering military assistance to Serbia. [59] One official said that by far the most troubling possibility raised in the memo was the chance that the NATO bombings would touch off a massive offensive by the Serbs. This would leave

Clinton vulnerable to charges that his air strikes had caused the very harm that they were intended to prevent. The official noted that the only solution to such an eventuality would be "to try to get the military resources" to win the war "as quickly as we could."[60] Ultimately, no serious contingency plans were made for positioning U.S. troops in the region for humanitarian purposes or for combat should the bombing strategy fail.

Defiance at Rambouillet

On February 6, an international diplomatic conference was opened at Rambouillet, France, to give Milosevic and the Kosovars one last chance to reach an agreement (and to convince the Europeans that all reasonable efforts had been taken to avoid the use of force). The United States wanted to protect ethnic Albanian Kosovars from Serbian repression but did not support independence for the province. It was thought that independence would be a destabilizing precedent calling into question the legitimacy of other multiethnic nations in central Europe, including Bosnia. The basic allied proposal at Rambouillet included a cease-fire, the removal of most Serbian security forces from Kosovo, the demilitarization of the KLA, a NATO peacekeeping force with access to all of Yugoslavia, and greater internal autonomy for Kosovo for at least three years.

Milosevic did not bother to attend the conference, and the Serb delegation refused to sign any agreement that included NATO peacekeeping troops in Kosovo. The Kosovar delegation also rejected the allied proposal, demanding instead a guarantee of complete independence for Kosovo. In late February, with both parties to the dispute obstructing agreement, the allies recessed the conference. Albright angrily announced that "if the talks crater because the Serbs do not say yes, we will have bombing. If the talks crater because the Albanians have not said yes, we will not be able to support them; and, in fact, will have to cut off whatever help they're getting from the outside."[61] After the talks reconvened in Paris on March 15, the Kosovars signed on to the proposal, but once again the Serbs refused. Albright later observed that the Kosovar's signing at Rambouillet was critical in two ways: solidifying the European allies' support for the use of force against the Serbs and selling the Albanians on the settlement.[62]

While the Rambouillet talks were stalled through much of February and March, preparations to increase the pressure on Milosevic continued in Washington. On February 13—one day after he was acquitted in his Senate impeachment trial—President Clinton announced his intention to include U.S. troops among the post-settlement implementation forces. A former NSC adviser observed, "Once the Lewinsky scandal ended, once the final political step in that torturous year-long process [was] over, the president [felt] able to commit to the deployment of ground troops. He wasn't able to commit beforehand." [63] Although in private Clinton had always agreed that U.S. troops would participate in the implementation of a Rambouillet settlement, this was the first public acknowledgment of that policy.

On March 13, Clinton and his top advisers met to assess the diplomatic situation. In two days talks would reconvene in Paris, and the Kosovars were expected to sign the agreement. Milosevic would now have to accept the terms of Rambouillet or suffer NATO air strikes. Most in the White House thought he would reluctantly acquiesce or perhaps take a few symbolic strikes from NATO before agreeing. The group contacted Ambassador Christopher Hill for his assessment of the likelihood that an accord could be reached. He answered, "Zero point zero percent." [64] One participant recalled "stunned silence in the room." [65] They now realized that Milosevic had decided to challenge NATO.

Two days later, at another White House meeting, final preparations were made for the air strikes. By this time, the Joint Chiefs of Staff had unanimously voted to support them. In spite of continuing reservations, they were swayed ultimately by the need to protect U.S. leadership in NATO and by the brewing humanitarian catastrophe in Kosovo. [66] Despite the military's acquiescence, General Shelton conveyed their fear that "[i]n the short term, military action would make things worse in Kosovo." [67] CIA director George Tenet had warned in early February that NATO air strikes might set off a wave of ethnic cleansing by the Serbs. [68] Shelton's and Tenet's assessment was supported by a March military intelligence report concluding that Milosevic intended to ethnically cleanse all 1.8 million Albanians within a week. [69] By the March 15 meeting, U.S. and NATO estimates indicated that there were now 30,000 Serbian forces in Kosovo—twice the limit allowed by the October agreement—and there were an additional 40,000 troops with 300 tanks massing on the Kosovo border. [70] The White House downplayed the prognosis of massive ethnic cleansing and assumed that if Milosevic attacked Kosovo his primary target would be the KLA, not the civilian population.

When on March 18 the Kosovars signed the Rambouillet agreement, Albright decided to send Holbrooke to Belgrade. No one was confident that he would have much success at this point; General Clark objected that a mission by Holbrooke gave Milosevic more time to deploy troops and equipment. Holbrooke and Hill met with Milosevic on March 22 to deliver the ultimatum that unless the Serbs signed the Rambouillet accord, NATO would begin bombing.

Milosevic refused.[71] Faced with Milosevic's intransigence, Holbrooke immediately recommended to Clinton and Albright that his mission be canceled.[72] The following night, Holbrooke briefed NATO secretary-general Solana in Brussels on the collapse of the talks. Solana then gave General Clark authorization for the air campaign. On March 24, Berger met with Clinton to discuss the failure of the Holbrooke mission. Berger informed Clinton, "We're going to go, unless you say otherwise." Clinton simply replied, "Let's do it."[73]

Despite Pentagon recommendations for a massive air campaign, a more limited option was chosen. Only ninety-one approved targets, restricted to purely military facilities, were on the bombing list for the first three days. The list was a compromise to maintain unity within NATO, as a number of members were uncomfortable with any bombing. In addition, most civilians in the Clinton administration felt that a moderate air campaign would be sufficient to bring Milosevic back to the table.

Clinton Addresses the Nation

On March 24, President Clinton addressed the nation on television to announce that NATO air strikes on Yugoslavia had begun. He portrayed the U.S. intervention as part of a moral imperative to protect the Kosovars. Furthermore, he said, the bombing would protect U.S. national interests by preventing the spread of war in this historically volatile region and helping create "a Europe that is prosperous, secure, undivided and free." He then outlined the objectives of the campaign:

> Our mission is clear: to demonstrate the seriousness of NATO's purpose so that the Serbian leaders understand the imperative of reversing course. To deter an even bloodier offensive against innocent civilians in Kosovo and if necessary to seriously damage the Serbian military's capacity to harm the people of Kosovo. In short, if President Milosevic will not make peace, we will limit his ability to make war.[74]

Clinton also said that should Milosevic agree to a settlement, NATO would provide peacekeeping troops. "If NATO is invited to do so, our troops should take part in that mission to keep the peace. But I do not intend to put our troops in Kosovo to fight a war."[75]

Clinton's declaration that he had no intention of using U.S. troops to fight a war in Kosovo had been carefully prepared. Berger had included this reference in the address. The ever-cautious Berger was "a pivotal voice against moving toward the use of ground troops" in any combat role in Kosovo.[76]

Berger saw a number of problems with a ground option. A U.S.-led ground war in Kosovo could split NATO, destroy U.S. relations with Russia, and devastate U.S. public support for efforts to stop Milosevic in Kosovo. In addition, Berger felt that NATO had far greater military advantages in the air compared to on the ground: "We had an advantage of 100-1, 1000-1 from the air.... If we were forced to go in on the ground in deep summer, it would have been maybe 3-1 or 2-1. Milosevic would have been able to be on much more equal grounds with NATO."[77] Defending the decision to explicitly rule out a ground option in Clinton's speech, Berger rationalized, "We would have been paralyzed by a debate in NATO, and paralyzed, in my judgement, by a debate in this country by what was at that point a hypothetical, distant option."[78]

President Clinton, too, had strong reservations about the use of U.S. ground troops in a combat role. Beyond his inclination to worry about his hold on public support, his advisers were also warning him of the danger of an open-ended commitment. One senior adviser said that if NATO sent troops into Kosovo, "Invade, occupy and stay there. You own this country."[79] Clinton echoed these concerns in an interview with Dan Rather in the first week of the air campaign, saying, "The thing that bothers me about introducing ground troops into a hostile situation, into Kosovo and into the Balkans, is the prospect of never being able to get them out."[80]

Clinton would later say that he was faced with "a bunch of bad options."[81] To Clinton and Berger, deploying ground troops was too dangerous—politically and militarily—while doing nothing was morally bankrupt and called into question the international credibility of the president, the United States, and NATO. With all its flaws, the choice of air strikes without ground troops seemed the only viable option.

Others in the administration saw a president torn by moral and pragmatic instincts—and his historical understanding of both. Clinton was morally unwilling to allow Serb forces to overrun and ethnically cleanse Kosovo, but he also was only willing to bear the political cost of air strikes, even though many advisers thought ground troops necessary.[82] Clinton had seen the terrible human consequences of delay and inaction in Bosnia and Rwanda and the political cost of Vietnam and Somalia. He had also witnessed the eventual success of intervention in Bosnia. Former senior adviser George Stephanopoulos observed, "You take Somalia, that's what forces you out. You take Bosnia, that's what pushes you in. It highlights how there are no good choices."[83]

The War

The Kosovo war lasted 78 days. Operation Allied Force consisted of strikes primarily targeted against Serbian military, paramilitary, and police units. Within the first ten days of the campaign, Serbian security forces took almost full control of Kosovo on the ground and pushed more than 500,000 Kosovars across the border into Albania and Macedonia, creating a massive humanitarian crisis. By the end of the war, 860,000 Kosovars had been expelled from the country and another 600,000 were internal refugees. A senior NATO military official acknowledged that the alliance always recognized that Milosevic might respond harshly to the air strikes, but he conceded, "We underestimated the ferocity and velocity of Milosevic's offensive to transform the ethnic balance in Kosovo."[84]

It soon became clear that Milosevic would not politely concede after a brief air war; the humanitarian crisis rapidly worsened. NATO leaders ordered the pace of the bombings escalated, but there were not enough aircraft in theater to sustain around-the-clock war for several more weeks. It was not until May that the augmented air campaign, Papa Bear, reached its full strength.[85] As the war dragged on, an increasing number of attacks were aimed directly at command and communications facilities and infrastructure inside Serbia, including high-profile targets in downtown Belgrade.

The United States was heavily engaged in Operation Allied Force. Its military contributed more than 725 aircraft, hundreds of artillery and multiple-launch rocket systems for theater ground attack, and about 5,500 supporting troops in the theater of operation. U.S. Navy ships fired 450 Tomahawk cruise missiles, and the Air Force launched 90 cruise missiles.[86] Tens of thousands of soldiers were committed to the air operation at military bases worldwide. President Clinton also activated 5,000 reservists to provide logistical support. Experts estimated that U.S. participation in the war totaled some $5 billion.[87]

Eleven weeks into the campaign, the war abruptly ended after Milosevic agreed to limited provincial autonomy for Kosovo, to remove Serb security forces from the region, and to a 50,000-strong NATO peacekeeping force under UN auspices. More than 600,000 Kosovars were repatriated. Seven thousand U.S. soldiers were deployed to Kosovo as part of the peacekeeping force, with an estimated operational cost of some $3.5 billion annually.[88] Peacekeepers and non-governmental organizations in Kosovo soon discovered that some 10,000 Albanian civilians had been killed during the conflict. The Clinton administration and NATO allies celebrated their military victory over Milosevic, but they were left to consider whether their actions in Kosovo had been a triumph of coercive diplomacy.

Conclusion: Defining the National Interest

Clinton administration decision making on the crisis in Kosovo was shaped by a number of factors. First, the complexity of the problem in Kosovo made decision making more difficult. Without cold war orientations that seemed to simplify perspectives on world events, administration officials had great difficulty defining the significance of the problem in Kosovo for U.S. national interests. Moreover, without the old bipolar forces shaping events and behavior, predicting the outbreak and pattern of conflict had become much more problematic.

Second, the administration long debated whether Kosovo was "merely" a human rights crisis or whether it had deeper implications for U.S. national security. The lack of agreement about the significance of the problem, in turn, made it less likely that a policy consensus could be achieved quickly. Secretary Albright and the State Department argued that Milosevic's actions were not only a grievous human rights violation, but also a threat to the stability of central Europe and hence vital to U.S. national interest. The Pentagon doubted that security interests were at risk. Only when the crisis boiled over during the winter of 1998–1999—with more brazen and severe acts of ethnic cleansing, a flood of refugees spilling into neighboring countries, and a growing recognition that NATO's impotence was on full display—was the administration able to agree that a policy of coherent, forceful coercive diplomacy was necessary.

Constructing that option, however, was further complicated by the inability of the administration to ascertain Milosevic's motivation and strategy in Kosovo and hence his likely response to efforts to limit his aggression. Without the cold war structural constraints to limit Milosovic's options, the Clinton administration could no more understand Milosevic in Serbia than it could Saddam Hussein in Iraq or Mohamed Farah Aideed in Somalia. The administration's efforts to agree upon the substance of a coercive diplomacy option were slowed by the inability to decide whether Milosevic was a wily international negotiator, a schoolyard bully, or a fanatical nationalist willing to fight to the end. Ultimately, its initial policy underestimated his resolve and his willingness to order horrific measures against the Kosovars.

Finally, the role of domestic politics was also significant in this case. At various times, the precarious political standing of President Clinton distracted the administration from paying sufficient attention to the burgeoning crisis in the Balkans. Even when policy makers focused on the crisis in Kosovo, the costs and benefits of policy options were often viewed through a domestic politics lens. Throughout the crisis, the White House consistently opposed the deployment of U.S. troops in a variety of roles on the basis of the domestic political costs. Concerns about congressional opposition, lack of public support, and electoral setbacks were abundant. As intervention in Kosovo was contemplated in the White House, contrasting historical analogies were raised. Clinton's desire to avoid another Rwanda—where the West passively accepted the slaughter of hundreds of thousands of innocent civilians—was more than balanced by the images of Vietnam and Somalia. Visions of the political debacles in Vietnam and Somalia consistently raised domestic red flags for intervention in Kosovo. Clinton's sensitivity to these events was no doubt heightened by the escalating partisan conflict that had plagued Washington since the mid-1980s. Ultimately the option chosen—an air war—seemed to be heavily determined by a desire to restrain Milosevic's aggression, but at the least possible domestic cost to the United States.

Notes

1. See John G. Stoessinger, *Why Nations Go to War* (New York: St. Martin's Press, 1998), 185–195.

2. Christopher Bennett, *Yugoslavia's Bloody Collapse: Causes, Course and Consequences* (London: Hurst, 1995); see also Laura Silber and Alan Little, *The Death of Yugoslavia* (London: Penguin, 1997).

3. Stoessinger, *Why Nations Go to War*, 191.

4. Noel Malcolm, *Bosnia: A Short History* (New York: New York University Press, 1994), 54–55.

5. See Susan L. Woodward, *Balkan Tragedy: Chaos and Dissolution after the Cold War* (Washington, D.C.: Brookings Institution Press, 1995).

6. Misha Glenny, *The Fall of Yugoslavia: The Third Balkan War* (New York: Penguin, 1992), 6.

7. See Sabrina Petra Ramet, "War in the Balkans," *Foreign Affairs* 71, no. 4 (fall 1992): 174–181.

8. See Steven L. Burg and Paul S. Shoup, *The War in Bosnia-Herzegovina: Ethnic Conflict and International Intervention* (Armonk, N.Y.: M. E. Sharpe, 1999).

9. "Maßnahmen zur Absicherung des Friedensvertrages für Bosnien-Herzegowina," *Reihe Stichworte für die Öffentlichkeitsarbeit und Truppeninformation* (Bonn: Bundesministerium der Verteidigung Presse- und Informationsstab Referat Öffentlichkeitarbeit, 1995).

10. William Hagen, "Kosovo: The History behind It All," *Foreign Affairs* 78, no. 4 (July/August 1999): 57.

11. Ibid., 58.

12. Roger Cohen, "Crisis in the Balkans: Kosovo Notebook," *New York Times*, July 2, 1999, A1.

13. "Chronology of Events Relating to the Kosovo Conflict," *New York Times*, March 24, 1999, A6.

14. Barton Gellman, "The Path to Crisis: How the United States and Its Allies Went to War," *Washington Post*, April 18, 1999, A1.

15. Ibid.

16. Elaine Sciolino and Ethan Bronner, "Crisis in the Balkans: The Road to War," *New York Times,* April 18, 1999, A1.

17. Doyle McManus, "Crisis in Yugoslavia: Debate Turns to Finger-Pointing on Kosovo Policy," *Los Angeles Times,* April 11, 1999, 1.

18. WGBH, "Interview with Ivo Daalder," *Frontline: War in Europe, 2000,* http://www.pbs.org/wgbh/pages/frontline/shows/kosovo/interviews/daalder.html.

19. Gellman, "The Path to Crisis." The Contact Group was made up of diplomats from France, Germany, Great Britain, Russia, and the United States, who attempted to coordinate their responses to the Balkan crises in the 1990s.

20. Gellman, "The Path to Crisis."

21. WGBH, "Interview with Ivo Daalder."

22. John Harris, "Berger's Caution Has Shaped the Role of U.S. in War," *Washington Post,* May 16, 1999, A1.

23. Sciolino and Bronner, "Crisis in the Balkans."

24. Ibid., A6.

25. Ibid., A1.

26. WGBH "Interview with Ivo Daalder."

27. Gellman, "The Path to Crisis."

28. Ibid.

29. Accounts of the September 30 meeting are from WGBH, "Interview with Ivo Daalder."

30. Sciolino and Bronner, "Crisis in the Balkans."

31. Ibid.

32. Ibid.

33. Jane Perlez, "Yugoslav Leader Is Not Complying with Kosovo Pact," *New York Times,* October 16, 1998, A1; and Jane Perlez, "Two Exempt Army Battalians Are Deployed by Milosevic," *New York Times,* October 20, 1998, A14.

34. Sciolino and Bronner, "Crisis in the Balkans."

35. Michael Mandelbaum, "A Perfect Failure: NATO's War against Yugoslavia," *Foreign Affairs* 78, no. 5 (September/October 1999): 2.

36. Sciolino and Bronner, "Crisis in the Balkans."

37. Gellman, "The Path to Crisis."

38. Ibid.

39. Michael Hirsh and John Barry, "How We Stumbled into War," *Newsweek,* April 12, 1999, 40.

40. Bradley Graham, "Joint Chiefs Doubted Air Strategy," *Washington Post,* April 5, 1999, A1.

41. WGBH, "Interview with William Cohen," *Frontline: War in Europe, 2000,* http://www.pbs.org/wgbh/pages/frontline/shows/kosovo/interviews/cohen.html.

42. Gellman, "The Path to Crisis."

43. Ibid.

44. Barton Gellman, "U.S. Has 'Vital Interests' in Containing Conflict," *Washington Post,* February 21, 1999, A1.

45. Ibid.

46. Ibid.

47. Barton Gellman, "In the End Allies See No Credible Alternative," *Washington Post,* March 23, 1999, A12.

48. Gellman, "The Path to Crisis."

49. John Harris, "Clinton Saw No Alternative to Air Strikes," *Washington Post,* April 1, 1999, A1.

50. Sciolino and Bronner, "Crisis in the Balkans."

51. WGBH, "Interview with Ivo Daalder."

52. Gellman, "The Path to Crisis."

53. Sciolino and Bronner, "Crisis in the Balkans."

54. Thomas Lippman, "State Department Miscalculated on Kosovo," *Washington Post,* April 7, 1999, A1.

55. Ibid.

56. Sciolino and Bronner, "Crisis in the Balkans."

57. Gellman, "The Path to Crisis."

58. Ibid.

59. Ibid.

60. Ibid.

61. WGBH, *Frontline: War in Europe, 2000,* http://www.pbs.org/wgbh/pages/frontline/shows/kosovo/etc/script1.html.

62. Sciolino and Bronner, "Crisis in the Balkans."

63. WGBH, "Interview with Ivo Daalder."

64. Hirsh and Barry, "How We Stumbled into War," 38.

65. Ibid.

66. Graham, "Joint Chiefs Doubted Air Strategy."

67. Hirsh and Barry, "How We Stumbled into War," 39.

68. Lippman, "State Department Miscalculated on Kosovo."

69. Craig Whitney and Eric Schmitt, "Crisis in the Balkans: NATO Had Signs Its Strategy Would Fail Kosovars," *New York Times,* April 1, 1999, A1.

70. Ibid.

71. WGBH, "Interview with Richard Holbrooke," *Frontline: War in Europe, 2000,* http://www.pbs.org/wgbh/pages/frontline/shows/kosovo/interviews/holbrooke.html.

72. Michael Hirsh, "He Was Calm, Unyielding," *Newsweek,* April 5, 1999, 37.

73. Michael Elliott, "Mission Uncertain," *Newsweek,* April 5, 1999, 30.

74. William Clinton, "Statement by the President to the Nation," March 24, 1999, http://www2.whitehouse.gov/WH/Newhtml/19990324–2872.html.

75. Ibid.

76. Harris, "Berger's Caution Has Shaped the Role of U.S. in War."

77. WGBH, "Interview with Sandy Berger," *Frontline: War in Europe, 2000,* http://www.pbs.org/wgbh/pages/frontline/shows/kosovo/interviews/berger.html.

78. Harris, "Berger's Caution Has Shaped the Role of U.S. in War."

79. Harris, "Clinton Saw No Alternative to Air Strikes."

80. Ibid.

81. Sciolino and Bronner, "Crisis in the Balkans."

82. John Harris, "In Handling of Crisis, a Different President," *Washington Post,* June 8, 1999, A1.

83. John Harris, "Stakes Are Growing for Clinton," *Washington Post,* April 2, 1999, A1.

84. Harris, "Clinton Saw No Alternative to Air Strikes."

85. Rebecca Grant, "Air Power Made It Work," *Air Force Magazine,* November 1999, 30.

86. Tom Raum, "Cost of Kosovo Conflict Said to Be $4 Billion," *Washington Post,* June 8, 1999, A1.

87. Eric Schmitt, "The World: The Bombs Are Smart, People Are Smarter," *New York Times,* July 4, 1999, D6; see also "*Frontline: War in Europe, 2000:* Facts and Figures," http://www.pbs.org /wgbh/pages/frontline/shows/kosovo/etc/links.html.

88. Raum, "Cost of Kosovo Conflict Said to Be $4 Billion."

4 The Colombian Drug Trade: National Security and Congressional Politics

Jennifer S. Holmes

Before You Begin

1. What should the United States do about drug smuggling and the countries involved?

2. What was President Bill Clinton's drug policy, and how did it change over time?

3. Will Clinton's 2000–2001 package to Colombia help or hinder the U.S. goals of promoting trade, democracy, and regional stability in Latin America?

4. Do Colombia's concerns with its social stability and democracy conflict with the strategic or political concerns of the United States? Where do they converge, or where do they conflict?

5. Does U.S. policy address Colombian social stability and democracy? What issues do U.S. lawmakers prioritize?

6. Why has U.S. aid to Colombia tended to be predominantly military in nature? Is this the most appropriate type of assistance?

7. Should human rights in Colombia be a prominent concern in crafting U.S. foreign policy where the drug trade is involved? Who is interested in this issue?

8. Is drug trafficking fundamentally a question of supply or demand? Which aspect of the problem does U.S. policy address?

Introduction: Existing Policies and the Clinton Challenge

Colombia has been singled out as "public enemy number one" in the debate over illegal drugs in the United States. Colombia is the world's leading producer and processor of cocaine: about 75 percent of all cocaine is processed there, and 98 percent of the cocaine that enters the United States originates in Colombia or passes through it. Opium poppies (for heroin) and marijuana are also produced in Colombia.

Several recent U.S. presidents have attempted to deal with drug smuggling in various ways. The drug trade was identified as a national security threat under President Ronald Reagan. His so-called war on drugs focused on production, processing, and trafficking abroad and was supplemented by First Lady Nancy Reagan's "Just Say No" campaign, which addressed U.S. consumption. Under President George Bush, the Andean Initiative provided countries with military support, economic assistance, and law enforcement advice to curb production and trafficking. Countries that did not cooperate with the United States faced possible U.S. military intervention, as Panama experienced in 1989.[1]

According to President Bill Clinton, "Continued drug production and trafficking puts Colombia's progress in peril. It also fuels addiction and violence in other countries, including ours."[2] Were the policy means and goals of the Clinton administration appropriate given Colombia's problems of drug-related violence, long-standing guerrilla conflict, corruption, and failing institutions, or did Clinton's policy merely reflect the complexity of U.S. politics?

Background: Battling the Colombian Producer State

Colombia is one of Latin America's oldest democracies, but it is a democracy in which political participation has been limited. Following a brutal civil war between liberals and conservatives, representatives of the two parties agreed to a power-sharing arrangement that lasted from 1958 to 1974. After this National Front agreement ended, until 1986 "adequate and equitable" representation was offered to the other party. Although this agreement was effective in ending the conflict between them, it left little chance for other political parties to be viable.[3]

Since the 1960s successive Colombian governments have faced rebel insurgencies. In addition, since the 1970s Colombia has been struggling against an illegal drug industry with expansive networks that have penetrated the economy, politics, and society. Adding to the conflict are the paramilitaries—private armies with varying degrees of loyalty to the Colombian government and military. The activities of guerrilla groups, drug cartels, and paramilitaries have made Colombia one of the most violent nations in the world. The damage done to the country and the people has been horrendous. Approximately 2 million of its citizens have fled the country since 1985—a significant number in a nation of less than 42 million—and hundreds of bombs have exploded in Colombian cities. The Unión Patriótica, a left-wing political party of former guerrillas, was practically eliminated, with thousands of its members "disappeared," or murdered, by right-wing paramilitaries. Four presidential candidates, half of the sitting Supreme Court justices, more than 1,200 police officers, 200 journalists and judges, and more than 300,000 Colombian civilians have been murdered since 1985.[4] Violence in Colombia is a pressing societal problem.

Guerrilla Groups and Drug Traffickers

Four major guerrilla groups are active in Colombia. The largest and best-equipped group is the FARC, the Armed Forces of the Colombian Revolution. Numbering between fifteen thousand and seventeen thousand members, the FARC wants to establish a Marxist/Leninist state. The group finances its organization by extorting part of the profits from businesses in areas under its control, including drug trafficking.[5]

For a time, the second largest group was M-19, or the Nineteenth of April Movement. M-19 formed in response to contested elections in 1970. In November 1985 M-19 seized the Palace of Justice in Bogotá and took the Supreme Court hostage. After a brief attempt to negotiate, the military stormed the building, killing most of M-19's leaders and half of the justices. In 1989 the remaining M-19 leaders signed an agreement with the government of President Virgilio Barco Vargas to turn over their arms in return for reincorporation into civilian life. Today M-19 is a legal political party called the Democratic Alliance/M-19.[6]

The third group is the EPL, the Popular Army of Liberation. This relatively small, but highly disciplined group consists of three hundred to five hundred members. The EPL has criticized the FARC's drug ties, but finances itself through kidnappings and violence against the landed elite.[7] The ELN, the Army of National Liberation, is a group of four thousand to five thousand guerrillas that gained notoriety by bombing the pipeline that carried most of Colombia's export oil from the eastern plains to the Caribbean.[8]

In addition to the rebel groups, the Colombian drug traffickers have also, at times, turned to violence. The drug trade in Colombia began with the small-scale cultivation of marijuana in the 1960s. By the 1970s some Colombians had begun to process and export cocaine. The necessary chemical supplies were brought in from Europe, and the cocaine paste was imported from Peru and Bolivia. The final product was smuggled into the United States. By 1982 the drug trade had become so big that it accounted for 10 percent to 25 percent of the country's exports. At this point, however, the trade did not appear to be a threat to Colombian democracy.[9]

U.S. Aid to Colombia

1986   With the passage of U.S. PL 99-570, the process of certification begins, in which countries are evaluated on the basis of their efforts to stem the illegal drug trade. If not certified, countries risk forfeiting U.S. economic and military assistance.

1989   President George Bush's Andean Initiative provides Colombia and other South American nations with military and economic assistance and law enforcement advice to curb production and trafficking of illegal drugs.

1994   Rumors circulate that Colombian president Ernesto Samper's election campaign had received millions of dollars from the Cali drug cartel.

1995   For the first time, Colombia fails to gain certification from the United States as a cooperating partner in the war on drugs. President Bill Clinton grants Colombia a national security waiver allowing the disbursement of U.S. aid.

1996   The United States decertifies Colombia but does not grant a national security waiver or impose sanctions.

1997   The United States decertifies Colombia and issues a list of drug-fighting measures that the Colombian government must implement in order to receive assistance, which was granted. The Leahy Amendment is passed, restricting units of security forces from receiving U.S. aid if the secretary of state determines that the unit has committed human rights violations, a measure that threatens aid to Colombia.

1998   Colombia fails to gain certification, but is issued its second national security waiver. President Andrés Pastrana elected.

1999   The United States certifies Colombia as a partner in the war on drugs.

2000   President Pastrana announces Plan Colombia, a program to reduce drug cultivation, strengthen Colombia's political and judicial institutions, and gain the upper hand against the guerrillas opposed to the government. Pastrana's government seeks U.S. and international assistance to carry out the $7 billion program.

January 11, 2000   President Clinton proposes $1.6 billion in aid for Plan Colombia (later reduced to $1.3 billion).

March 30, 2000   The House of Representatives approves $1.7 billion in aid for Plan Colombia.

continued on the next page

continued from the previous page

June 22, 2000 The Senate approves $934 million in aid for Plan Colombia. House and Senate conferees agree on $1.3 billion with a certification provision.

August 2000 Clinton waives the requirement that Colombia meet human rights standards and implement drug-fighting measures before aid dollars and equipment can be released. Colombia is certified as a partner in the war on drugs.

In the beginning, a few groups controlled the trade. One major group was the Medellín cartel, headed by Pablo Escobar and Jorge and Fabio Ochoa. This cartel was arguably at its strongest in the middle to late 1980s. When Escobar was killed in a shootout with Colombian police in December 1993, the Cali cartel took over most of cocaine production. Less violent than the Medellín cartel, the Cali cartel focused its attention on legalizing parts of its operations and moving into legitimate businesses. Colombian president Ernesto Samper Pizano was rumored to have received $6 million from legal Cali businesses during his 1994 campaign for office. Nevertheless, Samper pursued an antidrug strategy, and the main "cartel kingpins" were jailed by 1996, through with relatively light sentences.[10]

In addition to the well-known Cali and Medellín cartels, many other independent organizations produce, refine, and smuggle drugs. Sometimes these smaller groups cooperate and coordinate their activities with the larger organizations.[11] Since the targeting by law enforcement of the Cali and Medellín groups, others have quickly filled the void to meet demand. That same year a large number of cocaine labs were destroyed and the eradication of opium was stepped up, but these successes were short-lived. By 1999 the potential acres of coca harvest had almost quadrupled from 1993.[12]

The business of drugs is a complicated activity, and in the case of Colombia it has profoundly affected preexisting social dynamics. Before the emergence of drug trafficking, there had been an ongoing struggle between traditional landowners and popular groups concerning unused *latifundios* (large estates or ranches), demands by peasants for property titles, and disagreements caused by state support of rural modernization programs. Until the 1970s the large landowners usually won these disputes. The drug trade changed all that by introducing competition from the narcos into the mix. Many drug traffickers invested their assets in the land, becoming landowners. They were then able to sponsor armed groups to protect their holdings from landless peasants and rebel groups. By the 1980s armed protection of haciendas was reinforced "so that in the middle of that decade almost all of the struggle for land had been eliminated through a combination of military harassment and paramilitary terrorism" of the peasants.[13] The peasants who had earlier demanded land had clearly lost. The spread of the drug trade eliminated the obstacles to it, including judges, police, and so forth. The result was a growth in criminal groups and a change in the dynamics of the traditional conflict over land.

The growth of the drug trade also affected the operations of guerrillas opposed to the government and their control over territory. Colombian drug traffickers and the guerrillas have a complex relationship. Bloody conflicts between narco-traffickers and guerrillas are common in guerrilla-controlled areas that traffickers take over for cultivation and processing. When drug traffickers take over land, they commonly create death squads to eliminate the guerrillas, terrorize the local population, and limit the effectiveness of government authority. In short, they reorganize society by eliminating the existing social structure and creating their own social order. In areas where guerrillas cannot be defeated, a pragmatic relationship develops. In these cases, the producers and traffickers usually pay tribute to the guerrilla groups.[14]

Some have tried to label the guerrillas as nothing more than another drug cartel. For example, Gen. Barry McCaffrey, President Clinton's director of the Office of National Drug Control Policy, has called the FARC the "principal organizing entity of cocaine production in the world."[15] According to Marc Chernick, director of the Andean and Amazonian Studies Program at Georgetown University,

> Some have tried to obfuscate this issue by collapsing the two issues into one, saying that the guerrillas work with the drug traffickers and are therefore effectively "narco-guerrillas." However, this is a gross distortion of the situation in Colombia. The guerrillas do not constitute another "cartel." Their role in the drug trade is in extorting a percentage of the commercial transaction of coca and coca paste, just as they do with many other commercial products in the areas in which they operate, be it cattle, petroleum, or coffee.[16]

The nature of the trafficker-guerrilla relationship is significant because some policy makers have tried to link the guerrillas with the cartels in an effort to justify the use of drug war funds for counterinsurgency purposes. Regardless, the drug-related violence and guerrilla operations make Colombia's problems harder to solve.

Colombian Attempts to Control the Drug Trade

Since the late 1970s the Colombian government has tried to craft both political and military solutions to both the rebel and the drug conflicts, but so far few of these efforts have enjoyed lasting success. President Julio César Turbay Ayala (1978–1982) relied on the military and paramilitary units to try to control the violence. President Belisario Betancur (1982–1986) initiated talks with guerrillas that resulted in the formation of the Unión Patriótica by former FARC guerrillas. Paramilitary groups killed more than six thousand Unión Patriótica members, and a cease-fire agreement of 1984 failed. Both rural and urban violence escalated under President Barco (1986–1990). President César Gaviria Trujillo (1990–1994) attempted to restart talks, holding extensive negotiations in 1991 and 1992, but these discussions did not produce an agreement.

The Colombian government's response to the drug trade has varied. In its war on drugs, the United States had demanded the right to extradite Colombian citizens and charge them in U.S. courts, because it felt that the Colombian courts were too weak and corrupt to effectively prosecute drug traffickers. President Turbay signed an extradition treaty in 1979, but no extraditions were requested until the Betancur administration. Once they began, the extraditions created cycles of drug violence, followed by state retaliation, followed by more violence. The situation became so bad that President Gaviria stopped the extraditions. In 1991 he tried a policy of voluntary submission to justice, by which drug traffickers would be allowed to exit from crime and legalize their assets if they pled guilty to a few offenses and agreed to serve (light) sentences. The Samper administration (1994–1998) was hampered by the allegations that Samper had received contributions from the Cali cartel. During his term, the Colombian Congress passed an asset forfeiture law and resumed extradition of drug traffickers to the United States. Even so, Colombia's relationship with the United States was severely strained by the allegations of Samper's acceptance of drug-tainted campaign money.[17]

In 1998 newly elected president Andrés Pastrana began attempts to combat the drug problem and the guerrilla conflict. He initiated talks with the FARC and the ELN for the first time in eight years. Both were offered safe havens, free from government interference, as a precondition to the peace talks. The FARC received some forty-two thousand square kilometers of land in the center of Colombia, and the ELN received approximately five thousand square kilometers. Because these overtures did not produce a viable agreement, in 2000 Pastrana announced a three-year program called Plan Colombia. This plan aimed to reduce drug cultivation, including through promotion of an alternative development in coca-growing areas, strengthen Colombia's political and judicial institutions, and regain the initiative in the conflict with the guerrillas. The estimated cost of the program was more than $7 billion. The government committed $4 billion to the effort, and Colombia requested aid from the international community, including the European Union and the United States. [18]

Pre-Clinton U.S. Policy

There are two basic ways to fight drug use. One is to reduce the demand for drugs by increasing education and treatment programs. The other way is to attack the supply. Here the goal is to eliminate the production and trafficking. Because Colombia is the main source of cocaine supplied to the United States, U.S. foreign policy toward Colombia has focused on drug trafficking and developing supply-side tactics against it. One of the major components of this strategy has been tying aid, trade concessions, and external credits to the Colombian government's compliance with the U.S. goal of reducing the amount of cocaine produced and processed there. This supply-side strategy has in some instances led to the militarization of antidrug campaigns and armed intervention.[19] For example, in Panama, the United States under President George Bush intervened militarily to arrest the de facto Panamanian head of state, Gen. Manuel Noriega, for his involvement in drug trafficking. Noriega is currently imprisoned in the United States for drug-related crimes.

In 1989 the U.S. military presence in Colombia and aid to it were minor. After the assassination of leading Colombian presidential candidate Luis Carlos Galán by drug traffickers, the United States decided to strengthen the Colombian military and jump-start the war on drugs. Within a day, President Bush announced the release of $65 million in stockpiled Defense Department weapons and supplies to Colombia. Congress quickly approved a $200 million line of credit from the U.S. Export-Import Bank to the Colombian military. Three weeks later, Bush announced that $261 million more in aid would be given to the Andean nations of Bolivia, Colombia, and Peru, as part of the Andean Initiative. By 1992 U.S.-Colombian efforts had begun to concentrate on attacking the drug traffickers and cartels directly by focusing on the "kingpins" instead of crop eradication. As U.S. policy came to rely more on military and police efforts to combat the traffickers, many observers, including the U.S. General Accounting Office, became concerned that the United States would be drawn into counterinsurgency operations in the long-standing conflict between the Colombian government and the rebels.[20]

In 1999, according to the State Department's Bureau for International Narcotics and Law Enforcement Affairs, U.S. drug policy in Colombia had three main goals. The first was to eliminate the cultivation of illegal drugs, including opium, coca, and marijuana. The second goal was to strengthen Colombia's ability to disrupt and dismantle major drug trafficking organizations and prevent their resurgence. The third aim was to destroy the cocaine and heroin processing industries.[21] These goals needed to be accomplished without undermining regional stability or the already embattled Colombian democracy.

The Clinton Drug Policy

When asked by an MTV interviewer during the 1992 presidential campaign if he had ever tried marijuana, candidate Bill Clinton responded that he had, but, as he put it, "I didn't inhale." Clinton's comment helped create an atmosphere of distrust among many in Congress about the seriousness with which he would pursue an antidrug strategy. This impression gained strength on December 7, 1993, when Clinton's surgeon general independently suggested that the government study the idea of legalizing drugs in order to reduce violent crime. The response from the White House on this comment was less than warm, with the president's press secretary stating that such a study was not even being considered.[22] It was too late, however; many thought that the administration did not take the drug problem seriously. And difficulties were already shadowing its drug policy.

Clinton initially tried to craft an approach different from his predecessors by balancing supply-side and demand-side efforts. Between September 1992 and September 1995, Clinton reduced interdiction efforts and eliminated a thousand antidrug positions, shortened mandatory sentences for traffickers, and proposed cutting 80 percent of the staff of the Office of National Drug Control Policy and reducing the number of Drug Enforcement Agency agents by 227. Republicans viewed this policy as responsible for an increase in the supply of drugs from Colombia.[23]

When Republicans pointed to Clinton's policy as evidence of a lack of commitment to an antidrug strategy, administration officials protested that the statistics they cited took the president's policy out of context. Robert Gelbard, assistant secretary of state for International Narcotics and Law Enforcement Affairs, clarified some of the funding reductions:

> The President's 1995 National Drug Control Strategy continues our shift in focus to the source countries, so we are taking a more surgical view of how

to destroy major transit and transshipment operations. Both concentrations are occurring against the backdrop of enhanced efforts to strengthen anti-narcotics institutions of cooperating countries so they can shoulder more of the drug control burden.[24]

Despite such statements, others still disagreed with the approach, including William Olson, the former deputy assistant secretary of state for International Narcotics Matters, who said,

> It was clear from the outset that a decision had been made to distance the president from the drug issue. One of the first things that happened then was the national-level leadership at the top of the administration disappeared, leaving interagency rival[ry]—which had been corralled if not broken earlier—to throw off its commitment to a coherent drug strategy.[25]

According to Olson, the interdiction and international narcotics budget had fallen from $2.8 billion under George Bush in 1992 to $1.58 billion in 1996 under Clinton.

The truth was that although some programs suffered cutbacks, others enjoyed an increase in funding. In 1993 the international counternarcotics budgets of most U.S. agencies were cut. Gelbard's budget, for example, was cut by 30 percent. Overall, however, Clinton's aid request for drug control for fiscal year 1994 increased by $1.1 billion from the previous year, to $13.2 billion. Five areas were to receive more money:

- funding for drug prevention increased by $448 million;
- funding for drug treatment programs increased by $360 million;
- spending for drug-related criminal justice increased by $227 million;
- funding for other international programs increased by $76 million; and
- funding for drug-related research increased by $27 million.

Interdiction funding, however, was cut by $94 million, and antidrug intelligence programs were cut by $600,000. Some in Congress, such as Rep. Donald Manzullo, R-Ill., believed that these cuts reflected a lack of emphasis on interdiction by the administration, even though Clinton's stated policy was to shift funding from "transit zone interdiction" to stopping production in the source countries.[26]

In addition to the earlier disagreements over the components of Clinton's antidrug strategy, many House Republicans were also angry at delays in delivering promised aid to Colombia. For example, Rep. Dan Burton, R-Ind., said, "It is unfortunate that the Congress has had to fight tooth and nail with the administration, from the State Department to the United States Embassy and our Ambassador in Bogotá, in an attempt to try to get some form of assistance down to the brave people who are fighting the war on drugs."[27] In another example, Burton, along with Ben Gilman, R-N.Y., and Dennis Hastert, R-Ill., were upset about the lack of aid, specifically, getting Huey UH-1H helicopters to the Colombian national police in a timely manner.

Clinton received high marks for appointing Barry McCaffrey, a retired four-star U.S. Army general, to head the White House Office of National Drug Control Policy, a move that many saw as an attempt by Clinton to build up his credentials in the war on drugs.[28] McCaffrey took over as "drug czar" in February 1996, but his appointment did not produce the positive effects the president wished. In fact, McCaffrey contributed to interbranch squabbling by accusing some in Congress of attempting to micromanage U.S. foreign policy toward Colombia.[29] Adding to the dissension, different administration members and others in government preferred different aid strategies. Secretary of State Madeleine Albright emphasized supporting the peace process with the guerrillas. While some in the Pentagon favored an approach that focused on the military, many Republicans preferred more aid to the Colombian national police.[30]

Congressional concern would ultimately be important in crafting policy. Not only did Congress control how much aid would be sent to Colombia, it could override presidential decisions because of a certification policy adopted in 1986 based on Section 490 of the Foreign Assistance Act of 1961. The act was amended (PL 99-570) to give Congress a more active role in forging foreign policy in regard to drug-producing and transit countries. Since then, on March 1 of each year the president has had three options regarding countries known for substantial drug production or known to be transit points: to fully certify a country as cooperating to meet the goals of the UN Convention Against Illicit Traffic in Narcotic Drugs and Psychotropic Substances, also known as the Vienna Convention; to decertify a country as uncooperative, but grant it a national security waiver so that it does not suffer sanctions; or to decertify a country and impose sanctions. The sanctions could include an end to most U.S. foreign aid and votes against loans for that country in multilateral economic and development organizations. Depending on the country, other sanctions could be imposed, such as the elimination of the sugar quota for the U.S. market or the prohibition of tourist visas for the United States. The president could also levy trade sanctions, for example, the denial of preferential tariff treatment granted by the Andean Trade Preference Act of 1991, an increase of tariffs generally, and the withdrawal of the United States from any pre-clearance customs arrangements. Congress could overturn the president's decision within thirty days.[31]

Until 1995 Colombia had always received full certification, even though Sen. Jesse Helms, R-N.C., had repeatedly demanded that President Clinton decertify it. In 1995 Helms sponsored an amendment that would prohibit federal aid to Colombia until it began to fight more effectively against drug production and corruption. Despite Helms's efforts, Colombia received a national security waiver that year. In 1996 Clinton again decertified Colombia, but sanctions were not applied, and the government received the aid allocated that year. President Samper's acceptance of Cali cartel money for his presidential campaign seemed to be the reason for the decertification. In 1997 Colombia was decertified and given six months to improve its drug-fighting efforts before a decision on sanctions would be made. The United States demanded the following: the extradition of Colombian nationals (especially the Cali kingpins), the full implementation of asset forfeiture and money laundering laws, implementation of a bilateral agreement on maritime law enforcement (to aid in interdiction efforts), tightened security for Colombian prisoners, the use of more potent herbicides for drug crop eradication, and better efforts in combating corrupt officials.[32] Colombia did not meet the demands.

Another notable event of 1997 was the passage of an amendment sponsored by Sen. Patrick Leahy, D-Vt. His amendment to the Foreign Operations Act for Fiscal Year 1998 stated, "None of the funds made available by this Act may be provided to any unit of the security forces of a foreign country if the Secretary of State has credible evidence that such unit has committed gross violations of human rights." Passage of the amendment was an acknowledgment of the unofficial ties between the Colombian military and right-wing paramilitary groups in fighting the guerrillas, and it would later be included, in varying ways, in other security assistance programs in 1998, 1999, and 2000. Difficulty in applying it, however, would later arise over the definitions and compositions of military units. Representative Burton, among others, criticized the administration for not granting Colombia a national security waiver in 1996 and 1997. Samper's term ended in August 1998, and that year Colombia failed certification but was granted a national security waiver. In 1999, 2000, and 2001, under the Pastrana presidency, Colombia would again receive full certification.

The 2000–2001 Aid Plan

Congressional criticism continued to follow President Clinton's Colombian policy into the new millennium. Some Republicans, such as Sen. Mike DeWine, R-Ohio, wanted to shift the balance of funding away from education and prevention and back to supply-side efforts. Indeed, Congress added $870.2 million in extra monies for the drug war for fiscal year 1999 (PL 105-277). Again, many Republicans accused Clinton of not taking the problem seriously enough.[33] Political pressure continued to build for a stronger U.S. response to the Colombian drug problem, culminating in U.S. support for Plan Colombia.

On January 10, 2000, Speaker Hastert gave a speech in Chicago to the Mid-America Committee for International Business and Government Cooperation on the need to increase funding to Colombia. "Aggressive diplomacy, military assistance, continued military cooperation, intelligence activities, and counterdrug assistance will be necessary if we are to deter this growing threat.... The Republican-led Congress stands ready to support such a comprehensive strategy, but time is not on Colombia's side."[34] The next day Clinton announced plans to increase aid to Colombia. He proposed a $1.6 billion aid package designed to create two antidrug battalions (of one thousand troops each) within the Colombian military, control Colombian airspace, and wipe out coca fields.[35] The most expensive aspect of the 2000 aid plan was the addition of sixty-three Huey UH-1H combat helicopters. These aircraft would be used by the antinarcotics forces in southern Colombia, where the FARC was strong. After President Clinton announced his plan, Senator Leahy implored him not to dramatically increase the counterinsurgency aid in the name of counternarcotics policy. Leahy said, "We at least need to see a concerted effort by the Colombian army to thwart the paramilitary groups, who are responsible for most of the atrocities against civilians, and a willingness by the Colombian armed forces to turn over to the civilian courts their own members who violate human rights."[36]

Resistance

Criticism of the aid package focused on two matters. Many opponents, such as Leahy, were concerned that U.S. aid was being used for counterinsurgency purposes, thereby involving the United States in another country's civil war. Others wanted to make sure that U.S. aid would not be used to benefit groups implicated in human rights violations. Some critics asked why Plan Colombia focused on actions in southern Colombia, a traditional rebel stronghold, instead of the northern regions, where the paramilitaries sympathetic to the government were active in the drug trade. Critics suspected that the true purpose of U.S. aid was to assist Colombia in its internal conflict, in addition to reducing the drug trade. According to Brian E. Sheridan, the assistant secretary of defense for Special Operations and Low Intensity Conflict, there was no evidence to support this suspicion: "We are working with the Colombian government on counternarcotics programs. We are not in the counterinsurgency business." [37]

An earlier congressional staff report presented a somewhat different view:

In the past, the United States has tried to describe a bright line separating counterdrug and counterinsurgency support to Colombia, with no direct assistance for counterinsurgency. That line remains in law. Circumstances, however, are pushing the limits, making it difficult on the ground to make distinctions between insurgents and traffickers. [38]

Because of the lack of clarity in the aid packages and the messiness of Colombia's reality, it was impossible to deny with total certainty that U.S. aid was not being used for military support of counterinsurgency efforts, at least indirectly. Part of the controversy involved whether the Colombian military had ties to paramilitary groups, which were responsible for some 75 percent of all political killings. The largest such group was the AUC, the United Self Defense Groups of Colombia. Led by Carlos Castaño, this group, approximately five thousand to eleven thousand strong, was funded by landowners, businessmen, and drug dealers. Human Rights Watch, in its *World Report 2000,* documented the ties between the Colombian Army's Fourth Brigade and the Castaño group. Reportedly, Castaño's men were able to exchange civilian corpses for weapons from the brigade. The army would then dress the corpses as guerrillas and claim that they had been killed in combat. [39] Even the State Department, in its *1999 Country Reports on Human Rights,* said that Colombian "security forces actively collaborated with members of paramilitary groups by passing them through roadblocks, sharing intelligence, and providing them with ammunition." [40] Many human rights groups, as well as congressional Democrats, contended that the 2000–2001 aid package did not do enough to break these ties and prosecute those collaborating with the paramilitary groups.

To satisfy its critics, the Clinton administration reduced the amount of aid requested for Colombia from $1.6 billion to $1.3 billion. [41] To appease the Pentagon, it dropped the request for sixty-three Huey helicopters and requested instead thirty of the newer, more expensive, and more sophisticated Sikorsky UH-60L Blackhawk helicopters for combating drug trafficking. [42]

Congressional Passage

Despite the vocal opposition of its critics, the administration's modified proposal had solid support in the House, both from the rank and file and from the leadership. One of its most enthusiastic supporters was Speaker Hastert, who said, "The bill we're considering today is about our children and whether we want our children to grow up in a society free from the scourge of drugs."[43] It is safe to say that no representative wanted to be portrayed as condoning drug smuggling, but some spoke out against an aid package that seemed to move the United States closer to involvement in Colombia's internal conflict and a policy that did not sufficiently protect the human rights of Colombians. David Obey, D-Wis., invoked the Vietnam War: "This is the camel's nose under the tent for a massive long-term commitment to a military operation. I detest Vietnam analogies under most circumstances, but in this case there is a very real parallel."[44] Maxine Waters, D-Calif., objected for humanitarian reasons: "This bill gives money to drug traffickers who kill other drug traffickers and murder innocent civilians."[45] In the end, the House approved more aid for Colombia than the administration requested—$1.7 billion. On March 30, 2000, the House rejected any attempt to lower the amount by a vote of 239 to 186. It then passed the appropriations bill, 263-146, of which the Colombia aid was a part.[46]

Despite strong support and pressure for a large aid package in the House, the proposal faced problems in the Senate, with many senators fearing involvement in an escalating, Vietnam-like situation. Slade Gorton, R-Wash., and Paul Wellstone, D-Minn., led the debate in criticizing the Colombian military's human rights record, declaring that this aid package would pull the United States into Colombia's civil war.[47] Gorton stated, "There has been no consideration of the consequences, cost, and length of involvement.... This bill says let's get into war now and justify it later."[48] One of the concessions made to allay such fears was to limit the number of American military personnel in Colombia to five hundred at any one time, with exceptions made for carrying out a possible rescue mission.[49] The approved Senate bill called for supplying Huey helicopters, rather than the Blackhawks.[50]

The administration was not, however, without supporters in the Senate. Majority Leader Trent Lott, R-Miss., called for giving Colombians "the aid they need, the equipment that they need to fight these massive narcotics traffickers themselves."[51] Christopher Dodd, D-Conn., argued, "This package may not be perfect, but our delay in responding to a neighbor's call for help is getting old.... When we step up and offer the Colombian democracy a chance to fight for themselves, we're not only doing it for them, we're doing it for ourselves."[52]

On June 22 the Senate approved, 95-4, a Colombian aid package totaling $934 million, just slightly more than half of the $1.7 billion the House had approved. Later that day, House and Senate conferees met and split the difference between the two amounts.[53] The final package of $1.319 billion contained the additional requirement that the government of Colombia meet six conditions or obtain a national security waiver to receive the aid:

- The president of Colombia must issue a written order requiring that all military personnel facing credible allegations of human rights violations be tried in civilian courts.
- The commander general of the Colombian armed forces must promptly suspend those facing credible allegations of human rights violations or of participating in paramilitary groups.
- The Colombian armed forces must fully cooperate with the investigations of civilian authorities in the search for those accused of human rights violations.
- The Colombian government must actively prosecute in civilian courts paramilitary leaders and members and any military personnel who assist them.
- The Colombian government must craft a plan to rid the country of all coca and poppy production by 2005.
- The Colombian armed forces must develop and deploy a judge advocate general corps in field units to investigate military personnel misconduct.[54]

The majority of aid to Colombia under the 2000–2001 plan went to the police and the armed forces: $589.2 million for the military and $363.1 million for the police. The remaining $238 million in the package went for alternative development, aid to the displaced, human rights, judicial reform, law enforcement, and peace efforts. Also, the final package included the Blackhawks.[55]

The controversy did not end, however. The issues of Colombian army collaboration with paramilitary groups and deepening U.S. involvement in Colombia's internal conflict were not the only concerns of those opposed to the proposed aid package. Clinton was also being pressured to withhold aid because of human rights violations. Senator Wellstone wrote the president on July 28:

At present, the President of Colombia has issued no directive requiring that Colombian armed forces personnel accused of human rights violations will be held accountable in civilian courts, nor has the Colombian military taken the firm, clear steps necessary to purge human rights abusers from its ranks or ensure that its personnel are not linked to paramilitary organizations.... Given these facts, I believe your Administration cannot and should not certify Colombia to receive assistance under Plan Colombia.[56]

In another instance, representatives from thirty-three non-governmental organizations, including Amnesty International, the Washington Office on Latin America, and numerous church groups, requested that Colombia not be certified because of its lack of compliance with the human rights provisions of Section 3201 of the supplemental aid package. In an open letter to President Clinton on July 31, these groups stated, "A certification or waiver that ignores this critical human rights situation will send a clear message to the Colombian government and security forces, at the outset of this major increase in U.S. military involvement, that the United States' commitment to human rights does not go beyond empty rhetoric."[57]

These groups further stated that the Colombian government had not met the conditions for receiving aid in several areas. First, officers with a proven record of human rights violations and support for paramilitary groups had not been dismissed from duty or referred to civilian authorities for trial, despite credible accusations of army-paramilitary collusion. Second, the Colombian government had not enforced its own law that officers accused of human rights violations should be tried in civilian courts. Charges against these officers continued to be heard in the military courts, even though the Colombian Constitutional Court had ruled that human rights cases must be heard in civilian courts. Third, the groups charged that the Colombian government had not acted to restrain the action of the paramilitary groups or protect the population from attacks. Their letter concluded, "We have raised serious questions about its [the current aid policy's] efficacy as counter-narcotics policy.... It will be an unqualified disaster, however, if the human rights conditions prove meaningless at the very outset."[58] In the end, Colombia met only one of the U.S. requirements. Nevertheless, in August Clinton waived the requirement that the conditions of the aid be met, stating that the grave situation in Colombia dictated that aid could not be delayed any longer.[59] In this instance, drug control was the defining characteristic of the national interest, whereas human rights were not.

Just a week after passage of the package, Speaker Hastert announced that he was reviewing a request for an additional $99.5 million in aid to Colombia to provide more aircraft, ammunition, and other equipment to the Colombian police. Seventeen conservative lawmakers, including Burton and Gilman, had wanted more aid to the police to be included in the foreign assistance bill for the new fiscal year. They favored the police because they believed that they were less implicated in human rights violations and more effective at fighting drugs than the military.[60]

Conclusion: Supply or Demand—New Players and a New Agenda

In crafting his drug policy toward Colombia, President Clinton faced political pressure from Republicans in Congress and human rights groups. Originally, he wanted to pursue a policy that included more demand-side efforts and reduced interdiction efforts, but he quickly encountered stiff opposition from Republicans, who accused him of being "soft on drugs." After trying to fashion a policy balance between supply and demand, Clinton acquiesced to Republican pressure and shifted priorities. Unwilling to sustain conservative criticism of a new policy approach, he returned to a supply-side policy, symbolized by the appointment of General McCaffrey and the size of the 2000–2001 aid package. Clinton was also pressured from others in Congress and from non-governmental groups who feared that military aid to Colombia would result in more human rights violations. In the end, Clinton made concessions to both sides by increasing funds for the military and police and by including human rights provisions. For Colombia, the drug trade is a complex and intractable problem. Whether Clinton's 2000 package, greatly influenced by the U.S. political process, helps to solve the drug problem in Colombia remains to be seen.

The debate over Colombian drug policy exemplifies the conflict over intervention in Latin America in the post–cold war era and the increasing complexity in crafting foreign policy. No longer is the United States fighting communism in the region, but it faces new threats, such as the drug trade. History has changed how Americans view foreign intervention. A fear of entanglement in another countries' domestic conflicts is the legacy of the unsuccessful and painful intervention in Vietnam. In addition, non-governmental organizations such as Amnesty International are becoming more effective at making their voices heard in the policy debate. Concern for human rights has become an issue that Congress and the president cannot ignore. Whether human rights groups have successfully changed politics to include safeguarding civilians or if policies give only "lip service" to these ideals is debatable. What is clear is that no president can easily control the content of foreign policy. Political capital must be used to push the president's foreign policy agenda, as in other policy arenas. The present configuration of U.S. policy in Colombia demonstrates how foreign policy is shaped by lobbying by certain industries, non-governmental activism, and plain old politics.

Notes

1. For an excellent overview of U.S. drug policy from Nixon to Bush, see Bruce M. Bagley and William O. Walker, eds., *Drug Trafficking in the Americas* (Coral Gables, Fla.: University of Miami, North-South Center, 1996).

2. White House, Office of the Press Secretary, "Statement by the President (Plan Colombia)," November 10, 1999, http://www.state.gov/www/global/narcotics_law/991110_president_Colombia.html.

3. On contemporary Colombian history and politics, see Harvey Kline, *State Building and Conflict Resolution in Colombia, 1986–1994* (Tuscaloosa: University of Alabama Press, 1999).

4. Rafael Pardo, "Colombia's Two-Front War," *Foreign Affairs* 79, no. 4 (July/August 2000): 65.

5. Jonathan Hartlyn, "Colombia: The Politics of Violence and Accommodation," in *Democracy in Developing Countries*, vol. 4, ed. Juan Linz, Larry Diamond, and Jonathan Hartlyn (Baltimore: Johns Hopkins University Press, 1993), 291–334.

6. Ibid.

7. Ibid.

8. Ibid.

9. Francisco Thoumi, "Why the Illegal Psychodelic Drug Use Industry Grew in Colombia," in Bagley and Walker, *Drug Trafficking in the Americas.*

10. Alejandro Reyes, "Drug Trafficking and the Guerrilla Movement in Colombia," in Bagley and Walker, *Drug Trafficking in the Americas.*

11. Fabio Castillo, *Los nuevos jinetes de la cocaína* (Bogotá: Oveja Negra, 1996).

12. U.S. Department of State, Bureau for International Narcotics and Law Enforcement Affairs, *International Narcotics Strategy Report, 1999,* http://www.state.gov/www/global/narcotics_law/1999_narc_report/.

13. Reyes, "Drug Trafficking and the Guerrilla Movement in Colombia," 125.

14. Ibid., 122. See also Roberto Steiner, "Hooked on Drugs: Colombian-US Relations," in *The United States and Latin America: The New Agenda,* ed. Victor Bulmer-Thomas and James Dunkerley (London: Institute of Latin-American Studies/University of London, 1999), 171.

15. "U.S. Drug Chief Tries to Boost Colombian Resolve," *Washington Post,* November 21, 2000, A22.

16. House Committee on International Relations, *U.S. Narcotics Policy toward Colombia,* hearing, 104th Cong., 2d sess., 1996, 47.

17. For an in-depth overview of the responses to the guerrilla and drug conflict, see Reyes, "Drug Trafficking and the Guerrilla Movement in Colombia"; and Steiner, "Hooked on Drugs."

18. A copy of Plan Colombia is available online at http://www.usip.org/library/pa/colombia/adddoc/plan_colombia_101999.html.

19. Bruce M. Bagley, "Myths of Militarization: Enlisting Armed Forces in the War on Drugs," in *Drug Policy in the Americas,* ed. Peter Smith (Boulder: Westview Press, 1992).

20. In fact, the General Accounting Office audited the drug war expenses in Colombia in 1992 and 1993 and found that counternarcotics funds were being illegally used for counterinsurgency operations. The report concluded that this practice would continue due to the complexity of the Colombian situation.

21. Fact sheet provided by the Bureau for International Narcotics and Law Enforcement Affairs, April 23, 1999.

22. Stephen Labaton, "Surgeon General Suggests Study of Legalizing Drugs," *New York Times,* December 7, 1993.

23. Senate vote analysis, temp. record, 106th Cong., 2d sess., June 21, 2000, S5509.

24. House Committee on International Relations, Subcommittee on the Western Hemisphere, *A Review of President Clinton's Certification Program for Narcotics Producing and Transit Countries in Latin America,* hearing, 104th Cong., 1st sess., 1995, 33.

25. Ibid., 68.

26. House Committee on Foreign Affairs, Subcommittee on International Security, International Organizations, and Human Rights, *U.S. Anti-Drug Strategy for the Western Hemisphere,* joint hearing, 103d Cong., 2d sess., 1994.

27. House Committee on Government Reform and Oversight, Subcommittee on National Security, International Affairs, and Criminal Justice, *International Drug Control Policy: Colombia,* hearing, 105th Cong., 2d sess., 1998, 22.

28. For example, see "Choice of General as Drug Fighter Gets Enthusiastic Response," *New York Times,* January 28, 1996.

29. Stanley Meisler, "House OKs $3.2 Billion Measure to Bolster the Fight against Drugs," *Los Angeles Times,"* September 17, 1998, 8.

30. Miles A. Pomper, "Hastert Leads the Charge in Colombia Drug War," *CQ Weekly,* September 11, 1999, 2094.

31. *International Drug Trade and the U.S. Certification Process: A Critical Review,* Senate report prepared for the Caucus on International Narcotics Control, September 1996. The Andean Trade Preference Act of 1991 provided economic support to countries struggling to eliminate drug production by expanding the trade opportunities for legal crops. The ten-year program empowered the president to grant duty-free treatment to selected imports from Bolivia, Colombia, Ecuador, and Peru.

32. Subcommittee on National Security, International Affairs, and Criminal Justice, *International Drug Control Policy: Colombia,* Statement by Assistant Secretary of State for Inter-American Affairs Jeffrey Davidow, 19.

33. Jonathan Peterson, "Albright Pushes Anti-Drug Plan in Visit to Colombia," *Los Angeles Times,* January 15, 2000, A9. Despite Colombia's decertification, by 1997 aid to its military and police had doubled from $68.6 million in 1993 to $136.4 million (despite decreases in 1995 and 1996 to $51.4 million and $73.9 million, respectively). See also "Last Minute Spending Signals Shift in Drug War," *Congressional Quarterly Almanac,* 1998, 2–118.

34. Miles A. Pomper, "Clinton's Billion Dollar Proposal for Colombian Anti-Drug Aid Fails to Satisfy Republicans," *CQ Weekly,* January 15, 2000, 90.

35. Peterson, "Albright Pushes Anti-Drug Plan."

36. Pomper, "Clinton's Billion Dollar Proposal," 91.

37. Larry Rohter, "Cocaine War: A Special Report; A Web of Drugs and Strife in Colombia," *New York Times,* April 21, 2000.

38. Senate Caucus on International Narcotics Control, staff report, *On Site Staff Evaluation of U.S. Counter-Narcotics Activities in Brazil, Argentina, Chile, and Colombia,* January 28, 1998, 19.

39. Human Rights Watch, *World Report 2000,* http://www.hrw.org/wr2k.

40. U.S. Department of State, Bureau of Democracy, Human Rights, and Labor, *1999 Country Reports on Human Rights,* February 25, 2000, available online at www.state.gov/www/global/human_rights/1999_hrp_report/colombia.html.

41. Ester Schrader, "Congress Agrees on Funding for Colombia," *Los Angeles Times,* June 23, 2000, A1.

42. Tim Golden, "Colombia and Copters and Clash over Choice," *New York Times,* March 6, 2000.

43. Janet Hook and Ester Schrader, "Colombia Aid Package Gets House Approval," *Los Angeles Times,* March 31, 2000, A22.

44. Ibid.

45. Eric Pianin, "House Approves Additional $4 Billion for Defense; Nearing Passage, $12.6 Billion Emergency Spending Bill Has Funds for Colombia, Non-Emergencies," *Washington Post,* March 30, 2000, A6.

46. Hook and Schrader, "Colombia Aid Package." Included in the House bill was an endorsement of the administration's switch from the Huey helicopters to the Blackhawks. Intense lobbying efforts by the companies that make the helicopters helped influence the details of the final aid package. United Technologies, the Connecticut-based company that builds the Blackhawk, had contributed more than $700,000 to Republican and Democratic members of Congress between the 1996 and 1998 elections. Golden, "Colombia and Copters."

47. Karen DeYoung, "Colombia Aid Nears Approval in Senate; Lawmakers Back Bigger U.S. Military Role in Drug Fight," *Washington Post,* June 22, 2000, A1.

48. Anthony Lewis, "Abroad at Home: Into the Quagmire," *New York Times,* June 24, 2000.

49. Eric Schmitt, "$1.3 Billion Voted to Fight Drug War among Colombians," *New York Times,* June 30, 2000.

50. DeYoung, "Colombia Aid Nears Approval."

51. Ester Schrader, "Congress Agrees on Funding for Colombia," *Los Angeles Times,* June 23, 2000, A1.

52. Ibid.

53. Ibid.

54. PL 106–246, Section 3201.

55. DeYoung, "Colombia Aid Nears Approval."

56. Available online at http://www.ciponline.org/colombia/072801.htm.

57. Available online at http://www.ciponline.org/colombia/073101.htm

58. Ibid.

59. Marc Lacey, "Clinton Defends Colombia Outlay," *New York Times,* August 31, 2000, A1.

60. Eric Pianin and Karen DeYoung, "House Considers More Aid for Colombia; $99.5 Million Package Would Include Aircraft, Ammunition to Fight Drug War," *Washington Post,* September 9, 2000, A2.

5 The Demise of the Arms Control and Disarmament Agency: Arms Control Politics

Gregory P. Granger

Before You Begin

1. What were the arguments for and against the creation of the Arms Control and Disarmament Agency (ACDA)? Who were the key figures making these arguments?

2. In the post–cold war era, who argued for the abolition of the ACDA and why? Who argued to protect it and on what grounds?

3. Who "won" and who "lost" in this case?

4. What impact did the end of the cold war have on U.S. arms control policy making?

5. What impact did the domestic political context, especially divided government, have on the fate of the ACDA?

6. How did the decentralized nature of political power in the U.S. Senate provide context for challenges to the Clinton administration in foreign affairs?

7. Why might the future of U.S. arms control policy change now that responsibility for this issue falls within the State Department?

Introduction: The Context of Conflicts and Compromises

The collapse of the Soviet Union resulted in the end of the cold war and thrust U.S. foreign policy–making institutions into disarray. For more than forty years after World War II, U.S. foreign policy focused on one overarching objective—the containment of Soviet communism—a grand strategy that was primarily based on the deterrence of Soviet expansion. In the years since the tumultuous changes of 1989 through 1992, the U.S. foreign policy establishment has been in search of a strategy to succeed containment. In addition, the processes of deliberating and implementing foreign policy have become increasingly pluralistic and political. The return of divided government after the 1994 congressional elections ensured that President Bill Clinton would face determined opposition to his vision of international affairs, grounded as it was in Wilsonian internationalism. The six-year story of how the U.S. Arms

Control and Disarmament Agency (ACDA) met its ultimate demise clearly illustrates the heated conflict between Clinton's vision and the power of Congress.

What began as a proposal in 1993 to reorganize the U.S. foreign policy bureaucracy would soon escalate into a tug-of-war between the Clinton administration and the Republican foreign policy leadership in Congress. Caught in the middle was the ACDA, which fought an ultimately unsuccessful battle for its post–cold war survival. By 1999 "the only government bureaucracy in the world whose job [was] thinking up ways to halt the arms race"[1] had closed its doors, and John Holum, the last ACDA director, had taken up a new position in the State Department. Jesse Helms, R-N.C., the strong-willed, outspoken chairman of the Senate Foreign Relations Committee, had reason to celebrate, as his tenacity in seeking the demise of the ACDA was rewarded. Helms's victory was not, however, without cost: in exchange for ending the ACDA, Helms had to allow the Chemical Weapons Convention (CWC), which he opposed, to reach the Senate floor for a vote, where it was passed. In this chapter, we follow the winding path of a bureaucratic reshuffling proposal that exemplifies not only the contentious relationship between the Clinton administration and the GOP congressional leadership, especially in the realm of national security policy, but also the increasingly political emphasis on arms control and disarmament in the post–cold war era.

Background: The First Challenges to the ACDA

Although the concept of arms control is a creation of the nuclear era, the idea of disarmament has a richer historical pedigree, even if the actual practice of disarmament has been rare. Disarmament refers to the *elimination* of weaponry, either comprehensively or limited to a particular classification of weapons, and arms control refers to the attempt to *regulate* the number, type, and deployment of specific classes of weapons. The terms have not always been used in accordance with exact definitions. For example, the disarmament conferences of the 1930s were in reality attempts at naval arms control. More recently, the agreements resulting from the Strategic Arms Limitation Talks (SALT) of the 1970s, which designated exact numbers of specific types of nuclear weapons the superpowers could deploy, can be characterized as arms control. Alternatively, the Intermediate-Range Nuclear Forces Treaty (INF) of the 1980s is an example of disarmament, as it provided for the elimination of an entire class of weapons.

Origins of the ACDA

Created in 1961, the ACDA was the first government bureaucracy of its type—never before had an agency been created with any lasting success for the sole purpose of studying and negotiating arms control and disarmament matters and to do so within the context of U.S. national security policy. It was, however, not the first such attempt. In 1955 Republican president Dwight Eisenhower tapped Harold Stassen, a former governor of Minnesota, to head the new Office of the Special Assistant to the President for Disarmament. Stassen wasted no time in asserting an independent presence in the administration, but he did so at a cost. He resigned in 1958 after Secretary of State John Foster Dulles reprimanded him for exhibiting too much independence.[2] Professional rivalries aside, foreign policy at this time was not conducive to progress on disarmament matters. In particular, Eisenhower's New Look policy sought to exploit the cost-saving element of deploying nuclear weapons rather than conventional forces for containment of communism and deterrence of a Soviet first strike. Unlike personnel, nuclear weapons did not have to be paid, fed, housed, or clothed; relying on the threat of nuclear weapons was cheaper than maintaining a large standing force. In another attempt to institutionalize a presence for arms control voices, however, Eisenhower in September 1960 created the U.S. Disarmament Administration within the State Department, albeit with a small staff and budget.[3]

After the election of 1960, elements of President John F. Kennedy's administration and key members of Congress attempted to rectify the organizational dilemmas facing arms control proponents by proposing the creation of an arms control agency with an independent bureaucracy. John J. McCloy, the newly appointed head of the Disarmament Administration, took the lead in the executive branch. McCloy was well known in Washington circles and, most important, was not perceived to be "dovish," or soft" on national security. Administration officials who were suspicious of arms control felt they could trust McCloy. He was also aided by his personal friendships with the secretaries of state and defense and, by acting "as a critical link in fashioning a supportive coalition of diverse agencies, congressmen, interest groups, and individuals," McCloy overcame the opposition to a new and somewhat more robust arms control agency.[4]

Sen. Hubert Humphrey, D-Minn., took the lead on arms control in Congress and would eventually come to be known as "the father of the ACDA."[5] As chairman of the Senate Foreign Relations Subcommittee on Disarmament, Humphrey was in a position to steer arms control advocacy through the

The Arms Control and Disarmament Agency Debate

January 1993   President George Bush signs the Chemical Weapons Convention (CWC) banning all manufacture, possession, and transfer of chemical weapons; *State 2000: A New Model for Managing Foreign Affairs* recommends merging the Arms Control and Disarmament Agency (ACDA), created in 1961, into the State Department.

January 1995   Secretary of State Warren Christopher recommends merging the ACDA into State; the proposal is sent to Vice President Al Gore's National Performance Review (NPR) staff, charged with making the federal bureaucracy more efficient; ACDA director John Holum lobbies NPR against the merger.

February 1995   Gore's NPR rejects the plan for State's takeover of the ACDA; Sen. Jesse Helms, R-N.C., chairman of the Senate Foreign Relations Committee, proposes legislation to merge the ACDA into State.

August 1995   Clinton and Helms break off negotiations about the fate of the ACDA; Sen. John Kerry, D-Mass., takes over negotiating for the administration.

December 1995   Helms and Kerry strike a deal in the Senate to cut the foreign affairs budget, a move likely to lead to the elimination of the ACDA.

April 1996   Clinton vetoes H.R. 1561, which would have him choose the ACDA, USIA, or USAID for elimination as the result of budget cuts.

October 31, 1996   Hungary signs the Chemical Weapons Convention, beginning a countdown to the treaty's entry into force and giving the United States 180 days to become a convention member with input into the treaty's implementation.

April 24, 1997   In what appears to be a *quid pro quo* arrangement, the Senate votes to approve the CWC, and Clinton approves a plan to eliminate the ACDA within one year and USIA within two years and to grant the secretary of state more authority over USAID.

October 21, 1998   Clinton signs H.R. 4328 (PL 105-277), a $520 billion spending package that includes the abolition of the ACDA.

April 1, 1999   The ACDA is abolished, and the arms control bureaus are reorganized in the State Department.

legislative process. Resistance to this advocacy was quick to materialize, however, because opponents feared that an arms control agency would undermine, rather than support, U.S. national security policy. The "feeling that arms control and disarmament were suspect, that they were somehow different from national security, pervaded the entire process leading to ACDA's formation. It was to follow the Agency in one form or another, with varying levels of intensity, throughout its history." [6]

In Senate debate, Richard B. Russell, D-Ga., chairman of the Armed Services Committee, worried that creating an agency dedicated to disarmament could actually "provoke war" by misleading the Soviets into thinking that the Americans "are so confused that they are going in both directions at the same time," given the escalating arms race between the cold war rivals.[7] Additional opposition came from Sen. Barry Goldwater, R-Ariz., who argued that the agency's work would constitute costly and unnecessary redundancy, that is, would replicate work already being done in other bureaucracies.[8]

Conversely, support for the agency came from high-level political and military figures. Former president Eisenhower voiced support for the agency in a letter read to the Senate Foreign Relations committee by McCloy. Gen. Alfred N. Gruenther, former NATO supreme allied commander, argued that creating the agency would demonstrate to the world that "we are not a warlike group." [9] Also supportive was Secretary of State Dean Rusk, who pointed to the escalating cold war as a justification for the agency, asserting in particular that the "Berlin crisis brings into sharp focus the need for this agency and the urgency of its tasks." [10] Significantly, Rusk rejected the notion of placing the new agency in the State Department, arguing that the agency's responsibility would transcend departmental lines and thus it should be created as an independent structure, even though it would be under the direction of the secretary of state. Largely because of the support of these eminent leaders, the ACDA legislation successfully wound its way through Congress.

Once it became clear that an arms control agency would be established, its bureaucratic status became the subject of political wrangling. The Senate bill creating the ACDA placed it within the State Department, with a new undersecretary to lead it. After conference committee debates (similar to those that would take place more than thirty years later over the agency's demise), the requirement that it be under the State Department was dropped. Again, Senator Humphrey, arguing that the State Department did not give adequate priority to arms control considerations, was the leading congressional voice in support of bureaucratic independence for the agency. Secretary of State Rusk's views on this matter were also instrumental in defeating the Senate stipulation. In the end, the ACDA was created as an independent bureau, but housed in the State Department building. More important, H.R. 9118, the legislation that created the agency, stipulated that the ACDA director "shall serve as principal arms control and disarmament adviser to the President and Secretary of State and ... under the direction of the Secretary of State, shall be primarily responsible within the Government for arms control and disarmament matters."[11] Although advocates for an independent agency won the day, this wording would prove troublesome at various points in the ACDA's history. Simply put, the potential for conflict was inherent in the contradiction between the agency's independent status and its operation under the direction of the secretary of state. In other words, how much direction the secretary of state would exercise remained an open question and one prone to conflicting interpretations.

President Kennedy signed the Arms Control and Disarmament Act on September 26, 1961, and named William C. Foster as the agency's first director. Foster was a Republican with government and business experience whose appointment, like that of McCloy before him and most of his successors, was made to preemptively mute the ACDA's conservative critics.[12] In an attempt to better define the agency's bureaucratic status, in August 1962 Kennedy issued an executive order confirming the ACDA director's access to the president should the director become unable to resolve disputes with other policy actors. Specifically, the executive order stated:

> Differences of opinion ... arising between [ACDA] and other affected agencies with respect to such subjects which involve major matters of policy and cannot be resolved through consultation shall be promptly referred to the President for decision.[13]

The issuance of the executive order did not mean that the president would always decide in favor of the agency, but it gave the ACDA director a stronger hand in any potential disputes within the policy community.

Statutory Functions of the ACDA

The legislation creating the ACDA gave the new agency four primary functions, the first of which was to conduct research. Throughout its history the agency developed a well-regarded reputation for research and technical expertise. Second, the ACDA was responsible for the "preparation for and management of United States participation in international negotiations in the arms control and disarmament field."[14] During its four-decade life span, the agency was unable to carry out this function with the same level of consistency as its research mandate because of the shifting winds of cold war politics and foreign policy. For example, although the agency was widely commended for its efforts in successfully negotiating the Nuclear Non-Proliferation Treaty (NPT) of 1968, it confronted great challenges during the first Strategic Arms Limitation Talks, the bilateral arms control negotiations between the United States and the Soviet Union. In early 1973 President Richard Nixon removed the ACDA director from the chairmanship of the SALT delegation and justified the move by claiming that the talks were keeping the director away from Washington too much to adequately run the agency.[15] More likely, this diminution of the ACDA's negotiating role indicated "a sudden coolness in the White House's affection for the agency" and the consolidation of foreign policy under the leadership of National Security Adviser Henry Kissinger.[16]

The ACDA's third responsibility was for the "dissemination and coordination of public information concerning arms control and disarmament."[17] This task was usually carried out as an extension of the agency's research efforts and was most prominently manifested in the form of annual reports to Congress, as mandated in Article 50 of the law. Also, beginning in the late 1970s, Congress required the ACDA to submit impact statements detailing the arms control implications of weapons procurement decisions. Although on the surface this requirement would seem to be a vote of confidence in the agency's competence, in reality it often made the ACDA's job more difficult by arousing the ire of the Defense Department, which resisted threats to its dominance of the weapons procurement process.

Fourth, the law mandated the task of preparing and operating "such control systems as may become part of the United States arms control and disarmament activities."[18] Referring primarily to verification of compliance with arms control agreements, this task proved to be the least-often performed of the agency's functions, as most such matters were handled by the intelligence community or were otherwise provided for by the text of a given arms control treaty.[19] An exception was the ACDA's involvement in multilateral forums, especially in the NPT review conferences, which have been held every five years since the treaty's entry into force in 1970.

The ACDA's strongest performances were in research and publication, technical expertise and advice, and representation in multilateral negotiations. At the end of its existence, the ACDA had a staff of about 250 people and a budget of well under $50 million. The ACDA was among the smallest bureaucracies and thus was, indeed, a junior, although occasionally significant, player. As John Holum stated, with tongue firmly in cheek, "I suggest that by tangible returns, real value to the taxpayer, security added, defense costs avoided, ACDA has been one of the greatest bargains of all time. So, of course, we must get rid of it." [20] Throughout the ACDA's existence, the idea of "getting rid of it" surfaced and resurfaced, but with the cold war keeping the possibility of global nuclear annihilation on the front burner of superpower relations, the support for an independent voice for arms control considerations remained ample enough to ensure the agency's survival.

The Politics of Post–Cold War Arms Control, 1993–1999

The post–cold war path toward the ACDA's demise began with *State 2000: A New Model for Managing Foreign Affairs,* a State Department Management Task Force report. [21] The task force had begun its work under the Bush administration (1987–1991), but the report was released in January 1993, during the Clinton administration. With regard to the ACDA, the task force recommended that it be dissolved and its missions transferred to the State Department. The momentum for carrying out this proposal was sustained by elements within the newly staffed Clinton State Department. Indeed, the proposal was extended beyond the ACDA to include the dissolution of the United States Information Agency (USIA) and the United States Agency for International Development (USAID). Vociferous protests over the ACDA proposal arose from the Democratic majority in Congress and from non-governmental arms control advocates. Senate Foreign Relations Committee chairman Claiborne Pell, D-R.I., and House Foreign Affairs Committee chairman Lee Hamilton, D-Ind., expressed strong support for not only preserving the ACDA but strengthening it as well. Scholars at the Stimson Center reinforced their position in a report that favored strengthening the agency, [22] a position echoed by groups such as the nonpartisan Arms Control Association.

Enter the New Republican Majority

The 1994 midterm elections resulted in a Republican sweep of the House and Senate. The new majority party was eager for government reform, especially House Republicans under the leadership of Speaker Newt Gingrich, a Georgia conservative with a doctorate in history and a perceived mandate for the rapid devolution of federal power. Prior to the elections, conservative senator Orrin Hatch, R-Utah, had spoken in support of eliminating the ACDA, which he had referred to as an "anachronism in the post–Cold War world." [23] With the ascendance of a conservative majority in both houses of Congress, Hatch's sentiments soon became a congressional policy goal.

Early in the 104th Congress (1995–1996), with the White House and Congress focused on domestic matters such as welfare reform, the fate of the ACDA nevertheless became entangled in battles over defense policy and the federal budget. Secretary of State Warren Christopher in early 1995 revived the idea of merging the ACDA into the State Department, a move described as "a case of preemptive capitulation."[24] Put another way, the administration felt that the congressional Republicans were not only aiming to cut government spending but also were, in large measure, isolationist and highly disdainful of the foreign affairs bureaucracy. In an attempt to beat them to the punch, the State Department took the initiative to reform the bureaucracy.

Christopher was motivated to propose the merger by his ambition to participate in the streamlining of government in general and post–cold war foreign policy–making structures in particular. He also wanted to accomplish these goals in a way that took credit for reform away from the Republicans in Congress. In a January 5, 1995, White House meeting, the matter of foreign affairs restructuring was turned over for study to the National Performance Review (NPR) team.[25] The NPR staff, under the direction of Vice President Al Gore, was mandated with exploring means by which government bureaucracies could be guided to work more efficiently and, if possible, with a smaller staff and budget. The NPR embodied Gore's efforts at "reinventing government," although in this case reinvention would meet resistance. Reports from the deliberations on the ACDA emphasized the "high decibel infighting" over what ACDA supporters considered a "power grab" by the State Department. ACDA staff directed their ire at Lynn E. Davis, whose title of undersecretary of state for International Security Affairs had recently been changed to undersecretary for Arms Control and International Affairs.[26] In a memo to Gore's staff, ACDA director Holum expressed his concern that the State Department had historically failed to make arms control a priority matter, often subordinating such considerations to other diplomatic goals. He also pointed to the department's lack of technical expertise in handling the often arcane and highly technical details of arms control policy. Holum wrote, "It's sometime said that diplomacy isn't rocket science. Often, arms control diplomacy *is* rocket science."[27]

In the end, the NPR staff decided against the proposal to merge the ACDA into the State Department, but not for national security reasons. Rather, the decision resulted from concerns over a potential bureaucratic turf war. The NPR staff simply decided that the money a merger would save was not worth the "grief" that a merger would cause.[28]

Senator Helms Steps into the Fray

In a rapid and public response to the NPR staff's decision, Jesse Helms re-ignited the debate with a proposal to reform what he called an "incoherent mish-mash" of foreign policy organizations.[29] Refusing to allow Christopher's proposal for a merger to "be sacrificed on the altar of bureaucratic self-preservation," Helms also called for consolidating foreign affairs within the State Department.[30] In stark contrast to Holum's assertion that the State Department lacked both the expertise and the will to handle arms control policy, Helms argued that merging the agency into State was "the only way to ensure that proliferation is given adequate weight in our foreign policy."[31] These divergent strategies for achieving similar ends indicated the extreme polarization taking shape over arms control policy in early 1995.

In opposition to Helms's position, supporters of ACDA independence voiced concern that arms control issues might be lost in the myriad other tasks performed by the State Department. The following statement by Arms Control Association president Spurgeon Keeny Jr. clearly illustrates this concern:

> As the victim of an unfriendly takeover, ACDA will be in a poor position to bargain with the vastly larger institution that will absorb it.... With its budget; personnel; and its legal, public, and congressional relations in the hands of the State Department, the arms control function and its experienced practitioners will not fare well in the face of declining budgets and the department's many other pressing responsibilities as well as concern for furthering the careers of foreign service officers.[32]

For his part, Holum was forced to tread carefully between performing his duties as ACDA director and getting involved in the heated political debate over his agency. Beginning with its work on the Nuclear Non-Proliferation Treaty of 1968, the ACDA had developed highly respected talents not only in research, but also in multilateral arms control negotiations. The agency had been the cornerstone of the U.S. presence at the United Nations Conference on Disarmament in Geneva, Switzerland, the only multilateral arms control negotiating body in the world.

Following three years of preparatory meetings on the NPT, Holum and his staff participated in the April 1995 NPT Review and Extension Conference in New York. There, NPT members decided to indefinitely extend the life of the treaty, a decision hailed by Democrats and Republicans in Washington. Also on the ACDA agenda was the 1993 Chemical Weapons Convention (CWC), banning all manufacture, possession, and transfer of chemical weapons. The CWC had been negotiated by the Reagan administration, which had initiated the unilateral destruction of the U.S. chemical weapons arsenal, and signed by President Bush. President Clinton sent the CWC to the Senate on November 24, 1993, but in 1995 it was still stuck in the Foreign Relations Committee, languishing without consideration. Other matters on the ACDA's agenda included representing the United States at negotiations on a Comprehensive Test Ban Treaty (CTBT) to outlaw all explosive nuclear weapons testing. These negotiations were also being conducted under the auspices of the United Nations Conference on Disarmament. Although the decision to extend the NPT did not require explicit congressional approval, Senate consent was required for ratification of the CTBT and the CWC. Ultimately, U.S. accession to the test ban treaty would perish for its failure to garner sufficient Senate support, while the jockeying over the Chemical Weapons Convention's fate would take center stage in the battle over the ACDA.

The ACDA's Game of Survival

In the political impasse over restructuring the foreign affairs bureaucracy, Holum felt obliged to voice his opposition to Helms's proposal. In addition to concerns about the attention arms control would receive in the State Department, Holum indicated that Congress had become too dominant in this process, to the detriment of executive-legislative relations. Holum accused Congress of "trying to micromanage the executive branch" by making the unprecedented move of reorganizing the bureaucracy "over the objection of the executive branch." [33] Although Holum's statement probably overstated the cohesiveness of the Clinton administration's position, it is clear that the quarrels over foreign affairs' reorganization exemplified the reemergence of Congress as a voice in national security policy making.

During the summer of 1995 President Clinton and Senator Helms were engaged in direct negotiations over the issues in question. As chairman of the Senate Foreign Relations Committee—and with one of the safest seats in Congress—Helms was both in a position and in the mood to play hardball. Less an isolationist than a unilateralist, Helms was an avowed defender of traditional notions of national sovereignty and distrustful of international entanglements that might constrain unilateral foreign policy options. He was also concerned about the impact international agreements could have on the private sector in the United States. For example, he opposed the Chemical Weapons Convention, in part, because smaller firms in the U.S. chemical industry would be subject to expensive regulations and intrusive inspections.[34]

Helms's opposition to the chemical weapons ban remained steadfast throughout 1995, and he refused to allow the Foreign Relations Committee to take action on it. The START II nuclear arms reduction treaty between the United States and Russia, which Helms did support, was also "held hostage" in Helms's committee as leverage over the State Department's reorganization. From Helms's perspective, however, the Clinton administration held hostage the foreign affairs reorganization plan.[35] Regardless of the balance of blame for the impasse, Helms sat at the negotiating table with a strong hand. The Clinton administration was at a disadvantage not only because of its ambiguity on bureaucratic reform, but also and more generally because of its preoccupation with budget battles with Congress. The stalemate prompted one State Department official to decry the politicization of foreign policy by this conflict, "in which neither side has defined its objectives honestly and fairly.... The result could be deadlock for the duration of this administration."[36] By the end of summer 1995, Clinton's relationship with the Republican leadership in Congress had deteriorated, and the efforts of Clinton and Helms to reach an agreement had failed. In August the president turned to an ally in the Senate, Democrat John Kerry of Massachusetts, to continue negotiations with Helms.[37]

By December 1995 the budget crisis had taken a high political toll on the president and Congress. Although the House of Representatives had passed legislation to eliminate the ACDA, USAID, and USIA, the Senate was restrained by the Helms-Clinton impasse as well as the Democrats' use of procedural delaying tactics. In the foreign affairs arena, a compromise was achieved when Helms agreed to Kerry's offer to cut the budgets of the State Department and of the three targeted agencies by a total of $1.7 billion over five years. Earlier, Helms had attempted to force the administration's hand with a proposal to cut these budgets by $2.5 billion, ensuring that at least one of the agencies would be fatally wounded by such ax-wielding. Because of its focus on the ideologically charged topic of arms control and its relatively small staff and budget, the ACDA was the most likely candidate for elimination.[38]

The Helms-Kerry compromise took the form of an amendment to the State Department authorization bill (S. 908) for fiscal years 1996 and 1997. The language of the amendment did not rule out eliminating one or more of the agencies, but, more important, it did not mandate a retrenchment. Once the bill had made its way through the legislative process, however, it emerged from the conference committee with language wholly unacceptable to the president. In particular, the act's final wording mandated the elimination of at least one of the foreign affairs agencies, leaving to the president the decision of which one to cut. Arguing against the adoption of the bill, Sen. Joseph Biden, D-Del., declared

> If this act were anything more than a numbers game, it would not blithely give the President a waiver authority to save up to any two agencies of his choice. It is like picking draft choices. I will trade you one and you pick any two you want.... This bogus administrative reform, combined with purposefully punitive budget cuts, is no more than backdoor isolationism, in my view.[39]

The House's legislative strategy failed in April 1996, when President Clinton vetoed H.R. 1561. An attempt to override the veto failed by a significant margin in the House and was never scheduled for a vote in the Senate.[40] In his veto message to Congress, the president defended the independence of the agencies and criticized the "inflexible, detailed mandates and artificial deadlines included in this section of the bill" as unacceptable impositions on "any President."[41] Responding to the veto, the bill's sponsor in the House, Benjamin Gilman, R-N Y, cited the secretary of state's earlier proposal to merge the ACDA into the State Department and criticized the president for defending (in Gilman's assessment) obsolete bureaucracies.[42] Further criticism from congressional Republicans focused on the president's decision to veto the bill on a Friday night, allegedly to avoid extensive media coverage.[43]

Running in Place: The Chemical Weapons Convention

With foreign affairs reorganization settled for the time being, the issue of ratifying the Chemical Weapons Convention began to receive heightened attention in the Senate Foreign Relations Committee. From April to October 1996, Holum, bruised but not beaten by the encounter with Congress on bureaucratic reorganization, was the primary advocate for the weapons ban. On April 25 the Foreign Relations Committee voted 13-5 in favor of a resolution of ratification sponsored by Sen. Richard Lugar, R-Ind.[44] Furthermore, it was unanimously agreed to establish September 17 as the deadline for a vote of the full Senate.

As the deadline approached, however, it became abundantly clear that CWC supporters did not have the sixty-seven votes necessary for ratification. Opponents cited grave concern over two matters. First, the Russians had delayed implementation of a 1990 agreement between the United States and the then-Soviet Union, under which the latter was supposed to destroy its chemical weapons arsenals and permit frequent U.S. inspections of such activities. Holum had traveled to Moscow in August 1996 in an attempt to goad Boris

Yeltsin's government into greater compliance with this agreement and to appease CWC opponents in the Senate, but without much apparent success. Second, the treaty's opponents cited concern over the verifiability of the CWC, and over the possibility of so-called rogue states, such as Iraq, to remain outside the weapons ban regime or to dodge effective verification of their commitment to the CWC. Indeed, supporters of the treaty were offered an unacceptable deal on the CWC that imposed conditions for Senate approval: the CIA must certify with "high confidence" that the CWC can be verified, and the United States would not be obligated by the convention unless and until Iraq, Libya, and North Korea ratified it. Just days before the deadline for the Senate vote, Tom Daschle, D-S.D., the minority leader, requested that Majority Leader Trent Lott, R-Miss., call off the vote, because it was clear that the opposition had secured the thirty-four votes necessary to block Senate consent.[45] As the 104th Congress adjourned in late 1996, the president considered calling Congress into emergency session to address the CWC. The idea of calling "a lame duck Congress back into session" was scrapped because it was doomed to failure, but the battle over arms control continued.[46]

Two Fates Intertwined: The ACDA and the CWC

For the time being, the ACDA retained its independent status, and the CWC remained in the hands of the Senate Foreign Relations Committee. Through most of 1996, the issue of bureaucratic restructuring remained on the back burner while the administration and congressional leaders wrestled with welfare reform and more budget battles and prepared for the November elections. Meanwhile, the ACDA continued to represent the United States at the Conference on Disarmament, working toward completion of the Comprehensive Test Ban Treaty.[47]

Following his reelection to the Senate in November and return to the chairmanship of the Foreign Relations Committee, Helms in early 1997 aggressively revisited the question of foreign affairs reorganization. From this point in time, the matter of bureaucratic restructuring became even more entwined in executive-legislative bargaining over other foreign policy issues, especially over Senate action on the controversial CWC.

In January 1997 Helms demanded that the administration formally propose an agency reorganization plan before he would allow his committee to take up the CWC. At this time, Senator Biden dispatched a confidential memo to President Clinton suggesting that the president "needed to provide Senators Lott and Helms with some *quid pro quo*" for the CWC.[48] In the administration's view, time was getting short for ratifying the convention because of the stipulation that it would enter into force 180 days after the sixty-fifth country approved it. With Hungary's ratification of the CWC on October 31, 1996, the weapons ban would enter into force on April 29, 1997.[49] The administration was concerned because ratifying the CWC *before* its entry into force was a prerequisite for a state to participate in the Organization for the Prevention of Chemical Weapons (OPCW), the body that would implement the treaty.[50] In short, without a prompt vote, U.S. influence over CWC implementation would be lost.

Beyond this national interest, the president's personal interests were also engaged. His internationalist approach to foreign affairs and his need for a positive foreign policy legacy demanded that the United States become a member of the OPCW. These motivations, intensified by the demands of time, tilted the balance of options toward sacrificing the ACDA, ironically, for the sake of an arms control victory. Clinton worked with Senate leaders Lott and Daschle to pressure Helms into acting on the weapons ban.[51] On April 17, 1997, Helms agreed to allow the CWC to reach the Senate floor for debate and a vote on advice and consent within the following week. The process, however, was to involve sending the CWC to the floor with the stipulation that the Helms-authored Senate Resolution 75 be established "as the resolution of ratification for the CWC."[52]

Senate Resolution 75, also known as the Chemical Weapons Convention bill, included thirty-three conditions for Senate consent. The Senate agreed to the first twenty-eight conditions by voice vote on April 23, 1997. In accordance with the agreement with Helms, the five remaining conditions were subject to individual majority approval on the Senate floor. Each of these five were considered "killer conditions." Put another way, the survival of any one of these conditions would have the effect of preventing the president from depositing the U.S. instruments of ratification—leaving the United States a nonmember of the convention.

On April 24, 1997, Senator Biden introduced five amendments to Senate Resolution 75, each addressing a specific condition for Senate approval. Amendment 47 passed, 71-29, and eliminated Helms's condition Number 30, which withheld U.S. ratification until the president, in consultation with the CIA, could certify to Congress that "countries which have been determined to have offensive chemical weapons programs, including Iran, Iraq, Syria, Libya, the Democratic People's Republic of Korea, China, and all other countries determined to be state sponsors of international terrorism, have ratified or otherwise acceded to the Convention." Amendment 48, approved 66-34, struck out condition Number 29, which tied U.S. ratification to Russian ratification and other measures taken by Russia toward complying with all previous agreements on chemical weapons disarmament. Amendment 49, approved 66-34, eliminated condition Number 33, which held the president responsible for certifying to Congress that compliance with the CWC was "effectively verifiable." Amendment 50, approved 56-44, struck down demands made in condition Number 31, which specified criteria for the president to bar certain inspectors associated with verifying the CWC. Finally, Amendment 51, approved 66-34, overturned condition Number 32, which forbade the president from ratifying the CWC until treaty provisions regarding the transfer of chemical weapons defense technology were removed from it. After strong lobbying in favor of the CWC by Robert Dole, a former Senate majority leader and the 1996 Republican presidential candidate, and by retired generals Norman Schwartzkopf and Colin Powell, and with each of the "killer conditions" eliminated from the Chemical Weapons Convention bill, the ratifying resolution passed, 74-26.

Endgame: The ACDA Bargained Away

Within hours of the April 17, 1997, agreement to discharge the CWC from the Senate Foreign Relations Committee, President Clinton approved a plan that provided a two-year timetable for reorganizing the foreign affairs bureaucracies. According to this plan, the ACDA would be abolished by September 1998, and its functions transferred to the State Department. USIA would follow suit one year later. USAID would retain its institutional independence, but the secretary of state was given greater "direct authority and foreign policy guidance" over its functions.[53]

Not surprisingly, the close timing of the two decisions inspired much speculation about a *quid pro quo*, with staff members and higher officials in the administration and in Congress taking various positions. Whether there was an explicit and purposeful "grand bargain" is simply unknowable.[54] As one commentator pointed out,

> Undoubtedly, both sides factored these political agreements on arms control matters into a broader political puzzle that included unrelated issues high on their respective political agendas. *Securing Senate advice and consent inevitably involves this type of bargaining process.*[55]

What is certain is that shortly after these decisions, "the turf wars began."[56] Employees at all three affected agencies expressed fears for their jobs and for the missions of their respective institutions, often in harsh language against the State Department's priorities and way of doing business. In response, L. Craig Johnstone, State Department director for Resources, Plans, and Policy, stated, "It is a perverse rule of bureaucracy that people with a common set of goals and a common set of agendas are the ones most likely to end up at each others' throats."[57]

With the strong support of Secretary of State Madeleine Albright, the administration lived up to its agreement to supply Congress by September 1997 with a formal and detailed proposal for the foreign affairs reorganization. More delays in Congress, however, postponed consideration of the proposal, as legislators turned their attention to other battles with the Clinton administration, for example IMF and UN funding. For an extended period, therefore, the ACDA was left without a clear definition of its institutional status.[58] Holum remained as actively engaged in arms control matters as conditions allowed, including traveling throughout Europe to build support for strengthening the verification provisions of the 1972 Biological Weapons Convention.[59] But the ambiguity of the ACDA's status was beginning to take its toll, as it became increasingly difficult to discern who had authority over specific policy areas. For Holum, the institutional confusion was driven home by his holding two distinct titles; while still ACDA director, Holum had also become undersecretary of state for Arms Control and International Security.[60]

The budget was the primary obstacle to legislative progress. In this scenario, the president, despite being impeached earlier in the year, seemed to have a slight advantage over Congress, because public opinion in 1995 had held Congress, and specifically the Republican leadership, responsible for shutting down the government over a similar budget impasse. The "solution" in 1998 was not a high point in congressional history, to say the least. On October 21, 1998, President Clinton signed into law H.R. 4328, which provided for the appropriation of more than $520 billion in government spending for the 1999 fiscal year, combining into one huge omnibus bill "eight unfinished spending bills that provide funding for 10 Cabinet departments and scores of federal agencies."[61] Included in this massive election-year spending bill were the provisions for eliminating USIA and the ACDA, along with the reorganization of USAID.

In accordance with the requirements of Public Law 105-277, the president submitted a ninety-eight-page "implementation report" to Congress, detailing the precise plans for merging the functions and personnel of the ACDA and USIA into the State Department.[62] Holum's two positions were merged into one, as he accepted the position of undersecretary of state and senior adviser to the president and to the secretary of state for Arms Control, Nonproliferation, and Disarmament. In this capacity, the senior adviser would now oversee policy for three bureaus: Arms Control, Nonproliferation, and Political-Military Affairs. To carry out what was the ACDA's verification and compliance functions in a manner independent from those responsible for negotiating the arms control agreements, a special adviser for verification and compliance was instituted to assist the senior adviser. Newly created positions in the State Department included a scientific and policy advisory board on arms control, non-proliferation, and disarmament. In addition, former ACDA intelligence specialists were moved into the State Department's Bureau of Intelligence "to provide a robust interface with the Intelligence Community."[63]

The day of reckoning for the ACDA came on April 1, 1999, when it officially ceased to exist. The point of losing their bureaucratic home on April Fool's Day was not lost on the agency's staff members. Their farewell gathering included a costumed Grim Reaper.[64]

Conclusion: Function Follows Context

The events of ACDA's demise illustrate the complexity inherent in the United States' Madisonian system of separate institutions, checks and balances, and the necessity of interbranch deliberation and compromise. Within this context, the significance of political status—or lack thereof—becomes abundantly clear in the case of the ACDA. That is, the truly remarkable aspect of this story may not be that the ACDA was eliminated, but that it took so long after the end of the cold war to kill it, given that the agency was often caught in the middle of executive-legislative policy disputes without a strong constituent advocacy it could rely on for support. During the cold war, the voices of ACDA supporters were generally able to outweigh those opposing it, based on the idea that in the quest to avoid nuclear annihilation, all political and technical perspectives deserved attention. In the post–cold war era, however, attitudes changed. The absence of a hostile, nuclear-armed adversarial superpower combined with unprecedented challenges to executive branch preeminence in foreign affairs by powerful members of Congress meant that the rationale and steadfast support for the ACDA simply withered away. Indeed, some may find a sense of irony in this situation: the agency that participated in the arms control and arms reduction treaties of the 1980s and early 1990s, which arguably contributed to the peaceful conclusion of the cold war, became a victim of its own success.

Although many may find comfort in the old saying "politics stops at the water's edge," the serious analyst of post–cold war U.S. national security policy knows better. There can be no policy without process, there can be no process without an institutional framework, and, as this case illustrates, there can be no institutional framework without often grueling debates over what position, resources, and authority each element of the framework should be allotted. In turn, these debates are structured in accordance with the changing international and domestic political environments, and the post–cold war era has been nothing if not a time of change.

These matters are not easy to address, especially when the high-stakes priorities of national security are in question. In the end, no one comes away wholly pleased or wholly dissatisfied. The system at large is preserved, however altered, and the answers are found in the constitutionally designed struggle for institutional and policy preferences.

Notes

1. Peter Grier, "25 Years in Arms Control's Bureaucratic Trenches," *Christian Science Monitor,* September 26, 1996, 3.

2. Duncan L. Clarke, *Politics of Arms Control: The Role and Effectiveness of the U.S. Arms Control and Disarmament Agency* (New York: Free Press, 1979), 12.

3. "Senate Approves Disarmament Agency," *Congressional Quarterly Weekly Report,* September 15, 1961, 1575.

4. Clarke, *Politics of Arms Control,* 19.

5. Duncan L. Clarke, "Arms-Control Agency Retains Value in US Security System," *Christian Science Monitor,* March 11, 1993, 18.

6. Clarke, *Politics of Arms Control,* 18.

7. "Senate Approves Disarmament Agency."

8. Ibid.

9. "Disarmament Agency," *Congressional Quarterly Weekly Report,* August 18, 1961, 1456.

10. Ibid.

11. "Disarmament Agency," *Congressional Quarterly Weekly Report,* September 29, 1961, 1655.

12. "Disarmament: The U.S. Tries Again," *Time,* October 6, 1961, 23.

13. D. S. Greenberg, "Executive Order Boosts ACDA," *Science,* September 7, 1962, 738.

14. Section 2[b] of PL 87–297, *Arms Control and Disarmament Act,* U.S. Statutes at Large (1961): 631–639.

15. Nicholas Wade, "Arms Control: White House Whittles Down Peace Agency," *Science,* February 16, 1973, 668–669.

16. Ibid., 668.

17. Section 2[c] of the ACD Act.

18. Section 2[d] of the ACD Act.

19. Clarke, *Politics of Arms Control,* 24.

20. John D. Holum, "Remarks to the Arms Control Association Luncheon," Carnegie Endowment, Washington, D.C., March 29, 1999, www.state.gov/www/global/arms/speeches/holum/holac.html.

21. *State 2000: A New Model for Managing Foreign Affairs,* U.S. Department of State Publication 10029, December 1992.

22. Michael Krepon, Amy E. Smithson, and James Shear, *US Arms Control and Disarmament Agency: Restructuring for the Post–Cold War Era,* Stimson Center Occasional Paper no. 13, December 1992, http://www.stimson.org/pubs/allpubs.htm. The Henry L. Stimson Center, headquartered in Washington, D.C., is a non-profit, public policy institute focusing on security issues confronting the United States and other nations.

23. John Isaacs, "The 103rd Congress and Arms Control," *Arms Control Today,* January/February, 1994, 8.

24. George Moffett, "State Department Could Be Shuffled," *Christian Science Monitor,* January 13, 1995, 2.

25. John Goshko, " 'Super State Department' May Absorb Other Agencies," *Washington Post,* January 11, 1995, A15.

26. Thomas W. Lippman, "Entrenched Constituencies Help Kill Merger," *Washington Post,* February 3, 1995, A17.

27. Ibid.

28. Senior NPR staff member, quoted anonymously in ibid.

29. "Helms Opens Hearings on Abolishing ACDA," *Arms Control Today,* April 1995, 2.

30. Jesse Helms, "Christopher Is Right," *Washington Post,* February 14, 1995, A15.

31. Ibid.

32. Spurgeon M. Keeny Jr., "In Memoriam: ACDA (1961–1997)," *Arms Control Today,* April 1997, 2. This position was supported by a former State Department official, David Newsom, who questioned the ability of the department's leadership to effectively manage the increased workload following consolidation; see David D. Newsom, "A Mega-State Department?" *Christian Science Monitor,* April 26, 1995, 20.

33. Michael Rust, "GOP Remodels Foggy Bottom," *Insight on the News,* June 12, 1995.

34. See Jonathan S. Landay, "Senate May Nix Chemical Weapons Ban," *Christian Science Monitor,* November 21, 1996, 4.

35. George Moffett, "Who Holds Foreign Policy Hostage?" *Christian Science Monitor,* November 15, 1995, 4. The hostage-taking metaphor was widely used in media reports of these circumstances. For a scholarly view of the tactic, see Roger H. Davidson and Walter J. Oleszek, *Congress and Its Members,* 7th ed. (Washington, D.C.: CQ Press, 2000), 393.

36. Moffett, "Who Holds Foreign Policy Hostage?"

37. Ibid.

38. "Held for Ransom," *Washington Post,* December 17, 1995, C6.

39. "Against Backdoor Isolationism," *Congressional Record,* March 28, 1996, S3144.

40. See *Conference Report on H.R. 1561, Foreign Relations Authorization Act, Fiscal Years 1996 and 1997,* House of Representatives, March 8, 1996; and *American Overseas Interests Act—Veto Message from the President of the United States,* H. Doc. no. 104–197, April 15, 1996. The Foreign Relations Authorization Act and the American Overseas Interests Act are different titles of the same bill.

41. *American Overseas Interests Act.* It should be noted that the omnibus bill contained several other provisions that prompted the president to veto it.

42. See *Foreign Relations Authorization Act, Fiscal Years 1996 and 1997—Veto Message from the President of the United States, Congressional Record,* April 30, 1996, H4151–61.

43. Carroll J. Doherty, "GOP Not Giving Up on Agency Cuts," *Congressional Quarterly Weekly Report,* April 20, 1996, 1059.

44. Heather Podlich, "Senate Foreign Relations Committee Passes CWC Ratification Resolution," *Arms Control Today,* April 1996, 21; R. Jeffrey Smithy, "Chemical Arms Pact Backed," *Washington Post,* April 26, 1996, A18.

45. Thomas W. Lippman, "Senate Foes Derail Chemical Weapons Treaty," *Washington Post,* September 13, 1996, A1.

46. Ibid.

47. In late 1996 President Clinton became the first signatory to the Comprehensive Test Ban Treaty, but in 1999 the treaty would fail to garner sufficient consent in the Senate for ratification. See Lippman, "Senate Foes Derail."

48. Ibid.

49. Tom Pfeiffer, "Hungary Sets Clock Ticking for CWC Entry into Force," *Arms Control Today,* October 1996, 21.

50. Lawrence J. Goodrich, "World Views Clash on Weapons Treaty," *Christian Science Monitor,* April 15, 1997, 1.

51. Erik J. Leklem, "Majority Leader Emerges as Key to Fate of CWC in Senate," *Arms Control Today,* March 1997, 22, 27.

52. Erik J. Leklem, "Senate Gives Advice and Consent; U.S. Becomes Original CWC Party," *Arms Control Today,* April 1997, 32.

53. Jack Mendelsohn, "Clinton Announces Reorganization Plan, ACDA to Lose Independent Status," *Arms Control Today,* April 1997, 33. See also Stephen Barr and Thomas W. Lippman, "Turf Diplomacy at State Department," *Washington Post,* May 28, 1997, A17.

54. Thomas L. Friedman, "The Big Deal of the Day," *New York Times,* March 27, 1997.

55. John V. Parachini, "U.S. Senate Ratification of the CWC: Lessons for the CTBT," *The Nonproliferation Review* 5 (fall 1997), http://cns.miis.edu/pubs/npr/parach51.htm. Emphasis added.

56. Barr and Lippman, "Turf Diplomacy at State Department."

57. Ibid.

58. John Isaacs, "Arms Control in 1998: Congress Maintains the Status Quo," *Arms Control Today,* October 1998, 19.

59. Tim Butcher, "Move to Ease Threat of Biological Warfare," *Electronic Telegraph,* February 13, 1998, http://www.telegraph.co.uk.

60. Isaacs, "Arms Control in 1998."

61. George Hager and Charles R. Babcock, "President Signs Bill for Agency Funding; Lawmakers Decry Dealmaking Process," *Washington Post,* October 22, 1998, A1.

62. See *Reorganization Plan and Report,* part 2, *The Arms Control, Nonproliferation, and International Security Mission,* http://www.state.gov/www/global/general_foreign_policy/rpt_981230_reorg5.html; see also Thomas W. Lippman, "USIA and ACDA Workers All to Retain Employment; Agencies to Be Folded into State Department Operations," *Washington Post,* January 5, 1999, A9. The ACDA was formally abolished in

U.S. Code, Title 22 (Foreign Relations and Intercourse), Chapter 74 (Foreign Affairs Agencies Consolidation), Subchapter II (United States Arms Control and Disarmament Agency), Part A (Abolition and Transfer of Functions), Sec. 6511 (Abolition of United States Arms Control and Disarmament Agency).

63. *Reorganization Plan and Report,* part 2. See also "ACDA Prepares to Merge with State," *State Magazine,* March 1999, http://www.state.gov/www/publications/statemag/statemag_mar99/featur1b.html.

64. Al Kamen, "Grim Reaper at a Disarming Agency," *Washington Post,* April 5, 1999, A15.

6 India and Pakistan: Newest Members of the Nuclear Club

Christopher Allan McHorney

Before You Begin

1. What were the options available to the Clinton administration after India and Pakistan detonated nuclear devices in May 1998? Why did the Clinton administration decide to impose economic sanctions against them?

2. Why did the imposition of economic sanctions against India and Pakistan enjoy such strong support in Congress?

3. Why did Great Britain and France refuse to support the U.S. call for economic sanctions against India and Pakistan?

4. Could the international community have prevented India and Pakistan from conducting nuclear tests in May 1998?

5. Should the international community allow countries that have chosen not to participate in the nuclear non-proliferation regime to develop nuclear weapons?

6. How should the international community respond to efforts by so-called rogue states, such as Iraq and Iran, to develop weapons of mass destruction?

Introduction: The Nuclearization of South Asia

India shocked the international community by detonating three nuclear devices on May 11, 1998. Many analysts feared that the tests would lead to a similar action by Pakistan. Given the history of conflict between the two states, most members of the international community viewed the introduction of nuclear weapons into South Asia with alarm. Fueled by religious animosity and disagreements over their border, India and Pakistan had fought three major wars since the British partitioned colonial India into India, East Pakistan, and West Pakistan in 1947. Outbreaks of violence between India and Pakistan had become more frequent in the 1990s. The introduction of nuclear weapons into the region was particularly troubling when one considered reports alleging that the Pakistani air force may have armed several of its F-16s with nuclear weapons during the 1990 Kashmir crisis without informing Prime Minister

Benazir Bhutto.[1] The prospect of a fourth conflict raised the horrifying specter of a nuclear war in the second most populous region in the world (see map, p. 135).

Events following the 1947 partitioning of India placed most of Kashmir under Indian control, but because of its majority Muslim population Pakistan also claimed the province. By the mid-1990s, an increasingly familiar routine had developed. After virtually every spring thaw in the mountains, Indian military personnel would discover Pakistani military or paramilitary forces occupying disputed Kashmiri land inside the Indian border. Small arms fire and artillery exchanges would follow until the Pakistani forces withdrew. With India's testing of nuclear devices in 1998, these annual skirmishes took on a much more threatening appearance.

While the Clinton administration strongly condemned the decision of the Indian government to explode nuclear devices, the tests presented the United States with an opportunity to assess the effectiveness of the counterproliferation policy unveiled by Secretary of Defense Les Aspin on December 7, 1993, in a speech to the National Academy of Sciences' Committee on International Security and Arms Control. In his presentation Aspin identified an "increased threat of proliferation of nuclear weapons and other weapons of mass destruction" as one of the four primary national security threats that the United States would face in the post–cold war era. Aspin then unveiled the administration's response—the Defense Counterproliferation Initiative (CPI), a two-pronged approach to countering nuclear, chemical, and biological weapons.[2] The CPI consisted of four policy actions intended to prevent the proliferation of such weapons: dissuasion, arms control, international pressure, and denial.

Dissuasion involves the use of incentives, such as positive security assurances, to persuade a potential proliferator not to develop weapons of mass destruction. A positive security assurance would be, for example, a security guarantee offered by a nuclear weapon state to a non-nuclear state facing an adversary armed with nuclear weapons. The extension of the U.S. nuclear shield over Western Europe and Japan during the cold war is an example of a positive security assurance. Arms control agreements further the cause of non-proliferation by limiting or reducing the number of nuclear, chemical, and biological weapons in the arsenals of the signatories. The Chemical Weapons Convention is an example of an arms control agreement that limits the proliferation of weapons of mass destruction, in that each signatory agrees to destroy the chemical weapons in its arsenal, rather than retaining or transferring them to another country. International pressure would be used to change the behavior of a potential proliferator through threats of retaliation, such as the economic sanctions listed in Section 102 of the Arms Export Control Act of 1968, more commonly known as the Glenn Amendment of 1994. Denial would be used to prevent a potential proliferator from acquiring weapons of mass destruction by restricting access to the necessary technology and material. For example, the Enhanced Proliferation Control Initiative requires exporters to obtain an export license for any item that an importer could use to develop weapons.[3]

The CPI also identified four policy actions to reverse proliferation and protect military personnel and civilians during a conflict with an adversary armed with weapons of mass destruction: defusing, deterrence, defense, and offense. Defusing would involve the use of positive incentives, such as financial assistance, to persuade a country to eliminate some or all of its weapons. For example, the Nunn-Lugar Cooperative Threat Reduction Program, which began as an amendment to the Conventional Armed Forces in Europe Implementation Act of 1991, helped three newly independent states of the former Soviet Union—Belarus, Kazakhstan, and Ukraine—destroy their nuclear weapons. Deterrence would be enforced through the credible threat of the strategic and tactical use of nuclear weapons to reduce the probability of an attack by a state armed with weapons of mass destruction. Even after the cold war, the United States maintained a credible second-strike capability to dissuade an adversary considering a first strike. Defense would include all active and passive measures taken by the military to insure its ability to successfully engage an adversary armed with weapons of mass destruction. The U.S. Army's Patriot Advanced Capability Level 3 missile system, which provides a ballistic missile defense for ground troops, and the M21 Remote Sensing Chemical Agent, which detects and identifies chemical and biological weapons from long ranges, are examples of active and passive defenses. Offense would include preventive strikes intended to prevent the production of weapons of mass destruction, preemptive attacks prior to a crisis, and strikes that neutralize the adversary's weapons during a crisis or war.[4]

In 1998, the Clinton administration attempted to roll back proliferation in India and persuade the Pakistani government that responding in kind to India's tests would not further its national security or economic interests. Attempting to use international pressure, the administration tried threats of sanctions to force India to renounce further nuclear testing and reconsider its decision to become a nuclear state. The administration also tried to use international pressure through the threat of sanctions to stop Pakistan from testing a nuclear device. The administration also attempted to dissuade the Pakistani government with offers of economic and military aid. The Indian subcontinent continues to be one of the most unstable regions in the world because the administration failed to persuade India and Pakistan to remain non-nuclear states and tensions still run high between the two adversaries.[5]

Background: Prelude to Nuclearization

As noted above, the Indian subcontinent has a history of instability that dates back to 1947. The migration of more than 7 million Hindus into India and a comparable number of Muslims into Pakistan immediately after the partition of colonial India was only the first catastrophe to visit this troubled region during the past fifty years. With border issues and religion as constant sources of tension and almost irreconcilable differences, Hindu-dominated India and Muslim-controlled Pakistan fought major wars in 1947, 1965, and 1971 and a number of less serious border skirmishes. The cold war rivalry between the two superpowers only served to further inflame tensions on the subcontinent; India signed a treaty of friendship with the Soviet Union, and Pakistan received economic and military aid from the United States.[6]

In May 1998, as many as eleven nuclear devices would be tested on the Indian subcontinent. The weeks and months preceding the tests were a period of increasing tension, with threatening actions and inflammatory rhetoric flying across the Indian and Pakistani border. Jingoistic campaign rhetoric during the 1998 Indian parliamentary elections contributed to an increase in the animosity between India and Pakistan. The Bharatiya Janata Party (BJP) made the testing of a nuclear device one of its campaign promises. After the March 7 elections resulted in the BJP having a plurality of seats in the Lok Sabha, the lower house of the Indian legislature, the Hindu nationalist party formed a coalition government and continued to argue in favor of testing a nuclear device. On March 18, the BJP and its coalition partners presented the citizens of India with their National Agenda for Governance. Addressing the issue of Indian national security, the government, led by Prime Minister Atal Bihari Vajpayee, promised to exercise the nuclear option to deter potential adversaries.[7] In a television interview, while speaking with reporters, and during a formal lecture in New Delhi, Defense Minister George Fernandes identified China as the number one potential threat to India, igniting a political firestorm weeks before the first set of nuclear tests.[8] According to Fernandes, the Chinese military was stockpiling nuclear weapons aimed at India along the Chinese-Indian border in Tibet.[9] Fernandes also accused China of providing Pakistan

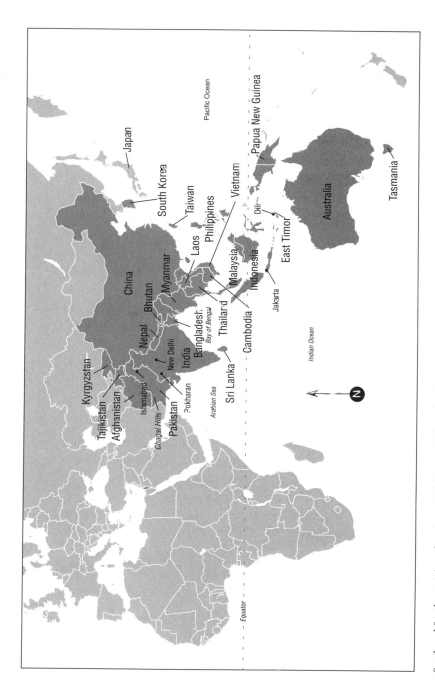

South and Southeast Asia and environs. In May 1998 India and Pakistan detonated as many as eleven nuclear devices, raising concerns that any future conflict between the two states might devolve into nuclear war.

The Nuclearization of South Asia

December 7, 1993   Secretary of Defense Aspin unveils the Defense Counterproliferation Initiative.

March 7, 1998   In India, the Hindu nationalist Bharatiya Janata Party receives a plurality of seats in the Lok Sabha.

March 18, 1998   The Bharatiya Janata Party and its coalition partners release the National Agenda for Governance.

April 6, 1998   Pakistan tests the Ghauri, a medium-range ballistic missile.

May 11, 1998   India tests three sub-kiloton nuclear devices underground in the Pokharan range.

May 12, 1998   President Bill Clinton speaks with Pakistani prime minister Nawaz Sharif and attempts to persuade him not to conduct nuclear tests.

May 13, 1998   Indian prime minister Atal Bihari Vajpayee writes a letter to Clinton in which he justifies India's nuclear testing. India conducts two more sub-kiloton nuclear explosions. Sharif meets with his cabinet's Defense Committee. Clinton issues Presidential Determination no. 98-22, imposing economic sanctions against India.

May 15, 1998   A high-ranking U.S. delegation meets with Pakistani officials.

May 22, 1998   Clinton and British prime minister Tony Blair phone Sharif.

May 27, 1998   Japanese prime minister Ryutaro Hashimoto phones Sharif. Clinton speaks with Sharif for the fifth time since India's May 11 tests.

May 28, 1998   Pakistan conducts underground nuclear tests in the Chagai Hills (though its claim that five devices were detonated is disputed). Clinton announces the imposition of economic sanctions against Pakistan.

May 30, 1998   Pakistan conducts another nuclear test.

with ballistic missiles and the technology required for the development and production of nuclear weapons.[10]

Pakistan contributed to rising tensions by testing the Ghauri, its latest medium-range ballistic missile on April 6, only weeks before India detonated nuclear devices. With a range of 930 miles, the Ghauri was capable of hitting most of India's major cities.[11] In fact, A. Q. Khan, regarded as the father of Pakistan's nuclear bomb, claimed that Pakistan could target twenty-six Indian cities.[12] Only days after it tested the Ghauri, Pakistan announced the impending test of a longer-range missile, the Ghaznavi.[13]

India Joins the Club

India conducted underground tests of fission, low-yield, and thermonuclear devices in the Pokharan range of Rajasthan at 6:45 a.m. EST on May 11, 1998.[14] The test of the three devices took place in the same area and almost twenty-four years to the day after India conducted its first underground test of a nuclear device, on May 18, 1974.[15] According to R. Chidambaram, chairman of the Indian Atomic Energy Commission, the thermonuclear device, or hydrogen bomb, produced a yield of approximately 43 kilotons (KT),[16] the fission device about 12 KT, and the low-yield device about 0.2 KT.[17] Chidambaram claimed that only concerns that the tests might damage homes in the surrounding area had prevented the detonation of devices with much higher yields.[18] The simultaneous blasts produced by the tests of the devices were approximately four times as powerful as the bomb dropped on Hiroshima.[19] Along the Indian-Pakistani border the explosions measured 4.7 on the Richter scale.[20] Prime Minister Vajpayee announced the successful completion of the tests in a six-sentence statement:

> Today at 15:45 hours, India conducted three underground nuclear tests in the Pokharan range. The tests conducted today were with a fission device, a low-yield device, and a thermonuclear device. The measured yields are in line with expected values. Measurements have also confirmed that there was no release of radioactivity into the atmosphere. These were contained explosions like the experiment conducted in May 1974. I warmly congratulate the scientists and engineers who have carried out these successful tests.[21]

India invoked national security concerns as a basis for the tests. On May 13, Vajpayee wrote a letter to President Bill Clinton in which he claimed to be very troubled about growing instability in South Asia. In an obvious reference to China, Vajpayee expressed his concern over an "overt nuclear weapon state on our borders" that had attacked India in 1962.[22] Vajpayee also criticized China for helping Pakistan become a covert nuclear weapon state.[23] Vajpayee went on to blame Pakistan for the deteriorating security environment in the region. According to Vajpayee, Pakistan had attacked India three times during the last half century and sponsored a nonstop campaign of terrorism in the Indian provinces of Punjab, Jammu, and Kashmir.[24] In previous statements, the government had argued that it had improved the security environment in its demonstration that India had developed a credible nuclear deterrent.[25] Asked to explain the tests during an interview, Vajpayee cited promises made by the BJP during the campaign; the tests were part of the National Agenda for Governance. Vajpayee professed a four-decade-long personal commitment to a nuclear India. After gaining power, Vajpayee believed his government needed to fulfill that campaign promise by testing a device.[26]

Resistance to existing non-proliferation treaties also appears to have influenced the government's consideration of nuclear testing. Prominent Indian leaders, expressing a perspective commonly held in developing countries, criticized existing non-proliferation treaties, like the Comprehensive Test Ban Treaty (CTBT) and Nuclear Non-Proliferation Treaty (NPT), as attempts to maintain the status quo of several Western, industrialized democracies with sizable nuclear arsenals and a southern hemisphere devoid of them. Vajpayee proclaimed that India would not sign the "discriminatory" CTBT or NPT.[27] BJP president Kushabhau Thakre called the tests a "repudiation of the policy of nuclear apartheid" imposed by the nuclear weapon states on India and other states capable of developing and producing nuclear weapons.[28] K. Subrahmanyam, former director of the Institute for Defence Studies and Analyses, took the argument further, claiming that the international community forced India to test nuclear devices by indefinitely extending the NPT.[29]

Indians reacted to the tests with almost universal support. According to an Indian Market Research Bureau poll, 91 percent of Indians surveyed supported the tests; only 7 percent opposed them.[30] With the exception of the Left, all the major political parties in India praised the tests. Forty-five organizations in India launched the Movement Against Nuclear Weapons on the same day as Gaurav Divas, or Day of Pride, which commemorates the first nuclear tests in 1974.[31] The Congress Party announced its support of the tests after Prime Minister Vajpayee met informally with party president Sonia Gandhi and other senior party leaders.[32] Sharad Pawar, the leader of the Nationalist Congress Party, congratulated the Indian scientists responsible for the blasts.[33] United Front spokesperson Jaipal Reddy also offered words of praise to the scientists.[34]

Bansi Lal, leader of the Haryana Vikas Party, categorized the tests as a "right step in the right direction."[35]

On the other hand, the Communist Party of India and Communist Party of India–Marxist questioned the motives of the government.[36] A. B. Bardhan and D. Raja of the Communist Party of India and Ramachandran Pillai and Prakash Karat of the Communist Party of India–Marxist signed a joint statement praising the scientists responsible for developing the nuclear devices but harshly criticizing the government for authorizing the tests.[37] Both parties called on the government to provide a rationale for the tests,[38] rejecting the justification already offered, and accused the BJP of using them for political gain. For example, Harkishan Singh Surjeet, general secretary of the Communist Party of India–Marxist, accused the BJP of using the tests to divert attention from the political problem of a shaky coalition.[39]

The Reactions

Pakistan initially reacted with caution to India's nuclear testing, stating that an analysis of the blasts would take place before the issuance of any reports.[40] Leading members of the government, however, quickly abandoned this wait-and-see attitude and adopted a more disapproving stance. Reading a statement on the floor of the Senate during an emergency session, Foreign Minister Gohar Ayub Khan accused India of placing the survival of the nuclear nonproliferation regime in doubt by covertly developing and testing nuclear devices.[41]

In addition to castigating India, Prime Minister Nawaz Sharif held the international community responsible for ignoring warnings from his government about the threat of India conducting nuclear tests.[42] Sharif also asserted that the international community encouraged India to test nuclear devices because of its willful ignorance and inequitable stance toward Pakistan.[43] Foreign Minister Khan criticized the international community for ignoring more than two decades of warnings from Pakistan about India's nuclear aspirations.[44] The Sharif government quickly reassured its citizens that India did not pose a threat to Pakistan. At the same time, it assured Pakistanis that the government would take all steps necessary to protect national security interests and that the military already possessed the ability to respond to any such threats.[45]

The United States Caught by Surprise

Acting on assurances by India, the United States had little reason to suspect that the government was planning to test nuclear devices. On March 26, 1998, senior Indian foreign policy adviser N. N. Jha had informed U.S. officials that his government would conduct a three- to six-month national security review. Jha assured the United States that India would not test a nuclear weapon before the completion of the review.[46] Thus, India's detonation of the three nuclear devices caught the United States unprepared and unable to intercede and attempt to prevent the tests.

According to several sources, a U.S. intelligence satellite had earlier detected evidence of renewed activity at the nuclear test site in the Pokharan range, including the presence of bulldozers.[47] On May 11, at 3:00 a.m. EST, only hours before the first test, an analyst examined a photograph that revealed that someone had removed the fences at the site.[48] The Central Intelligence Agency (CIA), however, did not issue an alert. Because of this failure, U.S. policy makers learned about the tests when watching Prime Minister Vajpayee read his statement on CNN about the success of the operation.[49] *Charhdi Kala International,* an obscure weekly Sikh separatist newsletter published in India, added to the United States' embarrassment by predicting the tests in its May 7 issue:

> Preparations for an Indian nuclear test have been further confirmed by our sources in India (who have never been wrong, having millions of pairs of eyes and ears fixed to the ground) who report all kinds of feverish night time activities in the vicinity of Pokharan in Rajasthan state 60 miles from the Pakistani border.[50]

Pakistani ambassador Riaz H. Khokhar brought along a copy of the newsletter when he met with Assistant Secretary of State for South Asian Affairs Karl F. Inderfurth.[51]

Several members of Congress reacted quickly, harshly criticizing the intelligence community. Richard C. Shelby, R-Ala., chairman of the Senate Intelligence Committee, referred to the inability of the intelligence community to anticipate the nuclear tests as "a colossal failure," "the intelligence failure of the decade." Shelby noted that the blunder had prevented the Clinton administration from attempting to intervene.[52]

CIA director George Tenet responded to the criticism by asking retired admiral David Jeremiah, a former vice chairman of the Joint Chiefs of Staff, to oversee a review panel to look into the failure to detect preparations for the tests.[53] After a ten-day investigation, the panel issued a report harshly critical of the CIA. It blamed the failure on poor leadership, inadequate human and on-the-ground intelligence, and improper assessment of data gathered from satellites. The panel recommended reform of the CIA, but also concluded that had the CIA provided the administration with advance warning of the tests, it would not have been able to persuade India to forego them. After the report was issued, Tenet decided not to punish anyone, saying that wrong decisions may have been made, "but nobody was asleep at the switch."[54] The Clinton administration publicly chastised the CIA. One senior administration official expressed disbelief that the agency had failed to detect preparations for the test, despite the fact that proliferation was its top priority and the Indian government had used the same site in 1974. The administration promised an immediate investigation.[55]

Speaking to reporters at the White House, Clinton refocused criticism on the Indian government for authorizing the testing. According to Clinton, the tests threatened the stability of South Asia and represented a direct challenge to international efforts to prevent the proliferation of weapons of mass destruction.[56] Unfortunately, the CPI provided the Clinton administration with few viable options. Given the unwillingness of the Vajpayee government to renounce further nuclear testing, the administration could not use positive incentives, such as offers of economic assistance, to defuse the situation by preventing further proliferation. The administration did not appear to have considered the offensive use of military force to destroy the nascent Indian arsenal, and the deterrence and defense components of CPI were not capable of reversing proliferation. Unfortunately for the Indian government, the decision to conduct nuclear tests would result in significant economic consequences. On May 11, the administration announced its intention of fully implementing the sanctions mandated by Section 102 of the Arms Export Control Act.[57]

Adding to the frustration of the Clinton administration was the fact that the Indian government had been more than adequately warned about the consequences of testing a nuclear device. During a press briefing on the day of the first set of tests, State Department spokesman James Rubin spoke about the sanctions imposed by the United States against two companies that had transferred missile technology to Pakistan. The Clinton administration thus believed that it had adequately communicated its willingness to use the threat of economic sanctions to prevent the spread of nuclear weapons technology and delivery systems to the subcontinent.[58]

Congressional leaders also harshly criticized India's actions. Sen. Sam Brownback, R-Kan., chair of the Senate Foreign Relations Subcommittee on Near Eastern and South Asian Affairs, called the tests "an enormous negative blow" to Indian-American relations.[59] Accusing the Indian government of making a "major miscalculation," Sen. Jesse Helms, R-N.C., chair of the Senate Foreign Relations Committee, said that the Indian government had "most likely shot itself in the head" by testing nuclear devices.[60] Helms also criticized the Indians for financing a nuclear weapons program in the pursuit of superpower status when its country was "tangled in economic knots, [and] disease and misery are rampant."[61] Senator Helms even characterized India as a potential nuclear threat to the United States.[62] According to Sen. Joe Biden, D-Del., India "thumbed its nose at the international community" by testing nuclear devices.[63] While professing a friendship with India, Sen. John Glenn, D-Ohio, described the tests as "a blatant slap in the face to the way the rest of the world is going."[64] The Clinton administration did not escape criticism in the aftermath of the tests. Attempting to understand why "a country suffering from rampant poverty and class instability" would "spend its valuable resources on a nuclear weapons programme," Sen. Tim Hutchinson, R-Ark., blamed the foreign policy of the administration. The Republican National Committee accused Clinton of exacerbating the missile crisis by ignoring Chinese military transfers to Iran and Pakistan.[65]

Following the Indian tests, the United States began an intensive campaign to pressure Pakistan into not responding in kind. Commenting on the tests, Clinton tried to impress upon the Pakistani government that reciprocating would only lead to a destabilizing arms race.[66] Clinton also spoke with Prime Minister Sharif on May 12 in an attempt to persuade him to exercise restraint.[67] After a positive conversation with Sharif, Clinton decided to send a mission headed by Deputy Secretary of State Strobe Talbott and Central Command commander in chief Gen. Anthony Zinni to meet Pakistani officials on May 15.[68] Assistant Secretary Inderfurth and Bruce Rydell, senior director of the National Security Council for South Asia, also traveled to Pakistan as part of the high-level mission.[69]

The U.S. delegation met with Prime Minister Sharif, army chief of staff Gen. Jehangir Karamat, and Foreign Minister Khan on May 15.[70] The American delegation delivered a two-pronged message. First, it conveyed a warning that a nuclear test by Pakistan would lead to the imposition of the same type of economic sanctions now facing India.[71] Second, it raised the possibility that the Clinton administration might reward Pakistan for showing restraint and not testing nuclear devices by, for example, possibly repealing the Pressler Amendment, which barred all economic and military assistance to Pakistan.[72] Repeal of the Pressler Amendment would also allow Pakistan to take delivery of twenty-eight F-16s.[73] Even though Pakistan had paid more than $650 million for the aircraft, the F-16s remained in the United States because President George Bush could not certify that Pakistan was not developing nuclear weapons as required by the Pressler Amendment.[74] With the tacit approval of the Clinton administration, and on the same day that the members of the U.S. delegation met with their counterparts in the Pakistani government, Senator Brownback and Sen. Tom Harkin, D-Iowa, proposed legislation that would repeal the Pressler Amendment.[75]

Pakistani leaders told the U.S. delegation that a decision to test nuclear weapons had not been made and might be avoidable.[76] Foreign Secretary Shamshad Ahmed, however, did express some doubts about the validity of the security guarantees proposed by the delegation. Arguing that a renunciation of the nuclear option might put the national security of Pakistan at risk, Ahmed questioned the wisdom of relying on the security guarantees offered by the United States because "all umbrellas have holes in them."[77]

Two More Indian Tests

India conducted two more nuclear tests at 12:21 p.m. on May 13 at the Pokharan range.[78] The sub-kiloton devices had yields of 0.2 and 0.6 KT.[79] According to an official press release from the government, the tests were fully contained and did not release any radioactivity into the atmosphere.[80] The government also announced its intention to stop testing such devices.[81] Adding fuel to an already intense fire, Pramod Mahajan, political adviser to the prime minister, announced the continuation of efforts to develop a long-range ballistic missile.[82]

Reacting angrily to the second series of tests, Pakistani foreign minister Khan accused India of a "consistent pattern of irresponsible behavior."[83] Reading a nine-page statement at a press conference, Prime Minister Sharif claimed that Pakistan continued to live "under the dark shadow of Indian nuclear sabre-rattling."[84] Discounting the claim by the Indian government that national security concerns justified its tests, Pakistan argued that India did not face a threat from any country in the region and accused it of developing and testing nuclear weapons in order to obtain the status of a Great Power and hegemon in South Asia.[85]

Prime Minister Sharif met with the Defense Committee of the cabinet on May 13 to decide how to react to India's tests.[86] Defense Minister Aftab Shahban Mirani, General Karamat, and others attended the four-hour meeting.[87] The committee released a statement accusing India and the international community of bringing to an end the possibility that South Asia might remain free of nuclear weapons and describing the tests as highly irresponsible provocations that had altered the balance of power in the region. In its statement the committee went on to blame the international community for ignoring Pakistan's warnings about India and pressuring Islamabad with threats of sanctions despite its "impeccable record of utmost restraint." [88]

Once again, the Pakistani government tried to reassure its citizens that India did not pose a threat. The statement released by the Defense Committee reasserted that the military could respond to the increased threat posed by an India armed with nuclear weapons.[89] Other members of the government, however, offered a different assessment of the security situation in the aftermath of India's second set of tests. Speaking to the Senate on May 13, Foreign Minister Khan claimed that the tests represented an "immediate and grave threat" to Pakistan's national security.[90]

The Defense Committee gave no indication whether Pakistan planned to test a weaponized nuclear device.[91] The committee did, however, reserve the right to take any steps necessary to safeguard the national security of Pakistan.[92] Other members of the government also refused to rule out the possibility that Pakistan might respond in kind to India's nuclear tests. Foreign Secretary Ahmed declared that the government continued to consider a test of nuclear devices as a possible option.[93]

In interviews and speeches, members of the Pakistani government and opposition leaders continued to argue that the response of the Western democracies to the Indian nuclear tests would influence whether Pakistan decided to test a nuclear device. A weak or timid response could lead to one or more detonations.[94] What Pakistan sought were sufficiently harsh sanctions against India. During an interview at his home, Information Minister Mashalof Hussein, a confidant of Prime Minister Sharif, said that "the core issue is whether there is a price tag to India's behavior." [95] Sharif initially adopted a cautious attitude, declaring that Pakistan would wait and see if the sanctions addressed a balance of power in South Asia that favored India.[96] According to Sharif,

> Pakistan has legitimate security concerns, which need to be recognized and addressed by the international community. If we can do that without testing a device and address our legitimate security concerns and satisfy ourselves that our security is not in jeopardy, that would be the ideal thing.[97]

Voicing his disappointment, Prime Minister Sharif claimed that if "the world punished India, I could have told my people that now there is no justification to detonate our nuclear device ... but this is not happening."[98] Concurring with Sharif, Foreign Minister Khan argued that the sanctions imposed by the United States "hardly constitute an effective response."[99] Khan added, "A rebuke and a couple of weeks of posturing is not going to be enough."[100]

International Reaction

State Department spokesman Rubin announced that the United States "deeply deplore[d]" the second set of "unfathomable" tests.[101] Despite its tough talk, the administration did not appear surprised by the second set of tests. Undersecretary of State for Political Affairs Thomas Pickering had met with representatives of the Indian government prior to the second set of tests to discuss the sanctions the United States might impose.[102] According to Rubin, Pickering did not leave the meeting with a commitment from the Indian government to stop testing nuclear devices.[103]

Clinton had few options other than to impose sanctions. Section 102 of the Arms Export Control Act did not provide him with the authority to waive them; only Congress has that authority, through the passage of a joint resolution, but congressional leaders showed no interest. The act did, however, permit Clinton to delay the imposition of sanctions for thirty days.[104] According to some officials, the National Security Council initially wanted to pursue the international pressure tenet of the CPI by delaying sanctions so that India might consider its options. The State Department, on the other hand, recommended their immediate imposition.[105]

Clinton decided to impose economic sanctions prior to India's second set of tests. Clinton issued Presidential Determination no. 98–22 on May 13, officially imposing economic sanctions on India. The determination authorized all relevant government agencies to take steps necessary to impose the sanctions described in Section 102 of the Arms Export Control Act.[106] He announced his decision on May 13 at a news conference in Potsdam, Germany, during a state visit. In his announcement—which was broadcast live by CNN—Clinton argued that the decision of the Indian government to test nuclear devices was an alarming misstep that required a clear and unmistakable response. He encouraged other members of the international community to support the U.S. response by also imposing sanctions.[107] Clinton's decision marked the first time that a president had implemented Section 102 of the Arms Export Control Act in response to a nuclear test by a non-nuclear weapons state.[108]

White House press secretary Mike McCurry released a statement detailing the sanctions. First, the United States would terminate all foreign aid provided to India under the Foreign Assistance Act of 1961, with the exception of humanitarian aid.[109] For example, the United States canceled $21 million in previously promised development assistance.[110] Second, the United States would cancel the sale of any military equipment and services.[111] Third, the administration would order every government agency to deny India credit and similar types of financial assistance.[112] Loans denied to India because of the sanctions included $4 billion from the U.S. Export-Import Bank and $10.2 billion in potential financing from the Overseas Private Investment Corporation.[113] Fourth, the United States would oppose the approval of loans to India from international financial institutions such as the World Bank and International Monetary Fund.[114] At the time, international institutions were considering $3.8 billion in assistance for India.[115] Fifth, the administration barred all U.S. banks from providing loans or other forms of credit that the Indian government might use for the purchase of goods other than food or other agricultural commodities.[116]

The Clinton administration could unilaterally enforce most of the provisions of Section 102 of the Arms Export Control Act, but restricting foreign aid provided to India by international financial institutions would require the cooperation of other members of the global community. For example, the World Bank requires that a proposal win a 50.1 percent share of a vote by the board of directors. The United States controls 16.7 percent of the vote share of the board, so it cannot unilaterally block funding proposals. Even with the support of Japan (8 percent) and Germany (4.6 percent), the pro-sanctions coalition controlled only 29.3 percent of the vote share.[117]

While the United States and other nations that favored the use of sanctions lacked the votes to block World Bank loans, the reliance of the bank on consensus rather than formal votes when making decisions allowed the Clinton administration to delay funding to India. For example, the administration forced the bank to delay indefinitely $865 million in loans, part of which the Indian government planned to use to construct a power grid. The United States also forced the bank to postpone a $130 million loan for building a number of small hydroelectric generators. The bank also delayed a third loan that would have provided $275 million for road construction in Haryana state.[118]

The imposition of sanctions enjoyed broad support in Congress. Despite being a strong supporter of India, Senator Helms claimed that he would never agree to the termination of sanctions unless India abandoned its aspirations of becoming a nuclear power.[119] Senator Glenn argued against a search for loopholes that might allow India to avoid the imposition of sanctions.[120] Senator Brownback called for the quick implementation of sanctions.[121]

Dozens of other countries condemned India's nuclear testing.[122] German foreign minister Klaus Kinkel called the tests a "slap in the face" to the 149 signatories to the Comprehensive Test Ban Treaty." [123] Japanese prime minister Ryutaro Hashimoto denounced the tests as "extremely regrettable." [124] The representatives of the only two cities ever to be devastated by nuclear weapons— the mayors of Hiroshima and Nagasaki—sent letters of condemnation to India.[125] Reading a statement in Copenhagen, Danish foreign minister Niels Helveg Petersen declared that his country "deeply deplores" the nuclear tests.[126] Calling the test "a very major regressive step backward," [127] Canadian foreign minister Lloyd Axworthy announced that his government was "deeply concerned and very disappointed" with the Indian government.[128] Russian president Boris Yeltsin said, "India has let us down with its test." [129] The Ministry of Foreign Affairs of the People's Republic of China issued a statement strongly condemning the Indian government for its "outrageous contempt for the common will of the international community." [130] The fifteen foreign ministers of the European Union condemned India's actions.[131] UN secretary-general Kofi Annan expressed his "deep regret" over the decision to test the devices.[132]

In addition to public statements of outrage, several countries expressed their displeasure with the Indian government by recalling their ambassadors. Japan recalled Ambassador Hiroshi Hirabayashi for consultations.[133] New Zealand prime minister Jenny Shipley recalled her country's ambassador, saying that India had "shattered" the dream of an "end of the nuclear arms race." [134] Prime Minister John Howard announced the recall of the Australian high commissioner from New Delhi for consultations.[135]

A number of countries followed the example of the United States and suspended much-needed economic aid. The issue of economic sanctions, however, deeply divided the cold war coalition of industrialized democracies. In addition to the United States, the other industrial nations that imposed sanctions were Denmark, Germany, Japan, the Netherlands, and Sweden.[136] Japanese prime minister Hashimoto announced the decision of his government to suspend 3.5 billion yen in new grant aid,[137] but decided not to suspend funds for humanitarian assistance and grassroots projects. Japan usually provides India with 133 billion yen in aid each year, so the suspension was a relatively small amount for India to lose. Japan also refused to host the World Bank–sponsored India Development Forum (IDF) meeting. At the previous gathering, developed countries attending contributed $6 billion in aid.[138] Germany froze $300 million of new development assistance.[139] In addition to freezing $28 million in aid,[140] Denmark canceled a high-level trade visit.[141] Sweden prematurely terminated a three-year $118 million aid agreement.[142] Dutch foreign minister Hans Van Mierlo announced that the Netherlands was freezing all economic aid and banning arms deliveries to India.[143]

A distinctly post–cold war coalition of France, Great Britain, and Russia opposed the imposition of sanctions. While supporting the goal of a nuclear weapons–free India, France, according to government spokesman Daniel Vaillant, felt that economic sanctions were not appropriate for persuading India to remain among the community of non-nuclear weapons states.[144] British minister of state for Foreign and Commonwealth Affairs Derek Fatchett justified his government's decision for forego sanctions on the grounds that they would punish "the poorest and the ordinary people of India for a decision taken by their Government."[145] Discussing the rationale behind his government's decision during an interview with Russian NTV, Foreign Minister Yevgeny Primakov characterized sanctions as an extreme and commonly counterproductive strategy.[146] During a meeting with senior Russian diplomats, President Yeltsin discussed his plans to exert diplomatic pressure on the Indian government during a visit scheduled for December 6 through 8, rather than relying on sanctions to coerce India into reversing its position on nuclear weapons.[147] In fact, the Russians claimed that they decided not to alter their plans to construct a nuclear power plant in Koodamkulam, India, because any change might appear to be sanctions related.[148] During an interview with *India Today,* Prime Minister Vajpayee complimented France, Great Britain, and Russia for showing "a commendable sense of realism" in their decision not to go along with the sanctions regime.[149]

India reacted with defiance and pride, rather than repentance, to the sanctions. Vajpayee, claiming that his country would not be intimidated by sanctions, accused the United States and its allies of hypocrisy for punishing India even though they had carried out more nuclear tests and built tens of thousands of nuclear weapons during the preceding fifty years.[150]

Pakistan Joins the Club

In the aftermath of India's second series of tests, the Clinton administration and other Western governments renewed their campaign of persuasion designed to prevent a nuclear test by Pakistan. Clinton spoke with Prime

Minister Sharif on May 22 and urged him to refrain from testing a device.[151] Likewise, British prime minister Tony Blair telephoned Sharif that same day and urged against responding to India's nuclear tests with more tests.[152] Japanese prime minister Hashimoto telephoned Sharif on May 27 and urged him to show restraint and not to respond in kind. Chinese president Jiang Zemin, responding to a request from Clinton during the first call on the hot line between Beijing and Washington, asked in a letter that Pakistan not conduct a test.[153] Sharif portrayed himself as a leader trying heroically to determine how to protect Pakistan's national security while under unrelenting pressure from domestic actors favoring or opposing a nuclear test.[154]

The Clinton administration, in addition to applying public pressure, attempted to implement the CPI policy of dissuasion by trying to allay some of Pakistan's security and economic concerns. According to State Department spokesman Rubin, the United States engaged Pakistan in a crucial dialogue in the days that preceded the first Pakistani nuclear tests.[155] Secretary of Defense William Cohen announced the willingness of the United States to offer Pakistan a wide-ranging package that would address some of its security and economic concerns if it would agree not to test a nuclear device. According to Cohen, the twenty-eight previously purchased F-16s would constitute only a small component of the package.[156] Other parts might include the conversion of $6 billion in short-term debt into long-term loans and the sale of battle tanks.[157] Pakistani analysts called the U.S. offer "flimsy": Pakistan had already paid for the F-16s and agreed to buy T-80 tanks from Ukraine. Finally, it wanted the United States to write off, rather than refinance, much of its debt.[158]

Clinton made a last-minute plea only hours before Pakistan detonated nuclear devices. He spoke with Sharif for twenty-five minutes on May 27 at midnight EST[159] and detailed the serious penalties that would follow a nuclear test.[160] White House press secretary McCurry described the conversation between Clinton and Sharif as intense.[161] Clinton had spoken with Sharif on four other occasions after India's first set of tests on May 11.[162] Responding to Clinton's personal appeal, Sharif said that the president had said all the right things,[163] but Sharif criticized the international community for "filing its fingernails" instead of taking action after India's tests.[164] Once again, Sharif cited significant domestic pressure as a reason that nuclear tests might be unavoidable. According to him, he was feeling pressure from opposition parties and ordinary citizens demonstrating in the streets.[165] Foreign Secretary Ahmed summoned Indian high commissioner Satish Chandra at 1:00 a.m. EST on May 27 and told him that Pakistan had reliable information of a plan by

India to launch an attack against Pakistani nuclear installations before sunrise. Chandra categorically denied the allegation.

Pakistan conducted five underground nuclear tests in the Chagai Hills in the western part of the country on May 28 at 6:30 a.m. EST.[166] While not providing details about the type of weapons involved or the power of the devices,[167] the Pakistani government did claim that the tests did not release radioactivity into the atmosphere.[168] Two groups measured the magnitude of the explosions at 4.8 to 4.9 on the Richter scale, with an explosive force somewhere between 8 and 17 KT. Again, by comparison, the atomic bomb dropped by the United States on Hiroshima had a force of 15 KT of high explosive.[169] Addressing the nation on television, Prime Minister Sharif boasted that Pakistan had "settled a score" by testing five nuclear devices.[170] Pakistan conducted a sixth test on May 30.[171]

Some U.S. military and intelligence analysts doubt that Pakistan actually tested five devices.[172] According to the Pentagon, the multiple explosions measured 4.2 on the Richter scale.[173] The Incorporated Research Institutions and National Earthquake Informational Center measured the magnitude of the explosions as 4.8 to 4.9, which equates to an explosive force ranging between 8,000 to 17,000 tons of high explosive.[174] One U.S. intelligence official speculated that Pakistan tested two, rather than five, devices.[175]

Speaking to reporters at a news conference held after his address to the nation, Prime Minister Sharif said that the decision of India to weaponize its nuclear program had fundamentally changed the balance of power in South Asia and that irresponsible decision making by India had forced his government to test nuclear devices in national self-defense. Sharif also acknowledged the impact of domestic pressure on the decision to approve the tests, commenting that the Pakistani people would not have tolerated any other outcome.[176] After all, might not India have thought Pakistan technologically inferior, and thus weaker, had it not detonated the devices? Would not India have interpreted the absence of a test by Pakistan as a lack of national resolve, thereby encouraging more reckless behavior during the next border conflict? Exacerbating the situation, Pakistan released a statement claiming that it had already armed the Ghauri missile with nuclear warheads so its military could respond "to any misadventure by the enemy."[177]

The Reactions

General V. P. Malik, Indian army chief of staff, categorically denied Pakistani allegations of an imminent attack on its nuclear facilities, claiming that the

Indian military did not even have plans for such a contingency.[178] Prime Minister Vajpayee also tried to ease tensions between the two countries, stating that India did not want to destroy Pakistan and suggesting that government representatives would be willing to meet with Pakistani officials to discuss a no-first-use of nuclear weapons policy and possible confidence-building measures to reduce tensions between the two states.[179]

More Sanctions

President Clinton reacted to the first set of Pakistani nuclear tests by harshly criticizing the government for failing to exercise restraint.[180] While acknowledging the role that India had played in the decision of the Pakistanis to test nuclear devices, Clinton still concluded that "two wrongs don't make a right."[181] Echoing the sentiment expressed by Clinton, Secretary of State Madeleine Albright referred to the Pakistani tests as a "serious error" of judgment.[182] Clinton then announced the imposition of economic sanctions on Pakistan. Deputy Secretary of State Talbott announced that the United States would treat India and Pakistan the same, regardless of the fact that India detonated the first nuclear device.[183]

The international community also reacted with outrage to the Pakistani tests. Japanese chief cabinet secretary Kanezo Muraoka described the tests as "extremely regrettable."[184] France, in a statement released by the Foreign Ministry, declared that it "deplores and condemns" the nuclear tests, which work against efforts by the international community to prevent proliferation.[185] The Russian Foreign Ministry lamented the fact that the Pakistani government had failed to "show prudence and good sense" at a critical point in its history.[186] Likewise, German government spokesman Otto Hauser and British foreign secretary Cook harshly condemned the Pakistani government for authorizing the tests.[187]

The coalitions that emerged in response to the Indian tests remained unchanged in the aftermath of the decision by Pakistan to test nuclear devices. Japan and Germany quickly announced their intention to impose economic penalties similar to those on India. A Japanese government official, speaking with reporters, said that Japan would "consider what we should do in parallel with what we did with India," and accordingly, Japan froze new loans and grants to Pakistan, which reduced Japanese aid to Islamabad by two-thirds. Germany canceled discussions scheduled for June about new development aid totaling approximately $45 million. The post–cold war coalition of France, Great Britain, and Russia refused to impose economic sanctions. Consistent with its decision not to limit $165 million in foreign aid promised to India, Great Britain decided not to reduce the $41 million in assistance committed to Pakistan.[188]

Attempting to put a positive spin on sanctions during an address to the nation, Prime Minister Sharif claimed that "by imposing sanctions, the Western powers will have done us a favor." He portrayed the sanctions as an opportunity for political and economic reform and a chance to end decades of corruption. He also argued that sanctions would force the government to end the squandering of natural resources and adopt a more fiscally responsible attitude toward the budget.[189] Accordingly, he announced several budget-cutting measures designed to address the decrease in foreign aid. All government ministers were ordered to vacate their official residences, and leading by example, Sharif announced his intention to vacate the $50 million prime minister's residence. After the residences were vacated, the government planned to turn them into schools, clinics, and welfare centers.[190] Commenting on the impact of the sanctions, A. Q. Khan declared that it would be "better to eat less and be free rather than be well fed but live the life of a slave." [191] The government also declared a state of emergency, suspending all fundamental rights.[192]

Conclusion: Counterproliferation in the Post–Cold War Era

Several observations can be gleaned from a careful analysis of the events that transpired in May 1998 in South Asia. First, the inability of the Clinton administration to prevent or reverse the nuclearization of South Asia suggests a significant flaw in current U.S. counterproliferation policy. The threat of economic sanctions should achieve maximum leverage when used against developing countries, such as India and Pakistan, in dire need of aid and assistance. Even after the imposition of sanctions following their testing of nuclear devices, however, both countries conducted missile tests in April 1999. On April 11, India launched from Wheeler Island a surface-to-surface Agni II ballistic missile with a range of more than 2,000 kilometers. In a pattern reminiscent of the events of May 1998, Pakistan reacted to the Indian test on April 14 by launching a Ghauri II missile, which also has a range of 2,000 kilometers. Pakistan went on to test a medium-range Shaheen missile twenty-four hours later.[193] Efforts by the Clinton administration to counter the arms race spiral in South Asia had clearly ended in failure.

Second, the seriousness of the threat posed by the nuclearization of the Indian subcontinent resulted in a relatively low level of partisan bickering for a foreign policy issue addressed by a divided government in the post–cold war era. Faced with the prospect of a nuclear war in the second most populous region of the world, Republicans and Democrats remained unified in their support of the imposition of sanctions against India and Pakistan. Even some of the most vocal supporters of India, such as Senator Helms, strongly condemned the Indian government for its decision to become a nuclear weapons state and argued against a premature termination of sanctions. The CIA became a victim of bipartisan cooperation, with Congress and the Clinton administration lambasting the agency for failing to provide advance warning about India's first set of tests.

Third, the cohesiveness of the cold war alliance of Western industrialized democracies ended with the collapse and disintegration of the Soviet Union and democratization of Eastern and Central Europe. The administration of George Bush benefited from the collapse of the alliance system when the Soviet Union sided with the United States and voted in 1990 and 1991 in favor of several resolutions passed by the UN Security Council in the aftermath of the Iraqi invasion of Kuwait. The Clinton administration did not likewise benefit from this more fluid alliance system in this instance. The issue of economic sanctions deeply divided the international community. Although Denmark, Germany, Japan, the Netherlands, and Sweden supported the U.S. response to the Indian and Pakistani tests, a distinctly post–cold war coalition of France, Great Britain, and Russia opposed the imposition of sanctions. The unwillingness of such major states as these to follow the example of the United States reduced the effectiveness of the sanctions. Thus even with domestic U.S. political actors in agreement about how to respond to the threat of a nuclear arms race in South Asia, political changes in the post–cold war international environment prevented the U.S. policy from being more effective.

Notes

Articles from the *Statesman* and the *Hindu* were located on Lexis-Nexis and therefore are cited without page numbers. The headlines are reproduced as they originally appeared in the newspapers.

1. Scott Sagan and Kenneth Waltz, *The Spread of Nuclear Weapons: A Debate* (New York: W. W. Norton, 1995), 82.

2. Les Aspin, "Counterproliferation Initiative," remarks to the National Academy of Sciences, Committee on International Security and Arms Control, December 7, 1993. Reprinted in Committee on Governmental Affairs, *Nuclear Proliferation Fact Book*, 103d Cong., 2d sess., 1994.

3. For a thorough discussion of the CPI, see Brian Bates and Chris McHorney, *Developing a Theoretical Model of Counterproliferation for the Twenty-first Century* (New York: Edwin Mellen Press, 2000).

4. Ibid.

5. Although the Clinton administration opposed the spread of nuclear weapons into South Asia, a number of scholars have argued that selective nuclear proliferation might contribute to a more stable international system by providing states with a credible deterrent. For a comprehensive discussion of both sides of the proliferation debate, see Sagan and Waltz, *The Spread of Nuclear Weapons.*

6. For an excellent overview of Indian-Pakistani relations during the last fifty years, see John Stoessinger, "Four Battles over God: India and Pakistan in 1947, 1965, 1971, and 1998," in *Why Nations Go to War* (New York: St. Martin's Press, 2001), 111–137.

7. "National Agenda for Governance," *India News,* April 7, 1998.

8. "India's New Defense Chief Sees Chinese Military Threat," *Statesman,* May 4, 1998.

9. Ibid.

10. Faced with criticism from political opponents, Fernandes claimed that reporters had misquoted him. "I Was Misquoted, Says Fernandes," *Statesman,* May 10, 1998.

11. "Pakistan Sets Off Nuclear Blasts; 'Today, We Have Settled a Score,' Premier Says," *Washington Post,* May 29, 1998, A1. The Ghauri is named after the Turkish invader who established the first Muslim kingdom in India, in 1193. "India's Choice, and Pakistan's," *New York Times,* May 29, 1998, A21.

12. "India's Choice, and Pakistan's," A21.

13. Ibid. Ghaznavi was a Turk who invaded western India from what is now Afghanistan.

14. "India Conduct Three N-Test," *Statesman,* May 11, 1998; "India Confirms Nuclear Capability with 3 Tests," *Chicago Sun-Times,* May 11, 1998, 3. The project code name was Shakti, after the Hindu goddess of destruction. "India Detonated a Hydrogen Bomb, Experts Confirm," *New York Times,* May 18, 1998.

15. "India Explodes Three Nuclear Devices at Pokhran," *Hindu,* May 12, 1998.

16. "Weaponisation Now Complete, Say Scientists," *Hindu,* May 18, 1998.

17. Ibid.

18. "India Detonated a Hydrogen Bomb, Experts Confirm."

19. Corrections, *New York Times,* May 15, 1998, A2.

20. "India Conduct Three N-Test."

21. "India Explodes Three Nuclear Devices at Pokhran."

22. "Vajpayee Writes to Clinton, Cites Reasons," *Statesman,* May 13, 1998.

23. Ibid.

24. "Indian's Letter to Clinton on the Nuclear Testing," *New York Times,* May 13, 1998, A14.

25. See the comments of the prime minister's principal secretary, Brajesh Mishra, in "India Conduct Three N-Test."

26. "Interview with Indian Prime Minister Atal Bihari Vajpayee," *India Today,* May 25, 1998.

27. "N-Tests in Supreme National Interest Vajpayee," *Hindu,* May 15, 1998.

28. "Fury at Indian Nuclear Test," *Guardian,* May 12, 1998, 2.

29. "India Explodes Three Nuclear Devices at Pokhran."

30. "Most Indians Hail N-Tests—Opinion Poll," *Hindu,* May 13, 1998.

31. "India Anti-Nuclear Movement Launched in Delhi," *Hindu,* May 17, 1998.

32. "Congress Backs Vajpayee," *Statesman,* May 14, 1998.

33. "Congress, UF Welcome Blasts, CPI-M, CPI Silent," *Statesman,* May 11, 1998.

34. Ibid.

35. "BJP, Allies Hail Tests," *Statesman,* May 11, 1998.

36. "Congress, UF Welcome Blasts, CPI-M, CPI Silent."

37. "Reasons Not Clear, Left Parties," *Hindu,* May 13, 1998; and "CPI-M, CPI Hail Scientists," *Statesman,* May 12, 1998.

38. "Reasons Not Clear, Left Parties."

39. "Left Parties Reject Government Justification for N-Tests," *Hindu,* May 20, 1998.

40. "USA Disappointed, Neighbours React Cautiously," *Statesman,* May 11, 1998.

41. Official statement from Pakistan following India's nuclear tests, May 12, 1998, http://www.clw.org/coalition/pako511.htm.

42. "Sharif Blames the West," *Hindu,* May 13, 1998.

43. Ibid.

44. Official statement from Pakistan following Indian nuclear tests, May 12, 1998.

45. "Sharif Blames the West," *Hindu,* May 13, 1998.

46. "U.S. May Have Helped India Hide Its Nuclear Activity," *New York Times,* May 25, 1998, A3. National Security Adviser Samuel Berger later disparaged India for conducting a campaign calculated to deceive the Clinton administration with promises of restraint. "India Denies US Charge of Deception," *Statesman,* May 18, 1998. According to a senior government official, the Clinton administration "made the mistake of assuming they [the Indian government] would act rationally." "U.S. Blundered on Intelligence, Officials Admit," *New York Times,* May 13, 1998, A1.

47. "U.S. May Have Helped India Hide Its Nuclear Activity," A3.

48. Ibid.

49. "The Day CIA Did Not Issue an Alert," *Statesman,* May 13, 1998.

50. "Scooped on Tests, U.S. Scorns a Sikh Journal," *New York Times,* May 16, 1998, A5.

51. Ibid.

52. "U.S. Blundered on Intelligence, Officials Admit," A1.

53. Ibid.

54. "U.S. Review Panel Blames CIA," *Hindu,* June 4, 1998.

55. "U.S. Intelligence Failed to Warn of India's Atom Test," *Los Angeles Times,* May 13, 1998, A1.

56. Excerpts of President Clinton's remarks on the Indian nuclear tests, May 12, 1998, http://www.clw.org/coalition/clino512.htm.

57. Ibid.

58. State Department, daily press briefing, May 11, 1998, http://www.clw.org/coalition/rubio511.htm.

59. "Defiance Endangers U.S.-India Relations; Administration Had Urged Cooperation," *Washington Post,* May 12, 1998, A15.

60. "Helms Targets CTBT," *Hindu,* May 15, 1998.

61. Ibid.

62. "Out of the Nuclear Closet," *New York Times,* May 17, 1998, 44.

63. "Gingrich Support Drowned in Chorus of Protest," *Statesman,* May 14, 1998.

64. "Lack of Response Forced U.S. Hand," *Hindu,* May 14, 1998.

65. "U.S. Govt. Urged to Clarify on Donations," *Hindu,* May 21, 1998.

66. Excerpts of President Clinton's remarks on the Indian nuclear tests, May 12, 1998.

67. State Department, daily press briefing, May 13, 1998, http//www.clw.org/coalition/rub0513.htm.

68. Ibid.

69. Deputy Secretary of State Strobe Talbott, on-the-record briefing, May 28, 1998, http://www.clw.org/coalition/talb0528.htm.

70. "Pakistan Evaluating U.S. Team's Deal," *Hindu,* May 16, 1998.

71. "U.S. Responds with Penalties, Persuasion," *Washington Post,* May 14, 1998, A1.

72. Ibid. Designed to dissuade Pakistan from acquiring nuclear weapons, the Pressler Amendment of 1985, which amended the Foreign Assistance Act of 1961, forbids the sale or transfer of any military equipment or technology to Pakistan unless the president can certify that Pakistan does not possess a nuclear explosive device and that the proposed assistance will significantly reduce the risk that Pakistan will acquire such a device.

73. "U.S. Responds with Penalties, Persuasion," A1.

74. Ibid.; and "Eight World Leaders Urge Suharto to Show Restraint in Handling Indonesian Turmoil," *New York Times,* May 16, 1998, A7.

75. "Bill in Congress for Repeal of Pressler Act," *Hindu,* May 16, 1998.

76. "Nuclear Anxiety in Pakistan," *New York Times,* May 16, 1998, A5.

77. "Pakistan Rules Out Giving Up N-Option," *Hindu,* May 17, 1998.

78. "Two More N-Tests, Sanctions Imposed," *Statesman,* May 13, 1998.

79. "Weaponisation Now Complete, Say Scientists," *Hindu,* May 18, 1998.

80. Official statement from the Indian government on the two tests of May 13, 1998, http://www.clw.org/coalition/ind0513.htm.

81. Ibid.

82. "India Conducts Two More Nuclear Tests at Pokhran," *Hindu,* May 14, 1998.

83. "Pakistan Says Sanctions Ineffective, Vows to 'Answer' India."

84. Prime Minister Nawaz Sharif, press conference, May 22, 1998, http://www.fas.org/news/pakistan/1998/05.

85. "Pakistan Accuses U.S. of Indifference," *Hindu,* May 25, 1998.

86. "U.S. Responds with Penalties, Persuasion," *Washington Post,* May 14, 1998, A1.

87. "Pakistan Says Sanctions Ineffective, Vows to 'Answer' India."

88. Press statement by the government of Pakistan on the two additional nuclear tests by India on May 13, 1998, http://www.un.int/pakistan/1498513a.htm.

89. "Pakistan Says Sanctions Ineffective, Vows to 'Answer' India."

90. Statement by the foreign minister in the Senate of Pakistan on two further nuclear tests carried out by India, May 13, 1998, http://www.un.int/pakistan/1498513c.htm.

91. "U.S. Responds with Penalties, Persuasion," A1.

92. Press statement by the government of Pakistan on the two additional nuclear tests by India on May 13, 1998.

93. "Pakistan to Keep N-Option Open," *Statesman,* May 16, 1998.

94. "Next-Door Neighbor Demands That World Powers Shun India," *New York Times,* May 14, 1998, A12.

95. "Pakistan Weighs Response to India; U.S. Team to Argue against Nuclear Test," *Washington Post,* May 15, 1998, A29.

96. "The Pressure on the Finger on the Nuclear Test Button," *Washington Post,* May 17, 1998, A1.

97. Ibid.

98. "Pakistan Reacts Sharply to Advani's Statement," *Hindu,* May 20, 1998.

99. "Next-Door Neighbor Demands That World Powers Shun India," A12.

100. "Pakistan Demands That World Powers Isolate India," *New York Times*, May 14, 1998.

101. State Department, daily press briefing, May 13, 1998.

102. "Clinton to Impose Penalties on India over Atomic Tests," *New York Times*, May 13, 1998, A1.

103. State Department, daily press briefing, May 13, 1998.

104. "What the Sanctions Are and What They Mean," *Statesman*, May 14, 1998.

105. "Clinton to Impose Penalties on India over Atomic Tests," A1.

106. Presidential Determination no. 98–22, http://www.clw.org/coalition/sanc0513.htm.

107. "U.S. to Press Allies to Act," *Hindu*, May 14, 1998.

108. "What the Sanctions Are and What They Mean."

109. Statement by the White House press secretary on U.S. sanctions against India for nuclear tests, May 13, 1998.

110. See "White House Fact Sheet on U.S. Sanctions of India and Pakistan as a Result of Their May Nuclear Tests," June 18, 1998.

111. Statement by the White House press secretary on U.S. sanctions against India for nuclear tests, May 13, 1998.

112. Ibid.

113. "Sanctions on India Hit U.S. Companies," *Washington Post*, May 14, 1998, E1.

114. Statement by the White House press secretary on U.S. sanctions against India for nuclear tests, May 13, 1998.

115. "U.S. Responds with Penalties, Persuasion," A1.

116. Statement by the White House press secretary on U.S. sanctions against India for nuclear tests, May 13, 1998.

117. "India Loans Will Continue, Says World Bank," *Hindu*, May 16, 1998.

118. "U.S. Delays World Bank Loans for India in Response to A-Tests," *New York Times*, May 27, 1998, A1.

119. "Gingrich Support Drowned in Chorus of Protest."

120. "Lack of Response Forced U.S. Hand."

121. "Defiance Endangers U.S.-India Relations; Administration Had Urged Cooperation," A15.

122. "India Sets Three Nuclear Blasts," *New York Times*, May 12, 1998, A1.

123. "India Sets Off Nuclear Devices; Pakistan Vents Outrage over Test Explosions, Delhi's First since 1974," *Washington Post*, May 12, 1998, A1.

124. Ibid.

125. "Indian Blasts Bring World Condemnation; Arch-Rival Pakistan Considers Staging Nuclear Test of Its Own," *Washington Post*, May 13, 1998, A1.

126. "India Conducts Two More Nuclear Tests at Pokhran."

127. "India Sets Off Nuclear Devices; Pakistan Vents Outrage," A1.

128. "Canada Asks India to Renounce N-Arms," *Hindu*, May 13, 1998.

129. "Germany Freezes $300 Million Aid to India, Clinton Pledges to Implement Sanctions," *Statesman*, May 12, 1998.

130. Statement of the Ministry of Foreign Affairs of the People's Republic of China, May 14, 1998, http://www.clw.org/coalition/chin0514.htm.

131. "E.U. to Delay Loans to India," *Hindu*, May 27, 1998.

132. "Outrage Greets India Nuclear Tests," *Daily Telegraph*, May 12, 1998, 1.

133. "Japanese Businessmen See Improved Climate in India," *Hindu*, May 22, 1998.

134. "India PM Writes to Western Leaders on Nuclear Tests," *Hindu,* May 13, 1998.

135. Ibid.

136. "Swift Punitive Action by USA and Japan," *Statesman,* May 13, 1998.

137. Three and a half billion yen equaled $26,100,000 on May 13, 1998.

138. "Denmark, Sweden Follow Suit Swift Punitive Action by USA and Japan," *Statesman,* May 13, 1998; and "Japanese Government Suspends Grants," *Hindu,* May 14, 1998.

139. "Germany Freezes Aid," *Hindu,* May 13, 1998.

140. "Denmark, Sweden Follow Suit Swift Punitive Action by USA and Japan,"

141. "India Conducts Two More Nuclear Tests at Pokhran."

142. "Denmark, Sweden Follow Suit Swift Punitive Action by USA and Japan."

143. "India Conducts Two More Nuclear Tests at Pokhran."

144. "Japan Freezes Some Grants; Other Nations Seem Doubtful," *New York Times,* May 14, 1998, A13.

145. Ibid.

146. "Russia to Oppose Sanctions against India," *Hindu,* May 14, 1998.

147. "Russians Favour Soft Approach," *Statesman,* May 13, 1998; and "Nuclear Deal with India Stays Russia," *Hindu,* May 20, 1998.

148. "Nuclear Deal with India Stays Russia."

149. "Interview with Indian Prime Minister Atal Bihari Vajpayee," *India Today,* May 25, 1998.

150. "N-Tests in Supreme National Interest Vajpayee," *Hindu,* May 15, 1998.

151. "U.S. Keeps Up Pressure on Pakistan," *Hindu,* May 24, 1998.

152. Ibid.

153. "China Asked Pakistan Not to Conduct Tests; Clinton Call Allegedly Led to Beijing Request," *Washington Post,* May 29, 1998, A36.

154. "Hashimoto Urges Sharif to Refrain from Nuclear Tests," *Daily Yomiuri,* May 28, 1998.

155. "U.S. Laws Curb Offers to Pakistan; Officials Look for Ways to Prevent Nuclear Test," *Washington Post,* May 28, 1998, A25.

156. "U.S. Ready to Offer Pakistan a Package," *Hindu,* May 26, 1998.

157. "Pakistan Analysts Term U.S. Package Flimsy," *Hindu,* May 27, 1998.

158. Ibid.

159. "Clinton Deplores Tests," *Hindu,* May 29, 1998.

160. White House press briefing on Pakistani nuclear tests, May 28, 1998, http://www.clw.org/coalition/whpro528.htm.

161. "Clinton Deplores Pakistan's Nuclear Testing," White House report, May 28, 1998, http://www.clw.org/coalition/who528.htm.

162. "Sharif Offers to Resume Dialogue," *Hindu,* May 29, 1998.

163. "After an Anguished Phone Call, Clinton Penalizes the Pakistanis," *New York Times,* May 29, 1998, A1.

164. Ibid.

165. Ibid.

166. "Pakistan, Answering India, Carries Out Nuclear Tests; Clinton's Appeal Rejected," *New York Times,* May 29, 1998, A1.

167. Ibid.

168. "Pakistan Also Detonates Five Nuclear Devices," *Hindu,* May 29, 1998.

169. "Nuclear Anxiety: The Blast," *New York Times,* May 29, 1998, A10.

170. "Pakistan Sets Off Nuclear Blasts; 'Today, We Have Settled a Score,' Premier Says," A1.

171. Press briefing by the foreign secretary of Pakistan, May 30, 1998, http://www.clw.org/coalition/paki0530.htm.

172. "Analysts Skeptical of Pakistan's Claims," *Washington Post,* May 29, 1998, A33.

173. "Pakistan Also Detonates Five Nuclear Devices."

174. "Explosion Is Detected by U.S. Scientists," *New York Times,* May 29, 1998, A10.

175. "Analysts Skeptical of Pakistan's Claims," A33.

176. "Pakistani's Words: 'To Restore the Strategic Balance,' " *New York Times,* May 29, 1998, A8.

177. "Pakistan Sets Off Nuclear Blasts; 'Today, We Have Settled A Score,' Premier Says," A1.

178. "No More Ambiguity," *Hindu,* May 29, 1998.

179. "India Open to Dialogue with Pakistan, Says Vajpayee," *Hindu,* May 30, 1998.

180. "Clinton Deplores Pakistan's Nuclear Testing."

181. Ibid.

182. Secretary of State Madeleine Albright press conference, May 28, 1998, http://www.clw.org/coalition/albro528.htm.

183. "Pakistan, Answering India, Carries Out Nuclear Tests."

184. "Pakistan Test, China Blames India, Japan to Suspend Aid," *Hindu,* May 29, 1998.

185. "Wealthy Nations Cut Aid to Pakistan over Nuclear Tests," *New York Times,* May 29, 1998, A10.

186. Ibid.

187. "Wealthy Nations Cut Aid to Pakistan over Nuclear Tests," A10.

188. Ibid.

189. "Pakistan, Answering India, Carries Out Nuclear Tests," A1.

190. Ibid.

191. "Pakistan Devices Can Be Turned into Warheads," *Hindu,* May 30, 1998.

192. "Emergency to Smother Dissent?" *Hindu,* May 30, 1998.

193. "India and Pakistan Missile Tests," *Disarmament Diplomacy,* no. 36 (1999).

7 Rejection of the Comprehensive Test Ban Treaty: The Politics of Ratification

Christopher M. Jones

Before You Begin

1. What actions illustrate President Bill Clinton's determination to reach a Comprehensive Test Ban Treaty (CTBT)?

2. Why did Clinton and members of his administration devote little attention to the CTBT once it was transmitted to the Senate?

3. Why did Clinton and Republican senators have different assessments of the treaty's importance? Did they have competing foreign policy agendas?

4. What direct and indirect legislative tools did senators use to advance their policy positions?

5. Did specific constitutional, political, or procedural factors shape the final outcome?

6. Ideally, what conditions should have been present to ensure ratification of the CTBT? Were any of these conditions present?

7. Who bears the greatest responsibility for the defeat of the CTBT?

8. Why was the treaty ultimately rejected? Was this outcome more a product of partisan politics or substantive policy differences?

9. As a senator, would you have voted for ratification of the CTBT in October 1999?

Introduction: A Landmark Treaty

A survey of U.S. foreign policy in the post–cold war era reveals few episodes as momentous as the Senate's rejection of the Comprehensive Test Ban Treaty (CTBT) on October 13, 1999. In a 51-48 vote, the resolution of ratification fell nineteen votes short of the two-thirds majority required for approval. In a challenge to the adage "politics stops at the water's edge," just four Republicans joined forty-four Democrats in support of the treaty, whereas fifty Republicans and one Independent opposed the measure. One Democratic senator voted "present."[1] The voting along party lines stood in sharp contrast to the strong bipartisanship traditionally associated with arms control agreements.

Besides challenging the notion that matters of national security are politically sacrosanct, the Senate action was imbued with historical significance. The repudiation of a treaty is a relatively rare event. At the time of the vote, the Senate had ratified 1,523 treaties and rejected only 20 during the course of its entire legislative history.[2] Furthermore, the defeat of the CTBT was the first time that lawmakers had failed to authorize a presidentially endorsed security-related pact since the Treaty of Versailles following World War I. As the oldest item on the international arms control agenda and a long-standing U.S. policy objective, the CTBT represented a landmark agreement. President Dwight D. Eisenhower first proposed a global test ban in 1958; President John F. Kennedy signed the Limited Test Ban Treaty in 1963, prohibiting nuclear tests in the atmosphere, in space, and underwater; and subsequent presidents agreed to limits and moratoriums on underground explosions. Thus President Bill Clinton's signing of a treaty banning *all* nuclear testing in September 1996 was considered a historic achievement, and his failure to win Senate ratification three years later was a major setback for his presidential legacy and the nuclear nonproliferation regime.

This chapter examines the Clinton administration's seven-year quest, from 1993 through 1999, to negotiate and then obtain legislative approval of the CTBT. From the time the treaty was sent to Capitol Hill in September 1997 until its rejection in October 1999, the political battle operated along three separate but interrelated lines: disagreement and substantive policy debate about the value of ratifying the treaty; disagreement over legislative procedures preceding the vote, including the timing of the critical ballot; and interbranch conflict intensified by partisan animosity in the wake of President Clinton's impeachment trial.

Background: Negotiating with the World

During the 1992 presidential campaign, Democratic candidate Bill Clinton, stressed his desire to achieve a CTBT during his administration.[3] Once in office, the new president wasted little time moving toward that goal. On March 3, 1993, an interagency review of U.S. nuclear policy and a draft CTBT were ordered. A month later, Clinton and Russian president Boris Yeltsin agreed at a summit in Vancouver, Canada, that "negotiations toward a multilateral nuclear test ban should commence at an early date."[4] In a Saturday radio address to the nation on July 3, Clinton indicated that the policy review initiated four months earlier was complete. The administration's conclusion was that further nuclear testing "could help ... prepare the [U.S. arsenal] for a CTBT" and "provide some additional improvements in safety and reliability."[5] Yet it was determined that the potential benefits from such tests would not be worth the cost of undermining the nation's non-proliferation goals. As a result, Clinton extended the 1992 moratorium on nuclear testing that his predecessor had adopted after it was determined that the end of the cold war and Russia's existing moratorium reduced the need for cutting-edge warheads.[6] He also directed the Department of Energy "to explore other means of maintaining ... confidence in the safety, reliability, and performance" of the United States' nuclear weapons.[7] These "means" would be encompassed within a new Stockpile Stewardship and Management Program (SSMP).

At the end of 1993, the administration shifted its attention to the international community. In December, the United States successfully co-sponsored a resolution in the United Nations General Assembly that specified the objectives of a CTBT and called for the negotiation of a verifiable multilateral agreement.[8] On January 25, 1994, the Conference on Disarmament (CD) convened in Geneva for that very purpose.[9] Despite past successes, such as the 1993 Chemical Weapons Convention, the CD had never faced a challenge as important as concluding a CTBT. An accord prohibiting tests of the world's most lethal weapons would prevent the nuclear powers from modernizing and expanding their arsenals (vertical proliferation), while non-nuclear countries would be deprived of the means necessary to begin such programs (horizontal proliferation). In essence, the state of nuclear weapons development would be permanently frozen.

From the perspective of the Clinton administration, the treaty was a way to preserve the United States' margin of superiority while preventing countries with small atomic programs, like India and Pakistan, and suspected nuclear aspirants, such as Iran, Iraq, and North Korea, from moving forward with their weapons plans. In addition, the agreement was viewed as a deterrent against Russia and China developing more sophisticated warheads. The pact also offered benefits beyond the realm of military security, such as sparing the global environment from the harmful effects of nuclear weapons testing.

Although the United States and many other countries recognized the advantages of a test ban, the process of reaching an agreement would be a long and difficult task. The CD's adherence to consensus decision making and

The Comprehensive Test Ban Treaty

April 4, 1993   U.S. president Bill Clinton and Russian president Boris Yeltsin agree that negotiations for a CTBT "should commence at an early date."

July 3, 1993   Clinton extends the moratorium on U.S. nuclear weapons testing established in 1992 and directs the Department of Energy to explore other means of maintaining the safety and reliability of the nation's nuclear weapons.

January 25, 1994   Negotiations on a CTBT begin in Geneva, Switzerland.

January 30, 1995   Clinton extends the U.S. moratorium on nuclear weapons testing until a CTBT enters into force.

August 11, 1995   Clinton announces that the United States will seek a true zero-yield CTBT.

September 24, 1996   Clinton becomes the first head of state to sign the CTBT.

September 22, 1997   Clinton transmits the CTBT to the Senate for advice and consent and asks for "early and favorable consideration of the treaty."

October 27 and 29, 1997   The Senate Governmental Affairs Subcommittee on International Security, Proliferation, and Federal Services and the Appropriations Subcommittee on Energy and Water Development hold hearings on the CTBT.

January 27, 1998   In the State of the Union address, Clinton urges the Senate to ratify the CTBT by the end of the year.

March 18, 1998   The Senate Governmental Affairs Subcommittee on International Security, Proliferation, and Federal Services holds a day of hearings on the CTBT.

May 1998   India and Pakistan announce detonation of nuclear devices.

January 20, 1999   In the State of the Union address, Clinton again asks the Senate to act on the CTBT.

September 8, 1999   Sen. Byron Dorgan, D-N.D., threatens to bring the Senate to a standstill unless the CTBT is placed on the agenda.

September 22, 1999   Senate Democrats agree to introduce a non-binding resolution calling for hearings on the CTBT in 1999 and a final vote by March 31, 2000.

continued on the next page

continued from the previous page

September 29, 1999 Senate majority leader Trent Lott, R-Miss., indicates he is willing to schedule a vote on the CTBT if Democrats drop the plan to introduce a resolution and refrain from tying up Senate business.

September 30, 1999 Lott proposes a procedure for bringing the CTBT to the Senate floor for ten hours of debate on October 6, followed by an immediate vote. Senate Democrats reject the offer.

October 1, 1999 Senate minority leader Tom Daschle, D-S.D., agrees to Lott's counteroffer, which provides for committee hearings during the week of October 3, eighteen to twenty-two hours of floor debate to begin October 8, and a final vote on October 12. (The vote ultimately occurs on October 13.)

October 2, 1999 The White House launches a high-level, full-scale effort to secure Senate approval of the CTBT.

October 5–7, 1999 The Senate Foreign Relations Committee and Armed Services Committee hold hearings on the CTBT.

October 8, 1999 Clinton asks the Senate to delay a vote on the CTBT, but his request is rejected.

October 11 and 12, 1999 Clinton and Daschle submit written requests to the Senate Republican leadership asking that consideration of the CTBT be deferred.

October 13, 1999 The Senate ends debate on the CTBT and rejects the resolution of ratification by a 51-48 vote.

several contentious issues resulted in two and a half years of negotiations. An early source of disagreement was the scope of the treaty. In 1994, the nuclear states sought exceptions to a complete and permanent test ban: Britain and France demanded periodic tests to ensure warhead safety; China insisted that the peaceful use of nuclear explosions within science and industry be permitted, even though both nuclear and non-nuclear states argued such activity would generate weapons design information; the United States pushed for a special clause to allow it to withdraw from a CTBT after ten years if the president determined testing was necessary. At the same time, the non-nuclear states moved in the opposite direction, calling for the prohibition *and* elimination of all nuclear weapons. As the CD concluded its first year of talks, the parties were separated by deep differences.

A Year of Decision

Proclaiming 1995 "a year of decision"[10] for global non-proliferation efforts, the Clinton administration took action to energize the languishing CTBT negotiations. In January, it was announced that the U.S. moratorium on nuclear testing would be extended until a CTBT entered into force. In addition, the U.S. bid for a ten-year "right to withdraw" clause was dropped. This retreat ended a long-standing political struggle within the executive branch. The Defense Department and Joint Chiefs of Staff (JCS) favored the provision, but some of President Clinton's top aides—National Security Adviser Anthony Lake, Secretary of Energy Hazel O'Leary, and Arms Control and Disarmament Agency chief John Holum—argued that the controversial exemption, which no other country supported, was a major impediment to the talks in Geneva.[11] The veracity of their position was confirmed when Britain and France responded favorably to the U.S. decision by abandoning their demands for a CTBT that ensured safety tests.

These developments had a positive effect on a separate set of negotiations related to nuclear proliferation. In May 1995, the Nuclear Non-Proliferation Treaty (NPT), which recognizes the exclusive standing of Britain, China, France, Russia, and the United States as nuclear weapons states, was extended indefinitely. The 178 countries at the NPT Review and Extension Conference also pledged their commitment to reaching a CTBT by "no later than 1996,"[12] but within a matter of days that goal was jeopardized by China's decision to explode a nuclear bomb as part of its ongoing testing program. Then, just weeks later, France announced that it planned to conduct as many as eight nuclear tests in the South Pacific between September 1995 and May 1996.[13]

As the summer of 1995 unfolded, progress toward a test ban was further complicated by the appearance that the nuclear states had decided to pursue a treaty that would permit some level of nuclear explosions. While the United States never departed from an official position of seeking a zero-yield test ban, it was well known in Geneva that the Defense Department was urging the Clinton administration to propose safety and reliability tests with yields as powerful as 500 tons of TNT. Russia and France also advocated test thresholds, which ranged from 10 to 200 tons, and China continued its insistence that peaceful nuclear explosions be allowed.[14] These positions prompted strong criticism from many non-nuclear states, which had only agreed to a permanent extension of the NPT after intense U.S. diplomatic pressure and a pledge by the nuclear powers to reach a CTBT by the end of the following year.[15] When Indonesia and India countered with proposals to eliminate *all* nuclear weapons testing, including non-explosive methods,[16] it was clear that the talks were nearing an impasse.

Once again, the United States sought to revive the negotiations. On August 11, 1995, President Clinton declared a CTBT was "one of [his] administration's highest priorities" and announced that he was seeking a true zero-yield agreement, which "would ban any nuclear weapon test explosion or any other nuclear explosion."[17] This statement ended the Defense Department's bid for a low-threshold test ban and the long-standing U.S. position in favor of extremely low-yield hydronuclear tests. The White House was confident in its decision, because an independent panel of scientists had recently reported that the United States had the requisite data—from 1,054 nuclear detonations between 1945 and 1992—and the technical means to ensure the safety and reliability of its nuclear weapons without further explosive testing.[18] On the advice of these same experts, President Clinton tied U.S. policy to specific safeguards (see Box 7.1). Most important was the understanding that the United States would be prepared to withdraw from the treaty under the standard "supreme national interests" clause if it was determined that testing was necessary to certify with a "high level of confidence the safety or reliability" of the nation's nuclear deterrent. Another key condition was the continued development and use of the Stockpile Stewardship and Management Program to ensure the safety and reliability of nuclear weapons through non-explosive, scientific techniques, such as computer simulations and laboratory experiments.[19]

U.S. leadership in supporting a zero-yield treaty produced immediate dividends. France quickly accepted the same position (partly to deflect international outrage over its testing in the South Pacific). Britain soon followed suit. Russia, while it did not fully embrace a zero-yield CTBT, agreed in October 1995 to work with the United States toward such a goal.[20] These actions addressed a major concern of the non-nuclear states and helped to improve the negotiating environment in Geneva.

The Final Details

As 1996 began, the parties were still far from a final pact. National representatives struggled to reach consensus on the treaty's scope and duration, the implementation organization, the means of verification, and the conditions under which the agreement would enter into force. There were also additional obstacles, such as France's ongoing tests, India's demand for a timetable on global nuclear disarmament, and China's support for peaceful nuclear explosions as well as its continued testing. Some countries still opposed *any* type of

> **Box 7.1**   Comprehensive Test Ban Treaty Safeguards
>
> In 1995, the United States established six safeguards for its entry into a Comprehensive Test Ban Treaty.
>
> **Safeguard A**   "Conduct of a science-based stockpile stewardship program to insure a high level of confidence in the safety and reliability of nuclear weapons in the active stockpile";
>
> **Safeguard B**   "Maintenance of modern nuclear laboratory facilities and programs";
>
> **Safeguard C**   "Maintenance of the basic capability to resume nuclear test activities prohibited by the CTBT";
>
> **Safeguard D**   "A comprehensive research and development program to improve ... treaty monitoring";
>
> **Safeguard E**   Intelligence collection and analysis for "information on worldwide arsenals, nuclear weapons development programs, and related nuclear programs"; and
>
> **Safeguard F**   The understanding that if the secretaries of defense and energy inform the president "that a high level of confidence in the safety or reliability of a nuclear weapon type which the two secretaries consider to be critical to our nuclear deterrent [can] no longer be certified, the president, in consultation with Congress, [will] be prepared to withdraw from the CTBT under the supreme national interests clause in order to conduct whatever testing might be required."
>
> Source: William J. Clinton, "Letter of Transmittal to the Senate of the United States," September 22, 1997, http://www.state.gov/www/global/arms/ctbtpage/ntbpage.html.

nuclear weapons testing, believing *non-explosive* techniques would allow nuclear states to make qualitative improvements to their arsenals. The five declared nuclear powers, however, refused to consider the issue, and the non-nuclear states were not prepared to sacrifice the treaty over computer simulations and laboratory experiments.

In the months that followed, negotiators made considerable progress toward resolving many of the differences related to the treaty's key provisions. Equally important were a series of developments that removed major impediments to a final agreement. In January, France ended its controversial nuclear testing program. Then, in late April, Russia officially committed itself to a zero-yield treaty. In early June, China abandoned its demand for peaceful nuclear explosions. That same month, the ambassador chairing the negotiations in Geneva tabled a draft of a final CTBT. The remaining differences over portions of the text were addressed during the summer. "While no [state] expressed unqualified support for the treaty, all but India ultimately supported it." [21] In August, India exercised its veto under the CD's consensus decision-making procedures, an action that prevented the final treaty from being transmitted to the General Assembly, where it could be opened for signing by member states.

India's decision, which was motivated by its desire to retain nuclear weapons as part of its national security strategy, led proponents of the treaty to search for an alternative. In late August, Australia went directly to the United Nations and sponsored a resolution that called upon the General Assembly to consider the draft treaty and open it for signing at the earliest possible date. By changing the forum from the Conference on Disarmament to the United Nations, the agreement could be adopted by a two-thirds majority rather than by unanimous consent. When the vote was held on September 10, 1996, the outcome was 158 states in favor, 3 states against (Bhutan, India, and Libya), 5 abstentions (Cuba, Lebanon, Mauritius, Syria, and Tanzania), and 19 states not voting. [22] Two weeks later, on September 24, the CTBT was opened for signing. Symbolizing his leadership role throughout the difficult negotiations, President Clinton became the first of more than fifty heads of state to sign the document that day. Wielding the pen that John F. Kennedy had used to sign the Limited Test Ban Treaty, Clinton inked what he called "the longest-sought, hardest-fought prize in the history of arms control." [23] The president also remarked that the agreement represented "a giant step forward" that would "help prevent the nuclear powers from developing more advanced and dangerous weapons" (see Box 7.2). By the end of the first week of signing, it was clear that the international community agreed. Ninety world leaders had placed their names on the CTBT. [24]

Negotiating with the Senate

Nearly a year after signing the CTBT, President Clinton announced during a speech to the Fifty-second UN General Assembly on September 22, 1997, that he was beginning the process of ratification. That same day he formally transmitted the agreement, Treaty Doc. 105-28, to the Senate for its advice and consent. In his letter to the Senate, Clinton stressed that the treaty, which now had more than 140 signatories, was of "singular significance to the continuing

Box 7.2   Major Provisions of the Comprehensive Test Ban Treaty

Scope	Each state that is a party to the treaty agrees not to conduct "any nuclear weapon test explosion or any other nuclear explosion," including those for peaceful purposes.
Implementing Organization	The agreement establishes the Comprehensive Test Ban Treaty Organization to ensure implementation and verification of the agreement as well as "to provide a forum for consultation and cooperation." The Executive Council, the organization's principal decision-making body, is comprised of fifty-one elected member states.
Monitoring Compliance	The treaty's verification regime encompasses four components: the International Monitoring System (IMS), consultation and clarification, on-site inspections, and confidence-building measures. IMS is a network of more than 300 seismological, radionuclide, hydroacoustic, and infrasound stations based in dozens of countries around the globe.
Inspections	An on-site inspection may be requested by any party to the agreement "to clarify whether a nuclear weapon test explosion or any other nuclear explosion" has occurred. Such a request can be based on information gathered from the IMS or a state's own technical means. Thirty members of the Executive Council must approve an on-site inspection request. The council must render its decision within four days of receiving a request.
Enforcement	If a country is found to be outside the terms of the agreement, the Executive Council or a larger conference of member states can suspend the violator's "rights and privileges under [the] treaty," recommend sanctions, or raise the issue within the United Nations.
Entry into Force	The treaty takes effect six months after its ratification by the forty-four states of the Conference on Disarmament that possess nuclear power and

continued on the next page

continued from the previous page

	research reactors. A state cannot ratify the treaty with reservations or unilateral amendments.
Review	Ten years after the treaty enters into force, a conference will be convened to review the agreement's operation and effectiveness. After that time, further review conferences may be held at intervals of ten years for the same purpose.
Duration	The treaty is of unlimited duration. Each party has "the right to withdraw from the treaty if it decides that extraordinary events related to the subject matter of [the CTBT] have jeopardized its supreme [national] interests."

efforts to stem nuclear proliferation" and enhance international security.[25] Perhaps anticipating the concerns of many senators, the president emphasized two additional points. First, the safety and reliability of the nation's nuclear arsenal could be ensured through an annual certification process and the six safeguards established in 1995. Second, the treaty's verification regime, coupled with U.S. diplomacy, intelligence, and science, "provided the ... means to make the CTBT effectively verifiable." [26] Clinton said that while very low-yield nuclear blasts could go undetected under the CTBT, such tests posed no threat to U.S. national security. He concluded his transmittal letter by appealing to the Senate "to give early and favorable consideration of the Treaty." [27]

The Republican majority was not receptive to his request. A spokesman for Sen. Jesse Helms, N.C., chairman of the Senate Foreign Relations Committee, stated soon after the CTBT was delivered to Capitol Hill that it was not a "front-burner issue." [28] Helms and other Republican leaders opposed the substance of the treaty, claiming that it was unverifiable and ineffective. Rather than engage in a serious debate of the pact, they used procedural justifications and their majority control over committees to block its consideration. For example, Senate Republicans indicated that there was no need to rush a review of the treaty, because the entry into force provision requiring its ratification by the forty-four nuclear capable states made it unlikely that the CTBT would become international law in 1997.[29] In addition, they pointed to the fact that the Foreign Relations

Committee was already scheduled to conduct a critical set of hearings on enlarging the membership of NATO. Most important, Senator Helms made no secret of his desire to bring the CTBT before his committee only after hearings were held on two other pacts, the Kyoto Protocol to the UN Framework Convention on Climate Change and two amendments to the Anti-Ballistic Missile (ABM) Treaty. The Clinton administration, aware of the senator's opposition to both these accords, refused to submit either agreement for ratification. Helms, for instance, saw a review of the ABM amendments as a way to scrap the entire 1972 treaty, thereby removing a major impediment to the establishment of a national missile defense system, which he believed was the only meaningful response to nuclear proliferation.

Since the chairman of the Senate Foreign Relations Committee has jurisdiction over all treaties, the CTBT became, in the words of one observer, "a political hostage." [30] The administration refused to give in to Helms on the Kyoto and ABM treaties, but failed to generate significant political pressure against the senator's position. Even though a majority of the American people supported the CTBT, there was no concerted effort to bring the issue before the public. Moreover, the administration did not designate a high-level official or task force to work with the Senate on CTBT ratification. In fact, the establishment of such a representative was not announced until November 10, 1999, a month *after* the Senate rejected the treaty. [31]

Although Helms was unwilling to schedule hearings in the Foreign Relations Committee, the CTBT did receive some consideration within the Senate in 1997. Collectively, the Governmental Affairs Subcommittee on International Security, Proliferation and Federal Services and the Appropriations Subcommittee on Energy and Water Development held two days of preliminary hearings in October. These bodies were not the preferable forums in which to begin an examination of a critical national security issue. Nonetheless, the proceedings did offer a small group of senators an opportunity to grapple with matters related to the CTBT and offered a preview of some of the arguments that would lie at the center of the ratification debate two years later.

The hearings on October 27 and 29 focused on whether the safety and reliability of the nation's nuclear weapons could be maintained under the CTBT and SSMP. Victor Reis, assistant secretary of energy for defense programs, testified, "We can maintain the safety and the reliability of the nuclear weapons in the stockpile indefinitely, without underground testing, and keep the risks to manageable levels." [32] To substantiate his point, Reis pointed to the "extensive data base" acquired from years of nuclear testing, a "cadre of experienced . . .

scientists and technicians," and the fact that nuclear weapons were safe and reliable five years after the last U.S. test.[33] Appearing before the Appropriations Subcommittee on Energy and Water Development, Secretary of Energy Frederico Pena added, "I have met with experts both within and outside [my] department. And I'm pleased to report ... there is strong consensus that stockpile stewardship is the right program to address the challenges of maintaining our nuclear deterrent without underground testing."[34] The secretary also stressed that the annual certification process and six safeguards established in 1995 would ensure the safety and reliability of U.S. nuclear weapons under the CTBT.[35]

Sen. Thad Cochran, R-Miss., chair of the Governmental Affairs Subcommittee and an opponent of the CTBT, was not swayed. He remarked, "I am skeptical of the stockpile stewardship program. Nobody yet knows if the program will ... become an acceptable alternative [to nuclear testing]."[36] Supporting the chairman's position was James M. Schlesinger, who had served in a number of prominent security posts—defense secretary, energy secretary, director of central intelligence, and chair of the Atomic Energy Commission. Schlesinger testified that it would be "many years" before the SSMP was fully operational and "many, many years" before an adequate evaluation of its success could take place.[37] Regardless of the effectiveness of the SSMP, Schlesinger added, "there is no substitute for nuclear testing."[38] Without the ability to test or replace weapons, he indicated, the U.S. nuclear arsenal will "be vulnerable to the effects of aging," and confidence in its reliability and the U.S. deterrent will decline substantially over time.[39]

The viewpoints of Reis, Pena, and Schlesinger were representative of the larger group of witnesses that appeared before the two panels. More important, their divergent positions reflected the partisan divide within the two subcommittees. Republican lawmakers were receptive to Schlesinger's critical testimony, whereas their Democratic counterparts were supportive of the Clinton administration's position as espoused by Pena and Reis. Although 1997 ended with no further consideration of the treaty, the October hearings revealed that a substantive policy debate along party lines was taking shape.

Stalled on Capitol Hill

Disappointed by the CTBT's lack of progress on Capitol Hill, the Clinton administration began 1998 with a renewed determination to achieve Senate ratification. In January, National Security Adviser Samuel Berger identified the CTBT as "one of the president's top priorities."[40] Later that month, President

Clinton used his State of the Union address to champion the treaty and urge Senate ratification by the end of the year. He also announced that the CTBT had the backing of four former chairmen of the Joint Chiefs of Staff—John Shalikashvili, Colin Powell, William Crowe, and David Jones.[41] In early February, the president publicly added the sitting chairman, Gen. Henry Shelton, to the growing list of supporters. It was at this point that Clinton traveled to Los Alamos National Laboratory to witness a simulation of a nuclear test. During his visit to New Mexico, the directors of the three nuclear weapons laboratories proclaimed in a joint statement, "We are confident that the [SSMP] will enable us to maintain America's nuclear deterrent without nuclear testing." [42] At the same time, senior administration officials, such as Secretary of Energy Pena, Secretary of Defense William Cohen, and Secretary of State Madeleine Albright, made public speeches and statements underscoring the value of the CTBT.[43]

Despite this flurry of activity, Senator Helms had no intention of abandoning the position he had staked out in 1997. With the full support of Senate majority leader Trent Lott, R-Miss., the powerful chairman maintained that he would not schedule hearings on the CTBT before the Foreign Relations Committee considered the Kyoto Protocol and the ABM amendments. In a January 21 letter to the president, Mr. Helms wrote:

> I feel obliged to make clear to you my concern that your Administration has been unwisely and unnecessarily engaged in delay in submitting these treaties to the Senate for its advice and consent. Despite your commitment, made nearly eight months ago, we have yet to see them.... Ironically, while the Administration has delayed in submitting these vital treaties to the Senate, some in your Administration have indicated the White House will press the Senate for swift ratification of the CTBT, immediately following the vote on NATO expansion. Such a deliberate confrontation would be exceedingly unwise because, Mr. President, the CTBT is very low on the Committee's list of priorities. The treaty has *no chance* of entering into force for a decade or more.[44]

While Senator Helms's statement was clearly motivated by his interest in reviewing and rescinding the ABM Treaty, his stance served two other purposes. On one hand, it allowed Republican leaders in the Senate to point to the White House for the lack of progress on the nation's foreign policy agenda. On the other hand, Helms's position and strong opposition to the CTBT "serve[d] to intimidate many Senate Republicans—who [were] characterized as undecided about the treaty—from openly expressing support for the test ban." [45]

In a February 10 response to Helms's letter, President Clinton reaffirmed his strong support for the CTBT and addressed the senator's claim that because the treaty must be approved by forty-four states it would not enter into force anytime soon: "Rather than waiting to see if others ratify the CTBT, I believe America must lead in bringing the CTBT into force.... I think it is important that when I travel to [India and Pakistan] this year I do so with U.S. ratification in hand."[46] After Clinton's reply, however, the administration's vigorous campaign on behalf of the CTBT simply dissipated.

Three factors were responsible for the administration's about face. First, the president's greatest priority had always been his domestic agenda. Three months into his administration, he remarked, "Foreign policy is not what I came here to do."[47] The 1998 midterm elections most likely reinforced this view. Since the White House was eager to usher a number of domestic initiatives through Congress, it made little sense to push the CTBT and risk antagonizing the Senate leadership. Second, the president's senior foreign policy aides were directing most of their energy toward securing Senate approval for NATO expansion. Third, the White House became seriously sidetracked in the early weeks of 1998 when the president was compelled to testify in the sexual harassment lawsuit brought against him by Paula Jones and confront the accusations that he had an intimate relationship with Monica Lewinsky, a White House intern. It was also at this time that an independent counsel was given the power to investigate the Lewinsky matter. These developments diverted high-level attention for the next fourteen months as the drama unfolded, the inquiry moved forward, and Clinton was impeached by the House and tried by the Senate.

Helms and Lott's control over the Senate agenda, coupled with a chief executive in crisis, produced a predictable result. With the exception of occasional statements, the CTBT received almost no attention on Capitol Hill; only one congressional hearing was held on the treaty throughout 1998. As in 1997, the forum was the Governmental Affairs Subcommittee chaired by Senator Cochran. On March 18, the panel met for a day, during which four senators and three witnesses sought to evaluate the effect of the pact on nuclear proliferation.[48] After the proceedings were concluded, no attention was devoted to the CTBT for two months. Instead senators focused on other foreign policy matters, such as NATO expansion and the ethnic conflict in Kosovo. Only in May—after India conducted three unexpected nuclear tests and Pakistan responded with five of its own—did the CTBT become a more salient issue. The troubling events in South Asia prompted the Senate's test ban proponents to speak out. First, as Sen. Joseph Biden, D-Del., the Foreign Relations Committee's ranking Democrat, stated on May 12, "The United States should urge India to sign the CTBT and refrain from further testing." [49] Second, as Sen. Tom Harkin, D-Iowa, remarked the following day, "I believe what happened in India more than anything indicates that we have to act now ... to ratify the CTBT." [50]

Although most senators who pushed U.S. approval of the treaty were Democrats, a small number of Republicans voiced their support for the first time. On May 13, Sen. Arlen Specter, R-Pa., said, "I think there is an urgent need that the Senate proceed to the consideration and ratification of the CTBT." [51] That same day, he urged Senator Helms, in a letter, to hold hearings and bring the treaty to a floor vote. Specter raised the possibility that the CTBT might be rejected, but stressed that action by the full Senate was necessary to demonstrate that the United States was not indifferent to nuclear testing and proliferation. He added, "From comments on the Senate floor and in the cloakroom, I know that many, if not most of our colleagues share my concern about action on the treaty." [52]

On May 19, Senators Specter and Biden circulated a letter asking senators to co-sponsor a non-binding resolution stating that the Foreign Relations Committee should hold hearings on the CTBT and schedule a floor vote "as expeditiously as possible." [53] Thirty-six senators immediately signed on. [54] At the same time, other lawmakers suggested that the Senate Armed Services Committee should hold hearings on the treaty's national security implications. Without expressing support for the CTBT, Sen. Olympia Snowe, R-Maine, made such a call on May 28. A week later, Sens. Jeff Bingaman, D-N.M., and Carl Levin, D-Mich., made a formal request to Chairman Strom Thurmond, R-S.C. In a separate statement, Senator Bingaman argued, "The era of nuclear testing is clearly not over. It is even more important today than it was yesterday to send a strong message to world leaders about the importance the United States Senate places on the CTBT. A committee hearing is central to getting the message across." [55]

Republican leaders were not swayed. Repeating long-standing concerns that the treaty was "unverifiable," "ineffective," and unlikely to enter into force, [56] they showed no willingness to move toward ratification. Moreover, they rejected any effort to urge India and Pakistan to sign the test ban. In a May 13 statement, Senator Helms said, "India's actions demonstrate that the CTBT, from a non-proliferation standpoint, is scarcely more than a sham. I hope that the Clinton Administration has learned from its mistakes sufficiently to refuse to allow India to paper over its actions by signing the CTBT." [57] Similarly, Senator Lott commented on May 28, "The nuclear spiral in Asia demonstrates the irrelevance of U.S. action on the CTBT." Instead of controlling the arms race between India and Pakistan, the majority leader claimed, "the Administration's push for the CTBT actually accelerated the greatest proliferation disaster in decades: two nuclear powers emerging in the last few weeks." [58]

The president and his senior advisers did not draw the same conclusion. Instead they temporarily renewed their efforts on behalf of the treaty. In a series of public statements in May and June, administration officials once again made the case for the test ban. Secretary of State Albright remarked on June 3, "If we want India and Pakistan to stop testing and keep others from starting, [Senate ratification of the CTBT] is the most basic, minimal, obvious step we can take on this critical issue at this perilous time. American leadership should be unambiguous, decisive, and clear." [59] A broad range of non-governmental actors reiterated the secretary's call. The Council for a Livable World, the Union of Concerned Scientists, Peace Action, Physicians for Social Responsibility, a coalition of religious groups, and several disarmament and environmental groups were among the many organizations that used letters, petitions, official statements, and demonstrations to lobby the Senate and educate the public. Additional pressure was generated when Senators Biden and Specter held a joint news conference on July 29 to announce the results of new public opinion polls, which revealed that 70 to 79 percent of Americans supported ratification of the CTBT. [60]

In early September, the two senators joined forces again. This time they co-sponsored an amendment to the FY 1999 Foreign Operations bill that restored nearly $29 million in funding to the CTBT Preparatory Commission—the body charged with establishing the global network of monitoring stations called for by the treaty. Biden and Specter made it clear that they viewed the measure as a "test vote" on ratification and a means for beginning "implementation of the CTBT prior to its [approval]." [61] The legislation passed on a 49-44 vote, but it was not the result Biden and Specter wanted. As Senator Lott observed before the vote, "Anything less than 67 votes in support of this amendment will send a strong signal the Senate is prepared to reject this treaty." [62] Lott would be proven correct. Clearly the amendment's narrow margin of victory foreshadowed the ultimate fate of the CTBT. For the time being, however, it was an indication that the pact would not receive serious attention in the remaining months of 1998. Given the close vote, Republican leaders were not under strong bipartisan pressure to place the CTBT on the legislative agenda, and the Democratic leaders, who were all advocates of the treaty, were reluctant to begin a battle they were far from certain they could win.

The Impasse Continues

The year began in a predictable fashion. Once again, National Security Adviser Berger publicly identified ratification of the CTBT as one of the president's "top priorities" for 1999.[63] Shortly thereafter, President Clinton made a pitch for the treaty in his January State of the Union address, declaring, "It's been two years since I signed the CTBT. If we don't do the right thing, other nations won't either. I ask the Senate to take this vital step, approve the treaty now to make it harder for other nations to develop nuclear arms, and to make sure we can end nuclear testing forever."[64]

The White House also announced that the Joint Chiefs of Staff still favored prompt ratification of the treaty based on the belief that arms control protects military personnel, reduces tensions, limits the potential for conflict, and conserves financial resources.[65] At the same time, the Senate leadership showed no inclination to change its stance. In a January 22 letter to the *Wall Street Journal*, Senator Helms restated his long-standing position that the Foreign Relations Committee would not hold hearings on the CTBT until it considered the Kyoto Protocol and the ABM amendments. Further, he wrote, "Mr. Clinton cannot demand quick action on the treaties he wants us to consider, and at the same time hold hostage other treaties he is afraid we will reject. The president must submit all of them, or we will consider none of them."[66]

Beyond the perennial obstacle posed by Senator Helms's control over the Foreign Relations Committee, there were new impediments. Many foreign policy issues—ambassadorial nominations, the nation's UN debt, the global convention on women's rights, and the CTBT—became overshadowed by national security crises. In the early months of 1999, U.S. warplanes were continuing to strike Iraqi targets in the aftermath of Operation Desert Fox. While most senators agreed with President Clinton's efforts to enforce the no-fly zones and contain Saddam Hussein, there was no consensus between the White House and Capitol Hill on how to respond to the worsening conflict in Kosovo. Many lawmakers were also distressed by the administration's response to alleged Chinese espionage at the nation's nuclear weapons laboratories.

Most important, as these events were unfolding the Senate was distracted by the time-consuming impeachment trial. The proceedings only deepened the personal and political antagonism between Clinton and many congressional Republicans that had developed as early as 1993. Clinton viewed the entire episode as a partisan witch-hunt, whereas Republicans considered it an inevitable consequence of Clinton's scandalous behavior. These feelings would persist after the president's acquittal, coloring interactions between the two branches of government, including the Senate's handling of the CTBT.

The cessation of hostilities in Kosovo in June marked an end to the crises that dominated the first half of 1999. Perhaps believing that too much of the year had been lost to foreign policy, Clinton did not use this opportunity to lobby for the treaty. Instead, CTBT advocates in the Senate took up the task. With active support from a broad range of interest groups, a campaign to pressure Senators Helms and Lott to permit consideration of the treaty was waged throughout the summer of 1999. One of the most vocal participants in this effort was Senator Byron Dorgan, D-N.D. In a series of passionate statements on the Senate floor, Dorgan repeatedly complained that the CTBT had languished on Capitol Hill far longer than other arms control pacts and stressed the Senate's obligation to act on treaties expeditiously.[67] Mr. Dorgan was also among the nine senators—seven Democrats and two Republicans—who held a joint news conference on July 20 to announce the results of bipartisan public opinion polling that showed 82 percent of Americans in favor of ratification.[68] That same day, all forty-five Democratic senators sent a letter to Helms asking that he hold hearings so the treaty could be reported to the full Senate for a vote. The correspondence underscored that it was important for the United States to participate in the treaty's inaugural conference of ratifying states in September.[69]

Frustrated by Senator Helms's negative response on July 26, in which he again referenced the Kyoto Protocol and ABM amendments,[70] Senate Democrats adopted a more aggressive posture. Senator Biden led the offensive with a series of strong statements extolling the CTBT and chastising Senators Helms and Lott for their obstructionism.[71] At one point Biden went so far as to taunt them, stating on July 30,

> I know that my good friends the chairman and the majority leader have raised arguments against the treaty, but they seem curiously unwilling to make those arguments in the context of a proper committee or floor debate. ... Could they be afraid of losing? Could they be afraid that, once the pros and cons are laid out with a resolution of ratification before us, two-thirds of this body will support ratification? ... I know ... the treaty can readily get that support.[72]

Senate minority leader Tom Daschle, D-S.D., seemed to share Biden's confidence. In late July, he indicated he was ready to force a confrontation over the CTBT by attaching a resolution for debate to other legislation.[73]

When the deadlock continued after the Senate's August recess, the Democrats intensified their efforts. Senators Daschle and Dorgan made it clear they were willing to bring the Senate to a standstill unless the treaty was placed on the agenda. Dorgan announced, "I intend to plant myself on the [Senate] floor like a potted plant and object ... to other ... business."[74] A short time afterward, he addressed the majority leader from the Senate floor and repeated his threat. Lott said he would speak to Helms about scheduling hearings and added that he was anxious to hear James Schlesinger's damning critique of the CTBT. Dorgan retorted confidently, "Mr. Schlesinger will be standing in a mighty small crowd."[75] That same month, Senator Biden spoke with equal assurance about the level of public backing. He warned, "If the Republican leadership does not handle this treaty responsibly, I have no doubt how the issue will play out in next year's elections."[76]

The Impasse Breaks

Believing the preponderance of elite and mass opinion was on their side, and certain that the sixty-seven votes necessary for ratification would fall into place, Senate Democrats decided to force the matter. In a meeting with National Security Adviser Berger on September 22, Daschle, Biden, and other Democratic advocates of the test ban agreed to introduce a non-binding resolution calling for hearings in 1999 and a vote on ratification by March 31, 2000. On September 28, Biden allowed Helms to see the measure. A day later, Lott suddenly indicated he was willing to schedule a vote on the treaty if the Democrats dropped the resolution and refrained from tying up Senate business. The offer was accepted, thereby ending the two-year impasse.[77] It appeared that the Democratic minority and their Republican supporters— namely Sen. James Jeffords, R-Vt., and Senator Specter—had finally secured what they wanted.

The Democrats were unaware that Helms and Lott had set a trap. Since April, they, along with Sens. Jon Kyl, R-Ariz., and Paul Coverdell, R-Ga., had secretly worked behind the scenes to line up enough Republicans to defeat the treaty. To go unnoticed, the group was careful to avoid senators who were inclined to support the treaty or might draw attention to their quiet campaign. Those lawmakers who were considered safe to approach were polled, lobbied, and provided briefing books by Kyl and Coverdell. By early May, a selective check of Republican senators identified twenty-four votes against the CTBT. Later that month, the count rose to thirty. In early September, thirty-four senators were on board—the exact number needed to reject a resolution of ratification. As the Democrats adopted more aggressive tactics, Helms and Lott did not want to gamble, so they continued to block the treaty and dispatched Kyl and Coverdell to round up more votes. The final push involved the use of experts and former governmental officials—most notably James Schlesinger—to sway undecided senators in small, group meetings. The effort produced immediate results. By the end of the month, forty-two Republicans were prepared to reject the treaty.[78] Senate Democrats, still uninformed about the backroom maneuvering, mistakenly believed as many as twenty-five Republicans might vote for ratification.[79]

Endgame

Given the opposition to the CTBT within the Republican caucus, there was no risk in Senator Lott allowing hearings and a vote. He and his colleagues were certain they were poised to hand President Clinton a major foreign policy defeat. In late September, the question was whether to do so immediately or wait. Through their threats to obstruct Senate business and make the test ban an election-year issue, the Democrats convinced the Republicans to move faster rather than slower. On one hand, Republican leaders had grown tired of the Democrats' prodding. Senator Coverdell later recounted, "They were a huge influence on the decision to say, 'Okay, let's just hold this vote.'"[80] On the other hand, there was a desire to avoid any problems associated with the Democrats' threats. For instance, a disruption in Senate business late in the fall could have jeopardized a number of critical spending bills, creating the potential for a budget crisis and a government shutdown.

When pressing the Republican leadership to act on the treaty, the Democrats failed to evaluate how quickly Senator Lott might actually proceed. This mistake proved costly. On September 30, a day after the deadlock ended, Mr. Lott caught the Democrats off guard when he proposed that consideration of the CTBT begin October 6. He specified there would be ten hours of floor debate followed by an immediate vote on ratification. A stunned Senator Daschle rejected the offer, raising concerns about the six-day notice, lack of hearings, and limited time for debate.[81] The next day, Lott made a final counteroffer. It provided for committee hearings during the week of October 3, an 18- to 22-hour floor debate to begin October 8, and a final vote on October 12.

(The Senate would actually vote a day later.) These terms were accepted by the minority leader and became part of an official unanimous consent agreement[82] that required the approval of every senator. It passed without objection.

The Democrats wanted to follow standard practice and consider the CTBT for several weeks or months. After all, the non-binding resolution they had crafted on September 22 and dropped five days later envisioned a final vote by March 2000. Nonetheless, all forty-five Democratic senators approved Lott's truncated schedule for several reasons.[83] Foremost, Senate Democrats had little choice. They had repeatedly, and at times vehemently, demanded hearings and a vote on the pact. Their statements were on the record. If they rejected the agreement, it would have appeared as though they had backed off the very thing they had requested. In addition, they did not have an accurate assessment of the votes on the Republican side and so were unaware that the treaty's defeat was a fait accompli. They were also confident that once the merits of the test ban were fully aired and understood, enough votes for ratification would fall into place. Furthermore, Senate Democrats knew that the Republicans did not want the CTBT to become an election-year issue. Thus they figured that if the treaty was not considered in 1999, it might be the middle of 2001 or later before the Foreign Relations Committee scheduled hearings. Last, the Democrats likely assumed that if they ran into trouble and could not muster the necessary support for ratification, they could always strike a last-minute deal with the Republican leadership to delay the vote.

The terms of the October 1 unanimous consent agreement meant the Clinton administration faced a vote on one of its top foreign policy priorities within a matter of days. The president would later remark, "This whole thing came as a complete surprise to us." [84] It was under these circumstances that the White House finally launched a high-level, full-scale effort to secure Senate approval of the CTBT. On the weekend of October 2, Vice President Al Gore, Secretary of Defense Cohen, and Secretary of State Albright were dispatched to Capitol Hill for two days of intense lobbying. The following week, they continued their campaign, using further meetings, statements to the press, letters to the full Senate,[85] and (in the case of Albright and Cohen) congressional testimony, to explain why the CTBT served the nation's interest. By October 4, the president had also assumed a central role. Knowing the treaty's ratification or rejection would have a significant impact on his legacy, Clinton held strategy sessions with his foreign policy advisers, lobbied undecided senators (namely moderate Republicans) in one-on-one and small-group meetings, and made his case for the CTBT before the news media. To draw further attention to the issue, the White House held a ceremony on October 6 where prominent backers of the treaty—national security officials, past and present lawmakers, former chairmen of the JCS, and eminent nuclear physicists (including Nobel laureates)—were paraded before the cameras. During the event, Clinton made a twenty-minute appeal for Senate approval.[86]

The belated engagement of the president coincided with the beginning of the brief set of legislative hearings on the CTBT. The Senate Armed Services Committee held three days of testimony from October 5 through October 7. The Senate Foreign Relations Committee restricted its hearings to a single day, October 7. In one sense, these proceedings did not break new ground. The senators and witnesses who participated made the same policy arguments for and against the treaty that had been offered in the past and would be reiterated during the floor debate. Much like the interest groups that lined up on either side of the issue, Senate Democrats and administration officials extolled the virtues of the test ban, whereas Senate Republicans and former Reagan and Bush administration officials criticized it.[87]

Amid this pedestrian testimony, however, there was a noteworthy development. Key moderate Republicans, who were the focus of the White House lobbying campaign, announced they would not support ratification. Sen. Richard Lugar, R-Ind., a senior member of the Foreign Relations Committee, declared, "I do not believe the CTBT is of the same caliber as the arms control treaties that have come before the Senate in recent decades."[88] He also noted, "Presidential leadership has been almost entirely absent on this issue. Despite having several years to make a case for ratification, the administration has declined to initiate the type of advocacy campaign that should accompany any treaty of this magnitude."[89] Lugar's opposition was a stunning political loss for the president and Senate Democrats. As an arms control advocate and respected bipartisan voice on international affairs, his support was considered critical for winning ratification of the treaty.

Equally important was the opposition of Sen. John Warner, R-Va., chairman of the Senate Armed Services Committee. His stance against the CTBT can be traced to testimony before his committee on October 7. When asked by Senator Levin, the directors of the three national nuclear weapons laboratories indicated they were "on board with [the] treaty," assuming the SSMP was fully funded and the six safeguards were in place.[90] Yet in response to other questions that day, they made it clear that explosive testing was the preferred means for ensuring the safety and reliability of nuclear weapons. The directors also said it would be anywhere from five to twenty years before the substitute for testing—the SSMP—was fully operational. Further, once in place, a successful SSMP would continue to require experienced personnel, adequate funding, and new scientific tools to track the unknown effects of an aging arsenal. So although capabilities and circumstances at the time of the directors' testimony gave them the confidence to certify the safety and reliability of the U.S. stockpile, they made no definitive promises about the future.[91]

These statements had two consequences. First, enough uncertainty was created to persuade some lawmakers to vote against the CTBT. Senator Warner concluded, "There are honest differences on both sides [of the issue], leaving, clearly, a reasonable doubt—and I come from the old school that it should be beyond any reasonable doubt if we're going to take a step that affects our vital security interests for decades to come."[92] The lab directors, in essence, furnished the reasonable doubt. Second, isolated portions of their October 7 testimony were seized upon by critics of the treaty in making their case against ratification. A day later, the directors issued a joint press statement to clarify and strengthen their support for the test ban.[93] It was too late. Some CTBT opponents were already referencing their earlier comments on the Senate floor.[94]

The Final Scramble

The three days of hearings also revealed that numerous lawmakers and witnesses favored postponing the vote on ratification.[95] While the White House was initially reluctant to retreat, both Secretary of State Albright and the new secretary of energy, Bill Richardson, recommended a delay during their October 7 testimony. Senate Democrats, who were eager to avert a major legislative defeat, espoused the same position. Most important, moderate Republicans joined the call. By the following day, it was clear several avowed internationalists—Sens. Lugar, Warner, Pete Domenici, R-N.M., Chuck Hagel, R-Neb., and Ted Stevens, R-Alaska—who were all prepared to vote against the treaty, wanted to avoid that outcome. On one hand, they had misgivings, as expressed by Senator Lugar when he complained, "I regret that the Senate is taking up this treaty in an abrupt and truncated manner that is so politicized."[96] On the other hand, there were concerns about how the world would perceive a rejection of the landmark pact. Beyond damaging the United States' standing as a global leader, there was fear of undermining international non-proliferation efforts.

Seeing inaction as preferable to an inevitable defeat, President Clinton brought himself on October 8 to ask the Senate for a delay, arguing that a repudiation of the treaty would give "a green light to every other country in the world" to test and develop nuclear weapons.[97] Two days earlier, Senator Lott had seemed receptive to a postponement. The majority leader stated, "I think it is unwise for the administration to have pushed for this treaty as they have when the timing is not right.... They, in effect, have forced this vote. Now, they're going to have to make a decision to go forward."[98] There was a catch, however. Senator Lott made it clear that he would only entertain a delay if two conditions were met. President Clinton and Senate Democrats would have to request that the pending vote be canceled. There also would have to be a commitment to delay a vote on ratification until after a new president and Senate entered office in January 2001. In his October 8 statement, Clinton said his administration would not revisit the CTBT "until we think we can pass it" and that the matter ought to be "taken out of politics." These ambiguous remarks were not enough to mollify Lott.

Senators Kyl and Helms further complicated the situation when they insisted that the president agree to the two conditions in writing.[99] Senator Daschle indicated the Democrats were not prepared to abandon the treaty until 2001, and added that he believed the president would request a delay in writing.[100] Clinton, however, scoffed at the Republicans' demand: "They want me to give them a letter to cover the political decision that they made that does severe damage to the interest of the United States and the interest of nonproliferation in the world? I don't think so. They have to take responsibility for whether they want to reverse 50 years of American leadership in nonproliferation."[101] Senator Helms was equally obstinate: "[The treaty] was forced upon us by the Clinton administration and all 45 of our friends on the other side of the aisle. But now ... [they] realize they don't have the votes to ratify the CTBT, and so they are hoping to dictate the terms of their own surrender. They want us to say something like this: 'Okay, let's call it a draw.' And I say to them, that ain't going to happen."[102]

Reluctance by the White House and Senate Democrats to accept Lott's proposal led to further negotiations on the matter. But as the floor debate got underway on October 8 and continued through the next several days, it seemed likely that any deal reached by Senators Daschle and Lott would be meaningless. Under the terms of the October 1 unanimous consent agreement, a *single* senator could block cancellation of the vote; and Sens. James Inhofe, R-Okla., Tim Hutchinson, R-Ark., and Robert Smith, I-N.H., all pledged on the record that they would not allow the vote to be rescheduled.[103]

On the Senate floor, Inhofe raised issues such as verification and the threat posed by rogue states as reasons to defeat the treaty. At one point, however, he could not contain his contempt for President Clinton, who he had recently labeled "the worst Commander in Chief in the history of America."[104] Specifically, he questioned whether Clinton could be trusted to exercise the supreme national interests clause (Safeguard F), "because we have a president who has a very difficult time telling the truth."[105] For Senator Smith, the goal was to deny the president any opportunity to escape from a major political defeat. He would later remark, "Postponing a vote on the CTBT will allow the White House to claim victory in saving the treaty, and will allow the White House to continue to spin the American people by blaming opponents for not ratifying the treaty." Thus Senator Smith reasoned that the best way to handle the pact was to "stick a knife in its heart and kill it."[106]

Still determined, proponents of the treaty continued to search for a way out. Senator Daschle announced on October 8 that the Democrats would seek to bypass the unanimous consent agreement through parliamentary procedure. The one available option was a non-debatable motion supported by a fifty-one-vote majority, which would move the Senate from its executive calendar—under which the CTBT was being considered—back to a legislative session, where other business would be taken up.[107] To be successful, however, the Democratic minority would have to persuade six Republicans to join them. As Daschle scrambled to avoid a vote, foreign leaders and envoys from nearly 100 countries lobbied the Senate in Washington and from overseas to approve the pact.[108] French president Jacques Chirac, British prime minister Tony Blair, and German chancellor Gerhard Schröder, who represented three of the twenty-six nuclear-capable states that had ratified the pact, made a rare pitch in a *New York Times* op-ed column cautioning that "rejection would give great encouragement to proliferators."[109]

President Clinton and his top national security advisers repeated the warning throughout the weekend of October 9 and 10, as the administration launched an aggressive media campaign to pressure Senate Republicans to postpone the fast-approaching vote.[110] Unable to sway his political opponents through the press, the president took another course of action. On October 11, Clinton submitted a formal letter to the Senate asking that consideration of the CTBT be deferred. Equally frustrated in his attempt to find six Republican senators to support his parliamentary maneuvering, Senator Daschle made a similar written request on October 12. More important, he went further than the president by addressing Republican concerns about the possibility of a vote during 2000. The minority leader pledged, "Absent unforeseen changes in the international situation, I will not seek to reschedule this vote."[111] Senator Lott objected to the wording of this commitment, forcing talks on a possible delay to continue, but Daschle's promise, coupled with Lott's propensity to cut deals, heightened expectations that a compromise would be reached. In fact, later that day an agreement appeared imminent when Daschle said he would modify the phrase "unforeseen changes" to "extraordinary circumstances."[112]

Signs of an impending deal led conservative Republicans to race to the majority leader's office. Senators Kyl, Helms, and Coverdell opposed what they saw as a "glaring escape clause," while Senators Inhofe and Smith insisted the vote go forward.[113] Kyl also argued that if the Senate did not reject the treaty, the United States—as a signatory—would be forced to abide by its terms. Further, Lott was told by his colleagues that there would be "personal political repercussions should he agree to delay the vote."[114] Under pressure, Lott informed Daschle that he would not allow a deal that provided any chance for the CTBT to be resurrected during an election year. This was a condition the minority leader was not prepared to accept.

With the floor debate winding down and a vote on ratification just hours away, President Clinton telephoned Senator Lott in a final effort to save one of his top foreign policy priorities. Remarkably, the conversation, in which Clinton once again asked for a postponement, was the first time since September 1997 that the president had spoken to the senator about the treaty. Lott, however, made it clear that the last minute appeal was too little, too late.[115] Wanting to avoid the political fallout, both domestically and internationally, that would come with a rejection of the CTBT, Sen. Daniel Patrick Moynihan, D-N.Y., and Senator Warner presented a letter to Lott and Daschle urging the two leaders to undertake a "statesmanlike initiative" to delay consideration of the treaty until 2001. Although sixty-two senators—twenty-four Republicans and thirty-eight Democrats—signed the letter,[116] it did not serve its intended purpose.

October 13 became the day of decision. Prior to voting on the resolution of ratification, senators concluded floor debate on the treaty. Their remarks followed the pattern of the previous five days.[117] First, there were complaints on both sides of the aisle that the Senate had not devoted enough time to the details and implications of the CTBT. Conservative Republicans argued, however, that there had been two years to pass judgment on it. Second, Democrats criticized the partisan nature of the proceedings, suggesting that some Republicans were more interested in handing them and President Clinton a major legislative defeat than doing what was best for U.S. and international security. Conservative Republicans responded that the White House and Senate Democrats were simply frustrated by their inability to win a vote that they had forced the majority to hold. Third, and most important, the floor debate encompassed a substantive policy dispute over the wisdom of ratifying the CTBT. Although the proceedings lacked all trappings of vigorous debate, with senators often delivering prepared statements before a "near-empty Chamber,"[118] the differences separating Democrats and Republicans could not have been sharper. The exchange of views also revealed a sharp divide among some senators over the very value of arms control (see Box 7.3).

Box 7.3   The Comprehensive Test Ban Treaty: The 1999 Debate

The Case for Ratification

- A ban on explosive testing will impede the rise of new nuclear weapons states and the modernization of existing nuclear arsenals, thereby making the world a safer place.
- By freezing nuclear weapons development, the Comprehensive Test Ban Treaty (CTBT) locks in U.S. nuclear superiority.
- By ratifying the pact, the United States will prompt other countries to follow its lead. By rejecting the treaty, it will encourage nuclear testing and proliferation.
- While no arms control treaty is perfectly verifiable, the CTBT is effectively verifiable. All militarily significant tests can be detected through national technical means (such as diplomacy, intelligence, and science), a global network of sensors, and on-site inspections.
- The thirty out of fifty-one Executive Council votes necessary to authorize an on-site inspection will not be difficult to gather.
- The U.S. nuclear deterrent is safe and reliable (seven years after the last explosive test). The nation's extensive database, coupled with the Stockpile Stewardship and Management Program's (SSMP) capabilities and future improvements, will sustain the status quo.
- In the event the safety and reliability of the U.S. stockpile cannot be certified, the United States can withdraw from the treaty under the supreme national interest clause.
- The treaty is the culmination of efforts by several administrations to reach a CTBT.
- The credibility of the U.S. nuclear deterrent is not at stake. Many of the treaty's strongest supporters are U.S. friends and allies.

continued on the next page

---

continued from the previous page

- As a signatory to the treaty, the United States is bound under customary international law to abide by its "object and purpose." By rejecting the treaty, the Senate cannot renege on this obligation. The only recourse is for the president to announce his intention not to seek ratification.

The Case against Ratification

- A ban on explosive testing will not dissuade countries from developing and modernizing nuclear weapons if they believe such behavior serves their national interest. U.S. ratification will not change this fact.
- By freezing nuclear weapons development, the treaty will disadvantage the U.S. militarily. Other countries will evade the ban and ultimately erode the United States' margin of superiority.
- Rejection of the CTBT will signal to the world that the United States will not accept flawed arms control pacts that run counter to its national security interests.
- The United States cannot adequately and confidently verify other states' compliance with the CTBT. Low-yield nuclear tests are not detectable, the global network of sensors is not ready, and the difficulty in gathering thirty Executive Council votes to authorize on-site inspections will invite delay and deception.
- A ban on explosive testing will make it extremely difficult for the United States to meet new military requirements, replace aging delivery systems, and improve the safety and reliability of its nuclear stockpile.
- The United States will not be able to withdraw from the CTBT under the supreme national interest clause, because domestic and international actors will claim the act is too provocative.
- Since the SSMP encompasses unproven technology and will need several more years to become fully operational, its viability as a substitute for explosive testing is not assured.
- No president before Clinton pursued a permanent, zero-yield CTBT.
- The absence of testing will undermine confidence in the U.S. nuclear deterrent, prompting some non-nuclear states that rely on U.S. security guarantees to consider developing their own nuclear weapons.
- The United States should not be bound by customary international law to uphold the CTBT's "object and purpose."

Conclusion: Politics or Principles?

When the debate was concluded and the roll was called, the CTBT fell nineteen votes short of winning the Senate's advice and consent. Just four Republicans joined forty-four Democrats in support of the resolution, whereas fifty Republicans and one Independent opposed the measure.[119] Sen. Robert Byrd, D-W.Va., did not cast a vote for or against the treaty. Instead he voted "present" for the first time in his forty-one-year career to protest the truncated and politicized process of deliberation.[120] Beyond the rebukes of bitter Senate Democrats, the repudiation of the landmark treaty drew a barrage of criticism from the international community, arms control advocacy groups, newspaper editorialists, and the White House. President Clinton complained that the rejection had been driven by "[partisan] politics, pure and simple." Senator Lott responded, "It was not about politics; it was about the substance of the treaty, and that's all it was."[121] Neither man was entirely correct.

Like most foreign policy issues involving significant congressional activity, the Senate's handling of the CTBT was a manifestation of both party and ideology. The fact that partisan politics and substantive policy differences are intertwined makes it difficult to distinguish where the influence of one force begins and the other ends. As a result, it is not surprising that even though both sides were motivated by politics *and* policy, Democrats viewed the rejection of the treaty as mere partisanship, while Republicans saw the outcome as a principled difference of opinion. Such reactions are typical in any public policy struggle that produces distinct winners and losers. Yet these attitudes were clearly intensified by the high-stakes battle over the CTBT, which unfolded within a political environment marked by divided government, personal rancor, veiled maneuvers, and acute policy differences. The case of the CTBT is an excellent example of how national security matters of the highest importance can be affected by the increasingly open, pluralistic, and partisan nature of contemporary foreign policy making.

Notes

The author wishes to thank Northern Illinois University undergraduates Lisa A. Meyers and Debra L. Olson for collecting documents used in this case study.
1. *Congressional Record*, October 13, 1999, S12548.
2. R. W. Apple Jr., "The GOP Torpedo," *New York Times*, October 14, 1999, A1.
3. Mark Stencel, "Clinton's Pledges," *Washington Post*, January 20, 1993, A19.

4. Office of the Press Secretary, "Joint Statement by President Bill Clinton and President Boris Yeltsin," April 4, 1993.

5. Office of the Press Secretary, "U.S. Policy on Nuclear Testing and Comprehensive Test Ban," July 3, 1993.

6. Jonathan Medalia, "Nuclear Weapons: Comprehensive Test Ban Treaty," *CRS Issue Brief for Congress,* April 26, 2000, 3.

7. Ibid.

8. UN General Assembly Resolution 48/70, December 16, 1993.

9. While the CD is associated with and financed by the UN, it is an autonomous intergovernmental body, considered the world's principal disarmament forum.

10. This statement was made National Security Adviser Anthony Lake. R. Jeffrey Smith, "Clinton Overrules Pentagon Objections to Win Backing on Treaties," *Washington Post,* January 31, 1995, A10.

11. Ibid.

12. Norman Kempster, "Nations Agree to Make Nuclear Pact Permanent," *Los Angeles Times,* May 12, 1995, A10; and U.S. Department of State, "Comprehensive Test Ban Treaty a Top Priority," *Fact Sheet,* http://www.state.gov/www/global/arms/ctbtpage/ntbpage.html.

13. William Drozdiak, "France Says It Will Stage Nuclear Tests," *Washington Post,* June 14, 1995, A27.

14. Spurgeon M. Keeny Jr., "U.S. Policy Decision on Testing Seen as Helping CTB Talks," *Arms Control Today,* September 1995, 25, 32; and R. Jeffrey Smith, "Administration Debates Pentagon Proposal to Resume Nuclear Tests," *Washington Post,* June 18, 1995, A17.

15. Julia Preston and R. Jeffrey Smith, "The Nuclear Treaty: Product of Global Full-Court Press by U.S.," *Washington Post,* May 14, 1995, A23; and William Drozdiak, "France's Nuclear Storm," *Washington Post,* July 8, 1995, A13.

16. Rebecca Johnson, "The In-Comprehensive Test Ban," *Bulletin of the Atomic Scientists* 52 (November/December 1996): 32.

17. Bill Clinton, "Statement on a Comprehensive Nuclear Weapons Test Ban," *Weekly Compilation of Presidential Documents,* August 14, 1995, 1432–1433, http://www.access.gpo.gov/nara/nara003.htm.

18. For a summary of the 1,054 U.S. nuclear tests, which include 24 British tests at the Nevada test site, see "Nuclear Weapons: the Comprehensive Test Ban Treaty," *Congressional Digest,* December 1999, 294. For a discussion of the report by the scientific panel, see Bureau of Arms Control, U.S. Department of State, "CTBT Facts and Fiction," *Fact Sheet,* October 8, 1999.

19. Ibid.

20. Office of the Press Secretary, "Comprehensive Test Treaty Chronology during Clinton Administration," *Fact Sheet,* September 10, 1996, 1.

21. Medalia, "Nuclear Weapons," 7.

22. United Nations, "Assembly Adopts Comprehensive Nuclear-Test-Ban Treaty," press release GA/9083, September 10, 1996.

23. John F. Harris, "Five World Powers Promise to Stop Nuclear Testing," *Washington Post,* September 25, 1996, A1; and "Test Ban: Ike Pined, Clinton Signed," *U.S. News & World Report,* October 7, 1996, 23.

24. For the figure and quotes, see Johnson, "In-Comprehensive Test Ban," 30.

25. William J. Clinton, "Letter of Transmittal to the Senate of the United States," September 22, 1997, 1, 6, http://www.state.gov/www/global/arms/ctbtpage/ntbpage.html.

26. Clinton, "Letter of Transmittal," 6.

27. Clinton, "Letter of Transmittal," 7.

28. Craig Cerniello, "Clinton Sends CTB Treaty to Senate; Hearings Set to Begin in October," *Arms Control Today,* September 1997, 25.

29. Ibid.

30. Stephen Schwartz, "Out Maneuvered, Gunned, and of View: Test Ban Debacle," *Bulletin of the Atomic Scientists,* 56 (January/February 2000): 25.

31. Secretary of State Madeleine K. Albright, "Remarks and Q & A before the Chicago Council on Foreign Relations," November 10, 1999, http://www.state.gov/www/global/arms/ctbtpage/ntbpage.html

32. *Nuclear Stockpile Safety,* hearing of the Governmental Affairs Subcommittee on International Security, Proliferation, and Federal Services, October 27, 1997, 15, at CIS Congress Universe, http://www.lexis-nexis.com.

33. Ibid., 15, 18.

34. *Nuclear Stockpile Reliability,* hearing of the Energy and Water Development Subcommittee, October 29, 1997, 2, at CIS Congress Universe, http://www.lexis-nexis.com.

35. Ibid., 2–4.

36. *Nuclear Stockpile Safety,* 2.

37. Ibid., 4.

38. Ibid., 5.

39. Ibid., 3–4.

40. Daryl Kimball, "What Went Wrong: Repairing the Damage to the CTBT," *Arms Control Today,* December 1999, 3.

41. Craig Cerniello, "Clinton Urges Senate to Act on CTB; Helms Calls Treaty 'Low Priority,'" *Arms Control Today,* January 1998, 28.

42. Daryl Kimball, "Holding the CTBT Hostage in the Senate: The 'Stealth' Strategy of Helms and Lott," *Arms Control Today,* June 1998, 4.

43. For excerpts, see Cerniello, "Clinton Urges Senate," 28; and Kimball, "Stealth Strategy," 4.

44. Senator Jesse Helms, letter to President Clinton, 21 January 2000, at Center for Security Policy, no. 98-P13, http://www.security-policy.org/nuclear.html.

45. Kimball, "Stealth Strategy," 4. On the intimidation factor, also see Bill Mesler, "Republican Strangeloves," *Nation,* October 1998, 6, 23.

46. President Bill Clinton, reply letter to Senator Jesse Helms on the CTBT, February 10, 1998, at Coalition to Reduce Nuclear Dangers, http://www.clw.org/coalition/ctbindex.htm.

47. Stephen E. Ambrose and Douglas G. Brinkley, *Rise to Globalism: American Foreign Policy since 1938,* 7th ed. (New York: Penguin, 1997), 399.

48. *Comprehensive Test Ban Treaty,* hearing of the Governmental Affairs Subcommittee on International Security, Proliferation, and Federal Services, March 18, 1998, part II, 2–6, at Coalition to Reduce Nuclear Dangers, http://www.clw.org/coalition/ctbindex.htm.

49. Sen. Joseph R. Biden Jr., "Senator Joseph R. Biden, Jr. (D-DE) Deplores Indian Nuclear Testing," press statement, May 12, 1998.

50. *Congressional Record,* May 12, 1998, S4680.

51. *Congressional Record,* May 13, 1998, S4775.

52. For a transcript of Specter's May 14, 1998, letter, see *Congressional Record,* September 1, 1998, S9731.

53. Sen. Joseph R. Biden Jr. and Sen. Arlen Specter, Dear Colleague letter, May 19, 1998, at Coalition to Reduce Nuclear Dangers, http://www.clw.org/coalition/ctbindex. htm.

54. *Congressional Record,* September 1, 1998, S9732.

55. "Statement by Senator Snowe on Nuclear Test Ban Treaty," news release, May 28, 1998; Sen. Carl Levin and Jeff Bingaman, letter on CTBT to the chairman of the Armed Services Committee, Strom Thurmond, June 3, 1998, at Coalition to Reduce Nuclear Dangers, http://www.clw.org/coalition/ctbindex.htm; and "Sen. Levin and Bingaman Call for hearings on the CTBT," *News from Carl Levin,* June 9, 1998.

56. Sen. Trent Lott, "Nuclear Arms Race in Asia Makes Test Ban Irrelevant, Lott Says," press release, May 29, 1998.

57. Sen. Jesse Helms, "Statement on India's Nuclear Tests," May 13, 1998, at Coalition to Reduce Nuclear Dangers, http://www.clw.org/coalition/ctbindex.htm.

58. Lott, "Test Ban Irrelevant."

59. "Senate Inaction on Test Ban Undercuts Effort to Address South Asia Crisis," *Issue Brief,* June 4, 1998, at Coalition to Reduce Nuclear Dangers, http://www.clw.org/coalition/ctbindex.htm.

60. Kimball, "Stealth Strategy," 8.

61. Center for Security Policy, "R.I.P. C.T.B.: Biden-Specter Amendment's Pyrrhic Victory Shows Decisive Senate Opposition to Clinton's Flawed Test Ban," *Decision Brief,* September 2, 1998.

62. Ibid.

63. "Nuclear Treaty Confirmation High on White House Agenda," *CQ Weekly,* January 1999, 153.

64. Transcript, "My Fellow Americans ... State of Our Union Is Strong," *Washington Post,* January 20, 1999, A12.

65. The White House, "The Joint Chiefs of Staff Call for Prompt CTBT Ratification," *Test Ban News,* March 4, 1999, 1.

66. Sen. Jesse Helms, "Amend the ABM Treaty? No, Scrap It," *Wall Street Journal,* January 22, 1999.

67. *Congressional Record,* July 12, 1999, S8206. Also see *Congressional* Record, May 24, 1999, S5792; *Congressional Record,* June 30, 1999, S7924; *Congressional Record,* July 16, 1999, S8737; *Congressional Record,* July 19, 1999, S8813.

68. "Eight in Ten Americans Support Test Ban Treaty," news release, July 20, 1999, at Coalition to Reduce Nuclear Dangers, at http://www.clw.org/coalition/ctbindex.htm.

69. Letter from all 45 Democratic senators to Sen. Jesse Helms, July 20, 1999, at Coalition to Reduce Nuclear Dangers, http://www.clw.org/coalition/ctbindex.htm.

70. Letter from Sen. Helms in response to July 20 letter from all 45 Democratic senators, July 26, 1999, at Coalition to Reduce Nuclear Dangers, http://www.clw.org/coalition/ctbindex.htm.

71. For example, see Sen. Joseph R. Biden, "Biden Urges Committee, Senate to Act on CTBT," press release, 27 July 1999; *Congressional Record,* July 27, 1999, S9321–9323; and *Congressional Record,* July 30, 1999, S9421–9423.

72. *Congressional Record,* July 30, 1999, S9422.

73. See Chuck McCutcheon, "Senators to Seek Vote on Nuclear Test Ban Treaty,"*CQ Weekly*, July 1999, 1814.

74. *Congressional Record*, September 8, 1999, S10541. For Daschle's position, see Miles A. Pomper, "Senate Showdown Expected over Nuclear Test Ban Treaty," *CQ Weekly*, September 1999, 2069.

75. *Congressional Record*, September 10, 1999, S10723; also see S10720–10722.

76. *Congressional Record*, September 24, 1999, S11426.

77. See Schwartz, "Out Maneuvered," 27; Kimball, "What Went Wrong," 4; Richard Lowry, "Test-Ban Ban," *National Review*, November 1999, 22; and John M. Broder, "Quietly and Dexterously, Senate Republicans Set a Trap," *New York Times*, October 14, 1999, A11.

78. Schwartz, "Out Maneuvered," 27; Kimball, "What Went Wrong," 4; Lowry, "Test-Ban Ban," 22; Broder, "Republicans Set a Trap," A11.

79. Broder, "Republicans Set a Trap," A11.

80. See Lowry, "Test-Ban Ban," 22.

81. Helen Dewar, "Lott Proposes Vote on Nuclear Test Ban Treaty," *Washington Post*, October 1, 1999, A4.

82. For the text of the agreement, see *Congressional Record*, October 1, 1999, S11820–11821.

83. The following overview is based largely on Schwartz, "Out Maneuvered," 28; Kimball, "What Went Wrong," 4; and Lowry, "Test-Ban Ban," 22.

84. Office of the Press Secretary, "Press Conference by the President," transcript, October 14, 1999.

85. For example, see Madeleine K. Albright, letter to all members of the United States Senate, October 5, 1999, http://www.state.gov/www/global/arms/ctbtpage/ntbpage.html.

86. See Helen Dewar and Roberto Suro, "Senate Conservatives to Demand Vote on Test Ban Treaty," *Washington Post*, October 7, 1999, A9; also see Charles Babington, "Clinton Campaigns for Senate Passage of Test Ban Treaty," *Washington Post*, October 5, 1999, A5.

87. See *Comprehensive Test Ban Treaty*, hearing of the Senate Foreign Relations Committee, October 7, 1999, panels I, II, and III (official transcript); and *Comprehensive Test Ban Treaty*, hearing of the Senate Armed Services Committee, October 7, 1999, panels I, II, and III (official transcript). Hearings of the Senate Armed Services Committee on October 5 and 6 were closed sessions.

88. Sen. Richard Lugar, "Lugar Opposes Comprehensive Test Ban Treaty," news release, October 7, 1999, 2.

89. Ibid., October 7, 1999, 1.

90. Senate Armed Service Committee, *Comprehensive Test Ban Treaty*, 7 and 20.

91. See ibid., esp. 4–7 and 12.

92. Senate Foreign Relations Committee, *Comprehensive Test Ban Treaty*, 1.

93. "Joint Statement by the Three Nuclear Weapons Laboratory Directors," Energy Department press release (R-99–276), October 8, 1999.

94. See Sen. James M. Inhofe, "Comprehensive Nuclear Test-Ban Treaty," Senate floor statement, October 8, 1999, http://www.state.gov/www/global/arms/ctbtpage/ntbpage.html.

95. See Senate Foreign Relations Committee, *Comprehensive Test Ban Treaty*, 1, 3–4, 12; and Senate Armed Services Committee, *Comprehensive Test Ban Treaty*, 8–10.

96. "Lugar Opposes," 1.

97. Helen Dewar, "As Debate Starts, Clinton Asks Senate to Delay Test Ban Vote; Democrats Threaten to Cut Off Treaty If Lott Doesn't Withdraw It," *Washington Post*, October 9, 1999, A4.

98. Reuters, "Clinton to Press Senate on Nuclear Pact," October 6, 1999.

99. "Press Conference with Senators Jesse Helms, John Kyl, and John W. Warner on their Opposition to the CTBT," Federal News Service transcript, October 6, 1999.

100. Chuck McCutcheon, "Senators Struggle to Put Nuclear Treaty Back in Bottle," *CQ Weekly*, October 9, 1999, 2393.

101. Reuters, "Clinton Asks Senate for CTBT Delay, Lott Declines," October 8, 1999.

102. "Press Conference with Senators Helms, Kyl and Warner."

103. See Helen Dewar and Roberto Suro, "Senate Conservatives to Demand Vote on Test Ban Treaty," *Washington Post*, October 7, 1999, A9.

104. See Eric Schmitt, "A Clinton Critic Pushes for a High-Stakes Vote," *New York Times*, October 12, 1999, A7.

105. Inhofe, "Comprehensive Nuclear Test-Ban Treaty."

106. The first statement was made on October 12 on the Senate floor. See Kimball, "What Went Wrong," 7; and McCutcheon, "Senators Struggle," 2394.

107. "News Briefing with Senate Minority Leader Tom Daschle including Statement on Comprehensive Test Ban Treaty," Federal News Service transcript, October 8, 1999.

108. See ibid.; William Drozdiak, "U.S. Allies Urge Senate to Ratify Test Ban," *Washington Post*, October 8, 1999, A1, A24; and Donald G. McNeil Jr., "Weight of U.S. Treaty Vote Emerges at Vienna Panel," *New York Times*, October 8, 1999, sec. A.

109. Jacques Chirac, Tony Blair, and Gerhard Schröder, "A Treaty We All Need," *New York Times*, October 8, 1999, sec. A. For a list of the twenty-six states, see Chuck McCutcheon, "Treaty Vote a 'Wake-Up Call,'" *CQ Weekly*, October 16, 1999, 2435.

110. William Claiborne, "Clinton: Test Ban Treaty Is Essential," *Washington Post*, October 10, 1999, A10; and Helen Dewar, "Cohen Warns against Rejection of Treaty," *Washington Post*, October 11, 1999, A10.

111. Schwartz, "Out Maneuvered," 29; also see Helen Dewar, "Democrats Push Delay on Treaty," *Washington Post*, October 13, 1999, A4.

112. Schwartz, "Out Maneuvered," 29.

113. Lowry, "Test-Ban Ban," 22.

114. Schwartz, "Out Maneuvered," 29.

115. See Lowry, "Test-Ban Ban," 22; Schwartz, "Out Maneuvered," 29; and Eric Schmitt, "Senate Kills Test Ban Treaty in Crushing Loss for Clinton; Evokes Versailles Pact Defeat," *New York Times*, October 14, 1999, A1.

116. "Letter Signed by 62 Senators Requesting a Delay on Consideration of the Comprehensive Test Ban Treaty," *Congressional Record*, October 12, 1999, S12549.

117. See *Congressional Record*, October 13, 1999, S12465–12550; and Congressional Research Service, "Nuclear Weapons: The Comprehensive Test Ban Treaty," *Congressional Digest* December 1999, 300–313. Also see *Congressional Record*, October 8, 1999, S12257–12316.

118. Senator Moynihan commented on the largely empty Senate chamber. For his statement, see Congressional Research Service, "Nuclear Weapons," 302.

119. *Congressional Record,* October 13, 1999, S12548.

120. Ibid., S12523.

121. Office of the Press Secretary, "Statement of the President," October 13, 1999; and Senator Trent Lott, "Response to President Clinton's Remarks," Federal News Service transcript, October 14, 1999.

8 The Clinton Administration's Strikes on Usama Bin Laden: Limits to Power

Ryan C. Hendrickson

Before You Begin

1. What is the traditional role played by Congress when the United States uses force abroad? What is the traditional role of the president? Why did President Bill Clinton consult with members of Congress prior to the missile strikes in retaliation for the bombing of the U.S. embassies in Kenya and Tanzania?

2. Why did senior Clinton administration officials initially stress that there was a high degree of unanimity regarding the intelligence information on Usama Bin Laden and the decision to use force?

3. Do you think the United States would have used force had Bin Laden's camps been in Belgium or Saudi Arabia?

4. Why did Congress so quickly back the strikes, and why did few members raise questions following the research and reporting that challenged the administration's information on the al-Shifa Pharmaceutical Industries plant in Khartoum?

5. Do you think Clinton used force to divert attention from his domestic problems involving the Monica Lewinsky scandal? How did the scandal affect the formation and implementation of foreign policy?

Introduction: The White House Faces Terrorism

Occasionally foreign policy making occurs in an environment involving a high degree of secrecy, in which the public, the media, and even most members of Congress are not privy to the decision-making process. One such case was when President Bill Clinton decided in August 1998 to launch missile strikes against the alleged terrorist facilities of Usama Bin Laden in Sudan and Afghanistan in response to the bombing of U.S. embassies in Nairobi, Kenya, and Dar es Salaam, Tanzania, earlier that month. The choice to use force, however, came at a controversial time for Clinton. Only three days before the strikes, the president had admitted to misleading the public about an extramarital affair he had with a White House intern, Monica Lewinsky. Moreover, in the aftermath of the strikes investigative journalists uncovered information indicating that considerable disagreement had existed among Central Intelligence Agency (CIA) and State Department officials over the intelligence gathered on Bin Laden and his supposed connections to the al-Shifa Pharmaceutical Industries plant, which the administration targeted on the grounds that it was involved in producing chemical weapons. Yet, with only a few exceptions, Clinton's decision to launch seventy-nine cruise missiles generated little controversy among members of Congress or opposition from other countries after the fact.

Background: Usama Bin Laden and the War Powers Resolution

During Bill Clinton's two terms as president, 1993 to 2001, the perceived threat of terrorism against U.S. interests grew to unsurpassed levels. Although the total number of terrorist strikes against the United States was higher in the 1980s than in the 1990s, Americans at home and abroad had been victims of a number of high-profile attacks that heightened the public's awareness. During the cold war, some U.S. presidents retaliated after such attacks with military force. When Usama Bin Laden's network struck U.S. embassies in Kenya and Tanzania on August 7, 1998, Clinton similarly employed the military as a foreign policy tool.

The Man and His Mission

Prior to the U.S. strikes in Afghanistan and Sudan, most Americans had never heard of Usama Bin Laden, who was, however, no stranger to the U.S. intelligence community. Bin Laden, the youngest of twenty children, was born in 1957 to a wealthy conservative family in Saudi Arabia.[1] His father earned an estimated $5 billion fortune in the construction business as a preferred client of the Saudi monarchy.[2] Two of his principal projects included the renovation of Islamic holy sites in Mecca and Medina. Usama Bin Laden received a degree from King Abdul Aziz University, and his first known foray into politics occurred after the 1979 Soviet invasion of Afghanistan. In 1980 Bin Laden left Saudi Arabia to go to Afghanistan and support the *mujahidin,* the Afghan fighters resisting the Soviet takeover and occupation. He assisted in the construction of roads and hospitals and provided other financial assistance to the rebels. He also created a network of Islamic radicals known as al-Qa'ida (The Base). This organization served as the core of what would become Bin Laden's network of supporters willing to advance their fundamentalist version of Islam using any means necessary.[3]

The Clinton Administration's Strikes on Usama Bin Laden

April 18, 1996   President Bill Clinton signs a new anti-terrorism law.

August 23, 1996   Usama Bin Laden issues his first *fatwa* against the United States.

February 23, 1998   Bin Laden issues his second fatwa against the United States.

August 7, 1998   Explosives are detonated at the U.S. embassies in Nairobi, Kenya, and Dar es Salaam, Tanzania.

August 12, 1998   Clinton holds his first meeting with senior advisers about the attacks on the embassies.

August 14, 1998   CIA director George Tenet presents his agency's assessment that Bin Laden was behind the attacks on the embassies.

August 17, 1998   Clinton admits to the nation that he misled the public about having an extramarital relationship with White House intern Monica Lewinsky.

August 18, 1998   Public opinion polls show a deep distrust of Clinton.

August 19, 1998   From his vacation on Martha's Vineyard, Clinton speaks with National Security Adviser Samuel Berger and other senior advisers about possible strikes on Bin Laden.

August 20, 1998   At 2:00 a.m. Clinton authorizes strikes against Bin Laden in a phone conversation with Berger. Seventy-nine missiles are launched against Bin Laden's alleged outposts in Afghanistan and Sudan, including the al-Shifa chemical plant. Clinton addresses the nation about the strikes.

November 4, 1998   A federal grand jury indicts Bin Laden on 224 counts of conspiracy to commit murder and orchestrating the bombing of the U.S. embassies.

October 27, 1999   The *New York Times* reveals dissention within the Clinton administration over the decision to use force against Bin Laden.

Bin Laden returned to Saudi Arabia after the Afghan war concluded in 1989. Upon his father's death, Bin Laden was estimated to have inherited between $200 million and $300 million, part of which he used to finance al-Qa'ida. In 1991, Saudi officials seized Bin Laden's passport after he was caught smuggling weapons into the country from Yemen. He then moved to Sudan, where he invested heavily in its impoverished economy and developed a close relationship with Sudanese president Umar Hassan al-Bashir of the National Islamic Front. Much of Bin Laden's financial support went toward Sudan's major export, gum, as well as pharmaceutical companies. He also assisted in the construction of an airport, a 750-mile highway, and a bank in the capital, Khartoum. While in Sudan, which was mired in civil war and whose government had little authority, Bin Laden may have also financed the training of three alleged terrorist groups.[4]

During his years in Sudan, Bin Laden was suspected of being involved in a number of high-profile attacks around the world. The first strike occurred in 1992 in Aden, Yemen, when alleged Bin Laden associates planted a bomb in a hotel where American military personnel lived; the Americans left before the bomb exploded. There would be a series of attacks over the next five years. Bin Laden is also blamed for a 1994 attack on a Saudi National Guard station that resulted in the deaths of five American military personnel. Four of five people arrested and beheaded by Saudi authorities for involvement in the bombing maintained that they had acted under Bin Laden's orders. Bin Laden has also been loosely linked to the 1996 strike on the Khobar Towers military living quarters in Dhahran, Saudi Arabia, that took the lives of nineteen American soldiers. He was also thought to be responsible for an aborted assassination plot on President Clinton when the president traveled to the Philippines in 1994.[5]

In addition to these events, Bin Laden's network is believed to have had connections to the bombing of the World Trade Center in New York City in February 1993. Bin Laden's followers from the war in Afghanistan were also convicted of an attempt to bomb U.S. passenger jets 1995. His network was affiliated with a failed attempt to assassinate Pope John Paul II in 1995. The Islamic Group, which maintains an alliance with al-Qa'ida, also claimed responsibility in 1997 for the worst terrorist attack in Egypt, which claimed the lives of fifty-eight tourists. By the mid-1990s, Bin Laden's reach was global, and in 1997 al-Qa'ida was placed on the State Department's list of terrorist organizations.[6]

Bin Laden's radicalism reached new levels on August 23, 1996, when he publicly issued a *fatwa*, or a decree (usually issued by a recognized religious leader), calling for a *jihad* (holy war) against the United States to oppose the U.S. military presence in Saudi Arabia that began with the Persian Gulf War. He argued that Muslims had a "legitimate right" to drive the United States out of the Islamic homeland, and he criticized Saudi Arabia for its alliance with the United States.[7] Under diplomatic pressure from the United States, in 1996 Sudan expelled Bin Laden, who returned to Afghanistan.[8]

In 1998 Bin Laden ascended the world stage and entered into U.S. foreign policy history. On February 23, he issued a second fatwa, in a fax to a London-based Arabic newsletter, in which he made three central points: the United States should leave the Muslim holy land; the United States should end the "great devastation inflicted" upon the Iraqi people through its continuation of economic sanctions; and the United States is engaged in a religious and economic war against Muslims, while simultaneously serving Israel's interests against the Muslim world. Bin Laden appealed to all Muslims to "kill the Americans and their allies—civilians and military" wherever possible.[9]

Terrorism and the Powers of the President

According to the U.S. Constitution, Congress has the power to declare war and possesses a host of other enumerated powers associated with the military. The president is given the explicit authority to act as commander in chief. Most constitutional scholars concur, however, that the president is empowered to use force without congressional approval in order to "repel sudden attacks" against the United States.[10] Otherwise, the president must gain Congress's approval prior to using force.

For much of U.S. history, Congress's war powers have been respected by the commander in chief.[11] With the onset of the cold war and the broad consensus that the Soviet Union and communism represented a threat to the United States, the president's perception of his power as commander in chief became increasingly omnipotent. Since 1945, presidents have asserted wide military powers, with few recognized limitations. Since Congress agreed that communism should be checked, and because it was politically safer to let a president assume full political responsibility for U.S. military endeavors, Congress often deferred.[12] This remained the norm until the 1973 passage of the War Powers Resolution, which was designed to reassert the authority that many felt Presidents Lyndon Johnson and Richard Nixon had usurped from Congress during the Vietnam War. The resolution requires that the president "consult with Congress in every possible circumstance," both prior to and after the use of force.[13] The president must formally notify Congress within 48 hours after the use of force has been initiated and must obtain Congress's approval within sixty days of the operation if it is ongoing, or U.S. troops must be withdrawn. Despite its intent, the War Powers Resolution has proved to be a failure. All presidents since 1973 have maintained that it is unconstitutional; Congress has often refused to enforce it.[14]

When dealing specifically with terrorist threats, U.S. presidents have on occasion responded with military force. In 1979, when Americans were being held captive by supporters of Ayatollah Ruhollah Khomeini at the U.S. embassy in Tehran, President Jimmy Carter planned a military rescue operation. No member of Congress was included in Carter's inner circle of decision makers.[15] In 1986, when President Ronald Reagan bombed Libya—including the compound of Libyan leader Mu'ammar Qadhafi because of Libya's alleged involvement in an attack on a Berlin dance club frequented by Americans—a few members of Congress were notified of the forthcoming military action. These members, however, were notified of the strikes only three hours before they occurred.[16] Both of these actions produced outrage among some members of Congress who perceived them as violations of the War Powers Resolution, but no legislative steps were taken to address their concerns.

As commander in chief, President Clinton also viewed his powers broadly. During his first term, Clinton bombed Iraq in 1993 for its association with a failed attempt to assassinate President George Bush in Kuwait and in 1996 for military actions against Kurdish rebels in the north, deployed 10,000 American troops to Haiti to assist in the return to power of elected president Jean-Bertrand Aristide, used aerial bombing under the North Atlantic Treaty Organization (NATO) to stop Bosnian Serb attacks on Sarajevo, and sent 20,000 American troops to Bosnia in a peacekeeping operation to enforce the Dayton Peace Accord. In all these cases, Clinton maintained that congressional approval was not required. When it came to the use of force, Clinton's behavior closely resembled that of his predecessors. In August 1998, however, his preference for presidential unilateralism as commander in chief was tested.

On August 7, 1998, the U.S. embassies in Nairobi and Dar es Salaam were bombed. The attackers detonated two truck bombs minutes apart. Two hundred sixty-three people were killed, including twelve Americans, and the embassies were severely damaged. These simultaneous strikes indicated the organizational capacity of the perpetrators, and in retrospect their global reach, while also illustrating the vulnerability of U.S. embassies abroad. Although the number of terrorist incidents against U.S. interests during the 1990s was smaller than in the 1980s, high-profile events in the United States and around the world captured the media and public's attention, heightening Americans' fear of attack. During Clinton's years in office, the world witnessed the bombing of the Alfred P. Murrah Federal Building in Oklahoma City, terrorist bombings in France in 1995, the release of deadly chemical substances in a Japanese subway by the Aum Shinruki group, as well as the events noted above in New York City,

Saudi Arabia, and Egypt.[17] The mysterious crash of TWA Flight 800 off the coast of New York shortly after takeoff on July 17, 1996, produced additional concerns among the American public that terrorists were targeting the United States. A month after the crash, with its cause still unknown, 29 percent of Americans indicated that they were worried that "a close relative or friend might be the victim of a terrorist attack."[18] Another poll conducted by CBS News found that 80 percent of Americans felt that the federal government should have "more authority" to fight terrorism.[19] Congress reacted in 1996 by passing new laws that gave additional power to the secretary of state and the secretary of the Treasury and other law enforcement officials to pursue terrorists more aggressively.[20] President Clinton also continued to push for additional security measures to improve airport security as the 1996 election drew closer.[21]

In mid-January 1997, opinion polls found that 32 percent of Americans viewed terrorism as one of the most important threats to world peace.[22] Later that month, 51 percent agreed that NATO should be used to combat terrorism,[23] and 63 percent in early April 1997 felt that U.S. anti-terrorism laws were too weak.[24] Thus, terrorism's place on the U.S. political agenda rose considerably as the Clinton administration entered its second term.

The Strikes on Bin Laden

Immediately after the bombings of the U.S. embassies, intelligence experts from the Federal Bureau of Investigation and the CIA rushed to the scene to determine responsibility for the attacks. In cooperation with the Kenyan and Tanzanian governments, they and other U.S. intelligence specialists examined the evidence.[25] Meanwhile, another group of experts from the CIA, National Security Agency (NSA), Defense Intelligence Agency, and other executive offices met at the White House to sift through the available information.[26] Senior administration officials soon began to argue that the evidence pointed to Bin Laden. Most of what the American public, foreign policy analysts, and journalists would initially know about the internal activities in the White House during the days before the U.S. military response came from a joint press conference by Secretary of State Madeleine Albright and National Security Adviser Samuel "Sandy" Berger, who answered a host of questions regarding the decision to use military force and the process by which this decision was made.[27]

On August 12 President Clinton flew home from a fund-raising trip to California to meet with his principal foreign policy advisers in the White House

Situation Room, where evidence was presented on Bin Laden's links to the attacks. Later that day, Chairman of the Joint Chiefs of Staff (JCS) Henry Shelton and Secretary of Defense William Cohen presented the president with preliminary plans in the event that a military response was approved. According to Berger, Secretary Albright was also being consulted as policy was being developed. Two days later, August 14, at another meeting at the White House, CIA director George Tenet presented his agency's analysis to the president. According to Berger, Tenet reached a "judgement about responsibility," indicating that Bin Laden was responsible for the attacks.[28] According to the CIA, there was evidence that Bin Laden was planning another attack on Americans, and that a large meeting of Bin Laden associates would take place in Afghanistan on August 20. At this meeting, Clinton gave tentative approval to a military response and authorized his senior military advisers to move forward with operational plans.[29]

The bombings and their aftermath occurred at a difficult time for Clinton. On August 17, he testified to the Office of the Independent Counsel and a grand jury by video conference, acknowledging that he had an extramarital relationship with former White House intern Monica Lewinsky. Later that evening in a national address, Clinton admitted that he had "misled" the American people about his relationship with Lewinsky.[30] Opinion polls following Clinton's admission found that one-third of Americans felt the president was "too damaged" by the Lewinsky affair to stay in office, and nearly one-half felt that Clinton might have lied when he told the nation that he encouraged no others to perjure themselves in their grand jury testimonies.[31] Thus, Clinton had created for himself a serious credibility crisis with the American public.

After his address, Clinton and his family left for a vacation on Martha's Vineyard, but planning for the military strikes continued. On Wednesday, August 19, while on Martha's Vineyard, Clinton discussed the strikes with Vice President Al Gore. Senior congressional party leaders were also notified of the possible strikes. Throughout the day, Clinton spoke on four occasions by phone with National Security Adviser Berger, who was in Washington. In a call around 2:00 a.m. Thursday, Clinton gave approval for the strikes. Once the decision was made, Donald Kerrick, an air force brigadier general and National Security Council staffer, arrived at Martha's Vineyard on a 6:00 a.m. flight to be with Clinton when the strikes began.[32]

The strikes, which began on August 20 around 1:30 p.m. Eastern Standard Time, involved the launching of seventy-nine cruise missiles at targets in Afghanistan and Sudan from ships stationed in the Arabian and Red Seas. The targets included the al-Shifa pharmaceutical plant in Khartoum, which the United States alleged was a chemical weapons factory. Six other sites were struck simultaneously in Afghanistan. Secretary Cohen declared that al-Shifa was chosen because Bin Laden was heavily involved in Sudan's military-industrial complex and had an interest in acquiring chemical weapons.[33] The Pentagon added that Bin Laden had excellent relations with the Sudanese military and that the plant was heavily guarded by Sudanese soldiers. A senior intelligence official noted that the CIA had found empta, a chemical compound used only in the production of chemical weapons, near the plant.[34] In discussing the sites hit in Afghanistan, General Shelton said that one "base camp" was struck, which served as the headquarters for Bin Laden's organization. Other targets included a support camp, which served as a weapons storage facility, and four other weapons and tactical training camps.[35]

Approximately twenty-five minutes after the strikes took place, Clinton addressed the nation and provided four justifications for his actions. First, he announced that "convincing evidence" indicated Bin Laden's responsibility for the attacks on the embassies. Second, the president pointed to Bin Laden's long history of terrorist activities. Third, Clinton argued that "compelling information" suggested that Bin Laden was planning another attack against the United States. Fourth, he said that Bin Laden sought to acquire chemical weapons.[36] Due to the gravity of the situation, Clinton flew back to the White House to phone foreign leaders, speak with congressional leaders, and prepare for a more comprehensive address to the nation that same evening. In his second speech, Clinton expanded on Bin Laden's previous declarations and activities and said that his senior military advisers had given him a "unanimous recommendation" to go forward with the strikes.[37]

That evening, in response to a question from CNN talk show host Larry King, Secretary Albright reiterated that universal agreement existed among Clinton's senior foreign policy advisers in support of the attacks. "There's absolutely no disagreement about this," said the secretary.[38] Similar sentiments were expressed by White House Press Secretary Mike McCurry in his first briefing with the press, when he noted that the "president acted on a unanimous recommendation" from his national security advisers.[39] As the War Powers Resolution requires, Clinton sent letters to congressional leaders, notifying them of his actions within the forty-eight-hour time limit. He wrote that Article 51 of the United Nations Charter—which allows member states to exercise "self-defense"—as well as his powers as commander in chief justified his actions.[40]

The press asked if any analogies existed between the recently released movie *Wag the Dog* and Clinton's strikes. In the movie, an American president hires a marketing specialist to create a fictional war in an effort to boost support for him in an upcoming election. A war involving U.S. participation is then concocted in Albania, which in 1998 was considered remote to many Americans.[41] After the president uses force in *Wag the Dog*, his approval ratings receive a quick boost, which is usually what happens in actual cases of the president using force abroad or when the United States becomes involved in a foreign policy crisis; the American public "rallies around the flag."[42] Clinton officials responded vehemently with denials that any linkages existed between the president's domestic troubles and the strikes on Bin Laden.[43]

Consulting Congress

National Security Adviser Berger noted "some degree of collective pride" in the secrecy that had been maintained throughout the entire planning and operational aspects of the strikes. The media learned of the attacks only after they had occurred.[44] As noted above, prior to the strikes the Clinton administration had contacted leading congressional Democrats and Republicans. The night before the attacks, Berger phoned Speaker of the House Newt Gingrich, R-Ga., and Senate majority leader Trent Lott, R-Miss., and presented them with the evidence implicating Bin Laden. Senate minority leader Tom Daschle, D-S.D., was phoned the morning of the bombing before the strikes occurred and were made public. Berger also attempted to call House minority leader Richard Gephardt, D-Mo., but Gephardt was traveling in France and was unable to establish a secured phone, so Berger could not speak directly with him; instead, Gephardt's staff was notified. Clinton also phoned the leaders, with the exception of Gephardt, as he flew back to Washington to deliver his second address to the nation.[45] Some reports contend that Gingrich had been consulted and was privy to intelligence on Bin Laden before Berger's first phone calls were made.[46]

In their press briefings, Berger and McCurry both stressed the "consultation" that took place between the president and Congress. McCurry specifically noted that all requirements of the War Powers Resolution had been met by the president.[47] Clinton's actions were markedly different from other presidents who have used force against "terrorist actors," such as when Reagan launched missiles against Libya and Carter attempted to rescue the hostages in Iran. In the aftermath of Clinton's use of force against Bin Laden, there were no complaints about violations of the War Powers Resolution or Congress's war-making powers. Congress gave essentially universal support to the president on constitutional grounds.

In addition to its constitutional backing, Congress also provided broad political support to Clinton. The vast majority of members, including nearly all of Clinton's harshest critics in the Republican Party, stood behind the president, including House majority leader Dick Armey of Texas and House minority whip Tom DeLay of Texas, who had frequently displayed profound partisan differences with the president. Senator Lott called the strikes "appropriate and just."[48] To help solidify support for the president, Speaker Gingrich made a conference call to senior Republicans, urging them not to criticize Clinton. Gingrich also delegated one of his closest Washington political consultants, Rich Galen, to contact all major conservative media critics of the president, urging them not to negatively spin the issue.[49]

Among Republicans in the Senate, two notable exceptions existed. Sens. Dan Coats of Indiana and Arlen Specter of Pennsylvania suggested that the president might be using the military to divert the public's attention from his considerable domestic political troubles with Monica Lewinsky. Recognizing that Coats and Specter posed a political threat to the administration, senior administration officials immediately began briefing in closed meetings all members of Congress who sought further information on the decision to bomb. Hours after their initial criticism, Coats and Specter had rethought their position and sided with the president. On August 21, only one day after the attack, Coats noted, "There does seem to be credible evidence to suggest that targeting an Usama Bin Laden terrorist training site was necessary."[50]

Like Congress, the public approved overwhelmingly of the attacks. A poll conducted by CNN found that 66 percent of the American public favored the strikes,[51] as a USA Today poll also found, while a Los Angeles Times poll found that 75 percent of Americans approved of the action.[52] Thus, Clinton faced almost no domestic criticism for the strikes.

International Response

As president, Bill Clinton frequently sought multilateral approval for major uses of force and deployments abroad. In the case of Bin Laden, however, the strikes were launched unilaterally and without seeking prior approval from the UN Security Council or NATO. Because U.S. forces fired on Afghanistan from the Arabian Sea, which entailed using Pakistan's airspace, the administration sent the air force's Gen. Joe Ralston, vice chairman of the Joint Chiefs of Staff, to meet with Pakistani military leaders prior to the attacks.[53] After leaving

Martha's Vineyard, the president did phone leaders around the world to request their support.[54]

A number of states quickly condemned the attacks. Of course, Afghanistan and Sudan were the first to denounce the administration's actions. In 1996, the United States had recalled its diplomatic corps from Khartoum for fear of terrorist strikes against Americans.[55] Ninety percent of Afghanistan was controlled by the Taliban, an Islamist group that had come to power in 1996 and had no formal diplomatic relations with the United States.[56] The Sudanese and Afghan complaints were soon followed by those of Iran, Iraq, Libya, and Yemen—all states whose diplomatic relations with the United States could best be characterized as "poor" (or virtually nonexistent).[57] Sudan maintained that the pharmaceutical plant targeted by the United States was a legitimate business and had no links to Bin Laden.

The twenty-two-member Arab League, of which Sudan is a member, also rebuked the United States for its military aggression against Sudan and for the attack's potentially destabilizing effect on the region. Outside the league forum, however, many of these states were much more reserved in their sentiments. For example, Egypt initially withheld public judgment on the strikes, and later, without openly criticizing the United States, spoke about the need to limit terrorism and suggested that the matter of the bombings be turned over to the United Nations for investigation. Syria condemned the United States for the strikes, but also denounced those who attacked the U.S. embassies. Saudi Arabia and Jordan were also noticeably restrained in their response to Clinton's actions.[58]

Most states in the Western world offered speedy and unconditional support for the U.S. action. France, Germany, and the United Kingdom, among others, stood beside the United States. Russian president Boris Yeltsin indicated his displeasure about being left out of consultations by the United States during the decision-making process but did not appear to be concerned about the actual strikes.[59] According to U.S. sources, China, through Foreign Ministry spokesman Zhu Bangzao, also signaled early support, but later criticized the administration for its actions in a press release.[60] China never verbally objected to the attack and was slow to respond to its spokesman's earlier apparent misstatement. At the United Nations, Sudan called for an international investigation of the attack on al-Shifa, but other than tentative backing from the Arab world, it received only limited support in the General Assembly. In the Arab League, Bahrain had criticized the United State for its actions, despite its generally good diplomatic relations with Washington. From its rotating seat in the Security Council, however, Bahrain proved hesitant to push forward with an investigation.[61]

Raising Questions

Although Clinton had the backing of Congress and the American public for the strikes against targets in Afghanistan and Sudan, in the days and months following the attacks journalists and others began to raise questions about the intelligence used to justify the action in Sudan. In response, Clinton administration officials in off-the-record interviews began suggesting that the Iraqi chemical weapons program had close ties to the Sudanese government and al-Shifa. In background discussions, intelligence officials suggested that Iraqi scientists were assisting Sudan in developing the nerve gas VX, of which empta is a key ingredient. The plant was already being investigated by the CIA and NSA before the August attacks on the U.S. embassies and had emerged as a source of serious concern for U.S. officials. Emad al-Ani, an Iraqi weapons specialist, was specifically noted as one individual whose links with the plant were strong.[62] A number of scientists who worked for al-Ani had attended the grand opening of the plant in 1996. Other pharmaceutical plants in Sudan had been frequently visited by Iraqi scientists.

Other intelligence that quietly surfaced subjected the Clinton administration to additional scrutiny. On August 29, the *New York Times* reported that the CIA's intelligence on al-Shifa may have been flawed, and at minimum incomplete. It was unclear whether the agency had reported to the president that al-Shifa had a pharmaceutical contract with the United Nations and was Sudan's largest producer of medicines. Moreover, the report suggested that the plant was not the tightly guarded facility described by Pentagon officials in the hours immediately following the strike. While journalists had begun exposing some of the controversial aspects of the intelligence gathered by the CIA, defenders of the strike continued to maintain that al-Shifa was a legitimate target and that even with questionable evidence it still would have been targeted.[63] The questions raised, however, were convincing enough for former president Carter to call for an investigation of the plant and the United States' decision to target it.[64]

The last major challenge in 1998 to the administration's actions again came from the *New York Times*. Reporters Tim Weiner and James Risen reiterated concerns about Bin Laden's precarious connection to al-Shifa and raised further questions about U.S. policy toward Sudan, which had been a major source of disagreement among Clinton officials during the preceding two years.[65] In 1996, the CIA pulled all its operatives from the country after concluding that its Sudanese informants had been supplying false information. The agents' withdrawal left the United States without any intelligence in Sudan. Some administration officials suggested that the information gathered on al-Shifa may have been outdated or simply wrong. Previously, tensions had risen over information passed along in 1995 from CIA informants who warned that Sudanese terrorists were planning an assassination on then-national security adviser Anthony Lake. The CIA's source for this information disappeared. Yet, in response, Lake had to move into the Blair House, the vice president's residence, and to other undisclosed locations to protect himself. Weiner and Risen contend that this information, coupled with earlier flawed intelligence, created a "climate of fear" among National Security Council staffers when it came to Sudan.

In 1996 Secretary Albright had referred to Sudan as a "viper's nest of terrorists."[66] The recall of U.S. embassy staff in 1996 produced considerable debate within the State Department about the appropriateness of such an action. Some preferred to isolate Sudan, while others continued to lobby for engagement. Thus, the journalists maintained, it was inference—not conclusive data—about al-Shifa and Bin Laden, coupled with internal disagreements over how to best deal with Sudan, that informed the Clinton administration's policy. The New York Times report prompted Congressman Edward Whitfield, R-Ky., to call for an investigation of the decision to strike al-Shifa, but no other members of Congress sought further enquiry.[67] The vast majority of members of Congress busied themselves with other issues—debate over whether to impeach Clinton for actions concerning the Lewinsky affair and congressional midterm elections, which were only two and a half months away. Many members had campaigns to conduct and constituents to see.

For the next year, questions about al-Shifa disappeared from the political map, but further concerns about the plant were raised in a front-page article by James Risen in the New York Times on October 27, 1999. Although a number of off-the-record interviews were again cited to confirm the differences among Clinton administration officials, this report provided names and specifically expressed concerns, which added credibility to its analysis. The CIA maintained that in 1995 Bin Laden had gained approval from Sudan to develop chemical weapons. In 1997, the al-Shifa plant surfaced as a site with which Bin Laden might have connections. That same year, the CIA obtained Sudanese soil samples taken from near the plant, which contained 2.5 times the normal amount of empta. The samples, however, were taken approximately sixty feet from the plant and from across the access road to the facility, on land that was unlikely to be owned by al-Shifa. Risen reported that in the month prior to the embassy attacks, the CIA believed that more information was needed before conclusive links could be drawn between Bin Laden and the plant.[68] On August 4, 1998, an additional CIA report was presented to the administration, indicating that Bin Laden might be planning a chemical weapons attack. When the State Department's Bureau of Intelligence and Research (INR) learned of the report, doubts about its content were raised, as well as concerns about the validity of the soil samples.[69]

Risen also reported that during the planning sessions on how and where to strike Bin Laden after the embassy attack, CIA director Tenet told senior national security advisers that Bin Laden's relationship to al-Shifa was only inferential, and that the CIA was still working to firmly establish a link. National Security Adviser Berger continued to deny that any disagreement existed over Bin Laden's connection to al-Shifa but did admit that significant "geopolitical" differences existed about where to strike. Berger may have been alluding to concerns expressed by General Shelton and the Joint Chiefs of Staff. On August 19, it was determined that two sites in Sudan, al-Shifa and a tannery, would be included on the target list. According to Risen, Shelton protested the inclusion of the tannery because of risks to civilians and because it had no association with chemical weapons. When he proved unable to convince other senior officials to eliminate the tannery from the list, Shelton expressed his concerns to the Joint Chiefs of Staff. The JCS supported their chairman. Shelton then phoned the White House to reiterate the military's opposition to striking the tannery, which was apparently enough to make Clinton change his mind.[70]

Risen also pointed to a meeting, among NSC staffers on the evening before the strikes, in which there was apparently opposition to striking al-Shifa. Richard Clarke, an NSC official, had called in NSC staff to help prepare the "paperwork" for the planned strikes. At the meeting, a number of the staff expressed surprise that al-Shifa was to be hit. Clarke, however, denied that any such discussions took place, although Risen's sources indicated otherwise.[71] After the strikes, INR expressed concerns about the intelligence on al-Shifa and asked Assistant Secretary of State Phyllis Oakley if it could proceed with its own investigation. Oakely relayed these concerns to Undersecretary of State Thomas Pickering, who told her that no such report was necessary. Secretary Albright likewise added her opinion that no further review was needed. Oakley relayed the decisions, which were followed. Meanwhile, according to Risen, some CIA analysts were asking the same questions as INR.[72]

A piece of evidence creating more skepticism was the United States' dealings with Salah Idris, the owner of al-Shifa. The CIA maintained that information gathered after the strike indicated that Idris had financial connections to Islamic Jihad, a group affiliated with Bin Laden. At the time of the strike, however, CIA officials had said that they did not know that Idris owned the plant. The Treasury Department froze $24 million of Idris's assets in Bank of America branches worldwide after the strike, but after Idris filed suit against the United States, Treasury released his holdings. Had hard evidence existed connecting Idris to Bin Laden or Islamic Jihad, it is doubtful that the United States would have released his assets.

James Risen found numerous reasons to question the Clinton administration's decision to strike al-Shifa, yet Congress remained silent. Risen indicates that the small group of officials who made the decision to strike al-Shifa was convinced that the circumstantial evidence still pointed conclusively to Bin Laden. The doubts expressed by midlevel administration officials were not convincing to senior Clinton officials, notably CIA director Tenet and Secretary of State Albright, especially with evidence suggesting that another attack seemed possible.

The Jihad Continues

In November 1998, approximately two and a half months after the strikes against Sudan and Afghanistan, a federal grand jury indicted Bin Laden on 224 counts of conspiracy to commit murder and charged him and his top military commander with orchestrating the bombings of the U.S. embassies. The United States also issued a $5 million reward for information leading to Bin Laden's arrest.[73] The United States, believing that Bin Laden remained in Afghanistan, put pressure on the Taliban to turn him over.[74] Their efforts failed, and Bin Laden remained at large throughout the Clinton presidency. On October 21, 2000, a former sergeant in the U.S. Army stated in a federal district court in New York City that he had provided information to Bin Laden on the U.S. embassy in Kenya in 1993 and 1994 and that Bin Laden had specifically indicated where a bomb could be placed.[75]

As 2000 had approached, Bin Laden was suspected of planning a number of attacks against U.S. citizens. According to reports, Bin Laden's associates were involved in terrorist activities to be carried out amid New Year celebrations, but they were foiled when they were uncovered by U.S. and Jordanian intelligence officials.[76] More recently, Bin Laden has been suspected of involvement in the attack on the USS *Cole*. On October 12, 2000, as the destroyer was refueling in the Yemeni port of Aden, a small boat pulled alongside it and two men in the boat on a suicide mission detonated explosives that killed seventeen Americans and injured thirty-nine others. In the days following the attack intelligence experts maintained that the Egyptian Islamic Jihad, a group that had been associated with al-Qa'ida, might have been responsible. Yemeni president Ali Abdallah Salih claimed initially that the attackers were Afghans who had fought in the war against Soviet occupation in the 1980s. Given Bin Laden's support of the mujahidin, his alledged connections to the Islamic Jihad, and his familial ties to Yemen, Bin Laden became a suspect.[77] Whether Bin Laden was responsible for the attack on the *Cole* remains unknown. Many analysts maintained that his network remained quite functional, despite the various policy approaches employed by the Clinton administration to limit his influence.

Conclusion: Deference to the President

The foreign policy–making process prior to the strikes on Usama Bin Laden demonstrates that the post–cold war era brought little change in how the United States deals militarily with terrorist challenges. President Clinton, after consulting with his closest security advisers, made the decision alone to use force against Bin Laden. Only a few government actors were involved in the decision-making process, and no non-governmental players played a role. In fact, Clinton's closest advisers went to great lengths to keep information from the public about the strikes. The process was not "pluralistic," as in other cases in this book.

Clinton's level of consultation with Congress prior to the strikes was somewhat different from past presidents when they chose to use military force against perceived terrorist threats. Clinton reached out to Speaker Gingrich, and to a lesser extent to Senate majority leader Lott, prior to the strikes to discuss the security issues surrounding Bin Laden. Yet, akin to cold war politics, Congress largely backed Clinton, with very little criticism of the president even though he was acting during precarious domestic political conditions. With the perceived threat of terrorism so high on the U.S. and international agenda, few politicians and foreign leaders questioned the missile strikes.

While the decision-making process produced little controversy among members of Congress, and the strikes themselves were politically popular, the media coverage in the aftermath raised questions about the targets chosen. Some administration officials quietly questioned the wisdom of striking the al-Shifa plant. Other administration officials and reporters implied that a serious mistake had been made in targeting the plant. Despite these reports, Congress did little to address these concerns. Clearly, Congress showed little interest in "checking" the president when it came to using force against terrorists, even if a serious mistake seemed possible. Despite the strikes, Bin Laden's influence appears unabated. He is alive and well, and it appears probable that he has been involved in other attacks since August 1998. Perhaps the 1998 military actions prevented the "second strike" that Clinton alluded to in his first address to the nation. That response, however, did not eliminate Bin Laden as a long-term threat to the United States.

Notes

1. Much of the information on Bin Laden's biography comes from Tim Weiner, "U.S. Hard Put to Find Proof Bin Laden Directed Attacks," *New York Times,* April 13, 1999, A1.

2. The current ruling family of Saudi Arabia, the Al Sauds, took power in 1902, when King Abd al-Aziz enlisted the support of local Wahhabis—believers in a strict, conservative interpretation of Islam—in taking control of its major city, Riyadh, later the birthplace of Bin Laden. His father came from Hadhramaut, an eastern province of Yemen known for its intense Wahhabism. See Michael C. Hudson, *Arab Politics: The Search for Legitimacy* (New Haven: Yale University Press, 1977), 171; John F. Burns, "Remote Yemen May Be Key to Terrorist's Past and Future," *New York Times,* November 5, 2000.

3. See Vernon Loeb, "A Global, Pan-Islamic Network; Terrorism Entrepreneur Unifies Groups Financially, Politically," *New York Times,* August 23, 1998, A1.

4. The mostly substantive reports researched by the *Washington Post* and *New York Times* provide different conclusions on the presence of terrorist training sites in Sudan. See Weiner, "U.S. Hard Put," and Loeb, "A Global, Pan-Islamic Network." Loeb states that Bin Laden supported terrorist camps in northern Sudan "for radicals from Egypt, Algeria, and Tunisia, as well as Palestinians."

5. Weiner, "U.S. Hard Put."

6. Loeb, "A Global, Pan-Islamic Network."

7. "Saudi Militant Is Said to Urge Forced Ouster of U.S. Troops," *New York Times,* August 31, 1996, A2.

8. See Loeb, "A Global, Pan-Islamic Network."

9. For a reprint and analysis of the declaration, see Magnus Ranstorp, "Interpreting the Broader Context and Meaning of Bin-Laden's Fatwa," *Studies in Conflict and Terrorism* 21 (1998): 321–330. See also Bernard Lewis, "License to Kill: Usama bin Laden's Declaration of Jihad," *Foreign Affairs* (November/December 1998): 14–19.

10. For example, see David Gray Adler, "The Constitution and Presidential Warmaking," *Political Science Quarterly* 103 (1988): 1–36; and Charles A. Lofgren, "War-Making under the Constitution: The Original Understanding," *Yale Law Journal* 81 (1972).

11. Francis D. Wormuth and Edwin B. Firmage, *To Chain the Dog of War* (Urbana: University of Illinois Press, 1989).

12. Louis Fisher, *Presidential War Power* (Lawrence: University Press of Kansas, 1995).

13. PL 93–148.

14. Michael J. Glennon, "Too Far Apart: The War Powers Resolution," *University of Miami Law Review* 50 (1995): 17–31; Edward Keynes, "The War Powers Resolution: A Bad Idea Whose Time Has Come and Gone," *University of Toledo Law Review* 23 (1992): 343–362.

15. Robert A. Strong, *Working in the World* (Baton Rouge: Louisiana State University Press, 2000), chap. 9. The absence of consultation *within* the administration prompted Secretary of State Cyrus Vance to resign.

16. Pat Towell, "After Raid on Libya, New Questions on the Hill," *Congressional Quarterly Weekly Report,* April 19, 1986, 838.

17. Walter Enders and Todd Sandler, "Transnational Terrorism in the Post–Cold War Era," *International Studies Quarterly* 43 (1999): 145.

18. Question 003, Roper Center, University of Connecticut, Public Opinion Online, August 5, 1996, Lexis-Nexis.

19. Question 008, Roper Center, University of Connecticut, Public Opinion Online, July 29, 1996, Lexis-Nexis.

20. PL 104-132. See also Holly Idelson, "Terrorism Bill Is Headed to President's Desk," *Congressional Quarterly Weekly Report,* April 20, 1996, 1044.

21. Peter Baker, "President Takes on Terrorism; Congress Challenged to Improve Package," *Washington Post,* September 10, 1996, A10.

22. Question 011, Roper Center, University of Connecticut, Public Opinion Online, January 18, 1997, Lexis-Nexis.

23. Question 006, Roper Center, University of Connecticut, Public Opinion Online, January 24, 1997, Lexis-Nexis.

24. Question 055, Roper Center, University of Connecticut, Public Opinion Online, April 11, 1997, Lexis-Nexis.

25. David L. Marcus and Andrea Useem, "Death Toll in Blasts Rises to 148," *Boston Globe,* August 9, 1998, A1.

26. Marc Lacey, "The U.S. Embassy Bombings," *Los Angeles Times,* August 9, 1998, A18.

27. "Press Briefing on U.S. Strikes in Sudan and Afghanistan," August 20, 1998, http://secretary.state.gov/www/statements/1998/.

28. Ibid.

29. Ibid.

30. Bill Clinton, "Address to the Nation on Testimony before the Independent Counsel's Grand Jury," *Public Papers of the Presidents,* August 17, 1998, 1638; James Bennet, "Testing of a President: The Overview," *New York Times,* August 18, 1998, A1.

31. Douglas Turner, "Credibility of President Is in Crisis, Polls Show," *Buffalo News,* August 19, 1998, 1A.

32. "Press Briefing on U.S. Strikes in Sudan and Afghanistan," August 20, 1998.

33. DefenseLINK News, DoD News Briefing, August 20, 1998, http://www.defenselink.mil/news/Aug1998/t08201998_t820brfg.html.

34. DefenseLINK News, Background Briefing, "Terrorist Camp Strikes," August 20, 1998, http://www.defenselink.mil/news/Aug1998/x08201998x820bomb.html.

35. DoD News Briefing, August 20, 1998.

36. Bill Clinton, "Remarks on Departure for Washington, DC, from Martha's Vineyard, Massachusetts," *Public Papers of the Presidents,* August 20, 1998, 1642.

37. Bill Clinton, "Address to the Nation on Military Action against Terrorist Sites in Afghanistan and Sudan," *Public Papers of the Presidents,* August 20, 1998, 1643.

38. Interview on CNN, *Larry King Live,* August 20, 1998, http://secretary.state.gov/www/statements/1998.

39. "Holds News Briefing Aboard Air Force One; Air Force in Route to Washington," FDCH Political Transcripts, August 20, 1998, Lexis-Nexis, transcripts file.

40. Bill Clinton, "Letter to Congressional Leaders Reporting on Military Action against Terrorist Sites in Afghanistan and Sudan," *Public Papers of the Presidents,* August 21, 1998, 1650–1651.

41. The research on such "diversionary military actions" by U.S. presidents is mixed at best, with a number of analysts concluding that no evidence indicates that presidents act in this manner. See Joanne Gowa, "Politics at the Water's Edge: Parties, Voters, and the Use of Force Abroad," *International Organization* 52 (1998): 307–324; James Meernik, "The Myth of the Diversionary Use of Force by American Presidents," *Political Research Quarterly* 49 (1996): 573.

42. Patrick James and Jean Sebastien Rioux, "International Crises and Linkage Politics: The Experiences of the United States, 1953–1994," *Political Research Quarterly* 51 (1998): 781–812; John T. Rourke, Ralph Carter, and Mark A. Boyer, *Making American Foreign Policy* (Madison, Wis.: Brown and Benchmark, 1996), 193.

43. For example, see Secretary Albright's statements, "Interview on NBC-TV *Today* Show with Katie Couric," August 21, 1998, http://secretary.state.gov/www/statements/1998; Bruce Westbrook, "War or a 'Wag'?" *Houston Chronicle,* August 25, 1998, 1; Marcella Bombardieri, "Wagging Dog? Fine, Some Say," *Boston Globe,* August 22, 1998, A8.

44. "Press Briefing on U.S. Strikes in Sudan and Afghanistan," August 20, 1998.

45. Ibid.

46. Mike McCurry, Office of the Press Secretary, "Remarks in Gaggle," August 20, 1998; see also Chuck McCutcheon, "Lawmakers Back Missile Strikes Despite a Bit of GOP Skepticism," *CQ Weekly,* August 22, 1998, 2289.

47. See McCurry, "Remarks in Gaggle."

48. Quoted in Guy Gugliotta and Juliet Eilperin, "Tough Response Appeals to Critics of President; Several Question Clinton's Timing of Raids," *Washington Post,* August 21, 1998, A17.

49. Ibid. See also Ryan Hendrickson, "American War Powers and Terrorists: The Case of Usama Bin Laden," *Studies in Conflict and Terrorism* 23 (2000): 161–174.

50. Quoted in Steven Lee Meyers, "President Swears to Use 'All Tools' against Terrorism," *New York Times,* August 23, 1998, 1.

51. Brian McGrory, "US Calls Terrorists' Losses Significant," *Boston Globe,* August 22, 1998, A1.

52. Bill Nichols, "U.S. Strikes Back: Hits Sudan, Afghanistan," *USA Today,* August 21, 1998, 1A; Mark Z. Barabak, "The Time Poll," *Los Angeles Times,* August 23, 1998, A1.

53. James W. Crawley, "U.S. Attacks on Bin Laden Detailed," *San Diego Union-Tribune,* August 20, 1999, A1.

54. "Press Briefing on U.S. Strikes in Sudan and Afghanistan," August 20, 1998.

55. Thomas Lippman and John M. Goshko, "U.S. Begins to Withdraw Personnel from Sudan," *Washington Post,* February 1, 1996, A4.

56. Ahmed Rashid, *Taliban: Militant Islam, Oil and Fundamentalism in Central Asia* (New Haven: Yale University Press, 2000).

57. John Daniszewski and Dexter Filkins, "Attack on Terrorism," *Los Angeles Times,* August 22, 1998, A19; Howard Schneider, "Radical States Assail Act," *Washington Post,* August 22, 1998, A22.

58. Elizabeth Bryant, "Targeting Terrorism," *Houston Chronicle*, August 22, 1998, A19.

59. Tim Butcher and Hugh Davies, "US Strike Was 'First Blow in War of Future,'" *Daily Telegraph*, August 22, 1998, 1.

60. Frank Ching, "China Feels Let Down by US," *Australasian Business Intelligence*, September 24, 1998, 38.

61. Craig Turner and Doyle McManus, "Sudan Gets Little Support for a U.N. Probe of U.S. Attack," *Los Angeles Times*, August 25, 1998, A6.

62. Steven Lee Meyers, "U.S. Says Iraq Aided Production of Chemical Weapons in Sudan," *New York Times*, August 25, 1998, A1; for the National Security Agency's role in gathering the intelligence on Iraq, see John Diamond, "U.S. Links Sudan Plant to Iraq," *Chicago Sun-Times*, August 26, 1998, 40.

63. Tim Weiner and Steven Lee Meyers, "Flaws in U.S. Account Raise Questions on Strike in Sudan," *New York Times*, August 29, 1998, A1.

64. "Carter Urges Inquiry into U.S. Raid on Sudan," *New York Times*, September 18, 1998, A4.

65. Tim Weiner and James Risen, "Decision to Strike Factory in Sudan Based on Surmise Inferred from Evidence," *New York Times*, September 21, 1998, A1.

66. Ibid.

67. *Congressional Record*, September 23, 1998, H8508.

68. James Risen, "Question of Evidence: A Special Report," *New York Times*, October 27, 1999, A1. See also Vernon Loeb, "Role of Targeted Plant in Making Nerve Gas Was Questioned by CIA," *Buffalo News*, August 21, 1999, 5A.

69. Risen, "Question of Evidence."

70. Ibid.

71. Ibid.

72. Ibid.

73. John J. Goldman and Ronald J. Ostrow, "U.S. Indicts Terror Suspect Bin Laden," *Los Angeles Times*, November 5, 1998, A1.

74. John J. Goldman, "U.S. Seeks Sanctions to Force Taliban to Expel Bin Laden," *Los Angeles Times*, October 7, 1999, A9.

75. Benjamin Weiser, "Bin Laden Linked to Embassy Blast by an Ex-Soldier," *New York Times*, October 21, 2000, A1. The sergeant, Alia A. Mohamed, pled guilty to participating in a terrorist conspiracy against the United States.

76. Stephen Kinzer, "Jordan Links Terrorist Plot to Bin Laden," *New York Times*, February 4, 2000, A4; David Storey, "U.S. Helped Foil Terrorists in 8 Countries, Berger Says," *San Diego Union-Tribune*, January 7, 2000, A8.

77. Alan Sipress and David A. Vise, "Cole Blast Probe Drawing Closer to Bin Laden," *Washington Post*, October 26, 2000, A1.

9 The V-22 Osprey: Pure Pork or Cutting-Edge Technology?

Christopher M. Jones

Before You Begin

1. What is the V-22 Osprey and why is it so controversial?

2. Why did the Office of the Secretary of Defense (OSD) try repeatedly to cancel the V-22 program?

3. Why did Congress restore V-22 funding each year?

4. Were congressional supporters of the program motivated by parochial priorities or substantive policy concerns?

5. Was OSD right to defy congressional authority?

6. What actors, interests, and strategies ensured the Osprey's survival?

7. Is the V-22 Osprey best characterized as a pork barrel program or critical cutting-edge technology?

8. Which institution of government is best equipped to make weapons procurement decisions?

Introduction: A Troubled Weapons Program

The beginning of the twenty-first century has been a difficult period for the V-22 Osprey, a tilt-rotor transport plane designated to replace the Marine Corps' aging helicopter fleet.[1] In April 2000, a crash of a MV-22 Osprey during a nighttime evaluation exercise killed all nineteen marines aboard. After an investigation revealed that the incident was the result of "human factors" rather than a design flaw or mechanical problem, the Marine Corps resumed flying its small squadron of Ospreys in June 2000.[2] Six months later, in December, another MV-22 crashed during a similar night training mission. All four crew members perished, and the marines' eight remaining Ospreys were grounded pending another probe. The December 2000 crash also delayed a decision on the V-22's full-rate production until the Pentagon's inspector general, an independent commission, and Congress complete program reviews sometime in 2001.[3]

These fatal crashes, however, were not the only bad news. In November 2000, the Pentagon's director of operational testing and evaluation had issued a report concluding that the plane "need[ed] further testing, seem[ed] unreliable and [was] costly to maintain."[4] Two months later, the marines were compelled to fire the commander of their Osprey squadron after it was disclosed that he had ordered subordinates to falsify maintenance records over a two-year period.[5] The officer's efforts to bolster the aircraft's performance rating prompted a separate criminal investigation of the V-22 program that encompassed the seizure of computers belonging to Marine Corps generals.[6] Then in February 2001, a report by the General Accounting Office (GAO) revealed that the marines had omitted and restricted operational tests in an effort to save money and move the project forward.[7] These events and the determination of the George W. Bush administration to review the program in light of other priorities have refocused attention on arguably the most controversial weapons system of the last two decades.

Over the course of its nineteen-year development and testing period, the Osprey has demonstrated a remarkable capacity to survive serious challenges and setbacks. Before the latest difficulties, the program had already endured the crashes of two prototypes, a fire in another model, the resignation of the chief test pilot, and the deaths of seven other crew members.[8] The project has also continued even though it has fallen years behind schedule and its scope (in projected units) has been drastically scaled back; the Pentagon's original plan to buy 913 planes has been trimmed to purchasing 458 Ospreys.[9] Remarkably the V-22 program has remained intact as its price tag has steadily risen. Between 1995 and 1998, the flyaway cost per unit jumped from $29 million to $39 million.[10] Today the Marine Corps puts the price tag at $44 million, while the GAO and other sources have reported that each aircraft will cost between $60 and $80 million.[11]

To illustrate how the Osprey has persevered in the face of such adversity, this chapter examines the period 1989 through 1992, when it confronted and ultimately survived its greatest challenge—four years of intense opposition from the Office of the Secretary of Defense (OSD). The program was initiated during President Ronald Reagan's defense buildup in the 1980s, and although the Clinton administration, 1993–2001, devoted less funding to the project, through a low-rate production commitment, than V-22 supporters preferred, it honored a campaign pledge to build the plane. The George Bush administration, 1989–1993, however, had tried repeatedly to cancel the Osprey. Each year Secretary of Defense Richard Cheney omitted money from the defense budget to develop the aircraft. Congress, the Marine Corps, and the primary contractors—the Boeing Company and Bell Helicopter Textron, Inc.—fought back jointly and effectively each year to allocate funding. This four-year battle stands as a powerful example of how difficult it is to reduce and restructure military spending in the post–cold war era. \

Background: Capability versus Cost

The Bush administration faced a dilemma when it came to office in 1989. There was intense pressure to cut the defense budget to reflect the changing realities in domestic and international politics. At the same time, there were a number of expensive weapons systems in development that stood to enhance U.S. military capability at the dawn of a new era. The V-22 was one such program.

A Revolutionary Plane

The V-22 Osprey, named for the diving bird of prey, is a cutting-edge transport plane designated to replace many of the U.S. armed services' aging helicopters. A special tilt-rotor design allows the odd-looking, futuristic aircraft to operate as a helicopter during takeoff and landing. Once airborne, its twin engines shift from a vertical to a horizontal position, allowing it to fly like a conventional turboprop airplane. The result is a machine that can fly twice as fast and twice as far as the military's Vietnam-era helicopters. The Osprey can carry twenty-four fully equipped combat troops internally or up to 15,000 pounds externally at a speed of more than 250 knots over a distance of 200 nautical miles. With less personnel and cargo, the Osprey's ferrying range extends 2,100 nautical miles, enabling it to fly independently to military bases, aircraft carriers, and "hot spots" throughout the world.[12] Although the navy and air force plan is to buy modified versions of the MV-22, for search and rescue, special warfare and operations, and fleet logistic support, the plane's main procurer will be the Marine Corps.

The Osprey's impressive capabilities are particularly well suited for the marines. As an amphibious expeditionary force, the marines are required to move rapidly to faraway places to perform a variety of duties. Moreover, the regional and non-traditional security threats of the post–cold war world require a more mobile and flexible military posture. In this environment, the V-22's capacity to self-deploy will enhance the marines' capacity to transport troops and equipment to distant combat zones. It will also facilitate quicker and more

The Battle over the V-22 Osprey

December 1982 The Department of the Navy officially launches the V-22 Osprey program.

April 1983 A preliminary V-22 design contract is awarded to Boeing and Bell Helicopter.

May 1986 The V-22 enters full-scale development.

March 1989 A V-22 prototype flies for the first time.

April 1989 President George Bush and congressional leaders reach a bipartisan budget summit agreement that reduces defense expenditures by $10 billion. Secretary of Defense Richard Cheney submits a FY 1990 defense budget that includes termination of the V-22.

November 1989 Congress overrides Cheney's cancellation of the V-22 and approves $255 million for research and development. An additional $330 million in unspent advanced procurement funding is released. A final decision on production is deferred, pending completion of a cost operational effectiveness analysis (COEA).

December 1989 The Office of the Secretary of Defense (OSD) orders the Department of the Navy to cancel all V-22 production contracts.

February 1990 Cheney submits a FY 1991 defense budget without a request for V-22 funding. He also proposes a deferral of 1989 funds, including $200 million for the V-22 program, and a transfer of funds from FY 1990 programs to pay for Bush administration priorities. The Tiltrotor Technology Coalition is established.

March 1990 The General Accounting Office rules against OSD's planned deferral of $200 million in FY 1989 funding.

June 1990 OSD releases a COEA study prepared by the Institute for Defense Analyses concluding that the V-22 Osprey is the most cost effective and capable option for the marines' medium-lift needs and the navy's search-and-rescue mission.

November 1990 Congress overrides Cheney and awards $403 million in V-22 funding, including $167 million for long-lead production. The Pentagon is ordered to manage the Osprey as an acquisition program.

February 1991 Cheney submits an FY 1992 defense budget without a request for V-22 funding. He also proposes a recision of previously appropriated money, but commits to completing the Osprey's development program with FY 1991 procurement allocations.

March 1991 Congress passes an FY 1991 "Dire Emergency" supplemental appropriations bill and orders OSD to release FY 1989 V-22 procurement funds.

June 1991 A V-22 prototype crashes in Delaware because of incorrect wiring. There are no casualties.

November 1991 Congress approves $790 million for the V-22: $625 million in FY 1992 funds and $165 million from prior-year accounts.

January 1992 Cheney submits an FY 1993 defense budget without a request for V-22 funding. OSD refuses to release FY 1992 V-22 funds. Cheney claims that the appropriations act makes it impossible for OSD to execute the law.

June 1992 The comptroller general concludes that OSD has illegally impounded the V-22's FY 1992 funding. OSD is ordered to obligate the funds or face court action.

July 1992 Congress accepts a Cheney compromise proposal that allows OSD to use most of the $790 million in FY 1992 funding and $755 million expected to be approved in FY 1993 to complete V-22 development. Some money is allocated to explore alternatives to the Osprey.

A V-22 prototype crashes in Virginia, killing all seven crew members. A subsequent investigation cites mechanical failure as the cause. The V-22's congressional supporters are angered by the Pentagon's efforts to change the plane's design requirements and performance standards.

August 1992 After a special hearing on the status of the V-22, the Bush administration drops its opposition to the Osprey.

October 1992 Vice President Dan Quayle visits Boeing's V-22 plant near Philadelphia to announce a $550 million engineering, manufacturing, and development contract.

November 1992 Congress awards $755 million in FY 1993 funding for the V-22.

More Recent Events

April 2000 An MV-22 Osprey crashes during a night operational evaluation exercise in Arizona, killing all nineteen marines aboard. The remaining nine Ospreys are grounded until June.

continued on the next page

continued from the previous page

November 2000   The Pentagon's director of operational testing and evaluation issues a report criticizing the Osprey's reliability and maintenance costs.

December 2000   A MV-22 Osprey crashes during a night training mission in North Carolina, killing all four marines aboard. The remaining eight Ospreys are grounded pending another probe. A decision on full-rate production of the V-22 is deferred until the marines, the Defense Department, and an independent commission conclude separate investigations sometime in 2001.

January 2001   The commander of the Marine Corps' Osprey squadron is fired after it is revealed that he ordered subordinates to falsify maintenance records over a two-year period.

effective responses to peacetime contingencies, such as the need to rescue hostages, strike at terrorists, or evacuate civilians in trouble spots.

A New Fiscal Environment

When the first V-22 prototype was rolled out in the fall of 1988 Marine Corps commandant Alfred M. Gray Jr. declared the plane his organization's "number one aviation priority."[13] In March 1989, Marine Corps officials testifying before the House Armed Services Committee reaffirmed the general's statement,[14] but

A V-22 Osprey in its takeoff and landing mode.

a month later the new secretary of defense, Richard Cheney, informed the marines that he intended to cancel the program.[15] The announcement came just weeks after the first flight of a V-22 production prototype.[16] Despite an appeal from the Marine Corps that included an offer to forego procurement of the M-1 tank,[17] Cheney submitted the Pentagon's FY 1990 budget to Congress without a request for V-22 funding.

The secretary's decision was not a complete surprise. The Bush transition team had held serious discussions in 1988 about postponing or eliminating major weapons programs.[18] The incoming administration's search for budget savings was driven by the reality that the massive defense spending of the Reagan era could not continue. After all, the Soviet threat was waning; the federal budget deficit was soaring; the president-elect had pledged "no new taxes"; and the Congress was eager to reduce overall defense spending. It was within this context that the new administration scrutinized several expensive weapons systems.

Once Bush took office, the pressure to make significant defense cuts intensified. In April 1989, the Republican president and leaders of the Democrat-controlled Congress convened a budget summit in an attempt to meet a legally mandated deficit reduction target. The subsequent bipartisan agreement led to a $10 billion reduction in the FY 1990 defense budget, which was $4 billion deeper than Cheney's original proposal. As a result, the FY 1990 defense budget fell from President Reagan's request for $305.6 billion to $295.6 billion.[19] Secretary Cheney decided to address this decline by ordering the navy "to absorb almost half of the $10 billion," with the major casualty being naval aviation.[20] As part of the Department of the Navy, the marines were affected in the worst possible way when the V-22 was placed at the top of the hit list.

Cheney's Decision

Executive branch opponents to the Osprey were not a new phenomenon. In fact, critics emerged shortly after the navy launched the program in 1982. The most consistent opposition came from Program Analysis and Evaluation (PA&E), the office within OSD responsible for monitoring the design and cost of weapons. Given its role and relative success throughout the 1970s, PA&E was unpopular with the service departments. To the delight of the services, PA&E's importance came to an abrupt end when the Reagan administration took control of the Pentagon. Seeing PA&E as an obstacle to the administration's massive defense buildup, including its plan for a 600-ship navy, Secretary of Defense Caspar Weinberger "muted its role, downgrading the office head's title from assistant secretary to office director. Moreover, his controversial decentralization of the Pentagon seriously reduced the influence of PA&E as well as that of other central offices."[21] When David S. C. Chu, the head of PA&E, argued that modified CH-53E and UH-60 helicopters could perform the same multiservice mission as the Osprey at half the cost, he was ignored.[22]

PA&E and its quest to eliminate the V-22 program were given new life when Cheney became secretary of defense in March 1989. Cheney assumed the post belatedly, after the first nominee, Sen. John Tower, R-Texas, failed to win Senate confirmation. Tower, who was from one of the two states where the Osprey was being built, was a major supporter of the plane. Faced with the challenge of reducing the FY 1990 defense budget by $10 billion, Cheney turned to PA&E for assistance. Chu, who had served in the Congressional Budget Office when Cheney was a representative from Wyoming, happily obliged. It was an opportunity for PA&E to regain its influence and strike back at the services, which in its view were spending too much on the wrong types of weapons.

Chu had opposed the V-22 since 1983, when it was awarded a preliminary design contract. Thus it came as little surprise that the plane was one of the first weapons systems he advised Cheney to cut. Specifically, Chu and his colleagues "recommended that the Marines substitute a 950-aircraft mix of CH-53 and UH-60 [helicopters] for 552 V-22s."[23] The Marine Corps was quick to point out that Chu's plan was more expensive than the purchase of 552 V-22s, to which Chu responded by changing his proposal to 650 helicopters.[24] This adjustment brought the cost below the V-22 package, but "these numbers were inadequate to lift the Marines and tonnage required."[25] After a number of confrontations with the Marine Corps over costs and military requirements, Chu softened his position and "recommended a one-year slip in the program."[26]

Constrained by the budget summit agreement and President Bush's preferred weapons projects—for example, the B-2 Stealth bomber and Strategic Defense Initiative (SDI)—Cheney saw no alternative. He therefore acted on Chu's earlier advice and cancelled the V-22. On April 25, 1989, the secretary told the House Armed Services Committee, "[I] cannot justify spending the amount of money . . . proposed when we are just getting ready to move into procurement on the V-22 to perform a very narrow mission I think can be performed . . . by using helicopters."[27]

Cheney in his testimony cited three points that OSD would repeatedly state in its efforts to kill the V-22 project. First, the V-22's primary mission, ship-to-shore transport, could be accomplished by less expensive helicopters. Second, although the Osprey had greater speed and range than helicopters, it would not add much to the Marine Corps' capacity to fight. Cheney argued, as an example, that the Marines would rarely, if ever, be asked to conduct operations like the 1980 hostage rescue mission in Iran, which proponents of the plane said the V-22 was well-suited to perform.[28] Third, the army, for reasons of cost and narrow mission applicability, had decided in 1987 to leave the program, so the V-22 would not be the multiservice, multimission aircraft it was intended to be.

Given who was to use the Osprey and what it was to be used for, OSD believed the program was not cost effective. At no time between 1989 and 1992 did the Pentagon's civilian leadership dispute the marines' contention that their helicopters needed to be replaced. Similarly, there was no criticism of the Osprey's capabilities or the tilt-rotor concept. Instead OSD consistently approached the development of the V-22 from the perspective of affordability.

Cheney's Opposition

By canceling the Osprey in April 1989, Cheney provoked a confrontation with a powerful group of political actors. Although some weapons systems Cheney cut, for example, the F-14D Tomcat fighter plane, did not have broad support, the V-22 was a popular program backed by an impressive number of lawmakers, a committed armed service, and two politically adept contractors.

Support for the plane within the House and Senate was not unanimous, but it was pervasive. Two letters sent to President Bush regarding the V-22, one from 218 representatives and another signed by 40 senators,[29] were indications of the program's broad bipartisan appeal. Since the Osprey was being built in Texas and Pennsylvania, the senators and large congressional delegations from these states were firmly behind the program. Two of the strongest advocates were Reps. Pete Geren, D-Texas, and Curt Weldon, R-Pa., each of whom had a V-22 assembly plant in his district. Weldon, a member of the Armed Services Committee, was a particularly fierce proponent of the plane. The contractors estimated that a production rate of three to four Ospreys a month would employ between 2,000 and 3,000 people at each of the two production facilities.[30] In addition to the two primary contractors, Bell Helicopter and Boeing, there were an estimated 1,800 to 2,000 subcontractors.[31] As of October 1994, nearly $353 million in subcontracts had been distributed to businesses in forty-two states and 258 congressional districts. Twenty-five of the forty-two states had purchase orders or letter contracts in excess of $500,000.[32] The contractors calculated that 10,000 jobs were tied to V-22 subcontracts.[33]

Employment was not the only constituent benefit that motivated proponents of the V-22. Sen. Ted Stevens, R-Alaska, whose state had no jobs tied to the Osprey, declared upon learning of Cheney's decision, "I don't intend to vote for a [defense] bill that doesn't have V-22 money in it."[34] Stevens, a powerful member of the Senate Appropriations Committee, argued that the commercial variants of the Osprey would revolutionize civil aviation. While some lawmakers saw tilt-rotor aircraft as a way to relieve congestion at metropolitan airports and better protect the environment, Stevens was most interested in how the Osprey's considerable speed and range would make remote areas of the country more accessible.[35] Thus the V-22 was championed as a national asset, capable of easing two transportation problems without the construction of new runways and airports.

The Osprey's congressional allies also included lawmakers who saw civilian spin-offs as a way for the U.S. aerospace industry to remain competitive in the international marketplace.[36] This issue even won over "deficit hawks," such as Rep. John Kasich, R-Ohio, and Sen. Warren Rudman, R-N.H.[37] Some senators and representatives also claimed that the V-22 could aid national security and law enforcement agencies with drug interdiction.[38] Still others were receptive to the military rationale behind the plane and reinforced the marines' view of the program.[39] This group of lawmakers was composed of defense hawks and members of the formidable "Green Machine"—a group of senators and representatives who were once active-duty marines. For example, Sen. John Glenn, D-Ohio, a retired colonel, astronaut, and influential member of the Armed Services Committee, was a major supporter of the Osprey. In fact, he joined Senator Stevens in sponsoring a sense of the Senate resolution on behalf of the V-22 before the Bush administration even reached a final decision in 1989.[40] Another retired marine, Rep. Jack Murtha, D-Pa., was chairman of the Appropriations Defense Subcommittee and one of the Marine Corps' staunchest congressional supporters.

The Marine Corps, with this type of backing and a reputation on Capitol Hill for being "conservative, realistic, and above all, honest in defining its needs,"[41] was confident it could refrain from public lobbying and not jeopardize its top aviation priority. This quieter approach became necessary when the secretary of defense announced in April 1989 that the Pentagon's official position was to eliminate the V-22. The marines were likely told by civilian leaders that they were not to make statements or take actions in public that contradicted OSD's stance. During authorization hearings, members of Congress referred to "the gag order" and "subtle pressures"[42] on the Marine Corps. The marines also feared that a public campaign on behalf of the V-22 might anger Cheney and affect how they fared in the interservice competition over roles and missions at a time when the army and marines were "contending for primacy as the nation's force for fighting low-intensity conflict."[43]

These constraints did not, however, preclude the marines from being a vital member of the coalition that opposed Cheney's cancellation. There is evidence to suggest that the marines engaged in a vigorous, behind-the-scenes campaign on Capitol Hill.[44] More important, they demonstrated an unwavering commitment to the plane through candid congressional testimony. During committee hearings, the marines made it absolutely clear that there was a real need to replace their aging helicopters, and the Osprey was the most capable option. Later, lawmakers would counter OSD's opposition by referencing the statements of Marine Corps officials. Congress has traditionally viewed the corps as the underdog of the four services, because its needs are often overridden by the budget priorities of the army, navy, and air force.[45] Consequently, when the marines repeatedly request a budget item, it is usually honored.

The final component of Secretary Cheney's opposition was the private sector, namely Bell Helicopter and Boeing, the V-22's primary contractors. Like the Marine Corps' steady commitment, the Bell-Boeing team's political skill helped broaden and sustain congressional support for the Osprey. To make the program more attractive, the two companies had begun full-scale development in May 1986 "without a contract and with [their] own funds."[46] They also invested in initial production tooling, accepted a fixed-price development contract, agreed to compete against one another for future production lots, and improved manufacturing techniques to make assembly more efficient and affordable.[47]

Bell and Boeing launched a range of promotional efforts on behalf of the V-22. These efforts included a guest pilot program, the Osprey Fax newsletter, full-page advertisements in newspapers and magazines, television commercials,[48] and a congressional awareness campaign that included events like Tiltrotor Appreciation Day and the landing of a demonstrator aircraft on Capitol Hill. The contractors made information about the program widely available.[49] Their tactics were designed to attract support, counter criticism and misstatements, and convince the media and public that the V-22 was worthy of finite defense dollars.

As stated above, subcontracts were awarded to close to 2,000 companies in more than forty states. Once involved in the project, V-22 suppliers were encouraged to make their congressional representatives aware of the program's impact on local employment.[50] The subcontractors, however, were only one part of the constituency Bell-Boeing strategists built. The labor unions were also recruited. Organizations such as the United Auto Workers and AFL-CIO lobbied Congress, because thousands of their members had jobs tied to the Osprey. Another significant patron of the V-22 was the Federal Aviation Administration (FAA). In 1985, the contractors realized that if the Osprey was to be billed as a civilian asset, FAA backing was critical.[51] Two years later, Bell-Boeing convinced the FAA to co-sponsor a civil tilt-rotor study and participate in the V-22's test flight program. FAA involvement in tilt-rotor research and evaluation activated other interested parties, such as the California Department of Transportation and the Port Authority of New York and New Jersey. The Tiltrotor Technology Coalition—a collection of contractors, subcontractors, members of Congress, retired marines, and private sector groups—was established in February 1990 and became a unified lobbying force, aggressively championing the Osprey as a national asset that would solve the marines' medium-lift need, create jobs, remedy domestic transportation problems, and become an attractive export.

The Battle over the Osprey, 1989–1992

While opposition to killing the program was expressed before and immediately following Secretary Cheney's April 1989 decision, the real battle over the V-22 began in early May, when the FY 1990 defense budget was subjected to the congressional authorization and appropriation process. On May 11, the proposed termination of the Osprey program was a focus of discussion during a hearing of the House Armed Services Committee. At the session, Lt. Gen. Charles Pitman, the marine's deputy chief of staff for aviation, was given an opportunity to explain why his service desperately wanted the V-22. Drawing comparisons with existing helicopters as well as enemy capabilities, the general highlighted how the Osprey's speed, range, safety, reduced noise, survivability, and operational flexibility would enhance the marines' capacity to fight in the emerging post–cold war world. He also remarked, "We only buy aircraft for Marine assault forces about every 35 years, and we have been waiting 15 years, working on this program, trying to get the V-22 on the street."[52]

At the same hearing, the navy's assistant secretary for shipbuilding and logistics testified, "We would like to carry . . . on [the Osprey program], but we don't have the money to do it."[53] The V-22's fiercest proponent, however, took issue with OSD's affordability argument. Representative Weldon commented,

"[T]he Marine Corps presented data to the secretary [of defense] showing . . . over a 20-year life cycle the V-22 was the more cost effective solution." When Weldon asked Pitman to respond to this statement, the general indicated Weldon was "correct."[54]

Not every member of the House embraced Weldon's strong support of the Osprey. Rep. Andy Ireland, R-Fla., a critic of the program, complained that the Pentagon routinely "undertakes more programs than can be covered by its budget."[55] Rep. John Rowland, R-Conn., whose district produced the helicopters that Cheney wanted to substitute for the V-22, was also an opponent. Most important, Rep. Les Aspin, D-Wis., the chair of the House Armed Services Committee and chair of the Procurement Subcommittee, strongly supported the Bush administration's FY 1990 budget. His position was motivated by what one lawmaker termed "pork-barrel deterrence."[56] In a memorandum to other members of the committee, Aspin argued that OSD had made some tough fiscal choices and deserved support. "There's no room for even the deserving add-ons," he wrote, "let alone the ones that go 'oink.'"[57] On June 20, Aspin insisted that the Procurement Subcommittee only vote on whether to accept or reject the procurement portion of Cheney's budget proposal. No substantive changes were allowed. Aspin prevailed when the subcommittee approved Cheney's recommendations by a 10-9 vote.[58]

Two days later, the House Armed Services Research and Development Subcommittee revived the V-22 when it voted to authorize $351 million for the program. The panel decided to shift funds from two accounts: $51 million would be drawn from the amount that Cheney had set aside for CH-53 helicopters to replace the Osprey, and $300 million would be taken from the B-2 development program. Representative Weldon succeeded in pushing the initiative because he promised to offer an amendment when the full committee met to "restore $300 million for B-2 bomber development, provided the same amount was transferred to the Osprey development account from the B-2 production account."[59] Weldon made the pledge after some of his colleagues raised the issue of "raiding the B-2 for parochial reasons."[60]

The opposing actions of Aspin and Weldon indicated that the House Armed Services Committee would be compelled to choose between preserving Cheney's recommendations and saving its favorite projects. The issue came to a head when the full committee convened June 27 and 28 to mark up the defense authorization bill, which approves the weapons the Pentagon can purchase and sets spending limits for each program. After a heated debate, the committee disregarded the chairman's plea to accept Cheney's proposal without add-ons. Instead it awarded $508 million to the Osprey—$351 million for development and $157 million for long-lead procurement.[61] Since the 1989 budget summit agreement placed a cap on total defense spending, money for the Osprey was shifted from other programs. The House Armed Services Committee reduced Cheney's CH-53 helicopter order in half, freeing up $157 million, and diverted $355 million from the B-2 account.

Interestingly, two liberal Democrats who had a reputation for opposing major defense spending rescued the V-22. Reps. Ron Dellums, D-Calif., and Patricia Schroeder, D-Colo., were not supporters of the V-22, but they were major opponents of the B-2. Their strong stance against that project led to a $4 billion cut in funding that released money for the V-22, the F-14D Tomcat fighter jet, and other endangered programs.[62] On July 19 and 20, the House Appropriations Defense Subcommittee met and approved the same level of V-22 funding adopted by the House Armed Services Committee.[63]

When the matter reached the floor of the House a week later, Rep. Bill Dickinson, R-Ala., the senior Republican on the Armed Services Committee, tried to remove the $508 million for the V-22, but the House Democratic leadership and the lawmakers whose districts had a stake in the program protected the plane along with the F-14D. After the 261-162 vote in favor of the FY 1990 defense bill, Rep. David Bonior, D-Mich., the chief deputy whip, remarked, "We had to give something to our people."[64] Secretary Cheney responded to the vote, which cut money for SDI and the B-2 bomber, by accusing the House of putting political pork ahead of critical national security needs. He threatened that "a [presidential] veto was a real possibility," if the final House-Senate conference bill failed to "restore the president's priorities."[65]

The Senate approached the V-22 issue differently than the House. After a series of closed-door meetings, the Senate Armed Services Committee largely accepted Secretary Cheney's FY 1990 budget proposal, including the decision to forego procurement of the V-22 in favor of CH-53 helicopters. The committee, however, did provide the V-22 program with $255 million in research and development money. Some senators successfully argued that completion of Osprey test flights might convince the army to rejoin the program or attract civilian customers, thereby making the V-22 a more affordable option for the Marine Corps.[66] This stance led one observer to suggest that the plane's proponents had "cooked up a civilian [tilt-rotor] mission" in which private industry had little interest.[67]

Somewhat surprisingly, the Senate Appropriations Defense Subcommittee provided no funding for the Osprey for FY 1990, but Sen. Arlen Specter, R-Pa., who fought hard to preserve money for the plane, was assured by Chairman Daniel K. Inouye, D-Hawaii, that the V-22 would be included in the final House-Senate conference bill. Inouye stated, "This [appropriations] bill does not write the last chapter on the V-22."[68] After receiving promises about other Pennsylvania projects, Specter remarked that he felt "a special obligation . . . to advance these causes," because of the state's high unemployment."[69] Specter, however, did not have to wait for the conference report. When the full Appropriations Committee convened two days later, it set aside $255 million for V-22 development. The panel also approved the purchase of only three CH-53s, at a cost of $62 million. Secretary Cheney had requested twenty-three helicopters.[70] The full Senate did not alter these figures.

When the House and Senate conferees reconciled their competing defense bills in early November 1989, the Senate version prevailed: $255 million was allocated to complete development of the Osprey; also, $330 million in unspent advanced procurement funds from previous years were released against the wishes of OSD.[71] The Osprey had survived for another year. The question that remained was whether the costly plane would be produced. Congress chose to defer that issue, indicating that it wanted to see the results of the flight test program and an independent cost operational effectiveness analysis (COEA) of all V-22 alternatives. OSD was ordered to submit the COEA with its FY 1991 budget request.[72]

From Policy Dispute to Constitutional Struggle, 1990

Work on the FY 1991 defense budget began in the final months of 1989; and it was clear from the beginning that OSD was determined to challenge Congress on the V-22. Just a month after lawmakers had saved the Osprey in the FY 1990 budget and agreed to defer a decision on production, Deputy Secretary of Defense Donald J. Atwood ordered the navy to terminate the V-22's production contracts. In a memorandum, Atwood indicated that it was not in the "public fiscal interest" to spend advanced procurement funds when OSD had no intention of moving beyond the Osprey's research and development stage.[73] Representative Weldon criticized the decision, which came while Congress was in recess, calling it "faceless, gutless [and] very ill-timed and ill-conceived."[74]

The challenge to congressional appropriation power, however, did not end with the refusal to spend V-22 production funds. When Secretary Cheney presented the president's budget request in February 1990, which included no money for the Osprey, he proposed transferring $1.4 billion from programs Congress had funded in FY 1990 to pay for FY 1991 defense priorities the Bush administration deemed more important. Cheney also indicated that he planned to defer the expenditure of $835 million from funds appropriated in 1989. This figure included $200 million tied to the V-22 program. Sean O'Keefe, the Pentagon's comptroller, summed up his department's position when he said, "We ain't going to spend the money [for the purposes Congress intended]."[75] This direct challenge angered many on Capitol Hill, including people with no stake in the V-22. One legislative aide remarked, "If they get away with it, it's tantamount to a line-item veto."[76]

Other developments also strengthened the Osprey's support on Capitol Hill. During a visit to Bell Helicopter in January 1990, the Japanese minister of trade and industry commented, "If you produce the aircraft, I guarantee you we will buy it; if you do not, I guarantee we will build it."[77] This statement, coupled with the knowledge that Japanese and European firms had already designed tilt-rotor planes,[78] heightened congressional interest in the commercial rationale behind completing the V-22 and moving to a civilian program.[79] In addition, the Tiltrotor Technology Coalition formed in February had immediately become a formidable lobbying and public relations organization.[80] That same month, Commandant Gray testified before the House Armed Services Committee that the Marine Corps had no more "pressing" priority than the need to replace its aging helicopters. He then outlined a strong case for the V-22's capabilities without directly referring to the plane or OSD's decision to cancel it.[81]

A week later, Osprey supporters received yet another boost. The General Accounting Office ruled in early March that OSD's planned deferral of FY 1989 V-22 funding was unauthorized.[82] OSD subsequently withdrew its deferral request, but Secretary Cheney voiced his concern about "a certain hypocrisy" in congressional calls to reduce military spending when lawmakers were unwilling to eliminate particular projects.[83]

Despite the GAO ruling, OSD continued its efforts to kill the V-22 program. A clear example was its behavior before and after the release of the COEA study conducted by the Institute for Defense Analyses (IDA), an organization funded by the Defense Department but technically independent. The Pentagon had commissioned IDA to complete the report on V-22 alternatives. As noted above, Congress had ordered that the analysis be submitted with the president's FY 1991 budget request. Once the study was complete, OSD ignored several requests to send the document to Capitol Hill.[84] It was no mystery why it stonewalled. The IDA report concluded that in the long run the Osprey was the most cost effective and capable option for satisfying the Marine Corps' requirements as well as the navy's search-and-rescue mission.[85] When the study was finally released on June 29, OSD immediately challenged its findings. Secretary Cheney told Congress, "[T]he investment cost to procure [the V-22] remains too high. In the current era of declining defense budgets we must give up certain capabilities."[86] David Chu and Pete Williams, OSD's chief spokesman, criticized a number of the study's underlying assumptions.[87] Representative Weldon, however, remarked, "The Pentagon's arguments about the high cost of the Osprey are no longer credible. The Osprey is head and shoulders above the competition."[88]

When it came time for Congress to reconcile these competing positions in the FY 1991 authorization and appropriation bills, Weldon's perspective prevailed. His victory was no surprise given how the V-22's "deeply committed, highly energized and ideologically diverse coalition"[89] had grown. A case in point was Representative Aspin, who the previous year had tried to preserve Cheney's budget request, including cancellation of the Osprey. In the summer of 1990, Aspin, chairman of the House Armed Services Committee, changed his position and fully supported V-22 funding. His shift appears to have been motivated by political and policy concerns. On one hand, Aspin reasoned, the Osprey's imposing congressional allies made it virtually impossible to kill the plane. He also believed that it made more sense to eliminate the B-2 Stealth bomber, which would yield far more budget savings than cutting the V-22. On the other hand, Aspin argued, with the demise of the Warsaw Pact there were compelling reasons for going forward with the Osprey.[90] That is, the plane would be well suited for the emerging post–cold war strategic environment where there was a need to send troops to regional "hot spots" to deal with a range of non-traditional security threats.

When the House and Senate finished their work on the FY 1991 defense appropriations bill, the V-22 had fared well. Against the wishes of the Bush administration, the program was awarded $403 million, including $167 million for long-lead production. More important, Capitol Hill made it absolutely clear where it stood on the "V-22 vs. helicopter" debate. Instead of funding even a portion of OSD's request for 23 CH-45 helicopters ($435 million), Congress used the proposed allocation to fund the Osprey.[91] Moreover, Congress wrote into law that the Pentagon was to manage the V-22 project as an acquisition program.[92] The plane had survived elimination two years in a row and was in a far stronger position politically than it had been at the end of 1989.

The year began well for the Osprey program. In early January, it was reported that the V-22 had successfully completed shipboard compatibility tests on a naval assault ship.[93] In addition, OSD was focused on the Persian Gulf War. As a result, Pentagon officials ignored the Osprey in early 1991. They did not, however, abandon their long-standing opposition to the aircraft.

In February, Secretary Cheney delivered the president's FY 1992 budget proposal to Congress. Following the pattern of the previous two years, the submission did not include a request for V-22 funding. Instead the Bush administration asked for $509 million for twenty CH-53 helicopters.[94] Cheney also indicated his intention to rescind $200 million in FY 1989 V-22 production funds, because the money could not be used for its intended purpose before it expired in six months. For the first time, Cheney *did* commit to completing the Osprey's development program, but there was a catch. He proposed the goal be met with the $167 million Congress had allocated for V-22 procurement for FY 1991.[95] This idea, coupled with the $200 million recision, meant Cheney was effectively eliminating all production funds. If he had his way, the plane would never move beyond the research and development phase.

Cheney's recommendations angered the program's many advocates on Capitol Hill, Representative Weldon most of all. Nonetheless, the secretary of defense told members of Congress on February 7, "Cost is the driving issue, and the V-22 is too costly. . . . At these budget levels . . . we can afford to deploy only those technologies that offer the greatest combat capability payoff per dollar invested. The V-22 is not such a system."[96] Two weeks later, Weldon again complained that OSD's stance was "absolutely unacceptable." In a tactic that would become common among congressional supporters of the plane, he argued that the Pentagon's own IDA study identified the Osprey as the best option.[97] Secretary of the Navy Larry Garrett responded, "As you know, the [defense] secretary canceled the program in 1990. It was canceled at that point in time for reasons of affordability. . . . I submit to you that in the context of the precipitous decline of the top-line, the secretary's decision is even more supportable [in 1991]."[98]

Garrett's words, however, did not sway Representative Weldon or the other V-22 supporters on the House Armed Services Committee. Rather it was the testimony of the Marine Corps commandant at the same hearing that had the greatest impact. General Gray told the panel that the marines needed the Osprey debate resolved: "The reason I say we need a decision now is because the MV-22 is not being procured for operations. The CH-53 and CH-46 helicopters that were discussed last year are not being procured. We are going further and further downstream with less and less capability at our disposal."[99]

A month later, when Congress passed the FY 1991 "Dire Emergency" supplemental appropriations bill on March 22, it inserted language explicitly stating that OSD was required to spend the V-22's FY 1989 procurement funds totaling $200 million. These resources were to remain available until they were spent.[100] Lawmakers were now using legislation to compel OSD to release Osprey allocations. Congress, however, failed to specify in the emergency bill that the money was to remain as production funds, so in the spring of 1991, OSD directed the $200 million to V-22 testing and development.[101] This action kept procurement on hold and provided no immediate remedy to the problem General Gray had identified in February.

OSD's pattern of obstructionism led the House Armed Services Committee on April 11 to explore what Representative Aspin called "a process problem."[102] Representative Dellums complained, "In effect, the Department [of Defense] is exercising a line item veto of Congress' intent, and that, as we all know, is against the law."[103] In a prepared statement, Rep. Marilyn Lloyd, D-Tenn., strongly reinforced her colleague's position:

> The [Defense] Department has ignored Congress and refused to carry out congressional directives. . . . This is not acceptable. . . . The Department of Defense is not the sole repository of wisdom when it comes to defense policy. If the Department's decisions were not meant to be examined, reviewed, and occasionally reversed, then the Constitution would not have provided for the legislative branch.[104]

The Pentagon refused to waver. In perhaps the best statement of OSD's overall position during the four-year period, Pentagon comptroller O'Keefe told the committee on April 11,

> The V-22 may appear to be superior to existing helicopters. . . . But our goal cannot be to spend whatever is required to achieve peak performance. . . . Our goal is to find ways of performing our most critical missions acceptably, at a funding level that does not draw excessively from our other critical missions.[105]

Not only was Secretary Garrett's view of the budgetary environment still influencing this stand, but time delays, some of which were tied to OSD's refusal to release procurement funds, were increasing the cost of development and deployment.[106]

Neither this reality nor the June 11 crash of a V-22 prototype in Delaware dissuaded lawmakers from supporting the plane. The two crew members suffered no injuries, but test flights were suspended.[107] By the fall, the test program had resumed and the Osprey once again moved smoothly through the congressional authorization and appropriations process. In November, the House and Senate agreed to provide more financing than in previous years, allocating $625 million in new research and development money and shifting $165 million from previously appropriated procurement funds.[108] Moreover, Congress inserted the following language in the FY 1992 conference report: "The conferees expect the Navy to embark upon this program as soon as possible, and neither the secretary of defense nor his subordinates may take action which will unnecessarily delay obligation of these funds."[109] Cheney and OSD had lost for a third time.

Compromise, Conflict and Capitulation, 1992

The year began in predictable fashion. The Bush administration submitted its FY 1993 defense budget to Congress in late January without a request for V-22 funding. Secretary Cheney made his perennial plea for helicopters, asking for the same twenty CH-53s ($513 million) that were requested in 1991.[110] By March, Congress was once again complaining about OSD's obstructive behavior. This time it was not a proposed recision or an attempt to cancel contracts. It was OSD's refusal to release any of the V-22's FY 1992 funding ($790 million), which lawmakers contended was a direct violation of the appropriations act.[111] After all, Congress had inserted special language to ensure that the money was spent.

When Cheney and other OSD officials were asked to explain their violation of the law, they stressed that their non-expenditure of the funds was not motivated by defiance, but an inability to implement another portion of the FY 1992 Appropriations Act.[112] Specifically, they referenced the language that called for the "development, manufacture, and operational test of three production representative V-22 aircraft" by December 31, 1996. OSD maintained that limited funds, time constraints, and engineering problems precluded this goal.[113]

Of course, the plane's congressional supporters viewed OSD's stance as nothing more than the latest attempt to hinder V-22 production. Representatives Weldon, Geren, and others reacted quickly. In March, they summoned Marine Corps brass to Capitol Hill to recount the desperate state of their helicopter fleet. In addition, lawmakers asserted that OSD's failure to move forward with the Osprey was placing Marine Corps personnel in danger. They referenced the age and safety of the helicopters in use, their limitations during training missions, and the fact that the V-22 was what Marine Corps aviators wanted to fly in the post–cold war era. Through direct questions and anonymous quotations during committee hearings, members of Congress emphasized that the Marines shared their viewpoint.[114]

Although lawmakers showed no indication of backing away from their commitment to V-22 production, OSD remained firm in its unwillingness to abandon its position. In fact, it proceeded to tell Congress in April that the program would not only exceed budget allocations and fall behind schedule, but the Osprey would have to be redesigned because it was too heavy and too slow.[115] V-22 supporters saw this action as a sign that OSD was once again preparing to push a helicopter option to meet the marines' medium-lift need. Rep. James Bilbray, D-Nev., who claimed his district had nothing to gain from the program, bluntly told Deputy Secretary Atwood, "[Y]ou can go back to the Marines or the Navy and come up with alternatives, but you are going to come back to this subcommittee and find out [it's] going to continue with the V-22."[116] Other lawmakers raised the prospect of taking Secretary Cheney to court over OSD's refusal to spend congressional appropriations.[117]

The House Armed Services Committee, however, used more than words to express its displeasure. When the panel completed its work on the FY 1993 defense bill in May, it approved $755 million for three more production representative Ospreys. It also denied the purchase of CH-53 helicopters to replace the V-22. Most notably, the committee inserted a provision in the bill reducing the Pentagon comptroller's budget 5 percent each month for every month that appropriations from the previous year were not spent.[118] As the battle between the two branches intensified, OSD refused to abandon its position.

When fifteen Republican lawmakers—all supporters of the Osprey—tried to arrange a meeting with President Bush to discuss the impasse, they were rebuffed. One White House official indicated that with the political conventions and presidential election approaching, it was important "to keep Bush out of the fray."[119] The V-22 advocates, however, were successful in securing meetings with the secretary of defense during the month of June. Led by Rep. Robert K. Dornan, R-Calif., a former air force pilot and ardent proponent of the armed services, the group pushed Cheney to drop his opposition to the program.[120]

These meetings and, more important, the U.S. comptroller general's ruling that OSD had violated the law by illegally impounding Osprey funding, led Cheney to offer a compromise. On July 2, he told Congress that he would release $1.5 billion in V-22 funds—$790 million (FY 1992) and $750 million

(FY 1993)—to build six production representative aircraft if he was allowed to use some of the money to explore alternatives. The alternatives would include updated versions of existing helicopters, a new medium-lift helicopter, and a modified, less costly version of the V-22. Cheney also asked that the requirement to manufacture three production representative planes by December 1996 be relaxed.[121]

Both sides claimed victory. In briefing reporters, OSD spokesman Williams indicated that there could now be "a head-to-head competition"[122] between the Osprey and more affordable options. In contrast, Representative Weldon proclaimed, "We have gotten everything we asked for," and dismissed the exploration of helicopter alternatives as "nothing more than a face-saver for the Pentagon."[123] In reality, both sides benefited from the deal: OSD avoided possible court action, and Congress and the contractors gained the additional time desperately needed to manufacture the three required aircraft.[124]

The compromise, however, provided only a brief respite in the four-year battle. On July 20, the program was dealt a major blow when a V-22 prototype crashed into the Potomac River at Quantico, Virginia. Now two Ospreys had crashed within thirteen months, and this time the results were tragic. All seven crew members died.[125] Reactions to the incident were predictable. The plane's strongest supporters lamented the loss of life but expressed confidence that the program would continue. Most lawmakers responded more cautiously, saying they were prepared to await the outcome of an investigation. In contrast, OSD made it clear that there were now "serious questions" surrounding the reliability of the aircraft.[126] Nonetheless, it pledged to abide by the terms of the July 2 compromise,[127] although days later, the Pentagon took three actions that seemed to contradict that commitment.

First, it ordered the Marines to reexamine their medium-lift requirement and suggested that performance standards could be lowered. Second, the Defense Department's Joint Requirements Oversight Council (JROC) decided that the medium-lift replacement no longer had to meet the speed and long-range requirements necessary for special operations and search and rescue—that is, the two missions for which the air force and navy wanted the Osprey. Third, JROC rejected a Marine Corps statement of operational requirements that corresponded to the V-22's capabilities. Instead it retained a statement of requirements that could be met by existing helicopters.[128]

The Osprey's congressional allies were outraged. They charged that OSD's actions amounted to nothing more than an attempt to stall the V-22 program and remove the plane from the medium-lift competition.[129] When the House

Armed Services Committee convened a special hearing on the matter in early August, lawmakers expressed doubts that the Pentagon ever intended to respect the intent of Congress. OSD countered that its latest efforts were not "duplicitous," but were simply aimed at finding the most capable and affordable replacement for the marines' aging helicopters.[130]

The controversy continued after the hearing but quickly became irrelevant. In late August, the Bush administration dropped its opposition to the V-22 and indicated that it would not stand in the way of spending $1.5 billion on the program. Even though the policy reversal coincided with a similar announcement related to the army's M-1 tank and a decision to sell $9 million worth of fighter jets to Taiwan and Saudi Arabia, the administration denied there was any connection to the upcoming presidential election.[131] Instead it took the position that the Osprey now complemented the emerging post–cold war strategy of projecting force into "hot spots."[132] This stance, however, became difficult to defend by late October, when Vice President Dan Quayle visited Boeing's V-22 plant near Philadelphia to announce a $550 million engineering, manufacturing, and development contract.[133] The event left little doubt that the Bush administration was attempting to attract political support in vote rich Texas and Pennsylvania with the promise of jobs at Boeing and Bell Helicopter. Moreover, as one Pentagon official noted, "The jobs argument has never been more powerful than now with the economy the way that it is."[134]

President Bush's policy reversal ended any uncertainty surrounding the continuation of the V-22 program. His challenger, Governor Bill Clinton, D-Ark., had already backed the plane. During an August 1992 campaign speech, Clinton stated,

> Our new military must be more agile. Because of the end of the nuclear standoff, new battlefields will likely be dominated by maneuver, speed, and out-thinking the enemy. That is why I support . . . the V-22. . . . [I]t is the only aircraft capable of certain special operations, including the rescue of Americans deep in hostile territory.[135]

Clinton repeated these themes and championed the Osprey's civilian market potential during the first presidential debate.[136] Yet Bush's policy change and Clinton's endorsement, while helpful, were not crucial. Their positions only reinforced what the Congress had always intended to do—fund and produce the aircraft. Over the course of the four-year battle, Capitol Hill repeatedly demonstrated its willingness and capacity to override executive branch opposition to the program.

As 1992 drew to a close, the V-22 had fared exceedingly well. Both presidential candidates backed the plane; navy investigators had attributed the July crash to mechanical failure rather than the tilt-rotor concept;[137] and a strongly committed Congress awarded the project another $755 million for FY 1993.[138] After enduring four years of ardent opposition from OSD, it seemed as though nothing could stop the Osprey.

Conclusion: New Challenges for an Old Program

Throughout the remainder of the 1990s there were no serious threats to the Osprey's survival. Events in 2000 and 2001, however, altered this circumstance. Two fatal crashes, the deliberate falsification of maintenance records, and on-going government inquiries have placed the program in grave jeopardy. If these problems were not enough of a challenge, the troubled plane now faces the new administration of George W. Bush and a very influential vice president, Richard Cheney. These realities and the Osprey's mounting cost of procurement certainly have the potential to scuttle the program. If the V-22 is discontinued in the near future, one will still have to marvel at its capacity to survive for nearly two decades without entering into full production. The aircraft is a powerful example of how difficult it is to stop a weapons system once it is under development. This is a particularly important consideration in the post–cold war era, when there is pressure to restructure the military and reduce defense spending.

If the Osprey can endure a political confrontation such as the one it faced from 1989 through 1992, then it may very well weather its current troubles and remain a viable weapons procurement program. The coalition of actors and interests that defended the plane in the past remains intact and fully mobilized. Moreover, this "iron triangle" has more at stake than it did a decade ago. Congress has invested billions of dollars over the years; the contractors have thousands of jobs more deeply tied to the plane and spin-off models;[139] subcontracts have been distributed to 276 congressional districts;[140] and the marines' helicopters are nearing the end of their life cycle with no ready replacement except the V-22. Moreover, the plane is well suited for the post–cold war security environment. Given these considerations, there is good reason to believe the Osprey is here to stay. The aircraft's supporters, however, will be pressed to defend the embattled program within a far more open, pluralistic, and partisan policy process than they encountered a decade ago.

Notes

1. Portions of this case study are drawn from Christopher M. Jones, "Roles, Politics, and the Survival of the V-22 Osprey," *Journal of Political and Military Sociology* 29, no. 1 (summer 2001).

2. See Matthew L. Wald, "Pilot's Rapid Descent Cited in Osprey Crash Fatal to 19," *New York Times,* May 10, 2000, A17; and "U.S. Marine Corps Disciplines Osprey Pilots for Contributing to V-22 Disaster," July 27, 2000, http://www.cnn.com.

3. James Dao, "After a Crash in North Carolina, Marines Ground Osprey Program," *New York Times,* December 13, 2000, A1, A25. For an overview of the many investigations, see John Wagner, "Neutrality at Issue in Review of Osprey," *News and Observer* (Raleigh, N.C.), January 21, 2001, 1A, 14A.

4. Bob Williams and Joseph Neff, "Crash-Prone Osprey Not Likely to Be Killed," *News and Observer* (Raleigh, N.C.), December 17, 2000, 20A.

5. Elizabeth Becker and Steven Lee Myers, "Pentagon Says Commander Admits He Altered Records," *New York Times,* January 20, 2001, http://www.nytimes.com; and Steven Lee Myers, "Marine Unit Raided in Criminal Inquiry on Troubled Craft," *New York Times,* January 19, 2001, A1, A25.

6. Mary Pat Flaherty and Thomas E. Ricks, "Osprey Probe Reaches Pentagon's Top Ranks," *Washington Post,* March 2, 2001, A1.

7. Mary Pat Flaherty and Thomas E. Ricks, "Key Tests Omitted on the Osprey," *Washington Post,* February 19, 2001, A1.

8. See "Fire in V-22 Prototype Delays First Test Flight," *Aviation Week & Space Technology,* March 20, 1989, 261; Stanley W. Kandebo, "Osprey Flight Tests Suspended after Crash of No. 5 Aircraft," *Aviation Week & Space Technology,* July 17, 1991, 53–54; Robert Pear, "Disputed Military Aircraft Crashes; 7 Aboard Lost," *New York Times,* July 21, 1992, A1, A16; "The Osprey Can't Do It," *Newsweek,* March 8, 1993, 6.

9. In 1983, the four services planned to order 913 Ospreys: marines, 552; navy, 50; air force, 80; and army, 231. Bell-Boeing, "V-22 Multimission, Multiservice Requirements History, 1982–1993," fact sheet, 1993, provided to the author. Today the figure stands at 458 planes: marines, 360; navy, 48; and air force, 50. Gidge Dady, V-22 Public Affairs Office, Department of the Navy, telephone interview and follow-up correspondence dated December 7, 1998.

10. These figures are based on FY 1994 dollars. Terry Arnold, manager, Tiltrotor Communications, Bell Helicopter Textron, telephone interview and follow-up correspondence dated October 2, 1995; and Dady, correspondence.

11. See Dao, "Marines Ground Osprey," A1; General Accounting Office, *Navy Aviation: V-22 Cost and Capability to Meet Requirement Are Yet to Be Determined,* October 22, 1997, GAO report, NSIAD-98-13.

12. Department of the Navy, "V-22 Osprey Key Facts," provided to the author on December 7, 1998, by Naval Air Systems Command at Patuxent River, Maryland.

13. See Molly Moore, "Pentagon May Lose Weapons," *Washington Post,* April 15, 1989, A5.

14. For example, see *Navy and Marine Corps RDT&E Fiscal Year 1990 Budget Request,* hearing before the House Armed Services Committee, March 2, 1989, 234 (official transcript).

15. Moore, "Pentagon May Lose Weapons," A1, A5.

16. Carole A. Shifrin, "Bell-Boeing V-22 Tilt-Rotor Prototype Makes First Flight," *Aviation Week & Space Technology,* March 3, 1989, 20–21.

17. Michael Crouch, "The V-22: Can the Nation Afford to Forgo Its Production?" M.A. thesis, Naval Postgraduate School, 1991, 51–52.

18. Patricia A. Gilmartin, "Bush Team Weighs Postponing, Canceling Weapons Programs," *Aviation Week & Space Technology,* December 19, 1988, 20.

19. George C. Wilson, "Cheney Outlines $10 Billion in 'Painful' Defense Cuts," *Washington Post,* April 26, 1989, A1. Also see Moore, "Pentagon May Lose Weapons," A1.

20. "Naval Aviation Modernization Hit Hard by Pentagon Cuts," *Aviation Week & Space Technology,* April 24, 1989, 23.

21. Dave Griffiths, "Weinberger Puts a Muzzle on a Pentagon Watchdog," *Business Week,* June 5, 1986, 84.

22. Ibid.

23. Robert M. Flanagan, "The V-22 Is Slipping Away," *U.S. Naval Institute Proceedings,* August 1990, 42.

24. "Modernization Hit Hard," 23.

25. Ibid.

26. Flanagan, "Slipping Away," 42.

27. Bert H. Cooper Jr., "V-22 Tilt-Rotor Aircraft (Weapons Fact)," *CRS Issue Brief,* February 25, 1991, CRS-3.

28. Douglas Waller, "Will the Osprey Ever Fly?" *Newsweek,* July 24, 1989, 16.

29. See *Status of the V-22 Tiltrotor Aircraft Program,* hearing before the House Armed Services Committee, August 5, 1992, 39 (official transcript); and Arlen Specter, "Letter Sent to President Bush Regarding the V-22," *Congressional Record,* June 4, 1992, S7576–7577.

30. D. W. Ferguson, "V-22 Production Employment," internal memorandum, Bell Helicopter Textron, August 25, 1992, provided to the author.

31. Mark Harrison, internal memorandum, Boeing Defense Space Group, Helicopter Division, December 12, 1994, provided to the author.

32. Bell-Boeing, "Status of V-22 Subcontracts (including EMD and Uprated Drive System)," interoffice memorandum and attachments, and "U.S. Map, V-22 EMD Supplier Dollars," interoffice memorandum, Bell Helicopter Textron, October 12, 1994, provided to the author.

33. In determining the number of jobs created by subcontracts, the contractors "use a ball park figure of one job for every $35,000." Terry Arnold, manager, Tiltrotor Communications, Bell Helicopter Textron, telephone interview and follow-up correspondence dated November 21, 1994.

34. Andrew Rosenthal, "Pentagon May Spend More on Plane It Plans to Cancel," *New York Times,* May 5, 1989, A23.

35. Waller, "Will the Osprey Ever Fly?" 16; and David Griffiths, "Congress May Ram a Chopper Down the Pentagon's Throat," *Business Week,* June 5, 1989, 92. For further information on civilian use, see *Civil Tiltrotor Missions and Applications, Phase II: The Commercial Passenger Market,* study by Bell Helicopter Textron and Boeing, sponsored by NASA and the Federal Aviation Administration, report NASA CR 177576, p. iv.

36. See Flanagan, "Slipping Away," 43; *Department of the Navy and U.S. Marine Corps Fiscal Year 1991 RDT&E Budget Request,* hearing of the House Armed Services Committee, March 7, 1990, 102 (official transcript); *V-22 Osprey Program Review,* hearing of the House Armed Services Committee, April 11, 1991, 206 (official transcript);

House Armed Services Committee, *Status of V-22*, 44; Giovanni de Briganti, "The Comet and the Osprey and Killing the Golden Goose," *Rotor & Wing International*, February 1992, 62; Robert K. Dornan, "The V-22: Are We Killing the Golden Goose?" Dear Colleague letter, February 20, 1992, provided to the author; and ABC News, "Your Money, Your Choice," *World News Tonight*, aired March 3, 1993.

37. For a statement by Representative Kasich, see House Armed Services Committee, *Status of V-22*, 43–44. For Senator Rudman's support, see Moore, "Pentagon May Lose Weapons," A5.

38. House Armed Services Committee, *Navy and Marine Corps FY 1991*, 109; and House Armed Services Committee, *Status of V 22*, 35.

39. *Navy and Marine Corps FY 1992 Budget Request*, hearing of the House Armed Services Committee, February 21, 1991, 412 (official transcript); *Procurement and Military Nuclear Systems Subcommittee Hearings*, hearing of the House Armed Services Committee, March 3 and April 28, 1992, 118–119, 124–126, 203 (official transcript); and House Armed Services Committee, *Status of V-22*, 24, 27.

40. Pat Towell, "Defense Spending Decisions Sure to Stir Controversy," *Congressional Quarterly Weekly Report*, April 22, 1989, 916.

41. Brenda Forman, "The V-22 Tiltrotor Osprey: The Program That Wouldn't Die," 1994 paper provided to the author by Bell-Boeing Team, 7–8.

42. See House Armed Services Committee, *Procurement and Military Nuclear Systems Subcommittee*, 126–128; and House Armed Services Committee, *Status of V-22*, 13.

43. John C. Scharfen, "U.S. Marine Corps in 1989," *U.S. Naval Institute Proceedings*, May 1990, 178.

44. Waller, "Will the Osprey Ever Fly?" 16; John Kasich, "Congress and Defense Decision Making," in *American Defense Annual, 1991–1992*, ed. Joseph Kruzel (New York: Lexington, 1992), 154; Kenneth Szczublewski, "The V-22: A Turning Point in Congressional Behavior?" M.A. thesis, Naval Postgraduate School, 1992, 55; and Richard J. Norton, commander, U.S. Navy, remarks to author, annual meeting of the International Studies Association, Los Angeles, March 18, 2000.

45. Crouch, "The V-22," 175.

46. Bell-Boeing, "V-22 Program History and Milestones," fact sheet, provided to the author by Bell Helicopter Textron, 1994.

47. Stanley W. Kandebo, "V-22 Team Lowered Osprey Production Costs," *Aviation Week & Space Technology*, November 15, 1993, 58.

48. Paul Farhi, "Weapons Firms Carry Out Ad Blitzes," *Washington Post*, July 29, 1989, F1.

49. An overview of these activities is provided by Forman, "Program That Wouldn't Die," 7–12.

50. Arnold, interview and follow-up correspondence, November 21, 1994; Richard L. Berke, "Lobbying Steps Up on Military Buying as Budget Shrinks," *New York Times*, April 9, 1990, A16; and Louis Uchitelle, "An Odd Aircraft's Tenacity Shows Difficulty of Cutting Arms Budget," *New York Times*, November 2, 1992, D4.

51. Forman, "Program That Wouldn't Die," 10.

52. *Navy Program Review*, hearing of the House Armed Services Committee, May 11, 1989, 254 (official transcript).

53. Ibid., 247.

54. Ibid., 282.

55. Griffiths, "Congress May Ram a Chopper," 92.

56. George C. Wilson, "Aspin, Contractors Trying to Save Defense Budget," *Washington Post,* June 15, 1989, A24.

57. Pat Towell, "Party Battle Lines Are Fuzzy in House Defense Debate," *Congressional Quarterly Weekly Report,* June 17, 1989, 1486.

58. Ibid.; and Pat Towell, "The Politics of Procurement Creates New Alliances," *Congressional Quarterly Weekly Report,* June 24, 1989, 1557–1558.

59. Towell, "Politics of Procurement," 1560.

60. Andrew Rosenthal, "New Steps for the Military Budget Dance," *New York Times,* June 27, 1989, A20.

61. Pat Towell, "Saving Some Projects, Panel Bites the Funding Bullet," *Congressional Quarterly Weekly Report,* July 1, 1989, 1637.

62. Molly Moore, "Cheney, Aspin Rebuffed on 2 Projects," *Washington Post,* June 29, 1989, A16; and Pat Towell, "With House Floor Debate Near, Cheney Argues for 'Stealth,'" *Congressional Quarterly Weekly Report,* July 15, 1989, 1803.

63. Pat Towell, "Defense Panel Axes Funding for Troubled New Fighter," *Congressional Quarterly Weekly Report,* July 22, 1989, 1884.

64. See Pat Towell, "House Deals Bush Team Blows on Missiles, Weapons Cuts," *Congressional Quarterly Weekly Report,* July 29, 1989, 1974, 1976.

65. George C. Wilson, "Cheney Warns Defense Bill Risks a Veto," *Washington Post,* August 13, 1989, A20; and Molly Moore, "Cheney Lambastes House on Defense Budget Cuts," *Washington Post,* August 24, 1989, A11.

66. Andrew Rosenthal, "Senate Committee Approves Cheney's '90 Military Plan," *New York Times,* July 15, 1989, 8; Dan Morgan, "Panel Backs Cheney on Navy F-14, B-2," *Washington Post,* July 15, 1989, A10; and Pamela Fessler and Pat Towell, "Senate Defense Measure Sticks Closer to Bush Blueprint," *Congressional Quarterly Weekly Report,* July 29, 1989, 1984.

67. Waller, "Will the Osprey Ever Fly?" 16.

68. Pat Towell, "Budget Squeeze Sets the Stage for Defense Money Fights," *Congressional Quarterly Weekly Report,* September 16, 1989, 2407.

69. Ibid.

70. Pat Towell, "Senate Panel Adds Its Support to Bush Defense Program," *Congressional Quarterly Weekly Report,* September 23, 1989, 2484.

71. Michael R. Gordon, "Lawmakers Agree on 'Star Wars' Cut," *New York Times,* November 3, 1989, A17.

72. David Brown, "Bell, Boeing Push V-22 Flight Test Program," *Aviation Week & Space Technology,* October 16, 1989, 38.

73. George C. Wilson, "Navy Ordered to Cancel Plane Popular on Hill," *Washington Post,* December 2, 1989, A4.

74. Scharfen, "U.S. Marine Corps in 1989," 180.

75. Pamela Fessler, "Cheney's Spending Blueprint Faces Welter of Changes," *Congressional Quarterly Weekly Report,* February 3, 1990, 335.

76. Ibid.

77. See House Armed Services Committee, *Navy and Marine Corps FY 1991,* 107.

78. See Scharfen, "U.S. Marine Corps in 1989," 181; and David A. Brown, "Japan's Ishida Group May Build Tilt-Wing Transport in U.S.," *Aviation Week & Space Technology,* January 1, 1990, 83–87.

79. House Armed Services Committee, *Navy and Marine Corps FY 1991,* 102, 105–107. Also see Flanagan, "Slipping Away," 43; House Armed Services Committee,

V-22 Osprey Program Review, 206; and House Armed Services Committee, *Status of V-22,* 44.

80. See Berke, "Lobbying Steps Up," A1, A16.

81. *Amended Defense Authorization Request for FY 1991 and the Fiscal Years 1991–1995 Five-year Defense Plan,* hearing of the House Armed Services Committee, February 28, 1990, 501–521 (official transcript).

82. See Cooper, "V-22 Tilt-Rotor Aircraft," CRS-5.

83. Pat Towell, "Hill Searching for Answers on Where to Make Cuts," *Congressional Quarterly Weekly Report,* March 24, 1990, 924.

84. "Senate Appropriators Blast Cheney for Not Releasing Data on V-22," *Inside the Navy,* June 1990, 4–5.

85. See Cooper, "V-22 Tilt-Rotor Aircraft," CRS-5; Eric Schmitt, "Cheney Disputed on Plane's Merits," *New York Times,* July 15, 1990, 15; and Floyd D. Kennedy Jr., "U.S. Naval Aircraft and Weapons Development in 1990," *U.S. Naval Institute Proceedings,* May 1991, 166.

86. Cooper, "V-22 Tilt-Rotor Aircraft," CRS-6.

87. Schmitt, "Cheney Disputed," 15; and Cooper, "V-22 Tilt-Rotor Aircraft," CRS-6.

88. Schmitt, "Cheney Disputed," 15.

89. Pat Towell, "House Panel's Diet Defense Bill Would Cancel B-2 Production," *Congressional Quarterly Weekly Report,* August 4, 1990, 2531.

90. Ibid.; and Patrick E. Tyler, "Bush Aides Deploy on Capitol Hill in Effort to Rescue Defense Budget," *Washington Post,* August 2, 1990, A12.

91. All the figures in this paragraph are drawn from Pat Towell, "Senate Clears Military Bill after Panel Squabbles," *Congressional Quarterly Weekly Report,* November 3, 1990, 3724, 3728–3729.

92. For a subsequent discussion of this issue, see House Armed Services Committee, *V-22 Osprey Program Review,* 123, 220.

93. Stanley W. Kandebo, "Shipboard Tests Confirm V-22's Operating Capability," *Aviation Week & Space Technology,* January 14, 1991, 36–40.

94. Pat Towell, "Bush Begins Effort to Shrink Military by One-Fourth," *Congressional Quarterly Weekly Report,* February 9, 1991, 379.

95. *Fiscal Years 1992–1993 National Defense Authorization Request,* hearing of the House Armed Services Committee, February 7, 1991, 85–86 (official transcript).

96. Ibid., 104.

97. House Armed Services Committee, *Navy and Marine Corps FY 1992,* 411–412.

98. Ibid., 413.

99. Ibid., 414.

100. George Hager, "'Dire Emergency' Spending Bill," *Congressional Quarterly Weekly Report,* April 6, 1991, 879.

101. "OSD, Contractors at Odds on Spending $200 Million Appropriated for V-22," *Inside the Navy,* April 1991, 1, 7–8.

102. House Armed Services Committee, *V-22 Osprey Program Review,* 121.

103. Ibid., 123.

104. Ibid., 220.

105. Ibid., 146.

106. On cost overruns, see "Pentagon Cites Boeing Costs," *New York Times,* December 12, 1991, D19.

107. Stanley W. Kandebo, "Osprey Flight Tests Suspended after Crash of No. 5 Aircraft," *Aviation Week & Space Technology,* June 17, 1991, 53–54.

108. Floyd D. Kennedy Jr., "U.S. Naval Aircraft and Weapons Development in 1991," *U.S. Naval Institute Proceedings,* May 1992, 170.

109. Senator Arlen Specter, R-Pa., quoted the FY 1992 conference report during a subsequent committee hearing. See *Department of Defense Appropriations for Fiscal Year 1993: Marine Corps,* hearing of the Senate Appropriations Committee, March 3, 1992, 184–185 (official transcript).

110. Pat Towell and Andrew Taylor, "Aspin, Cheney Spar Face-to-Face but Stay Far Apart on Budget," *Congressional Quarterly Weekly Report,* February 8, 1992, 325.

111. Senate Defense Appropriations Subcommittee, "Defense Appropriations for FY 1993: Marine Corps," 184–185.

112. See ibid., 185; House Armed Services Committee, *Procurement and Military Nuclear Systems Subcommittee,* 115; *Department of Defense Appropriations for Fiscal Year 1993,* hearing of the Senate Defense Appropriations Subcommittee, May 21, 1992, 929–930 (official transcript); and House Armed Services Committee, *Status of V-22,* 1–52.

113. See House Armed Services Committee, *Status of V-22,* 3, 6.

114. House Armed Services Committee, *Procurement and Military Nuclear Systems Subcommittee,* 88, 118–128.

115. Eric Schmitt, "Grim Reaper for Military Budgets," *New York Times,* May 7, 1992, D8.

116. House Armed Services Committee, *Procurement and Military Nuclear Systems Subcommittee,* 121, 202.

117. Forman, "Program That Wouldn't Die," 17.

118. Pat Towell, "Aspin Wants $274 Billion, $3 Billion Below Cap," *Congressional Quarterly Weekly Report,* May 30, 1992, 1544.

119. Eric Rosenberg, "White House Rejects Republican Advances to Meet on Osprey," *Defense Week,* June 1, 1992, 3.

120. Robert K. Dornan, "Dornan, Cheney to Meet on V-22," news release, June 4, 1992, provided to the author; and Robert K. Dornan, "Dornan Cautiously Optimistic about V-22," news release, July 8, 1992, provided to the author.

121. Steven Pearlstein, "Cheney to Release Funds for Marine Tilt-Rotor Plane," *Washington Post,* July 3, 1992, A15; and John D. Morrocco, "Pentagon Reaffirms Narrow V-22 Mission, Reaffirms Medium Lift Need," *Aviation Week & Space Technology,* July 27, 1992, 25. For an excerpt of Cheney's letter to Congress, see House Armed Services Committee, *Status of V-22,* 49.

122. See Pearlstein, "Cheney to Release Funds," A15.

123. See Pat Towell, "Big-Ticket Projects Remain Intact as House Passes Spending Bill," *Congressional Quarterly Weekly Report,* July 4, 1992, 1979; and Pat Towell, "Osprey Fans Keep the Faith," *Congressional Quarterly Weekly Report,* July 25, 1992, 2182.

124. Sean O'Keefe, telephone interview, January 13, 1997.

125. Robert Pear, "Disputed Military Aircraft Crashes; 7 Aboard Lost," *New York Times,* July 21, 1992, A1, A16.

126. Clifford Krauss, "New Doubts Voiced over Disputed Plane," *New York Times,* July 22, 1992, A12.

127. Towell, "Osprey Fans," 2182.

128. See Morrocco, "Pentagon Reaffirms," 25; Forman, "Program That Wouldn't Die," 19; and Robert K. Dornan, "Dornan Criticizes Pentagon Panel over V-22," news release, 27 July 1992, provided to the author.

129. Morrocco, "Pentagon Reaffirms," 25.

130. House Armed Services Committee, *Status of V-22,* 3, 21.

131. Eric Schmitt, "Jet Sales to Saudis and Taiwan Weighed," *New York Times,* August 25, 1992, A14; and John Lancaster, "Military Moves with Political Overtones," *Washington Post,* September 3, 1992, A1.

132. Sean O'Keefe emphasized this point during a guest lecture at the Maxwell School of Citizenship and Public Affairs at Syracuse University, August 2, 1995.

133. Reuters, "Boeing and Textron Get $550 Million Contract," *New York Times,* October 24, 1992, 37.

134. Schmitt, "Jet Sales," A14.

135. Statement before the Los Angeles World Affairs Council, August 1992, reprinted in Boeing Defense & Space Group, "The V-22 Osprey: America's Airplane," 1993.

136. Uchitelle, "An Odd Aircraft," D4.

137. Bill Miller, "Navy Says Flash Fire Caused Osprey Crash," *Washington Post,* September 30, 1992, D3.

138. Pat Towell, "Spending Bill Trims Some Now, Sets Bigger Cuts in Motion," *Congressional Quarterly Weekly Report,* October 10, 1992, 3189; and Pat Towell, "Bill Shaves Personnel Spending but Slices Weapons Purchases," *Congressional Quarterly Weekly Report,* October 17, 1992, 3264.

139. On other models, such as the Bell Quad Tiltrotor, see Michael D. Towle, "Osprey's Big Cousin Excites Pentagon," September 26, 1999, www.helis.com.

140. The number of congressional districts is based on subcontracts awarded since 1992. John Wagner, "War for the Osprey: The Money and the Machine," *News and Observer* (Raleigh, N.C.), March 27, 2001, 1A, 6A.

10 The U.S.-EC Beef Hormone Dispute and U.S. Trade Strategy

Carolyn Rhodes

Before You Begin

   1. Why did the European Community institute a ban on beef produced with the aid of hormones, and what was the U.S. position on the ban?

   2. How did U.S. domestic interest groups influence government policy toward the EC ban, and what role did "organic beef" producers play in formulating U.S. policy?

   3. Why were the Office of the United States Trade Representative and the Department of Agriculture involved in negotiating and setting policy in this dispute?

   4. Why did the United States and European Community pursue bilateral negotiations throughout this dispute as well as appeal to the World Trade Organization?

   5. What are the limits of multilateral dispute settlement procedures?

   6. How much of a role should consumer perceptions play in determining public policy? Should international standards for product safety and healthful food production govern trade?

   7. What was the U.S. strategy for opening the EC market to U.S. beef? Who is most affected by U.S. trade retaliation? Is retaliation an effective way to change EC behavior?

Introduction: Trade Policy and Food

When you go to McDonald's to buy a Big Mac or sit down with your family for a roast beef dinner, do you stop to think about where the meat you are eating came from, whether it is safe and healthy, or why it costs what it does? Probably not. As consumers we rarely think about where food originates or how it was produced, but the choices available in the supermarket and restaurants are largely determined not only by domestic farming practices but also by national policies regulating food production and trade. The same is true in other countries as well, and an interesting aspect of international commerce is that when one nation's farming practices and public policies are different from another's, trade between them may be inhibited. Even if consumers abroad want to buy certain U.S. food products, their countries' policies may restrict access to them. Products that American consumers may be accustomed to and consider healthful may not be regarded that way elsewhere. This has been the situation for the past fifteen years in the case of beef produced in the United States and destined for the European Community.[1]

Consumers in Denmark, France, Germany, and the other of the fifteen member states of the European Community cannot buy the beef that is available in the United States. With minor exceptions, all the beef consumed in these countries must be produced in them as well. Even though U.S. producers are among the most efficient in the world and are capable of exporting beef to Europe at prices often lower than that produced locally, EC regulations block their full access to European markets. Why is this the case? Who are the interested parties? What does the dispute mean for U.S. foreign policy?

To answer the above questions and others, this case study explores the dispute between the United States and the European Community over hormone-raised beef, a long-standing trade issue. It specifically looks at how U.S. strategy aimed to achieve major policy goals and the side effects that strategy produced. Punctuated by acts of retaliation and highly charged rhetoric, as well as by sincere efforts by trade negotiators to reach an agreement, the beef hormone dispute has raised many questions about the effectiveness of U.S. trade policy in the face of different standards for food. Is the U.S. government able to keep open export markets for its producers? How credible is multilateral trade dispute settlement under the World Trade Organization (WTO)? How effective are international standards in the face of stiff societal opposition and widely divergent opinions?

Background: Origins of the Trade Dispute

Since 1985 the United States and the European Community have been engaged in a trade dispute over whether U.S. beef produced with the aid of hormone implants should be allowed into the European market. This disagreement not only has created mistrust between the world's two largest trading partners but has also threatened to undermine the World Trade Organization's dispute settlement procedure, to which the matter was submitted. The WTO was established in 1995 to encourage free trade through the reduction of trade barriers. Given the WTO's mission, and because the United States has long been the leading force behind developing free trade rules among member nations, the WTO's legitimacy and effectiveness are considered vital to U.S. trade policy. In addition, some of the EC states are among the United States' closest allies. It is therefore important to U.S. foreign policy that this trade dispute not damage bilateral relations.

Hormone Use in Food Production

For years, growth-promoting hormones have been used in Argentina, Australia, Canada, Mexico, New Zealand, the United States, and Uruguay to enhance the efficiency of beef production. According to agriculture specialists, "Livestock producers use hormones because they speed up growth rates and produce a leaner carcass more in line with consumer preferences for diets with reduced fat and cholesterol."[2] The hormones approved for use in the United States include estrogen and testosterone or "other similar natural compounds" that exist naturally in an animal or have been produced to mimic naturally occurring compounds.[3] A small pellet of the compound is implanted just under the skin at the back of the animal's ear. The hormone is released slowly over time, simulating the animal's natural hormone production. The hormones not only encourage more rapid growth, but also more efficient use of feed. The U.S. Meat Export Federation, an interest group representing meat exporters, claimed that "animals that are implanted with these growth-promoting hormones grow as much as 15 to 20 percent faster than untreated animals."[4] The industry, therefore, has a keen interest in using the implants.

Thirty years of experience with hormone implants, under the regulatory and scientific oversight of the U.S. Department of Agriculture (USDA), support the cattle industry's position that hormone use is safe for consumers of beef. Studies conducted since the 1950s by the USDA and other agencies, including the Food and Drug Administration and the Center for Veterinary Medicine, have consistently shown that hormone implants in beef do not present a risk to human health.[5] Analysts point out that hormones occur naturally in all animals and are necessary for growth and other physiological functions and that naturally occurring hormones—even in plants—exist at rates many times higher than the hormone levels used to promote growth in cattle. As one official report notes, "Some of the hormones are found naturally in concentrations from ten times higher than in beef to hundreds of times higher in eggs, butter, and broccoli."[6]

The beef industry argues, therefore, that hormone use is not only safe, but that it also replicates nature and is used in much smaller amounts than occur in nature. Quoting a local veterinarian, one Midwest newspaper reported, "An implanted animal will gain the same amount on about 10 percent less feed. By

The U.S.-EC Beef Hormone Dispute

1980 Reports in Italy link diethyl stilboestrol (DES), an illegally used hormone, with enlarged genitals in children. Green parties press for the prohibition of all growth hormones in livestock production.

1981 The EC Council of Ministers prohibits the use of two DES hormones presumed to be harmful to humans.

1984 Scientific research in the European Community concludes that natural hormones are safe when administered in proper dosages.

1985 The Council of Ministers issues a directive banning the use of all hormones in slaughter animals. The council also prohibits the importation of such animals from third-party states.

January 1987 The Reagan administration announces retaliatory tariffs against European exports.

The United States requests creation of an investigative committee and a panel of experts within the General Agreement on Tariffs and Trade (GATT) to assess the legality of the European ban on hormone-treated beef. The European Community blocks the investigation, but offers to allow beef imports if it can be certified to the community's satisfaction that they are hormone free.

January 1988 Third-party states (including the United States) whose processing facilities have not been approved by the European Community are banned from exporting *any* beef to community states. The United States has no approved facilities.

March 1988 After temporarily lifting the ban on hormone-treated beef, the EC Council of Ministers re-adopts the ban directive in unaltered form to go into effect in January 1989.

January 1989 The United States responds to the EC ban with retaliatory tariffs affecting more than $100 million in products.

February 1989 The European Community and the United States take their disputes to GATT, but each blocks the formation of panels to judge the other's complaint. A bilateral task force is formed to negotiate a compromise solution to the ban.

May 1989 The bilateral task force results in an interim agreement to set up a certification system for U.S. producers of hormone-free beef. U.S. retaliatory tariffs are to be reduced as access to the EC market warrants.

continued on the next page

continued from the previous page

1995 The World Trade Organization (WTO) is established through the Uruguay Round of trade negotiations, and a number of supplemental agreements are reached, including the Sanitary and Phytosanitary Agreement (SPS), which governs trade in food. The WTO includes a binding dispute settlement procedure.

April 1996 The United States and several other countries file a complaint with the WTO over the European ban.

August 1997 The WTO dispute settlement panel rules that the EC ban is inconsistent with EC obligations under the SPS agreement. The community appeals the ruling to the Appellate Body of the WTO.

January 1998 The WTO Appellate Body finds that the EC ban contravenes the SPS agreement, but allows the community to conduct its own risk assessment of hormone-treated meat.

April 1999 The European Community offers to expand the U.S beef quota and to consider labeling as options for settling the dispute. Bilateral negotiations ensue.

May 1999 Still working to complete its risk assessment, the European Community refuses to alter its ban on hormone-treated beef imports; ongoing negotiations result in an impasse. In accordance with WTO provisions, the United States, along with Canada, requests authorization to suspend certain trade concessions to the community as compensation.

July 1999 The United States and Canada are authorized by the WTO to suspend trade concessions to the European Community. The United States withdraws concessions on EC products worth $116.8 million.

May 2000 The European Commission announces its intention to implement a permanent ban on one beef hormone and continue the provisional ban on five others. Meanwhile, Congress passes legislation requiring the Office of the United States Trade Representative to review and rotate tariffs used for retaliation.

September 2000 The Clinton administration announces a list of "carousel tariffs" to rotate against the European Community but does not implement them, pending further negotiations with the community.

January–June 2001 The George W. Bush administration continues the Clinton policy of postponing implementation of carousel tariffs.

slaughter, the hormone has been all used up and there's only a trace level difference between implanted and non-implanted meat."[7] The article also compares estrogen levels of implanted beef with a number of other foods to make this point:

> 3 oz. of non-implanted beef has 1.3 nanograms (a nanogram is one billionth of a gram) of estrogen; 3 oz. of implanted beef has 1.9 nanograms of estrogen; 3 oz. of potatoes has 225 nanograms of estrogen; 3 oz. of garden peas have 340 nanograms of estrogen; 3 oz. of cabbage have 2,000 nanograms of estrogen, and 3 oz. of soybean oil has 1,680,000 nanograms of estrogen.[8]

Most American consumers have shown little concern about the safety of this practice, either because of a general acceptance or ignorance of the issue.[9]

Because the use of hormone implants in U.S. beef is so widespread, any bovine meat destined for the domestic consumer is likely to have been produced with them. According to a senior specialist in agricultural policy with the Congressional Research Service, "approximately 63 percent of all cattle and 90 percent of the cattle in feedlot" in the United States are implanted with growth hormones.[10] Consequently, most of the beef exported to Europe when this dispute erupted in the mid-1980s was likely produced with hormones.

Apprehensions in Europe

Meat produced from cattle implanted with hormones was not a subject of controversy in Europe until 1980, when the Italian government revealed that the hormone diethyl stilboestrol (DES), not licensed for use in food products, had been discovered in baby food. In the ensuing controversy over the presence of this hormone, it was reported that babies who had eaten the food were growing breasts and enlarged genitals. Across Europe, advocates for natural foods seized upon the reports from Italy as evidence against producing food with the aid of hormones.[11] In another highly publicized case, similar compounds (derived from stilbenes or thyrostatic substances) "were reported to have been injected into the rump of a veal calf just before slaughter. The substance was thus concentrated in a small quantity of meat, which was eaten by a young boy who later began to develop breasts."[12] None of the substances in question in these cases were (or are) legal for use in meat production in the United States, but the outcry against hormones in Europe targeted all hormone implants, regardless of whether scientific studies had endorsed them.

Responding to pressure from European consumer groups worried that the Italian cases indicated a more widespread problem, in 1981 the European

Community acted. The Council of Ministers, the community's main legislative body, prohibited the use of two hormones (from the DES category) that were presumed to be harmful to humans, pending results of research that was then being conducted in Europe. Concerned that such an approach was too conservative, Green parties, especially the West German Green Party, argued that all so-called growth hormones should be banned.[13] As the debate continued, in 1984 research by European scientists showed that natural hormones, meaning hormones obtained from natural sources, did not constitute a health risk. If the hormones were administered in proper dosages, these studies reported, there should be no adverse effects in consumers.[14] This finding corroborated what had been concluded in the United States years prior.

Nevertheless, the controversy raged on in Europe, as Green activists worried that over time hormone use could produce ill effects in humans. This concern led Europeans to be wary of all hormone-implanted meat, and the perception that meat produced with the aid of hormones was harmful began to overshadow scientific evidence. As one analyst explained, "Different cultures and attitudes influence the legal determination of when there is a food safety risk and how to respond to such a risk." She added, "With regard to comparative notions of what constitutes a food safety risk, it is interesting to contrast European and U.S. attitudes toward traditional production methods on the one hand, and modern technological processes on the other."[15] For example, in Europe unpasteurized cheese is not a concern to consumers who value traditional methods of production, yet high-technology applications to agriculture are met with suspicion and distrust. In the United States those attitudes are reversed. Americans are generally much more receptive to and comfortable with high-tech applications that make food more abundant or safe. In both cases, "attitudes follow through into the entities' respective legal regimes." The differences in culture lead to different laws and help to explain why the European Commission, the EC executive body, would argue that a "social factor—in addition to science—must be considered in food legislation."[16] It was largely this social factor that caused the Council of Ministers to take action to protect its citizenry.

Defenders of U.S. interests have argued that EC beef producers may be more concerned about protecting themselves from beef imports than with public health. Although the ban of hormone use domestically in the European Community preceded the import ban, the entire process, they argue, was motivated by different reasons. By the mid-1980s the community's Common Agricultural Policy (CAP) had produced too much beef due to two decades of price supports, which encouraged domestic production even when it was not competitive on the international market. As one observer noted, "By 1985, these surpluses were so large that [EC] policy makers were supportive of any measure that would limit beef imports likely to compete with domestic production and interfere with the operation of the CAP."[17] The ban on hormone-treated beef was an obvious solution.

Even if one could not prove that the hormone issue was the result of protectionism, it is probably fair to say that policy makers were more receptive to actions that restricted beef production in general and imports in particular. The Council of Ministers, therefore, issued a directive in 1985 banning all hormone use in slaughter animals within the community. The council also prohibited the importation of such animals (or the meat derived from them) from third-party states.[18] Because the United States exported approximately $100 million worth of beef annually to the European Community, the ban was a serious threat to U.S. economic interests, especially because at the time beef prices were low and any contraction of the market was viewed with alarm.

U.S. Reactions and EC Responses

Urged to act by the National Cattlemen's Beef Association (NCBA), the U.S. government complained that the European Community had no right under GATT international trade rules to impose such a restriction. The NCBA is a highly active group representing the vast majority of beef producers in the United States, but is dominated, its critics argue, by large and corporate ranchers who use a $1 fee per head of cattle from members to fund their lobbying efforts to "support liberalized trade, the World Trade Organization, hormone-ridden beef, and the overall corporate agenda for cattle."[19] Focusing on the administration's legal authority to have the Office of the United States Trade Representative (USTR) investigate the European ban and determine appropriate responses, the NCBA pressed for action. In January 1987 the Reagan administration announced that it would invoke Section 301 of the Trade Act of 1974, which authorizes the USTR to investigate alleged unfair trading practices of U.S. trade partners and to impose retaliatory tariffs. A set of goods exported from the European Community to the United States would have new import taxes imposed on them with the purpose of pricing the goods out of the U.S. market. Congress, which is much more subject to pressure from domestic interests than is the executive branch, had passed the provision in response to industry demands for action against trade partners who engaged in alleged unfair practices. The use of Section 301 was a signal to U.S. beef producers that something was being done and to the European Community that it could not take protectionist action with impunity.

While the United States was pursuing this unilateral strategy, it also requested that an investigative committee and a panel of experts be created within the General Agreement on Tariffs and Trade (GATT) to assess the legality of the EC ban. GATT, a multilateral cooperative regime created to govern trade in 1947 (and incorporated into the WTO in 1995), had provisions against the erection of new trade barriers. The United States hoped that GATT would consider the beef import ban an unfair trade restriction and rule in its favor. The European Community, insisting that it had the right to determine whether beef produced with hormones posed a health risk and to protect its citizenry, opposed the undertaking of any investigative effort on the part of GATT. Under GATT rules prior to 1995, the unwillingness of either disputing party to submit to arbitration automatically blocked the formation of an investigative panel, so the merits of the case were never considered under GATT auspices.

As a compromise, the European Community offered to allow imports of beef from the United States if U.S. officials could certify to EC satisfaction the meat to be hormone free. There were two problems with this offer. First, because most U.S. beef producers used hormone implants, it would take a major regulatory effort to segregate this meat from hormone-free beef, and it would exclude established beef-producing interests. Second, the European Community had never considered the testing of meat for detectable hormone residue to be reliable.

Instead, the entire beef production process was to be monitored and affidavits signed along the way to verify that no implants were used. At the time, the United States had no procedures to police beef production to ensure hormone-free status, and the European Community had no confidence in the USDA's commitment to do so anyway. Although some enterprising cattle producers in the United States saw the EC ban and certification requirement as an opportunity to create a niche market for organic beef, the unrealistic certification process made exporting to the European Community nearly impossible. In addition, the community added a January 1988 deadline for beef-processing facilities in the United States and elsewhere to meet EC requirements. Otherwise, no beef imports would be allowed. When the deadline came and went and the European Community had not certified any U.S. facilities, the offer to allow market access for hormone-free beef appeared pretty hollow to the U.S. beef industry and trade advocates. They continued to press the U.S. government to persuade the community to restore imports of beef produced with hormones.

In the meantime, interest groups within the European Community were divided about the council's ban on hormone-assisted meat production. British beef producers, backed by the British Ministry of Agriculture, demanded that the ban be lifted because of the lack of scientific evidence. The British position was that legal and appropriate use of growth hormones should be allowed, because their safety had been proven for many years. British farmers were angry that illegal hormone use in Italy had incited such an extreme response from the community, and they lobbied their government to pressure the Council of Ministers to change its directive. In response to a complaint by the United Kingdom, the council on procedural grounds temporarily nullified the ban in January 1988, but reinstated it in March 1988 to go into effect in January 1989.[20] In response to beef industry pressure, the United States again invoked Section 301 of the Trade Act of 1974, which had been strengthened in 1988, to immediately retaliate by imposing tariffs on a range of EC products, including tomatoes, citrus fruit, pasta, and ham, amounting to more than $100 million.[21]

In February 1989 both parties took the dispute to GATT, logging formal complaints. In its filing, the United States claimed that the ban created unnecessary obstacles to trade. As before, the European Community blocked the formation of a GATT technical panel to hear the case. In its own separate complaint, the community claimed that U.S. retaliatory tariffs violated GATT Articles I and II, which commit signatories to most favored nation treatment and nondiscrimination. The Europeans requested that the GATT council rule directly or appoint a panel for settlement. In turn, the United States blocked the formation of a panel unless the community lifted its objection to a hearing of the U.S. complaint.[22] The stalemate, therefore, continued.

The United States and the European Community were concerned, however, that the hormone dispute would derail the ongoing Uruguay Round of GATT trade negotiations, which had begun in 1986. These negotiations held the promise of further liberalization of global trade, especially in areas not fully governed, such as agricultural products, services, and intellectual property. The stakes on both sides of the Atlantic were high, as business and export interests lobbied their respective governments for the successful completion of the negotiations. Consequently, the trading partners created a bilateral task force in February 1989 to find a solution, and on May 3 an interim agreement was announced, aimed at facilitating the export of hormone-free U.S. beef to the EC market. The EC was to

> set up a certification system that would generate a list of U.S. producers of
> hormone-free beef who would qualify to export to the [European Commu-

nity]. Animals would arrive at U.S. slaughterhouses accompanied by affidavits to support the producers' claims of hormone-free beef. The Food Safety and Inspection Service (FSIS) of the U.S. Department of Agriculture (USDA) would insure that animals came from producers certified by the [EC] system.[23]

This interim agreement contained three important goals that reflected the U.S. strategy of keeping the conflict from escalating out of control. First, it prevented the hormone dispute from becoming a mini trade war, which in turn could have disrupted the Uruguay Round and prevented progress on other pending agreements. These included an agreement that U.S. policy makers hoped would create a clear set of international rules to govern trade in plant and animal foods. Second, the agreement maintained some trade (eventually about one-fifth the amount before the ban) in U.S. beef to the EC market, which would partially mollify the U.S. beef industry. Third, it kept U.S.-EC negotiators involved in dispute settlement rather than allowing the relationship to deteriorate into tit-for-tat trade restrictions and non-communication. Thus, for the time being, the U.S. administration accepted a compromise that did not fully satisfy domestic interests, but demonstrated an effort to assist them, while at the same time maintaining good relations with the European Community during the crucial Uruguay Round of negotiations.

In the interests of their strong bilateral trade relationship, as well as in the interest of the multilateral trading regime then undergoing reform, neither the United States nor the European Community wanted the beef hormone dispute to do too much damage. The U.S. strategy, therefore, was to accept this temporary agreement but continue to insist that the EC ban on beef raised with hormones was a form of "regulatory protectionism" that discriminated against U.S. producers without "any legitimate public health objective."[24]

New Rules: The WTO Takes on the Beef Hormone Dispute

In 1995 the Uruguay Round of trade negotiations culminated in the creation of the World Trade Organization and the completion of a number of supplemental agreements, including the Sanitary and Phytosanitary Agreement (SPS) to govern trade in food. These developments were significant for the U.S.-EC beef hormone dispute because they created a new set of rules and procedures for dealing with trade disputes in general and with health regulations in particular. Specifically, the WTO included a *binding* dispute settlement procedure that made it illegal for either party to a dispute to block a formal complaint from being considered. Because blocking complaints was the EC strategy for avoiding a GATT review of its ban, this change was significant.

In addition, agricultural products were placed under GATT rules. Previously, signatories to the agreement could sidestep GATT in some cases if agricultural trade was at issue, but this would no longer be possible after the Uruguay Round. The SPS agreement, a major priority of U.S. negotiators, set "rules that require a scientific basis for measures that restrict imports on the basis of health or safety concerns." Accordingly, "each country may set its own food safety and animal and plant health standards based on risk assessment and its determination of an acceptable level of risk. Alternatively, countries may use international standards."[25] Under the SPS agreement, a country may apply even stricter standards than those set internationally, but it must justify the stricter standards scientifically. In July 1995 the Codex Alimentarius Commission, the international organization that develops standards for safe food and guides the WTO in determining the legitimacy of nations' food standards, announced that it would base its food trade standards on science.[26] As one analyst commented,

> The Uruguay Round's SPS Agreement is significant for its attempt to discipline food safety measures, such as the Community's hormone ban, that are neither facially discriminatory nor patently discriminatory as applied. The principal vehicle for accomplishing this purpose is a scientific test, which marked the first time that scientific integrity has been identified as an explicit component of the GATT/WTO multilateral regime.[27]

Another trade law observer claimed that the SPS agreement was purposely drafted by U.S. negotiators to ensure that the European Community would lose in future dispute settlements of the beef hormone ban.[28] It is obvious why the United States did not want the beef hormone dispute to prevent the SPS agreement from being completed.

In April 1996, armed with the WTO's new dispute settlement procedure, as well as with the SPS agreement, the United States, joined by Australia, Canada, and New Zealand, filed a complaint against the EC hormone ban. It became the first WTO dispute settlement case brought under the SPS agreement. U.S. policy makers hoped that since import restrictions based on health safety concerns must now be backed by scientific evidence, this time the dispute would be resolved in their favor. Their hopes were further buttressed by two separate events. An EC conference in Brussels in November 1995 concluded that on the basis of experience and published data, there was "no evidence of human health risk arising from the controlled use of five hormones: oestradiol beta 17, progesterone, testosterone, zeranol, and trenbolone."[29] Also, the Alimentarius commission, which the SPS agreement identified as the authority on such matters, had voted in July 1995 to approve the use of natural hormones in meat production.[30]

In the meantime, however, unrelated developments in the British beef industry were causing alarm in Europe about the safety of beef in general and adding to skepticism about the healthiness of hormone-implanted beef. In 1994 connections were being made between bovine spongiform encephalopathy (BSE), commonly known as mad cow disease, which destroys brain tissue in cattle, and brain disease in humans. Reports from London linked people who had eaten McDonald's hamburgers with the contraction of a variant form of Creutzefeldt-Jakob Disease (CJD), a debilitating brain disease. This variant CJD is associated with BSE, and researchers suspect that it is passed from bovine species to humans through eating affected beef. Mad cow disease had been known to exist in Britain since 1985, but not until 1994 was a possible connection made with brain disease in humans. As British scientists attempted for two years to definitively establish a link, controversy raged in Europe over the safety of eating British beef. When British scientists announced in March 1996 that they "could not rule out a link between BSE and cases in Britain of a new strain of Creutzefeldt-Jakob Disease," the European Commission moved to ban shipment of British cattle and beef to other EC states.[31]

Although unrelated to the hormone implant issue, the mad cow scare added to European fears about modern feeding practices and the safety of their food supply.[32] This development was particularly ironic for the U.S. beef industry, which had a much more rigorous regulatory regime in place under the USDA for feeding cattle. Many American beef producers thought the mad cow problem in Europe might create a strong demand for "safe" U.S. beef, but the opposite happened. Coupled with unanimous support from the European Parliament, the elected body of the European Union, which "cited consumer worries, questions of animal welfare, meat quality and effects of hormones on the EU's beef and milk sectors, [EC] farm ministers responded to the U.S. threat [to take the hormone ban to the new WTO] . . . by voting 14 to 1 to maintain the ban."[33] In Europe, extending the ban was greeted with enthusiasm by many vocal groups. For example, in France, where farmers had for years rallied in demonstrations against McDonald's as a symbol of U.S. economic hegemony, the rallying cry was, "Foie gras will prevail! Hormone beef will not!" Other headlines read, "Stop McDonald's, Halt Coca-Cola, Down with . . . hormone treated beef!"[34] Clearly, concerns about the healthfulness of hormone-treated beef were intertwined with larger concerns about economic globalization and U.S. market dominance.

The WTO Decides

When the WTO announced the creation of an investigatory panel in response to the complaint filed by Australia, Canada, New Zealand, and the United States in April 1996, Agriculture Secretary Dan Glickman stated,

> The evidence is overwhelming that proper use of these hormones poses no danger to human or animal health. Even scientific groups composed by the EU have found that these hormones are safe when used properly. We hope that the panel process will lead to a re-opening of the EU market to U.S. beef—which would benefit consumers and producers on both sides of the Atlantic.[35]

According to the Dispute Settlement Understanding, panels would consist of three or five "well-qualified governmental and/or non-governmental individuals" who possess considerable trade law experience and who are not from the disputing parties.[36] These individuals would be nominated by the WTO Secretariat in Geneva. Such a panel was constituted to hear the complaints against the European Community, and in 1996 and 1997 each side presented its case before the WTO panel. In August 1997 the panel ruled that the EC ban on the use of hormones to promote the growth of cattle was inconsistent with EC obligations under the SPS agreement, citing in particular the position that the ban was not supported by scientific evidence, risk assessment, or relevant international standards. The panel stated, "By maintaining sanitary measures that do not rest on a scientific 'risk assessment,' the [European Community] has acted inconsistently with Article 5.1 of the SPS Agreement."[37]

U.S. policy makers were pleased with the outcome. U.S. Trade Representative Charlene Barshefsky said, "This final report confirms the value of the new WTO Agreement on the Application of Sanitary and Phytosanitary Measures in distinguishing legitimate food safety requirements from unscientific and unjustified barriers to U.S. exports. I am pleased that the WTO agreed that the [European Community] has no scientific basis for blocking the sale of American beef in Europe."[38] Secretary Glickman echoed her sentiment, saying, "The final report issued today by the WTO is welcome news for the U.S. beef industry. The WTO dispute settlement panel has affirmed what we have known for over nine years: that European consumers are being denied a high-quality and safe product due to an import regulation that cannot stand up to the test of good science."[39]

The European Community immediately appealed the ruling to the Appellate Body of the WTO, arguing that "it was entitled to select a risk level of no risk and that, having chosen that level of risk, the precautionary principle entitled [it] to ban the import of hormone-treated beef because there was a perception (among European consumers) that such beef created a health risk."[40]

In January 1998 the Appellate Body concurred with the panel's ruling that the ban contravened EC obligations under the SPS agreement because neither available scientific evidence nor international standards supported the reasoning behind it. The Appellate Body, however, left open the option of the community conducting its own risk assessment of hormone-treated beef. The implications of the latter opinion were twofold. First, it demonstrated that the European Community was not bound by existing international standards. Second, if the community could establish unacceptable risk based upon scientific evidence, it could legally keep the ban in place, regardless of what other nations or international organizations considered acceptable.

The Europeans announced that they would implement the finding in "as short a time period as possible." The United States, on the other hand, found such a vague commitment unacceptable and kept the pressure on. It demanded that the Europeans have fifteen months—the usual time for WTO signatories in past cases to implement the Appellate Body's finding—to come up with its own risk assessment. The European Commission then asked for four years. While the debate over the time frame raged, the European Community offered to negotiate compensation for its continuing ban, as is allowed under the WTO dispute settlement procedure. Hoping to limit U.S. compensation to beef and not allow U.S. retaliation to spill over into other areas of transatlantic trade, the community offered to double its import quota for hormone-free beef. Ambassador Barshefsky and Secretary Glickman met with Sir Leon Brittan, EC trade commissioner, to discuss possible solutions. "We are prepared to label U.S. meat to enable European consumers to make their own choice," Barshefsky said. "And, we are willing to discuss a temporary compensation package to provide the [European Community] a reasonable time to change its laws. But the question is whether [it] will respect the clear and unambiguous WTO ruling to lift its ban on U.S. meat."[41]

U.S. beef interests were not impressed with the EC offers, since U.S. exports only "fulfill[ed] about half of the existing hormone-free beef quota" as it was. A second offer, "which would allow imports of hormone-treated beef, but make them subject to labeling, foundered due to disagreements over the label's language."[42] Supporters of the EC ban argued that the reason the United States did not want to label its beef as containing hormones was that "if it goes on sale in European supermarkets . . . people over there wouldn't buy it," and there would be demands in the United States for similar labeling—a costly and potentially disruptive possibility for U.S. beef producers.[43] U.S. beef industry spokesmen argued that they were willing to allow the labeling of U.S. beef, but they wanted to be sure that the labeling was fair and accurate.

Meanwhile, a WTO arbitration panel gave the European Community until May 13, 1999, to comply with its ruling. As the deadline approached, negotiations stalemated and U.S.-EC relations sank to new lows. Reports from Brussels claimed that agriculture authorities had found traces of growth hormones in imported U.S. beef that had supposedly been certified hormone free. The community threatened that it would again ban all imports of beef from the United States if its officials did not "address the issue."[44] The U.S. beef industry saw the EC announcement as a negotiating tactic and diversion from the real issue—the legality of the EC ban.

Claiming that it had insufficient time to produce a risk assessment for its zero-tolerance policy, the European Community was unable to comply with the WTO requirement of reporting by May 13. Rather than accept that it could not make a case for its policy, the community refused to alter its ban on hormone-treated beef imports until the risk assessment was completed the following year. The announcement, made by EC consumer affairs commissioner Emma Bonino, "dropped a bombshell into the hubbub of predictions and expectations," according to one press account. "Citing the interim results of the first of the 17 studies, the chain-smoking Ms. Bonino said hormone-treated beef is so unsafe that it must continue to be banned from the EU market."[45]

That such conclusions were voiced so early in the process left many observers skeptical about the validity of the studies. Barshefsky said that although the United States remained open to talks to resolve the dispute, "we will absolutely protect our rights and we will without question retaliate if the [European Community] persists in disregarding the rules."[46] Following through later in the month, the United States, along with Canada, requested that the WTO "authorize suspension of the application to the European Union and its member states of Canadian and U.S. tariff concessions and related obligations in the amount of $202 million for the United States and $51 million for Canada."[47] The National Cattlemen's Beef Association commended the Clinton administration for its actions. NCBA president George Swan said, "NCBA applauds the U.S. government for announcing it will retaliate in the amount of $200 million against the European Union's ban on U.S. beef. While retaliation is a necessary step to force EU compliance, the only real resolution to this issue is access to the EU market for U.S. cattle producers."[48]

The Europeans disputed the amount of compensation requested by the United States, so the matter was again referred to an arbitration panel. In July 1999 the arbitration panel awarded the United States and Canada compensation—for the United States this amounted to $116.8 million worth of tariffs against EC products—because "the [European Community] had failed to comply within the reasonable period of time and no mutually acceptable temporary compensation has been agreed to, the United States had the right to request compensation."[49] WTO rules allow compensation to be taken in the form of the withdrawal of tariff concessions, which the United States did. EC officials still hoped to persuade the United States to accept some other form of compensation rather than resort to retaliation. Brittan expressed the hope that "Washington would agree to accept monetary compensation" for lost beef sales rather than impose tariffs.[50] The European Commission offered to expand access to the EC market for U.S. exporters in other product categories as compensation, but pressure from the U.S. beef industry, as well as a commitment by Barshefsky to punish the Europeans for the ban, prevented a softer compromise.[51] The Office of the United States Trade Representative, in consultation with the Commerce Department, USDA, and others, drew up a list of EC products that would have tariffs so high as to prevent them from entering the U.S. market. Notably, the list of goods did not include any products from the United Kingdom, the EC member that opposed the ban on growth-promoting hormones.

In 2000 Congress involved itself directly in U.S. trade enforcement strategy. Lobbied heavily by the NCBA, in the spring Congress passed new legislation governing Section 301 retaliations. Under Section 407 of the Trade Development Act of 2000, the Office of the United States Trade Representative must periodically review retaliatory actions and modify the targeted product lists if deemed necessary, mainly for maintaining the desired punitive effect against the European Community.[52] Dana Hauck, a cattle producer from Kansas and chair of the NCBA International Markets Committee, explained the NCBA's support: "The U.S. government should take an aggressive stand to demonstrate that these unfair trade practices will not be tolerated," she said.[53] Her statement was included with other NCBA testimony to support the bill in Congress, which the NCBA argued was an "effective tool to bring the European [Community] into compliance with international trade law." Barshefsky, however, cautioned that "changing the retaliation list [annually] could negatively affect negotiations with the European Union" and might adversely affect U.S. consumers and businesses.[54]

In May 2000 the European Community announced that it had no intention of lifting the hormone ban. In fact, it announced its intention to make the ban permanent, because it had "scientific evidence that confirms health risks posed by eating hormone-treated beef," and "to challenge U.S. and Canadian sanctions at the World Trade Organization as early as July 2001."[55] The European Commission was—as U.S. policy makers expected—displeased with the rotating tariff concept and protested it in the WTO. Arguing that the development was "contrary to the basic principle of the WTO, as Washington could act unilaterally in changing the targets of the sanctions at will," the commission said that it "created uncertainty for importers and exporters, and had an effect much larger than the trade retaliation authorized."[56] In September 2000 the Office of the United States Trade Representative drafted a new list of goods on which retaliatory tariffs would be imposed absent a mutually satisfactory agreement with the Europeans on the hormone ban. The 100 percent tariffs, which would affect about $117 million a year in EC exports to the United States, were aimed largely at products from Denmark, France, Germany, and Italy. A news release from the NCBA said that these "countries were chosen because they would be influential in the [European Community's] efforts to try to meet the WTO ruling. While Denmark is a relatively small EU member, it is a major meat (pork) exporter to the U.S."[57] The United States again made it clear that the United Kingdom was purposely excluded from retaliatory tariffs because of its "consistent voting record against the [EC] import ban."[58] Dubbed the "carousel sanctions" because of their rotating nature, these tariffs were aimed specifically at increasing the pressure on the European Community to reform its policy.

Despite the announcement of new tariffs, the Clinton administration never imposed them. In October 2000 Clinton sent a letter to European Council president Jacques Chirac personally urging "a renewed effort to resolve two festering trade disputes (the beef hormone dispute and the banana regime dispute)" before a U.S.-European summit scheduled for December.[59] As was allowed under the 2000 legislation, the president held off implementing the new tariffs pending progress on these issues. The George W. Bush administration continued the policy, and as of June 2001 the carousel tariffs had yet to be imposed.

Conclusion: The Efficacy of a Retaliatory Strategy

The retaliatory tariffs imposed by the United States have the potential to raise the costs of the EC policy on beef hormones even higher than before. EC consumers were already paying higher prices for beef because they did not have access to more efficiently produced beef from abroad. On top of that, the new tariffs could also impose costs on EC producers unrelated to the beef industry. These producers, it is argued in Washington, losing part of their market to a trade war over beef hormones, will pressure EC policy makers to bend. The U.S. strategy is to maintain retaliatory tariffs not so much as compensation for lost exports, but to create pressure. The National Cattlemen's Beef Association and the U.S. Meat Export Federation pushed this strategy, arguing for a punitive approach that might have some political effect within the European Community. In response to these interest groups, officials in the Office of the United States Trade Representative, in consultation with the Commerce and Agriculture Departments, specifically targeted "high-end" food products with a prominent presence in the U.S. market. In addition, EC countries that acted most visibly in favor of the hormone ban were singled out for retaliation. For example, Danish hams, French Roquefort cheese, and Italian tomato products were purposely and strategically included on the list.[60]

If the strategy works, it would achieve U.S. export policy goals, but at a cost to U.S. interests as well. If EC reform is not forthcoming—and there is no evidence that it is—the cost will be extensive and long term. When the United States imposes retaliatory tariffs, its strategy is guided by the idea that EC producers will want continued access to the U.S. market, and that by cutting them off the United States creates the atmosphere for domestic pressure on EC policy makers. The imposition of tariffs, however, does not impose costs only on EC producers. In the United States, importers, distributors, retailers, and consumers are also deprived of desired goods. Consequently, retaliation in the form of tariffs is a two-edged sword. The pressure points that the United States seeks to establish in Europe are also created within the United States against the retaliatory actions. Beef producers and exporters may find the policy appealing, but, as innocent bystanders, importers, and consumers of affected European products will no doubt find it frustrating and unfair.

The U.S.-EC trade dispute over beef hormones has stalemated. Neither side wants the dispute to escalate into a full-blown trade war, but at the same time neither side wants to concede. In the United States this means never officially encouraging the "organic" beef option, but instead adopting the trade groups' position that the EC ban is unacceptable and that the Europeans should be punished until they alter the practice. At the same time, however, U.S. strategy includes the larger foreign policy goal of containing the dispute so that U.S.-EC relations in general and broader foreign policy and trade policy goals are not threatened. For fifteen years the two trading partners sought bilateral and multilateral negotiations and arbitration to prevent the dispute from escalating, while each side pursued unilateral policies aimed at protecting its respective interests. The U.S. strategy irritates EC and member country officials and disrupts trade in areas not related to beef, but it has not forced EC policy makers to yield.

This friendly but highly competitive, relationship between the United States and the European Community has existed for decades, and it has been remarkably consistent. Both sides clearly value their transatlantic relationship at all levels, from trade to investment to security. Still, as democratic polities, they are subject to the pressures of their domestic interests. This case study demonstrates how, despite the changing global environment—the end of the cold war, which altered the character of the Atlantic alliance, and the creation of the European Union, which broadened and deepened Europe's belief in regional integration—these transatlantic partners maintain a high commitment to mutual cooperation even as they continue to squabble over trade issues.

Notes

1. Throughout this case study I have chosen to use the term *European Community*, even when referring to the European Union, which was created in 1992. Technically, all trade issues come under the purview of the European Community—one of the three pillars of European integration—not the European Union. The European Commission is the executive body that negotiates trade issues for the European Community. Students should be aware that writers may apply different rules to their use of the term, so it is possible to see European Union used interchangeably with European Community.

2. Charles E. Hanrahan, "The European Union's Ban on Hormone-Treated Meat," *Congressional Research Service Report for Congress*, February 8, 1996, 1.

3. Ibid.

4. Memorandum submitted by the U.S. Meat Export Federation (S 4) to the Select Committee on Agriculture, Appendices to the Minutes of Evidence, House of Commons, October 5, 1999. See http://www.parliament.uk.

5. Ibid.

6. Kathleen A. Ambrose, "Part II: Review of Key Substantive Agreements: Panel II D: Agreement on Technical Barriers to Trade (TBT) and Agreement on the Application of Sanitary and Phytosanitary Measures (SPS): Science and the WTO," *Law and Policy in International Business* 31 (2000): 863.

7. Phyllis Jacobs Griekspoor, "The Skinny on Fattening Beef," *Wichita Eagle,* January 9, 2000, 1B.

8. Ibid.

9. Speculation has arisen from time to time that hormones may have some ill effects, such as contributing to early puberty, but no scientific evidence has been produced in the United States to verify such speculation. *Time,* November 6, 2000, 84.

10. Hanrahan, "The European Union's Ban," 1.

11. *Financial Times,* December 29, 1988, 3.

12. Hanrahan, "European Union's Ban," 2.

13. Ibid.

14. George H. Rountree, "Raging Hormones: A Discussion of the World Trade Organization's Decision in the European Union–United States Beef Dispute," *Georgia Journal of International and Comparative Law* 3 (summer 1999): 608.

15. Marsha Echols, "Food Safety Regulation in the European Union and the United States: Different Cultures, Different Laws," *Columbia Journal of European Law* 4 (summer 1998): 530.

16. Ibid.

17. Charles E. Hanrahan, "RS20142: The European Union's Ban on Hormone-Treated Meat, Update," *CRS Issue Brief,* December 9, 1999.

18. Echols, "Food Safety Regulation," 530.

19. Rob Scott, "Exported to Death," *Dollars and Sense,* January/February 2000, 17.

20. Ibid.

21. Hanrahan, "European Union's Ban," 3.

22. Rountree, "Raging Hormones," 608.

23. Hanrahan, "European Union's Ban," 3.

24. Alan O. Sykes, "Regulatory Protectionism and the Law of International Trade," *University of Chicago Law Review* 6 (winter 1999): 3.

25. Hanrahan, "European Union's Ban," 4.

26. Rountree, "Raging Hormones," 614.

27. David A. Wirth, "International Decisions: European Communities' Measures Concerning Meat and Meat Products. WTO Doc. WT/DS26/AB. R&WT/DS48/AB/R. World Trade Organization Appellate Body, January 16, 1998," *American Journal of International Law* 92 (October 1998): 756.

28. Gary Horlick, "Sovereignty Revisited: Sovereignty, Trade, and the Environment—A U.S. Perspective," *Canada–United States Law Journal* 24 (1998): 179.

29. Hanrahan, "RS20142," 4.

30. Ibid.

31. Deutsche Presse-Agentur, March 25, 1996.

32. Many scientists speculated that mad cow disease developed in cattle as the result of a cross-species transmission. Because cattle in Britain had been fed offal from sheep with scrapie, a similar brain disease, the speculation is that the cattle acquired a mutated version from eating diseased offal. Always interested in cutting the costs of production, beef producers worldwide have experimented with feed of all sorts of animal by-products. The British case is apparently more extreme than others, but it raised objections among the public about what animals destined for human consumption should be fed.

33. Hanrahan, "RS20142," 2.

34. United States Information Agency, "U.S.-EU Trade Disputes: Hamburger, 'Frankenstein' Food vs. Foie Gras?" *Daily Digest,* August 25, 1999, 1.

35. Office of the United States Trade Representative, "WTO Panel to Review EU Hormone Directive," press release, May 20, 1996, http://www.ustr.gov/releases/1996/05/96-43.html.

36. Rountree, "Raging Hormones," 616.

37. Ibid.

38. Office of the United States Trade Representative, "WTO Hormones Report Confirms U.S. Win," press release, August 18, 1997, http://www.ustr.gov/releases/1997/08/97-76.pdf.

39. Ibid.

40. Ambrose, "Part II: Review of Key Substantive Agreements," 863.

41. Office of the United States Trade Representative, "USTR Barshefsky Committed to Resolving Beef Hormone Dispute," press release, April 19, 1999, http://www.ustr.gov/releases/1999/04/99-37.html.

42. Sean Murphy, "Contemporary Practice of the United States Relating to International Law," *American Journal of International Law* 93 (October 1999): 879.

43. Ian Cobain, "The Inside Scoop on American Feedlot Beef," *Daily Mail,* June 12, 1999.

44. *New York Times,* April 22, 1999, 8.

45. *Journal of Commerce,* May 11, 1999, 4A.

46. *New York Times,* May 15, 1999, 1.

47. Murphy, "Contemporary Practice," 879.

48. National Cattlemen's Beef Association, "Statement Regarding U.S. Retaliation against the EU Beef Ban by George Swan, President, National Cattlemen's Beef Association," May 14, 1999, http://hill.beef.org/ft/swstate.htm.

49. Memorandum submitted by the U.S. Meat Federation, 6.

50. Jennifer Walsh, "The Pate Hits the Fan: U.S. Imposing Beef Tariffs," *Houston Chronicle,* July 20, 1999, 1.

51. Ibid.

52. John R. Schmertz Jr. and Mike Meier, "US Preparing Sanctions for EU Failure to Implement WTO Reports in Beef Hormones and Bananas Cases," *International Law Update* 6 (June 2000): 1.

53. National Beef Cattlemen's Association, "Administration Examines Benefits of Carousel Retaliation," February 9, 2000, http://hill.beef.org/ft/aebo.htm.

54. Ibid.

55. *Wall Street Journal,* May 25, 2000, 21.

56. *European Voice,* June 8–14, 2000, 29.

57. National Beef Cattlemen's Association, "Retaliation against EU Ban on U.S. Beef," March 15, 2001, http://hill.beef.org/ft/eubeef.htm.

58. Ibid.

59. *Financial Times,* October 16, 2000, 12.

60. Ibid.

11 The Helms-Burton Act: Congress and Cuba Policy

Patrick J. Haney and Walt Vanderbush

Before You Begin

1. Who were the key players during the debate over the Helms-Burton Act? What were their motivations? How did these actors and their methods differ from their cold war counterparts?

2. What role has the U.S. president traditionally played in determining the course of U.S. foreign policy toward Cuba? What role did the president play in determining the course of Helms-Burton? What do the differences tell us about foreign policy making in the post–cold war era?

3. Describe the influence of the Cuban American National Foundation on Congress. How much influence has it had on legislation?

4. How did Congress gain momentum over U.S. Cuba policy? How did it lose it? Why did it regain momentum? What do you think of the behavior of Congress in this case?

5. Who ultimately "won" with the passage of Helms-Burton: Congress or the president? Why?

6. What was the political context within which Helms-Burton was crafted? How did U.S. policy toward Cuba change from the cold war to the post–cold war era?

7. What do you think about the efficacy of Helms-Burton and the U.S. embargo of Cuba? In what kinds of situations do you think economic sanctions would be a powerful instrument of foreign policy? When would you recommend their use? When would you not?

Introduction: Crafting Cuba Policy

On February 24, 1996, Cuban air force MiG fighter jets shot down two unarmed planes approaching Cuba from across the Florida Straits, killing four Cuban Americans: three U.S. citizens and one U.S. resident.[1] The planes were operated by members of the group Brothers to the Rescue, who fly over the waters separating Florida and Cuba looking for people fleeing Cuba by raft. The group was also known to fly over Cuba from time to time to drop anti-Castro leaflets.[2] On March 12, President Bill Clinton signed into law the Cuban Liberty and Democratic Solidarity Act of 1996, or LIBERTAD, also called the Helms-Burton Act.[3] The measure tightened and codified into law the long-standing U.S. economic embargo of Cuba that had previously existed by executive order.

At the signing of the act, Clinton said, "Today I sign [this bill] with a certainty that it will send a powerful, unified message from the United States to Havana, that the yearning of the Cuban people for freedom must not be denied." He continued, "The legislation I sign ... sends a strong message to the Cuban Government. We will not tolerate attacks on United States citizens and we will stand with those both inside and outside Cuba who are working for a peaceful transition to freedom and democracy." He concluded by saying that he signed the bill, "in the name of the four men who were killed when their planes were shot down on February the 24th: Armando Alejandre, Carlos Costa, Mario de la Pena, and Pablo Morales. In their memory, I will continue to do everything I can to help the tide of democracy that has swept our entire hemisphere finally, finally reach the shores of Cuba. The Cuban people must receive the blessings of freedom they have been so long denied. And I hope and believe that this day is another important step toward that ultimate goal that so many of you in this audience have worked so hard for, for so very, very long."[4]

The road to passage of Helms-Burton was not as simple as it might at first appear. Indeed, at one point Secretary of State Warren Christopher argued that he would urge President Clinton to veto the bill if it ever came before him—and that was in regard to a softer version of the bill Clinton ultimately signed. This is the story of a bill that, with a little help from the Cuban air force, would not die, and the forces that crafted it.

Background: U.S.-Cuba Cold War Policy

Over the course of the first two decades following the 1959 revolution that brought Fidel Castro to power in Cuba, the president of the United States, largely through executive orders, tightly controlled U.S. policy toward that island nation. As Castro consolidated power and joined forces with the Soviet Union as a communist state, President Dwight D. Eisenhower imposed an embargo on Cuba (excepting food and medicine) in 1960. President John F. Kennedy tightened the embargo in 1962, banning Cuban imports and the re-export of U.S. goods to Cuba via third countries; in 1963 he prohibited travel by U.S. citizens to Cuba. U.S. policy toward Cuba in the 1960s and 1970s was quintessential cold war policy making. That is, it was devised and directed by the president.

Although President Gerald R. Ford opened secret talks with Cuba in 1974 about normalizing relations, and President Jimmy Carter reached a few agreements in 1977—including the opening of interest sections in Washington and Havana in lieu of formal diplomatic exchanges and allowing travel to Cuba by U.S. citizens—U.S.-Cuban relations stayed in a deep freeze throughout this period.[5]

U.S. policy toward Cuba would get tougher in the 1980s. As a presidential candidate, Ronald Reagan made it clear that he saw Cuba as the source of U.S. difficulties in Latin America. "The troubles in Nicaragua [where communist Sandinistas were gaining power] bear a Cuban label. . . . There is no question but that most of the rebels are Cuban-trained, Cuban-armed, and dedicated to creating another Communist country in this hemisphere."[6] The Reagan team wanted to make the embargo even stricter if it got the chance and wanted other nations to join it to choke the Cuban economy and drive Castro from power. In Congress and among the public, however, there was little support for Reagan's view of Latin America.[7] Although Reagan pulled off a big victory at the polls in November 1980, he needed help lobbying Congress, especially the Democrat-controlled House of Representatives, and the public on this issue. As luck would have it, Miami-based Cuban Americans—who had been attempting to challenge Castro's regime for years—decided to take their political activities to Washington. The Cuban American National Foundation (CANF) was founded in 1980–1981 for the purpose of lobbying the government and the broader public on U.S. Cuba policy.[8]

CANF, and its charismatic founder and leader, Jorge Mas Canosa, emerged as a powerful force in the 1980s. CANF worked with the Reagan administration to lobby Congress for a government-sponsored radio station aimed at Cuba. In October 1983, President Reagan signed into law the bill that established Radio Marti, named after Cuban hero Jose Marti, who led the final push for Cuban independence from Spain starting in 1895. Radio Marti began broadcasting in May 1985. CANF would later follow this victory with the establishment of a TV station, TV Marti, which aimed its signals at Cuba in 1990. (The Cuban government jams most of the signals, but the broadcasts continue.) CANF also worked closely with the National Endowment for Democracy (NED), founded during the Reagan administration as a vehicle for government financial support for democracy movements around the world. CANF was also active in U.S. immigration policy with respect to Cubans fleeing the island, and a host of other issues related to Cuba. Throughout the 1980s CANF became an increasingly powerful player in U.S. policy making toward Cuba.

As the end of the cold war unfolded in Eastern Europe and the Soviet Union during the first part of George Bush's presidency, Cuba policy was moved to the back burner. It moved to the front burner during the latter part of the Bush administration for two reasons. First, Haitians fleeing their country en masse were being returned to Haiti, which raised the specter of a double standard vis-à-vis Cuban exiles, who gained easy entry to the United States.[9] Second, in 1991 a major legislative initiative on U.S. policy toward Cuba, the Cuban Democracy Act (CDA), was moving through Congress.[10] It is also important to note that in 1989 Cuban-American Ileana Ros-Lehtinen, R-Fla., was sworn into the House of Representatives. Fellow Cuban Americans Lincoln Diaz-Balart, R-Fla., and Robert Menendez, D-N.J., joined her in 1993.

Post–Cold War Cuba Policy: The Cuban Democracy Act

The end of the cold war suggested two opposing directions for U.S. policy toward Cuba. On the one hand, a number of developments indicated that the embargo of the island should be lifted. The Soviet Union ceased to exist, and Cuban troops stationed abroad returned home. The Bush administration seemed to have little interest in making a big deal out of Cuba, given all that was changing around the globe. Many suspected that Bill Clinton had even less interest in maintaining the long-standing U.S. embargo.[11] On the other hand, with the cold war over and communism in retreat, some saw conditions as ripe to continue or even strengthen the embargo to finally force Castro from power. Having lost its major trading partners, Cuba might even be more vulnerable to a tighter embargo.[12] Many in Congress seemed more in line with the latter view.

With the demise of the Soviet Union, Cuba needed new trade relationships with the West, which seemed to open the door for subsidiaries of U.S. companies in foreign countries to do business there. In response to this loophole in the embargo, for three years in a row, beginning in 1989, Sen. Connie Mack, R-Fla., proposed a bill prohibiting subsidiaries of U.S. firms from trading with Cuba. The Bush administration consistently opposed the so-called Mack Amendment. Laying out the administration's reasoning in testimony before Congress in July 1991, Bernard Aronson, assistant secretary of state for Inter-American Affairs, argued, "The ban on subsidiaries of U.S. multi-nationals would create a foreign policy problem with a lot of allies who rightly believe that that would be an assertion of U.S. law into their territory and who would be prepared to retaliate in direct ways. Our analysis is that the benefits that we

U.S.-Cuban Relations and the Helms-Burton Act

January 1959 Revolutionary forces take over the Cuban government. The United States recognizes the new government.

October 1960 President Dwight D. Eisenhower imposes an embargo on Cuba, with food and medicine excepted, following Cuba's move into the Soviet orbit.

January 1961 Eisenhower severs diplomatic relations with Cuba.

February 1962 The United States bans Cuban imports and the re-export of U.S. products to Cuba from third countries.

February 1963 President John F. Kennedy prohibits travel to Cuba by U.S. citizens.

November 1974 President Gerald Ford authorizes secret talks with Cuban officials on normalizing relations.

August 1975 Ford eases the trade embargo by allowing U.S. subsidiaries based in third countries to trade with Cuba.

March 1977 President Jimmy Carter lifts the ban on travel to Cuba by U.S. citizens.

September 1977 The United States and Cuba open interest sections in the other's capital.

May 1985 Radio Marti, a U.S.-sponsored radio operation, begins broadcasts to Cuba.

October 1992 Congress passes the Cuban Democracy Act prohibiting foreign-based subsidiaries of U.S. companies from trading with Cuba. President George Bush signs it.

February 1995 Senator Jesse Helms, R-N.C., introduces the Cuban Liberty and Democratic Solidarity Act (LIBERTAD), also known as the Helms-Burton Act, which would allow U.S. citizens to sue foreign companies that profit from the use of seized property in Cuba. It also would deny entry into the United States of company executives who do business involving seized property.

April 1995 President Bill Clinton argues against passage of Helms-Burton on CNN.

September 1995 The House of Representatives passes Helms-Burton by a vote of 294-130.

October 1995   The Senate passes a version of Helms-Burton with controversial Titles III and IV omitted.

February 24, 1996   Cuban MiG fighters shoot down two planes belonging to the U.S.-based organization Brothers to the Rescue as they fly toward Cuba.

February 26, 1996   Clinton proclaims his support for Helms-Burton.

February 28, 1996   Congressional supporters of Helms-Burton meet with Clinton administration officials to negotiate final terms of the act.

March 12, 1996   Clinton signs Helms-Burton into law.

March 1998   Clinton announces new measures to facilitate visits to Cuba by U.S. citizens and the sale of medical products.

January 1999   Clinton announces additional measures to increase people-to-people contact between Cubans and Americans.

September 1999   The Ashcroft Amendment, which would largely lift the embargo on food shipments to Cuba, passes the Senate but is blocked from the final agricultural appropriations bill by House opposition.

March 2000   The Senate Foreign Relations Committee votes to ease the embargo on the sale of food to Cuba.

October 2000   Clinton signs a bill allowing the sale of agricultural goods and medicine to Cuba and codifying restrictions on travel there by U.S. citizens.

would gain in terms of embargo enforcement are relatively minimal."[13] With the president opposed to it, the Mack Amendment was easily defeated each time it was presented.

In early 1992, the impetus came from the other side of the aisle. Rep. Robert Torricelli, D-N.J., and then senator Bob Graham, D-Fla., introduced the Cuban Democracy Act in their respective chambers. The CDA had two tracks. One track—like the Mack Amendment—sought to increase economic pressure on Cuba by prohibiting trade with foreign subsidiaries of U.S. companies and by making it more difficult for ships that had stopped in Cuba to enter U.S. ports. The other track tried to reach out to the Cuban people by facilitating communication and family visits to Cuba. CANF was a prominent player in the life of this bill—a bill opposed by the Bush administration for the same kinds of reasons that it opposed the Mack Amendment. Representative Torricelli had developed close ties to CANF. Torricelli's New Jersey district had almost no Cuban Americans, but if he decided to run statewide for the Senate, Cuban American support throughout the state would be helpful. Among the original twenty-two House sponsors of the CDA, fourteen had received donations from CANF's Political Action Committee of more than $1,000 each.[14] Bipartisan support in Congress notwithstanding, President Bush was probably going to veto the bill. In April 1992, Robert Gelbard, principal deputy assistant secretary of state for Inter-American Affairs, offered several objections to the CDA before Congress. Among the most important were that the bill would cause diplomatic problems for the United States and impinge "on the President's constitutionally mandated powers to conduct foreign affairs."[15]

With the November 1992 presidential election looming, and disappointed that the Bush administration was opposed to the CDA, CANF leader Jorge Mas Canosa met with Rep. Stephen Solarz, D-N.Y., and apparently offered through him to help Clinton's presidential campaign if Clinton would endorse the CDA.[16] Clinton adviser George Stephanopoulos and Representative Torricelli negotiated a deal.[17] With a campaign short on funds, and needing to be competitive in Florida against President Bush in the general election, candidate Clinton signed on in Miami: "I have read the Torricelli-Graham bill and I like it."[18] Clinton raised $275,000 from Cuban Americans in Coral Gables and Miami that day. Suddenly outflanked on the "right" on Cuba, the Bush camp tried to cut its political losses by working with Congress to fashion a CDA that the president could sign into law. In October 1992, just weeks before the election—which he would lose—Bush signed the Cuban Democracy Act. Although Clinton failed to carry Florida, he got many more Cuban American votes than Democratic candidate Michael Dukakis received there in 1988. Clinton would go on to win Florida in 1996.

Clinton supported the CDA at the outset of his administration. In November 1993, for example, he argued that his Cuba policy was working, stating that "gestures of openness that have come out of the Castro regime in the last several months have been the direct result of our policy of pressure and firmness."[19] He went on to note that "no Democrat in my life time, in the White House at least, has come close to taking the strong position I have on this, agreeing with the Cuban-American community."[20]

While Clinton in public supported continuing the embargo, a number of officials in the administration were asserting the need to reevaluate, if not change, U.S. policy toward Cuba. According to one critic of the administration, "On the entire Clinton foreign policy team—Bill (and Hillary); Anthony Lake and Richard Feinberg at the National Security Council; Warren Christopher, Strobe Talbott, and Tarnoff at the State Department—there isn't one single person who favors a hard line against Castro."[21] Skepticism would grow when, in the summer of 1994 in the face of a large exodus of Cubans heading for Florida in boats, the administration reversed the nearly three-decade policy of automatically granting asylum to all arriving Cubans.[22] Since the mid-1960s, all Cubans who left the island had immediately been given refugee status, thus avoiding the process of hearings that those fleeing other countries (like Haiti) were required to have. The reaction to the new policy by Cuban Americans was one of shock and outrage.[23]

A New Initiative: Congress and Helms-Burton

The November 1994 elections resulted in Republican majorities in the U.S. House and Senate, which would weaken the position of those in the Clinton administration interested in at least softening the embargo. The impetus for a new legislative initiative had begun to emerge even before the elections. Many on Capitol Hill were frustrated that Castro had survived the wave of democratization that had swept Latin America in the late 1980s and early 1990s, including Chile, Guatemala, and Nicaragua. Furthermore, some Republicans felt that Clinton was not doing enough to try to remove Castro from power. From the perspective of Dan Fisk, a former staffer for Sen. Jesse Helms, R-N.C., Clinton had run to the right of President Bush on the CDA only then to ignore Cuba or send signals of possible rapprochement. The contrast of Cuba policy with Clinton's Haiti policy—on which Clinton invested significant time and resources and even committed the military in 1994 to help remove a dictator and restore democracy—also frustrated many in Congress. The view for some on the Hill was that Haiti and Cuba were both countries with dictatorships, but that Clinton only seemed interested in dethroning the Haitian regime that refused to relinquish power after elections had been held. A key factor in the Haitian case, however, was the activism of the Congressional Black Caucus. Senator Helms and others decided that similar congressional activism was needed on Cuba.[24] It was in this context that the Cuban Liberty and Democratic Solidarity Act, LIBERTAD for short, and also known as Helms-Burton for its sponsors—Helms in the Senate and Dan Burton, R-Ind., in the House—began to take shape.

The proposed legislation picked up steam in early 1995 at the direction of Senator Helms, the new chair of the Senate Foreign Relations Committee. Dan

Fisk was the point man on the legislation, the basic aim of which was to drive Castro from power. Fisk constructed the bill by bringing together all the pieces of Cuba legislation that had been floating around the Hill for years. He formed a coalition of staffers from the House and Senate to review these past initiatives and to draft the new bill.[25] Notably absent from the drafting coalition was CANF. Although it was the biggest and most important lobbying group in town on Cuba policy, and the drafting coalition wanted CANF's help in pushing the bill once it was drafted, Congress was growing more autonomous in approaching Cuba policy, in part because of its three Cuban American members.

The original idea was to add Helms-Burton onto another bill, but pressure and momentum caused Senator Helms to unveil Helms-Burton as stand-alone legislation in February 1995. The bill included several controversial components to tighten and expand the embargo on Cuba. Perhaps most controversial was the bill's Title III, which would give U.S. nationals the right to sue in U.S. courts foreign companies that "traffic" in "stolen property" in Cuba. For example, a foreign company doing business in Cuba on or with property of U.S. nationals that was seized following the revolution could be taken to court. This "extraterritorial" element of the bill was highly controversial; its standing in international law was questioned by many, and it promised to pose diplomatic headaches for President Clinton that were even bigger than the ones Bush feared from the CDA. Canadian officials protested Title III by way of a strongly worded letter to the State Department in April, stating that it "would constitute an illegitimate intrusion upon third countries."[26] Also controversial was Title IV of the bill, which would deny visas to executives of foreign companies "trafficking" (doing business) in confiscated properties in Cuba. As Helms-Burton was moving through Congress in the spring and summer, it is important to note, others took more direct action to challenge Castro, as boats and small airplanes made periodic runs toward Cuba from Miami.

Hearings on Helms-Burton in the House were marked by suspicion about the Clinton administration's intentions toward Cuba. Administration witnesses were grilled about an article in the *Washington Post* claiming that an internal National Security Council paper had circulated that suggested the embargo of Cuba be lifted.[27] This was compounded by leaks from the administration and from abroad that the Clinton team was considering loosening or lifting the embargo.[28] Clinton's unilateral move to lift the economic embargo against Vietnam and to normalize relations in 1995, plus his actions to reverse U.S. policy automatically granting asylum to fleeing Cubans during the 1994 immigration crisis, suggested to congressional proponents of the Cuban embargo that they might need to restrain the president. Representative Diaz-Balart, for example, was concerned that the administration was going to normalize relations with Cuba before political reforms were enacted there. He said that he had received a number of signals suggesting such a situation, including a statement from a British diplomat who told him his government had been assured by Clinton officials that the president would normalize relations after the 1996 elections.[29]

The administration came out publicly against Helms-Burton. In an April 1995 interview on CNN, President Clinton argued that it was unnecessary because of the existing CDA.[30] Undersecretary of State for Political Affairs Peter Tarnoff testified against the bill in the Senate, claiming that it would limit the president's flexibility in conducting foreign affairs. He, like Clinton, argued that the two tracks of the CDA were sufficient.[31] Secretary of State Christopher sent a letter arguing against the bill to Speaker of the House Newt Gingrich, R-Ga., the day before the House vote. Christopher wrote that if Helms-Burton was passed he would urge the president to veto it on the grounds that it was overly inflexible for dealing with a rapidly developing situation as in Cuba. He also said Title III was counterproductive.[32] The House passed Helms-Burton by a vote of 294-130 on September 21. The action then moved on to the Senate, where the bill's passage promised to be more difficult.

According to Fisk, President Clinton never actually threatened to veto Helms-Burton, leaving it to the State Department to try to keep the bill from ever reaching his desk. Since there was no "heavy-handed White House presence" against the bill, in the Senate its supporters did not think Helms-Burton was necessarily a "killer" for Clinton.[33] A former administration official confirmed that their strategy was not to threaten a veto but rather to prevent the bill from ever getting to the president.[34] The administration also tried to cultivate corporate opposition to the bill. On October 6, Chief of Staff Leon Panetta and foreign policy advisers met with a group of about fifty U.S. business executives about taking a trip to Cuba. The problem with such a visit was that according to Treasury Department regulations, only certain categories of U.S. citizens and residents could legally travel to the island. People receiving permission to travel to Cuba typically were journalists and academics.[35] To meet these restrictions, the executives were classified as "journalists"; among those making the trip, which included meeting Castro, were heads of Time Warner, Hyatt Hotels, General Motors, and Zenith.[36] Representative Diaz-Balart challenged the one-day trip: "There is an abhorrent, unscrupulous, carefully planned strategy by administration officials to use the business community as a means of putting pressure on Congress."[37] Sen. Phil Gramm, R-Texas, described Clinton's maneuvers as "putting out the welcome mat to Castro instead of tightening the noose around his aging neck."[38]

Despite a plea by Senator Graham by way of an earlier "Dear Colleague" letter to Senate Democrats urging their support of the bill,[39] attempts to move Helms-Burton toward a Senate vote failed twice in mid-October 1995. As the White House strategy jelled and corporate opposition grew, support for Helms-Burton faltered. In the meantime Clinton moved forward under the two tracks of the CDA. He announced measures to expand contacts between Cuban and American residents, including opening news bureaus, relaxing travel restrictions, and allowing more activities in Cuba by non-governmental organizations.[40] Unable to move the bill as drafted, the Senate removed Titles III and IV. Even though Helms-Burton had passed overwhelmingly in the House, the president seemed poised to win the showdown. Once Helms-Burton passed the Senate in its weakened form, it still appeared dead as it went to the conference committee for resolution of the differences between the House and Senate versions of the bill. The future of the embargo looked bleak to some.

While events unfolded in Washington, activities in the Florida Straits caught everyone's attention. Brothers to the Rescue were regularly flying search missions over the waters between Cuba and Florida, but also reportedly flying over Cuba on occasion to drop anti-Castro leaflets. Tension over these flights had grown by February 1996, as the Cuban government became increasingly angry. Matters reached a dramatic and tragic crescendo when jet fighters from the Cuban air force shot down two small, unarmed Brothers to the Rescue planes over the Florida Straits on February 24, 1996, killing the four people aboard and breathing new life into the Helms-Burton Act.[41]

Helms-Burton's Second Chance

The downing of the Brothers to the Rescue planes produced strong reactions in Congress. Representative Ros-Lehtinen characterized the shooting as "an act of war" and called for a naval blockade.[42] On February 26 President Clinton condemned the attack and ordered a number of actions against Cuba; he also announced his intention to reach an agreement with Congress on Helms-Burton, as the advantage had now clearly shifted to the Hill.[43] At a strategy meeting the next day attended by Representatives Burton, Diaz-Balart, Patrick Kennedy, D-R.I., Robert Menendez, D-N.J., Ros-Lehtinen, Torricelli, and others, Titles III and IV were reinserted in the bill. Diaz-Balart insisted that a new measure be added as well: codification of the embargo into law. This addition, inserted in Title I, would take the full body of the U.S. embargo policy toward Cuba, which existed by executive order—and make it law. Thereafter the embargo could only be lifted through a repeal by Congress (making impossible a unilateral policy change like Clinton did with Vietnam). Diaz-Balart told the gathering that he would insist on codification and that he wanted their support; they all agreed.[44]

From the perspective of congressional supporters of Helms-Burton, Clinton now had no choice but to accept LIBERTAD, which was "the only game in town."[45] A House staffer noted that the events in the Florida Straits "changed everything," and left the administration "no position to bargain."[46] Patrick Kennedy argued, "Now is not the time to relax on Castro. Shooting down unarmed civilian planes is just one more in an escalating and disturbing pattern of human rights violations by the Castro regime, desperately clinging to power in its final days."[47] Diaz-Balart, adopting a populist tone at the same press conference, said, "Sometimes Main Street's got to . . . speak up and [tell] Wall Street where to go."[48] Even Richard Nuccio, the president's special adviser for Cuba policy, admitted that "President Castro created a veto-proof majority for the Helms-Burton bill."[49]

At 8:00 a.m. on February 28 in Representative Menendez's office, the coalition from the Hill met with several members of the administration, including Nuccio. Diaz-Balart recalls that the administration officials emphasized that they wanted to include in the legislation a presidential "waiver" for Title III that would essentially allow the president to sign the bill but then waive its enforcement, at least temporarily, for reasons of "national security." They negotiated most of the day. When the issue of codification was brought up, the Clinton team objected on the grounds that it was "new" to the bill. Diaz-Balart then asked, "Well, are you going to lift the embargo?" When the Clinton team said that they would not, Diaz-Balart's response was, "Good, then we have no problem; next issue." This go-round happened a few times through the day, but Diaz-Balart argues that there was never any negotiation on this point, plus the Clinton team seemed more concerned with Title III, for which they ultimately got a waiver. When it came time to negotiate on Title IV, for which the Clinton administration also wanted a waiver, Diaz-Balart recalled that Torricelli "played the bad guy and said there would be no waiver there." He further noted that the Clinton team had virtually no bargaining power and few options. "What were they going to do, veto a bill after a terrorist government's air force shot down

American citizens? Not even Qadhafi has done exactly that."[50] Fisk confirmed that the deal was "you get waivers on Title III, and we get codification."[51]

The Clinton team then met to decide how to proceed. The group included Attorney General Janet Reno, Secretary of Defense William J. Perry, Secretary of State Christopher, Chairman of the Joint Chiefs of Staff General John M. Shalikasvili, Director of Central Intelligence John Deutch, and others. As they discussed the policy issues, none of them appeared to know about the codification provision; when they were told about it they objected on the ground that it took away too much prerogative from the president and might be unconstitutional. Political advisers Stephanopoulos and Chief of Staff Panetta overruled the policy people and argued that Clinton should sign the bill because his administration could be weakened politically if he vetoed it following such a dramatic event in the straits. Clinton's reelection prospects could also be hurt if he were to anger the politically strong Cuban American populations in Florida and New Jersey. When National Security Adviser Anthony Lake agreed, the policy discussion was over; political calculations carried the day. Rather than argue against codification, the Clinton team focused on the waiver to Title III, so they could explain their reversal on the bill and salve the wounds of allies, who were not going to take well to Title III. They then agreed to sign the bill.[52]

Not everyone on the Hill was happy about the deal. Rep. Charles Rangel, D-N.Y., assessed the new law, saying, "This bill has nothing to do with Castro; it has everything to do with our friends and our voters in Florida."[53] Sen. Christopher Dodd, D-Conn., warned that the bill "totally ties the hands of this president and future presidents to respond flexibly to change in Cuba when it comes."[54] Rep. Lee Hamilton, D-Ind., shared Dodd's concern and argued that codification would "lock in the president of the United States in the conduct of foreign policy."[55] Beyond these concerns, critics of the bill continued to worry about how Helms-Burton would set the United States and its allies at odds over the extraterritorial nature of the bill. Supporters of the bill nevertheless argued that international opposition should not affect U.S. policy making. Sen. Paul Coverdell, R-Ga., declared, "We can't retreat because this is disruptive to some of our European allies."[56] Representative Ros-Lehtinen added, "The United States must stop hiding behind international public opinion and stop wavering."[57] Representative Burton concluded that agreement on Helms-Burton "makes it clear that Fidel Castro and his blood-soaked, dictatorial, corrupt tyranny is about to end."[58] After the new bill passed both houses, Clinton signed Helms-Burton on March 12, 1996.

The Politics of Cuba Policy since Helms-Burton

A number of interesting developments followed the passage of Helms-Burton. In July 1996, President Clinton announced that although he would allow Title III to come into force on August 1, as the act specified, he would waive enforcement of that part of the measure for six months.[59] He thus "put on notice" companies doing business in Cuba with the seized property of U.S. nationals that they could end up in a U.S. court, although he delayed such legal action. He thereafter continued to invoke the waiver every six months, including in January 2001, his last month in office. Helms-Burton allows the president to waive enforcement of Title III (1) if the president deems the waiver "necessary to the national interests of the United States" and (2) if waiving it "will expedite a transition to democracy in Cuba."[60] The act's framers thought that under the prevailing circumstances, the president could not in good faith exercise the waiver because there was no transition to democracy underway in Cuba.[61] That Clinton did so frustrated Helms-Burton proponents.

There has been little action on Title IV since 1996. A limited number of company executives have come under scrutiny for possible exclusion from entry to the United States, including from the Canadian firm Sherritt International, the Mexican firm Grupo Domos, and the Italian company Stet International.[62] Only officials with Sherritt and the Israeli BM group have been barred entry as a result of Title IV.[63] Early estimates had 100 to 200 foreign ventures under way in Cuba vulnerable to Helms-Burton's definition of "trafficking in confiscated property."[64] If the estimates are correct, enforcement efforts thus far would seem to be weak.

The bulk of the activity on Cuba policy since 1996 has been the expansion of the president's "licensing power" to relax some parts of the embargo. Although Helms-Burton froze all restrictions on trade and travel already in force, one part of the act, Section 112, gave the president limited licensing power to revise sanctions on family remittances—money that U.S. residents and citizens send to their families on the island—and travel to Cuba if specified steps are first taken by the Cuban government to liberalize political and economic life on the island (for example, releasing political prisoners). President Clinton used this licensing power provision to make a number of unilateral changes in policy. The first of these were announced just before Pope John Paul II visited Cuba in 1998 and included the resumption of direct humanitarian charter flights to Cuba, a higher remittance level ($300 per quarter), and easier shipping and sales of medicines and medical supplies to Cuba.[65]

A second set of changes followed in January 1999. Clinton expanded the use of remittances by allowing any U.S. resident to send money to Cuban families and independent organizations. He also sought to expand people-to-people contact through exchanges among academics, athletes, scientists, and others (including the publicized baseball games between the Baltimore Orioles and the Cuban national team). He authorized the sale of food and agricultural products to independent family restaurants, religious groups, and private farmers. He permitted charter passenger flights to cities in Cuba other than Havana and from cities in the United States other than Miami. Finally, he pledged to establish direct mail service.[66]

Supporters of Helms-Burton were not happy with Clinton's actions. After the 1998 reforms, for example, Representative Diaz-Balart said, "We are not going to let Clinton proceed along the path of normalization."[67] Following the January 1999 reforms, Representative Ros-Lehtinen said, "We want to know where is the legal controlling authority that authorizes them to change the law. The way we read Helms-Burton, they do not have any such authority."[68] Frustration aside, there was little Congress could do to reverse Clinton's decisions.[69] In some ways, Clinton acted as if Helms-Burton never existed.

Other activity in Congress on U.S. Cuba policy has centered around the efforts of the farm lobby to join forces with other business interests to weaken the embargo and allow increased sales of food to Cuba. In the summer of 1998, Sen. Chuck Hagel, R-Neb., proposed an amendment to the agricultural appropriations bill allowing the sale of food products to countries against whom the United States alone has an embargo. Torricelli successfully limited the impact of Hagel's amendment by adding an exemption to the bill for "terrorist" nations, among which Cuba is counted.

A number of farm state senators (in large part Republicans) and farm groups, such as the American Farm Bureau Federation and the U.S. Grains Council, welcomed Clinton allowing limited sales of U.S. agricultural products to non-governmental agencies and independent farmers and advocated even greater openings.[70] By the end of the summer of 1999, the momentum in the Senate to help distressed U.S. farmers by opening the Cuban market produced an amendment to the agriculture spending bill that would largely lift the embargo on food sales to Cuba. It would also prohibit the president from imposing such bans in the future without the consent of Congress.[71] The measure was co-sponsored by Hagel and one of the Senate's most conservative members, John Ashcroft, R-Mo. While the spending bill was sitting in the Senate-House conference committee, prominent non-agricultural business organizations such as the U.S. Chamber of Commerce offered support for what was known by then as the Ashcroft Amendment.[72] In the end, House opposition—largely from the Cuban American and Republican leadership—successfully kept the opening to Cuba out of the final bill.

In 2000, facing a third consecutive year of depressed global commodity prices, the farm lobby and its Senate allies resumed the battle to open the Cuban market. When prominent embargo supporter and LIBERTAD sponsor Senator Helms dropped his opposition to easing the embargo, the Senate Foreign Relations Committee voted in March to authorize sales of food and medicine to the island.[73] The Cuban American members of Congress and their allies nevertheless fought hard in the House against a farm lobby that saw the potential sale of $1 billion in goods to Cuba.[74] The measure stalled during the summer, but by the fall members of Congress reached agreement on a bill that would allow Cubans to buy food and medicine from the United States. Iran, Libya, North Korea, and Sudan—countries also subject to U.S. economic sanctions—were affected by the new legislation as well. Of these five countries, however, only Cuba was denied the right to pay for goods with U.S. government credits or loans from U.S. banks. Congressional supporters of the embargo, especially the Cuban American members of Congress, were able to get included in the bill a measure codifying all existing travel restrictions to Cuba. At the end of October, a little more than a week before the presidential election, Clinton signed the bill into law.[75] Presidents are now unable to change current travel restrictions without congressional approval. President George W. Bush, who won the 2000 election, in which Florida figured prominently, appears to be aligned with the members of Congress opposed to any easing of the embargo.

Conclusion: The Struggle to Control Cuba Policy

The post–cold war period in U.S.-Cuban relations began with a president who demonstrated little interest in changing policy toward the communist-led island. President George Bush's hand, however, was forced by the combined efforts of members of Congress, CANF, and an opportunistic opposing candidate in the 1992 presidential election. The resulting Cuban Democracy Act was the product of a variety of domestic political actors operating openly in an election year to promote the tightening of the embargo, even as international events might have favored a change of policy in a different direction.

In 1996 the Helms-Burton bill that was enacted was even more clearly driven by members of Congress dealing with a president whose decision making on

Cuba policy was overwhelmingly based on electoral and other domestic political calculations. Republican members of Congress, led by Cuban American representatives from Florida, not only refused to defer to the chief executive in the wake of the downing of the Brothers to the Rescue planes, but they effectively usurped decision-making authority on Cuba from the president.

Since the signing of Helms-Burton, the number of actors engaged in Cuba policy has continued to increase. A range of economic interest groups, including the U.S. Chamber of Commerce and leading agricultural organizations, has promoted loosening the embargo. Farm-state legislators on both sides of the aisle have supported them—from conservative Republican senator Ashcroft, who put forward such a bill, to Sen. Tom Daschle, D-S.D., who traveled to the island in 1999. Former government officials working under the auspices of the Council on Foreign Relations have twice issued reports suggesting possible changes in the direction of more open relations with Cuba. This impressive array of domestic political forces has yet to succeed in the face of the determined resistance of legislators led by a couple of Cuban American Republican members of the House. As this case study suggests, U.S.-Cuban relations are rooted in the struggles among a growing number of domestic political actors to publicly shape a policy that once was almost exclusively driven by presidents debating the national interest with their advisers behind closed doors.

Notes

1. Much of the material for this case study has been adapted from Walt Vanderbush and Patrick J. Haney, "Policy toward Cuba in the Clinton Administration," *Political Science Quarterly* 144 (fall 1999): 387–408. We would like to thank Ralph Carter, anonymous reviewers, and Amy Briggs at CQ Press for their helpful comments.

2. See Carl Nagin, "Backfire," *New Yorker,* January 26, 1998, 30–35.

3. 22 U.S.C. 6021 and following (H.R. 927, PL 104–114, March 12, 1996).

4. William Jefferson Clinton, "Remarks on Signing the Cuban Liberty and Democratic Solidarity (LIBERTAD) Act of 1996," *Weekly Compilation of Presidential Documents,* March 12, 1996, 478. The compilations are available at http://www.access.gpo.gov/nara/nara003.html.

5. See the chronology of U.S.-Cuban relations, 1958–1999, at http://www.state.gov/www/regions/wha/cuba_chronology.html. See also Philip Brenner, *From Confrontation to Negotiation: US Relations with Cuba* (Boulder: Westview Press, 1988); Gillian Gunn, *Cuba in Transition* (New York: Twentieth Century Fund, 1993); Donna Rich Kaplowitz, *Anatomy of a Failed Embargo: US Sanctions against Cuba* (Boulder: Lynne Rienner, 1998); and William M. LeoGrande, "From Havana to Miami: U.S. Cuba Policy as a Two-Level Game," *Journal of Interamerican Studies and World Affairs* 40 (spring 1998): 67–86.

6. Holly Sklar, *Washington's War on Nicaragua* (Boston: South End Press, 1988), 57.

7. Brenner, *From Confrontation to Negotiation*; Gunn, *Cuba in Transition*; Kaplowitz, *Anatomy of a Failed Embargo*, 117–143.

8. A number of different versions of the founding of CANF have appeared in the literature. For an analysis of these, see Patrick J. Haney and Walt Vanderbush, "The Role of Ethnic Interest Groups in US Foreign Policy: The Case of the Cuban American National Foundation," *International Studies Quarterly* 43 (1999): 341–361.

9. House Committee on the Judiciary, Subcommittee on International Law, Immigration, and Refugees, *Cuban and Haitian Immigration*, hearing, 102d Cong., 1st sess., November 20, 1991.

10. House Committee on Foreign Affairs, Subcommittees on Europe and the Middle East and on the Western Hemisphere, *Cuba in a Changing World: The United States-Soviet-Cuba Triangle*, hearing, 101st Cong., 1st sess., April 30 and July 11 and 31, 1991, 154. For the first statement of the Cuban Democracy Act, see Robert G. Torricelli, "Let Democracy Shine through an Open Door," *Los Angeles Times*, August 18, 1991, M5.

11. For example, see Wayne Smith, "Shackled to the Past: The United States and Cuba," *Current History* 95 (February 1996): 49–54; Gail DeGeorge with Douglas Harbrecht, "Warmer Winds Are Blowing from Washington to Havana," *Business Week*, August 2, 1993, 42; Peter Hakim, "It's Time to Review US Cuba Policy," *Brookings Review* 13 (winter 1995): 47.

12. For example, see Susan Kaufman Purcell, "Cuba's Cloudy Future," *Foreign Affairs* 69 (summer 1990): 113–130; and idem, "The Cuban Illusion: Keeping the Heat on Castro," *Foreign Affairs* 75 (May/June 1996): 159–161; Charles Lane, "TRB from Washington," *New Republic*, February 6, 1998, 6, 41; Michael G. Wilson, "Hastening Castro's Downfall," *Heritage Foundation Backgrounder*, July 2, 1992. For other views, see Bob Benenson, "Dissonant Voices Urge Clinton to Revise Policy on Cuba," *Congressional Quarterly Weekly Report*, August 24, 1994, 2498; Saul Landau, "Clinton's Cuba Policy: A Low-Priority Dilemma," *NACLA Report on the Americas* 26 (May 1993): 35–37; David Rieff, "Cuba Refrozen," *Foreign Affairs* 75 (July/August 1996): 62–75; Andrew Zimbalist, "Cuba, Castro, Clinton, and Canosa," in *Cuba in the International System*, ed. Archibald R. M. Ritter and John M. Kirk (New York: St. Martin's Press, 1995), 23–36.

13. House Committee on Foreign Affairs, *Cuba in a Changing World*, 128.

14. Peter H. Stone, "Cuban Clout," *National Journal*, February 20, 1993, 451.

15. House Committee on Foreign Affairs, *Consideration of the Cuban Democracy Act of 1992*, hearing, 102d Cong., 2d sess., April 8, 1992, 359.

16. Jane Franklin, *Cuba and the United States: A Chronological History* (New York: Ocean Press, 1997), 290.

17. Former Clinton administration official, telephone interview, June 1, 1998.

18. Ann Bardach, "Our Man in Miami," *New Republic*, October 3, 1994, 20.

19. William Jefferson Clinton, "Media Roundtable on NAFTA," *Weekly Compilation of Presidential Documents*, November 12, 1993, 2350.

20. Ibid.

21. Elliott Abrams, "Castro's Latest Coup," *National Review*, June 12, 1995, 37.

22. Burt Solomon, "Clinton's Fast Break on Cuba . . . or Foreign Policy on the Fly," *National Journal*, September 3, 1994, 2044.

23. David Rieff, "From Exiles to Immigrants," *Foreign Affairs* 74 (July/August 1995): 87, describes Cuban Miami as "stupefied." See also Jonathan C. Smith, "Foreign Policy for Sale? Interest Group Influence on President Clinton's Cuba Policy, August 1994," *Presidential Studies Quarterly* 29: 207–220.

24. Dan Fisk, telephone interview, June 16, 1998.

25. Patrick J. Kiger, *Squeeze Play: The United States, Cuba, and the Helms-Burton Act* (Washington, D.C.: Center for Public Integrity, 1997), chap. 5. See also Dick Kirschten, "Raising Cain," *National Journal*, July 1, 1995, 1714–1717.

26. Steven Greenhouse, "Allies of U.S. Seek to Block Bill on Cuba," *New York Times*, April 13, 1995, A9.

27. See House Committee on International Relations, Subcommittee on the Western Hemisphere, *The Cuban Liberty and Democratic Solidarity (LIBERTAD) Act of 1995*, hearing, 104th Cong., 1st sess., March 16, 1995, 31–34.

28. Fisk, telephone interview, June 16, 1998. See also Senate Committee on Foreign Relations, Subcommittee on the Western Hemisphere and Peace Corps Affairs, *Cuban Liberty and Democratic Solidarity Act*, hearing, 104th Cong., 1st sess., May 22 and June 14, 1995, 76.

29. Representative Lincoln Diaz-Balart, R-Fla., telephone interview, July 2, 1998.

30. William Jefferson Clinton, "Interview with Wolf Blitzer and Judy Woodruff on CNN," *Weekly Compilation of Presidential Documents*, April 14, 1995, 624–625.

31. Senate Committee on Foreign Relations, *Cuban Liberty and Democratic Solidarity Act*, 16–30.

32. Kiger, *Squeeze Play*, 54.

33. Fisk, telephone interview, June 16, 1998.

34. Former Clinton administration official, telephone interview, June 1, 1998.

35. For more detail on these regulations, see http://www.state.gov/www/regions/wha/cuba/travel.html.

36. Kiger, *Squeeze Play*, 54; Christopher Marquis, "New Clinton Strategy Eases Rules on Travel, Cultural Ties to Cuba," *Tampa Tribune*, October 6, 1995, 1; and Norman Pearlstine, "To Our Readers," *Time*, October 25, 1995, 4.

37. Mark Matthews, "Congress Divided on Clinton Move to Thaw Cuba Policy," *Baltimore Sun*, October 7, 1995, 9A.

38. William L. Roberts, "Clinton Draws Mixed Review on Cuba Policy," *Journal of Commerce*, October 10, 1995, 2A.

39. Pamela Falk, "U.S.-Cuba Deal Seems Close to Fruition," *Denver Post*, October 19, 1995, B7.

40. William Jefferson Clinton, "Remarks at a Freedom House Breakfast," *Weekly Compilation of Presidential Documents*, October 6, 1995, 1780–1781.

41. See Nagin, "Backfire."

42. Nancy Mathis, "New Sanctions against Cuba; U.S. Plans Action after 2 Civilian Planes Downed," *Houston Chronicle*, February 26, 1996, A1.

43. William Jefferson Clinton, "Remarks Announcing Sanctions against Cuba following the Downing of Brothers to the Rescue Airplanes," *Weekly Compilation of Presidential Documents*, February 26, 1996, 381–382. See also Nagin, "Backfire."

44. Diaz-Balart, telephone interview, July 2, 1998.

45. Fisk, telephone interview, June 16, 1998.

46. Steve Vermillion, Office of Representative Lincoln Diaz-Balart, telephone interview, June 19, 1998.

47. Federal News Service, "Press Conference: Reaction to Cuban Shootdown of Civilian Aircraft," February 27, 1996.

48. Ibid.

49. Carroll J. Doherty, "Planes' Downing Forces Clinton to Compromise on Sanctions," *Congressional Quarterly Weekly Report,* March 2, 1996, 565.

50. Diaz-Balart, telephone interview, July 2, 1998.

51. Fisk, telephone interview, June 16, 1998.

52. Former Clinton administration official, telephone interview, June 1, 1998. See also Nagin, "Backfire," 34.

53. "House, in 336-86 vote, Passes Bill Increasing Economic Sanctions on Cuba," *Buffalo News,* March 7, 1996, 4A.

54. "Clinton, Congress, Agree on Bill to Hit Cuba," *Montreal Gazette,* February 29, 1996, B1.

55. "House Passes Bill Increasing Economic Sanctions on Cuba," 4A.

56. Helen Dewar, "Clinton, Hill Agree on Cuba Sanctions; New Curbs May Be Enacted Next Week," *Washington Post,* February 29, 1996, A16.

57. Ibid.

58. Federal News Service, "Hearing of the House International Relations Committee: Cuba Shootdown Incident," February 29, 1996.

59. William Jefferson Clinton, "Statement on Action on Title III of the Cuban Liberty and Democratic Solidarity (LIBERTAD) Act of 1996," *Weekly Compilation of Presidential Documents,* July 16, 1996, 1265–1266.

60. See the full text of the act at http://thomas.loc.gov/cgi-bin/query/z?c104:H.R.927.ENR:.

61. See Jesse Helms, "Helms Slams Decision to Waive Cuba Provision," press release, July 16, 1996.

62. John Pearson, "Just Who's Getting Punished Here?" *Business Week,* international edition, June 17, 1996, 28. See also Juan O. Tamayo, "U.S. Poised to Bar Execs of Firm Operating in Cuba," *Miami Herald,* July 3, 1999, http://www.herald.com/content/today/docs/038483.htm; and Tim Golden, "U.S., Avoiding Castro, Relaxes Rules on Cuba," *New York Times,* July 7, 1999, A1.

63. Michael E. Ranneberger, coordinator for the Office of Cuban Affairs, statement before hearings of the Subcommittee on the Western Hemisphere of the House International Relations Committee, March 24, 1999.

64. Craig Auge, "Title IV of the Helms-Burton Act: A Questionable Secondary Boycott," *Law and Policy in International Business* 28, no. 2 (winter 1997): 575.

65. William Jefferson Clinton, "Statement on Cuba," *Weekly Compilation of Presidential Documents,* March 20, 1998, 475–476.

66. William Jefferson Clinton, "Statement on United States Policy toward Cuba," *Weekly Compilation of Presidential Documents,* January 5, 1999, 7–8.

67. Christopher Marquis, "US to Cut Sanctions on Cuba," *Pittsburgh Post-Gazette,* March 20, 1998, A1. See also Steven Erlanger, "US to Ease Curbs on Relief to Cuba and Money to Kin," *New York Times,* March 20, 1998, A1.

68. Juan O. Tamayo, "Eased Cuba Sanctions Questioned," *Miami Herald,* January 7, 1999, A12.

69. An attempt was made to form a presidential "blue ribbon" commission on U.S. policy toward Cuba, which may have suggested dropping the embargo, but the effort was halted in 1999 due to a variety of political pressures. See, for example, Thomas W. Lippman, "Group Urges Review of Cuba Policy," *Washington Post,* November 8, 1998, A10; and http://uscubacommission.org.

70. Ann Radelat, "Farmers Hurting in Cuba, U.S. Want to Help Each Other," *St. Louis Dispatch*, February 7, 1999, B4.

71. Thomas W. Lippman, "Senate Votes to Lift an Embargo on Cuba; Measure to End Most Unilateral Export Bans Would Allow Food, Medicine Sales," *Washington Post*, August 7, 1999, A15.

72. Kevin G. Hall, "Outlook Brightens in Washington for Resuming Trade," *Journal of Commerce*, September 30, 1999, 4.

73. "Senate Panel Clears Sales of Food to Cuba," *Chicago Sun-Times*, March 24, 2000, 30.

74. Lizette Alvarez, "U.S. Farm Groups Join Move to Ease Cuba Embargo," *New York Times*, May 24, 2000, A10.

75. Edwin McDowell, "Correspondent's Report: Traveling to Cuba Is as Tricky as Ever," *New York Times*, November 5, 2000, sec. 5, 3.

12 Sino-American Trade Relations: Privatizing Foreign Policy

Steven W. Hook and Jeremy Lesh

Before You Begin

1. In what ways did the U.S. engagement policy toward China reflect general changes in U.S. foreign policy after the cold war?

2. Which interest groups and non-governmental organizations became active as advocates or opponents of closer economic relations between China and the United States?

3. To what extent did the outcome of the debate over Sino-American trade relations—the normalization of trade and U.S. support for China's entry into the World Trade Organization—reflect economic disparities between business interests and non-profit non-governmental organizations?

4. What does this case tell us generally about the formulation and content of U.S. foreign policy after the cold war?

Introduction: The Chinese Challenge

Making U.S. foreign policy has become more complicated in many ways since the cold war ended. The nation's goals have become more diffuse and ambiguous, as have the means available to accomplish them. A wider array of state and non-state actors has become engaged in the policy-making process, and the historic rivalry between the executive and legislative branches has intensified, reflecting unresolved differences over the global roles and responsibilities of the United States. The course of Sino-American relations is representative of this increased complexity.

From the founding of the People's Republic of China (PRC) in 1949 through the end of the cold war, the PRC's relations with the United States were overshadowed by ideological competition and the East-West balance of power. Sino-American tensions moderated in the 1970s, when the Nixon-Kissinger "opening" to China was followed by the rise of reformist Deng Xiaoping as China's leader. Bilateral relationship remained plagued, however, by U.S.

291

complaints about Beijing's repression of human rights, neglect of environmental problems, transfer of weapons, and maintenance of protectionist trade policies. Conversely, Chinese leaders frequently opposed the United States at the United Nations and openly criticized Washington for its "hegemonic" world role.

Upon taking office early in January 1993, President Bill Clinton wanted to revive Sino-American relations. Specifically, he sought to "engage" the PRC, primarily through closer economic ties, in hopes that a more interdependent relationship would benefit U.S. firms and consumers while also eliciting greater cooperation from Beijing on issues of concern to the United States. Clinton's engagement strategy played an important part in his overall foreign policy, which shifted the nation's strategic focus from the military concerns of the cold war to the "geoeconomics" of the new era. In the president's view, the United States needed to exploit its status as the world's largest economy by making U.S.-based firms more competitive in the rapidly integrating global marketplace. Toward that end, his administration identified several "big emerging markets," including that of China, that should be given special attention in guiding U.S. foreign economic policy.[1]

Engagement required severing the link between China's human rights policies and its status as a trading partner. As Clinton stated in May 1994:

> That linkage has been constructive during the past year. But I believe, based on our aggressive contacts with the Chinese in the past several months, that we have reached the end of the usefulness of that policy, and it is time to take a new path toward the achievement of our constant objectives. We need to place our relationship into a larger and more productive framework.[2]

The president's policy was based on the neo-liberal presumption that China's inclusion in global economic and political regimes would encourage Beijing to moderate its internal behavior and conform with international standards. The alternative policy of estrangement—isolating China diplomatically and economically—was viewed as less likely to produce compliance and restraint in Beijing. Economic integration, in the view of the Clinton administration, would benefit the Chinese and world economies. In this context, China could no longer remain an island separated from the forces of global capitalism. The world had become "smaller" through economic integration, the unprecedented diffusion of technology, and greater recognition of shared problems, including environmental destruction, overpopulation, and weapons proliferation. Beyond increasing bilateral trade and promoting restraint in China's internal behavior, engagement raised the possibility of also eliciting China's cooperation in solving transnational problems.

A general shift in U.S. foreign policy in the 1990s produced concrete changes in policy formulation. During the cold war, the State and Defense Departments largely controlled the machinations of foreign policy. The end of the cold war not only altered the mission of these institutions, it also involved other agencies in shaping the foreign policy agenda. These included the Treasury and Commerce Departments, the Office of the United States Trade Representative, and a variety of federal agencies attached to law enforcement, environmental protection, and health and labor policy. As the foreign policy profile of these institutions grew, so did that of non-governmental organizations (NGOs) based in the United States and abroad. With a greater capacity to shape the U.S. foreign policy agenda, NGOs on both sides of the engagement debate mobilized in the late 1990s. Their efforts—often highly visible but frequently behind the scenes—typified the increased activism and policy advocacy of hundreds of NGOs in myriad issue areas after the cold war.

Business interests in particular benefited directly from the new opportunities inherent in the engagement policy. Dozens of U.S.-based multinational corporations (MNCs) praised and actively supported the engagement strategy. From their perspective, China's population of more than 1.2 billion was a vast potential market for goods and services that could only be tapped if the governments of China and the United States maintained cordial relations. Echoing the Clinton administration's logic, they predicted that expanded economic contacts would force China's leaders to maintain stable relations overseas and to cooperate on political issues. Many non-profit NGOs, meanwhile, strongly opposed engagement. Human rights groups argued that Beijing should not be "rewarded" for its defiance of human rights standards. Environmental NGOs demanded that engagement only proceed after the Chinese government implemented stronger measures to protect air and water quality at home and embraced multilateral environmental initiatives overseas. Religious groups also became vocal on the issue, calling attention to the PRC's suppression of spiritual movements and religious institutions. Finally, U.S.-based labor groups feared that engagement would lead to the exodus of U.S. jobs and manufacturing capacity to the PRC.

This case enhances understanding of post–cold war U.S. foreign policy through analysis of the engagement policy toward China. Its primary focus is on legislative processes that led to the establishment of permanent normal trade relations (PNTR) between China and the United States and U.S. support for China's entry into the World Trade Organization (WTO). Both measures were viewed as critical by the Chinese leadership and by the Clinton administration, both of which viewed Sino-American trade relations as a foreign policy priority. Private interest groups on both sides of this trade issue resorted to a variety of tactics to achieve their objectives. The mobilization of these NGOs, their respective links to domestic interests, and their widely varying levels of funding and institutional capacity all played key roles in determining the outcome of this process.

Background: The Course of Sino-American Relations

The rise of the PRC in 1949 came at a time of worsening relations between the United States and the Soviet Union, the two World War II allies that became cold war superpowers. As the newest communist country, and the world's most populous state, the PRC was to Washington a primary source of concern. The Sino-Soviet friendship treaty of 1950 and the Korean War exacerbated these fears, so U.S. leaders soon incorporated the PRC into the anticommunist containment policy designed in 1946 to prevent the spread of Soviet influence and power. Asia evolved as an arena of ideological competition in the 1950s and 1960s, with the wars in Korea and Vietnam assuming central stage in the global cold war.[3] The United States refused to recognize the communist regime in Beijing and instead considered Nationalist Party exiles in Taiwan the true rulers of China. This policy of non-recognition lasted until the 1970s, when the Nixon administration initiated bilateral relations with the PRC. Although Mao Zedong's hold on power remained strong at that time, China had suffered badly under his key programs—the Great Leap Forward and the Cultural Revolution. Millions of Chinese entrepreneurs, intellectuals, and citizens with connections abroad were purged as the Chinese economy experienced repeated failures.

By the time the PRC was formally recognized by Washington in 1979, under the Carter administration, key changes in the political and economic structures of China had been made. Following Mao's death in 1976, Deng Xiaoping, a leader of the growing technocratic movement, assumed power and initiated a series of market-oriented economic reforms geared toward bringing China into the modern era.[4] In 1978, Deng began privatizing a small percentage of state-owned enterprises and overhauled the agricultural sector by permitting the sale of surplus commodities at market prices. The PRC under Deng continued to punish dissidents, however, and political rights in general were denied to the Chinese people.

When it recognized the PRC, the United States adopted a trade policy that required annual reviews of China's behavior in several areas, including foreign economic relations and the protection of human rights. These reviews rendered China's most favored nation (MFN) trade status—which allowed Beijing the same terms of trade accorded other major trading partners of the United States—dependent upon its overall behavior. The MFN reviews became an annual ritual in Congress and were routinely criticized by China's leaders. The Chinese felt the PRC was being unfairly singled out among U.S. trading partners and that the United States was unduly interfering in their domestic and foreign affairs. Despite widely publicized violations of human rights by the PRC, Congress renewed China's MFN trade status every year in the 1980s. This was largely due to fast-growing trade with the United States and the rapid growth of the Chinese economy as Deng's economic reforms took effect.[5] Security concerns also figured in U.S. calculations; closer Sino-American relations were seen as a vital instrument in furthering containment of Soviet expansionism.

The Chinese government's assault on pro-democracy protesters in June 1989 sparked renewed debate within Congress and among the general public regarding human rights in China. Approximately 1,300 protesters were killed in the assault on Tiananmen Square, and thousands more were arrested and imprisoned.[6] Questions regarding the PRC's treatment of political opposition, its suppression of political and religious freedoms in Tibet, and its ongoing hostility toward Taiwan were also raised in Congress. Of additional concern to U.S. leaders was the government's conduct of bilateral trade with the United States. The Chinese domestic market had become open to some foreign goods, particularly the high-technology products that facilitated the PRC's modernization drive. China, however, remained largely closed to foreign goods that were also produced by Chinese workers. Foreign-based MNCs were limited to establishing joint ventures with Chinese firms in order to gain access to Chinese consumers.

U.S. complaints related to a wide range of barriers that prevented U.S.-based firms from competing in the PRC. The most common barriers were high tariffs, which averaged nearly 20 percent on all imports but were much higher on selected goods, such as automobiles and agricultural products. In addition, the Chinese government imposed a variety of non-tariff barriers—such as quotas, import licenses, technical standards, and domestic-content provisions—that further discouraged foreign competition. Corporate leaders also complained

Sino-American Trade Relations

October 1949   Mao Zedong's communist forces defeat the Chinese nationalist government. The United States refuses to recognize the People's Republic of China (PRC), recognizing instead the nationalist exiles in Taiwan.

February 1972   President Richard Nixon visits Beijing, opening relations between the United States and the PRC.

September 1976   The death of Mao leads to a two-year transition of power to Deng Xiaoping, who launches a series of market-oriented economic reforms while maintaining strict control over the PRC's political system.

January 1979   President Jimmy Carter formally recognizes the PRC and abrogates the U.S. treaty with Taiwan.

June 1989   Tiananmen Square protesters advocating democracy are crushed by government forces. The United States and other foreign governments respond by imposing economic sanctions against China.

May 1994   President Bill Clinton adopts the policy of engagement toward China, arguing that closer economic relations are more likely to produce cooperation from Beijing than is isolation.

February 1997   Jiang Zemin assumes leadership of the PRC and continues Deng's policies of economic reform and political repression.

1998   China applies for membership in the World Trade Organization.

November 1999   Clinton endorses China's entry into the World Trade Organization in return for a series of bilateral trade concessions from Beijing.

May 2000   The House of Representatives approves H.R. 4444 by a 237-197 vote, granting permanent normal trade relations to China.

September 2000   The Senate approves the trade bill by a vote of 83-15.

October 2000   Clinton signs the legislation formally establishing normal trade relations between the United States and China.

about the limited number of import-export companies in the PRC, which further impaired their ability to gain commercial licenses and establish transportation networks in the country.

In October 1991, the Bush administration authorized the Office of the United States Trade Representative to launch the most sweeping market-access investigation in that agency's history. In August 1992 the investigation confirmed a wide range of direct and indirect trade barriers hindering U.S. competition. The United States threatened to impose an unprecedented $4 billion in trade sanctions against Beijing if the protectionist measures remained in place. The threat of sanctions was dropped two months later, however, after Chinese officials promised to reform their trade policies and make their regulations more "transparent" and understandable to foreign MNCs and governments. The symbiotic relationship—one of mutual need and opportunism—between Washington and Beijing led to MFN renewals every year during the Bush administration.

Campaigning against Bush in 1992, Clinton vowed to make MFN legislation truly conditional. He viewed the human rights issue as central to U.S. foreign policy and demanded that China's MFN renewal be accompanied by strict legislation requiring reforms in Chinese law and in its behavior at home and overseas. Candidate Clinton promised to impose trade sanctions against China if its leaders did not adhere to internationally recognized standards of human rights. Clinton argued on the campaign trail that Bush had coddled the "butchers of Beijing" and tolerated their repressive rule and persecution of pro-democracy advocates.

Soon after his election in November 1992, however, Clinton's approach toward China changed. As president he adopted a more cooperative stance based on closer economic ties between the PRC and the United States. Clinton then became a strong supporter of China's entry into the WTO, the global trade body whose advocacy for open markets was strongly supported by the president. In addition, Clinton endorsed the establishment of normalized trade relations that would abolish the annual reviews of China's MFN status.

Clinton's shift on Sino-American relations must be placed squarely within the context of the PRC's emergence as a global economic superpower. Between 1979 and 1999, real gross domestic product (GDP) in China grew at an annual rate of 9.7 percent, one of the fastest rates in the world.[7] Between 1978 and 1999, the country's annual trade volume increased in absolute terms from $21 billion to $361 billion. China had become the tenth largest trading economy by 2000 and was projected by the World Bank to become second only to the United States in total trade by 2020. As China's trade volumes grew steadily, it maintained a large trade surplus—estimated at $21 billion in 1999—and a level of foreign reserves that exceeded $150 billion by the turn of the century. China also became the world's second largest destination of foreign direct investment (FDI) in the 1990s, attracting more than $45 billion in 1998 alone, primarily from the United States and Japan. This trend reflected strong investor confidence in the sustainability of the Chinese economy, even as real GDP growth slowed modestly and China's neighbors continued to recover from the regional economic crisis of 1997 and 1998. The scope of private investing in China widened throughout the decade, as the government loosened restrictions on capital transfers and became increasingly receptive to FDI as well as portfolio investments (trade in stocks, bonds, and international currencies).

The U.S. market was a major stimulant for the Chinese economy. In terms of bilateral trade, China exported more than $81 billion in goods to the United States in 1999. Of this total, $17 billion was in the form of manufactured goods. Footwear, office machines, telecommunications equipment, and apparel represented the other major Chinese exports. Sino-American trade grew more lopsided during the 1990s as China's trade surplus grew each year—from $10 billion in 1990 to nearly $70 billion by 1999. The United States exported just $13 billion in goods to the PRC in 1999, primarily in the form of aircraft, electrical machinery, fertilizers, computers, and industrial equipment.[8] Noticeably absent from this list are automobiles and agricultural products, both of which were subject to rigid trade barriers. It was argued that this would likely change, however, if China were to be granted permanent normal trade relations status with the United States. The U.S. Department of Agriculture estimated that U.S. exports of wheat, rice, corn, cotton, and soybeans to China would increase by $1.5 billion annually between 2000 and 2009 if barriers were removed.[9]

The large and growing bilateral trade gaps between Beijing and Washington stimulated widespread protests by the U.S. government, which faced strong pressure from labor unions, farmers, and corporate leaders to reverse the imbalance. Many members of Congress and non-profit NGOs, meanwhile, questioned why the United States continued to tolerate the Chinese government's ongoing violations of human rights, its neglect of environmental standards, and its transfers of military equipment to so-called rogue states. Their criticism was punctuated by the disparities in trade that only widened after the engagement policy was put into practice.

Clinton's Engagement Policy

As noted, President Clinton's critical rhetoric toward China softened after his election. While still calling for improvements in the PRC's human rights record, Clinton argued that Sino-American trade relations should not depend upon political concerns. In May 1994 he renewed China's favorable trade status, and by executive order proclaimed that future U.S. trade with China would not be linked directly to human rights. He predicted that U.S. engagement of the PRC, largely through closer economic ties, would elicit greater respect for human rights in China. Toward this end, the basis of Sino-American trade would be redefined in legislation formalizing the change in policy.

As Clinton announced the change in policy, the link between human rights and Sino-American trade economy was effectively severed.[10] Concerns over China's human rights policies persisted, however, along with economic tensions. In 1995, China exported $48.5 billion worth of goods to the United States, while receiving only $10 billion in U.S. imports.[11] A trade war had to be avoided, a conclusion drawn by the Clinton administration and Congress, which after the November 1994 midterm elections was dominated by the Republican Party.

Debates regarding Sino-American trade relations intensified in 1995. Human rights groups became more outspoken in February, when Human Rights Watch (HRW) released its annual report, which concluded that Chinese officials had failed to improve their human rights record following Clinton's proclamation of the engagement policy. In addition to human rights and labor groups pressuring Washington, U.S.-based MNCs, which had opposed isolating China for its human rights practices, pushed for sanctioning China over its trade practices. The bilateral trade deficit had become a serious problem, and an estimated $500 million in potential profits had been lost since the early 1980s by U.S.-based music and software companies as a result of alleged piracy of intellectual property. Even with these issues, many of Clinton's economic advisers felt that a return to estrangement would be more harmful than the potential damage of all the problems associated with engagement.

The controversy over intellectual property rights proved especially divisive. Washington threatened a 100 percent tariff on certain items if piracy continued. The result was a $3 billion package of sanctions. In retaliation, Beijing imposed higher tariffs against the U.S. automobile industry, which was already denied access to the Chinese market on a large scale. Further, the Chinese Civil Aviation Administration contracted with European aircraft manufacturers in a deal that exceeded $1.5 billion, spurning Boeing, which had taken its export monopoly in China for granted.[12] U.S. officials also expressed concerns about China's sales of nuclear technologies to developing countries, but the engagement strategy remained intact.[13]

After the death of Deng Xiaoping in February 1997, the new premier, Jiang Zemin, pledged to maintain Deng's formula of economic integration abroad and tight political control at home. Public opinion began to swing against engagement as Chinese officials continued to defy international human rights standards.[14] The PRC's burgeoning trade surplus with the United States provoked outrage among U.S. workers and trade unions. As a result, liberals motivated by human rights and conservatives opposed to the large U.S. trade deficit created ad hoc anti-engagement coalitions (see Box 12.1). Clinton again argued that economic withdrawal from China would have disastrous consequences for the U.S. economy and would only make matters worse for Chinese dissidents and workers.

NGOs Favoring the Engagement Strategy

Outside the U.S. government, most advocates of the Clinton administration's engagement strategy came from the business sector. This was no surprise given the immense size of the Chinese consumer market, which remained largely untapped because of the incremental nature of the country's economic reforms and restrictions on foreign competition. Among the pro-engagement advocates were individual MNCs, trade groups, and multisector organizations such as the U.S. Chamber of Commerce. Much of their efforts in the area of Sino-American trade relations took the form of traditional lobbying, but they also committed large sums of money to support the reelection campaigns of like-minded members of Congress and promote candidates challenging incumbents opposed to normalized trade relations between China and the United States. In addition, these groups were also able to advance their interests through the use of soft-money donations to the major political parties.

One of the first groups to promote expanded Sino-American trade was the U.S.-China Business Council, which played an active role in commercial relations between Nixon's visit to China in 1972 and formal U.S. recognition in 1979. Created in 1973 as the National Council for U.S.-China Trade, this group consisted of about 270 corporate executives who maintained economic interests in China. The council in the late 1990s supported PNTR status for China and its accession to the WTO. A similar group, the Business Roundtable, composed of the chief executive officers of major U.S.-based MNCs, spent nearly $6 million on an advertising campaign to promote normalized trade relations. Another $4 million was budgeted for campaign contributions in 1996 and 1998 to congressional candidates supporting free trade with China.[15] Finally, the U.S. Chamber of Commerce also launched a major effort to support China's entry into the WTO and PNTR status in the United States. Called TradeRoots China, the effort mobilized the organization's federation of state and local chambers

Box 12.1	Interest Groups in the Sino-American Trade Relations Debate	

Supporters	Opponents
Business groups	Human rights advocates
Transportation industries	Environmental groups
Telecommunications sector	Religious groups
Financial markets	Trade unions

of commerce. The national chamber also distributed a newsletter, *China Insider,* to keep its members informed about the progress of the trade legislation in Congress.[16]

The prospect of normalized Sino-American trade relations prompted U.S.-based MNCs to form alliances across economic sectors. For example, the San Francisco–based Wine Institute teamed up with the Semiconductor Industry Association, headquartered in San Jose, to form the Agriculture–High Technology Alliance, whose primary mission was to guarantee the passage of the free trade bill in Congress. The semiconductor group represented 150 technology companies, including such Silicon Valley giants as Intel and Hewlett-Packard. In combination with the agriculture groups, the high-tech trade association created a formidable political force in California. Similar multisector economic alliances were established in other states to pool resources for the lobbying effort that was seen as essential for the trade legislation to pass.

Among the most active corporate-based supporters of normalized trade relations were the transportation industries, primarily aircraft and automotive firms, which eagerly sought greater access to the Chinese domestic market. Boeing was one of the earliest U.S.-based MNCs to do business in China. Following Nixon's 1972 visit, the Chinese Civil Aviation Administration ordered ten passenger jets from the Seattle-based manufacturer. Since then, the Chinese government has purchased about 300 Boeing aircraft. Despite being snubbed in favor of European contractors in 1996, in 1998 Boeing held 72 percent of the market share in China. Commercial flights to and from China increased by more than 20 percent annually from 1988 to 1998, so free trade with China would undoubtedly benefit Boeing.[17]

Meanwhile, the "big three" U.S. automakers contributed large amounts of capital and time in an attempt to open the Chinese automobile market to foreign competition. The Chinese domestic auto market was still in the early stages of development in the 1990s, and the import of foreign-made cars was highly restricted. Nonetheless, the vast potential of the domestic market in China attracted great attention from U.S.-based manufacturers. Private automobile purchasing in China grew more than 300 percent in the 1990s, but there remained vast amounts of room for additional growth in this sector. According to a survey by the Beijing-based Meilande Information Co., by the end of 1999 nearly 8 percent of Chinese households in fourteen major cities owned private vehicles. The same survey indicated that an additional 7 percent intended to purchase vehicles in 2000.[18]

The General Motors Corporation (GM) was the most instrumental among U.S.-based automotive firms in developing the auto market in China. In 1997, GM entered into a joint venture with the Shanghai Automotive Industry Corporation, creating nearly 2,000 manufacturing and administrative jobs. Together, the participating companies invested $1.5 billion in the project.[19] General Motors officials hoped that its participation would not only increase its market share, but also improve the competitiveness of the Chinese auto industry internationally. In addition, GM launched a joint venture with Jinbei Automotive to produce a version of its Chevrolet Blazer as part of an effort to market sport utility vehicles in China. Predictably, GM strongly supported normalized trade relations and China's entry into the WTO.

The Chrysler Corporation entered the Chinese market in 1987 by forming a partnership with Beijing Auto Works. The company manufactured two Jeep Series models: the Cherokee and the BJ 2021. Unfortunately for Chrysler, the city of Beijing passed stringent traffic regulations in 1994 that made these vehicles illegal on some roadways during peak hours. These restrictions, combined with additional regulations, caused Jeep sales to fall by 40 percent by 1996.[20] The 1998 merger of Chrysler and Daimler Benz, the German automaker, was expected to increase the conglomerate's market share in China. The Ford Motor Company had yet to maximize its potential in China by 2000. Although Ford had entered the Chinese automotive market prior to the 1949 revolution, its reentry was slow. In 1993, Ford opened its first dealership on the mainland but in 1998 controlled less than 1 percent of overall market share in China.[21]

China, like much of the developing world, was also fertile ground for growth in the technology and communications sectors. In this respect U.S.-based MNCs played a key role in facilitating China's development and application of information technologies, a cornerstone of the PRC's development strategy. The San Diego–based Qualcomm Corporation, for example, partnered with two of the three largest state-owned communications companies, China Telecom and China Unicom, in an effort to develop the Chinese wireless communications market. By 2000 only a small part of the market had been penetrated, but as sharing information becomes a necessity in the rapidly integrating business environment, the use of wireless phones and satellite communications networks will prove vital. Qualcomm's assistance helped standardize the industry by licensing intellectual property and creating a prototype system, Code Division Multiple Access, that all domestic telecommunications firms could use. Not only did Qualcomm reap royalties for its services, but its assistance also made wireless communications more accessible to the business sector. Other major communications and high-technology firms followed Qualcomm into China. Nortel, Motorola, and Lucent Technologies invested in joint ventures with Chinese counterparts. It was commonly estimated that the total wireless market would exceed $16 billion in annual sales once fully exploited.[22] These companies had much to gain financially from their partnerships, and from free trade in general between the PRC and the United States.

Other proponents of normalized trade relations came from the financial markets, which may be viewed as something of a collective MNC. Investors can be individual stockholders, corporations, brokerage firms, or mutual fund managers. Recipients of these private investments use this capital to develop new products, expand production, and open new retail outlets. As noted earlier, FDI and portfolio investments played a key role in spurring the PRC's economic growth. As more MNCs set up shop in China, even through mandated joint ventures with Chinese firms, the country attracted additional private investment. As a result, leaders of U.S.-based financial institutions were among the most ardent supporters of normalized trade relations and Chinese entry into the WTO.

NGOs Opposing the Engagement Strategy

Many conservative members of Congress argued that Clinton's engagement policy would merely reward a "revisionist" Chinese state bent on military expansionism at the expense of U.S. interests. In their view, a policy of isolating the PRC was preferable to one actively "engaging" its government. Nonprofit NGOs were also active in the debate over Sino-American trade, though in most cases their views differed strongly from the pro-engagement stance adopted by business-related groups. Among other issues, they demanded that political, environmental, and labor disputes between China and the United States be resolved before trade relations were normalized. The non-profit NGOs were highly fragmented because of their wide range of interests and policy preferences. With more limited resources than the business groups and MNCs, these NGOs faced an uphill battle in the policy debate. Nonetheless, they posed a strong challenge to the Clinton administration's engagement policy and were able to shape the terms of the legislation ultimately passed by Congress and signed by President Clinton [23]

Private groups interested in human rights played an active role in the trade debate. Lacking the economic clout of U.S.-based MNCs and trade groups, the human rights organizations promoted their positions primarily through the release of detailed studies of the Chinese government's conduct in this area. Their reports were especially vital given the severe press restrictions in the PRC, which prevented Chinese journalists from investigating and exposing human rights violations. Among these groups, Human Rights Watch was particularly critical of the engagement strategy, claiming that the Chinese government's repression of political and civil rights would actually increase as the PRC became more integrated in the global economy. In addition to its annual reports on human rights, HRW published studies on China's strict control of religion, child abuse in state-run orphanages, and violations of women's reproductive rights. In one study, HRW argued that by separating human rights concerns from Sino-American trade relations, the United States gave Chinese leaders even less incentive to tolerate democratic movements.[24]

Another human rights NGO that played a major role in the debate over Sino-American trade relations was Freedom House, based in New York City. Freedom House's annual reports, along with those published by Human Rights Watch, were closely monitored within the U.S. government, by corporate leaders, and by non-profit interest groups. The reports were especially critical of the Chinese government's human rights policies; the PRC consistently received the group's lowest ranking in its annual surveys of political and civil rights. In its 1997–1998 report, Freedom House declared that the Chinese Communist Party "holds absolute power, has imprisoned nearly all active dissidents, uses the judiciary as a tool of state control, and severely restricts freedoms of speech, press, association, and religion."[25]

Amnesty International (AI) also published reports and sponsored demonstrations regarding human rights abuses in the PRC. Most notably, AI launched a media campaign in 1999 commemorating the ten-year anniversary of the Tiananmen Square massacre and circulated a list of 241 political prisoners still detained by the Chinese government. Members of AI continued to write to political prisoners in China as well as to government officials, urging the prisoners' release. While AI maintained the status of a non-political organization, the group cited continuing human rights abuses as evidence that the engagement policy had failed. "Hundreds, possibly thousands of activists and suspected opponents of the government were detained during the year," AI declared in its 1999 annual report. "Thousands of political prisoners jailed in previous years remained imprisoned, many of them prisoners of conscience."[26]

Another concern expressed by NGOs regarding the engagement policy was its lack of regard for the environment in China, where air and water pollution had steadily worsened during the country's modernization drive. This trend was especially regrettable given that environmental quality was one non-economic issue on which the Chinese and U.S. governments could potentially agree. China, however, made a Faustian bargain on the environment to achieve economic growth.[27] In particular, Chinese officials relied on coal-burning power plants as the primary source of electricity, a practice that led to high levels of fossil-fuel emissions that affected air quality far beyond China's borders.

Greenpeace, arguably the most influential environmental group in the world, urged the U.S. government to include environmental provisions in the PNTR legislation and in any U.S. endorsement of Chinese entry into the WTO. In China, Greenpeace sponsored protests in 1999 against genetically engineered food imports. Of particular concern to Greenpeace late in 1999 was Nestlé's use of genetically engineered soya milk in products sold in Hong Kong. The group sponsored a boycott of Chinese toy exports made with the toxic chemical polyvinyl chloride and organized mass demonstrations against a proposed waste incinerator in Hong Kong. Also of concern to the group was the worsening water quality in the Dongjiang River, the Pearl River Delta, and the South China Sea. Finally, Greenpeace joined with other environmental NGOs in opposing the massive Three Gorges Dam in Hubei Province, which was expected to force the relocation of 2 million people by the time of its completion in 2009.

Most of these environmental concerns remained outside the PNTR and WTO debates, primarily because of the Chinese government's rejection of foreign interference in what it considered its sovereign authority over internal economic development. The environmental groups did succeed, however, in raising the profile of these issues and putting pressure on U.S.- and other foreign-based MNCs to consider the ecological effects of their projects in China. As in other parts of the world, the environmental groups were most effective in appealing directly to public opinion through Internet campaigns and the sponsorship of mass protests and demonstrations.[28]

Religious groups were also active in the debate over Sino-American trade relations. Of particular concern to them was the persecution of individuals and groups that expressed support for religious principles and institutions. By their nature, such expressions are contrary to the ideology of the Chinese Communist Party. "Freedom of religion is under threat in China," proclaimed the United Methodist Church's General Board of Church and Society. "Catholic churches, mosques, Buddhist temples and indigenous religions are being harassed. . . . We call on Congress to vote against the extension of permanent normal trade relations to China until substantial improvements in religious freedom are achieved."[29] Religious groups in the United States were particularly outraged at the Chinese government's outlawing in July 1999 of Falun Gong, a spiritual movement that promoted "truthfulness, benevolence, and forbearance" through a combination of Buddhist and Taoist meditation practices. An estimated 10,000 Falun Gong followers surprised Chinese authorities in April 1999 by surrounding the government compound in Beijing to protest their lack of official recognition. The group was banned in July, and Chinese leaders arrested large numbers of its followers, closed its facilities, and confiscated its literature.[30]

American labor groups were vocal in their opposition to engagement. Lacking the economic clout of MNCs, these groups sought to sway public opinion against normalized trade relations with China through public information campaigns and public demonstrations. In an unusual demonstration of unity, more than 10,000 labor union advocates from different industrial sectors held a rally in April 2000 at the U.S. Capitol. Their show of force was designed to convince undecided members of Congress that public opposition to normalized trade relations was extensive and that normalized relations would have real human cost in the form of displaced workers. Their presence also reinforced that the trade unions represented a large and potentially crucial voting bloc.

The AFL-CIO and the United Auto Workers (UAW) led in promoting the trade union position, often invoking reasons beyond the economic self-interest of their members. AFL-CIO president John Sweeney frequently spoke out against Chinese entry into the WTO and normalized trade relations. Testifying to Congress in March 2000, Sweeney argued that an affirmative vote on PNTR "would reward the Chinese government at a time when there has been significant deterioration in its abysmal human rights record."[31] The AFL-CIO devoted much of its lobbying effort—and its budget—to the China trade issue. Advertisements it ran in eleven congressional districts were crucial in garnering public support for its position. For its part, the UAW initiated a lobbying campaign to oppose PNTR for similar reasons and cited the use of child labor and forced labor by political prisoners as justification for a reversal in U.S. trade policy. Of particular concern to the UAW was the opposition of the Chinese government to the formation of independent trade unions in the country.

With the U.S. trade deficit widening in China's favor, labor leaders also argued that normalized trade relations would jeopardize the country's long-term economic growth and harm thousands of firms as well as workers. Labor cited piracy of intellectual property, global environmental destruction, and the treatment of workers in China as additional reasons to oppose PNTR and China's entry in the WTO. Their primary focus in pressing the issue before Congress, however, was on the effects of normalized trade relations among their members. This appeal carried considerable weight among members of Congress who represented urbanized districts with large blue-collar populations.

Final Debates and Congressional Action

As all these NGOs were engaged on both sides of the debate over Sino-American trade relations, the U.S. government played a paradoxical role in informing the debate. Under a congressional requirement to report on all countries' human rights practices, the State Department released annual reports consistently critical of the Chinese government. According to the department's 1999 report,

> The Government's poor human rights record deteriorated markedly throughout the year. The government intensified efforts to suppress dissent, particularly organized dissent. . . . Abuses included instances of extrajudicial killings, torture and mistreatment of prisoners, forced confessions, arbitrary arrest and detention, lengthy incommunicado detention, and denial of due process.[32]

The State Department's findings were affirmed by human rights NGOs. Freedom House's review of human rights in China during 1999 noted that Chinese "authorities escalated a crackdown on political dissidents, labor and peasant activists, and religious leaders."[33] To President Clinton, the arguments made by non-profit NGOs as well as the State Department only strengthened his argument that the Chinese government should be "engaged." Thus in 1999 and 2000 the president intensified his efforts to apply the engagement policy by supporting Chinese accession to the WTO and normalized trade relations between China and the United States.

China's Drive for WTO Membership

The WTO had barely come into existence when Chinese officials declared their interest in joining. They took the first step in this direction in 1995 by forming a working party to prepare a formal application. This part of the process was completed in 1998, after which China began formal negotiations for membership. All applicants must undergo a two-part screening. First, they negotiate directly with the WTO on compliance with the trade body's regulations for open markets, protection of foreign firms and capital, and transparency for commercial regulations. These terms were originally set forth in the 1947 General Agreement on Tariffs and Trade (GATT), which was revised several times before GATT became the WTO after the completion in 1994 of the Uruguay Round of global trade talks. In the second phase, WTO applicants negotiate directly with their primary trading partners. These bilateral negotiations are often the primary hurdle facing prospective WTO members. Chinese officials acknowledged that gaining the blessing of the United States would be its highest hurdle in the WTO accession process. Once applicants complete bilateral talks, they draft a protocol of accession to be considered by WTO member states (which numbered 135 at the time China's application was under review). Two-thirds of the states must approve the protocol for the applicant to gain entry into the organization.

Talks between Chinese and U.S. trade negotiators progressed early in 1999 despite a series of unrelated political controversies and diplomatic crises that strained relations. The full extent of the 1996 presidential campaign scandals, many of which involved Chinese contributors, was widely known by 1998. The scandals provoked charges within Congress of undue Chinese influence in the Clinton administration. Making matters worse, U.S. bombers mistakenly destroyed the Chinese embassy in Belgrade in May 1999 as part of the North Atlantic Treaty Organization's effort to stem Serbia's crackdown against Kosovo. Chinese officials condemned the attack, and some even alleged that the bombing was deliberate. Trade talks were suspended for four months after the incident, during which the two governments again clashed over Taiwan's status, weapons proliferation in North Korea, and other regional issues.

These incidents compelled Clinton to step up his efforts to conclude a trade pact with China. Once talks resumed in September, progress was made, leading to a comprehensive bilateral agreement that was signed by both governments in

November 1999. Under the terms of the deal, the United States endorsed China's WTO membership in return for a wide range of Chinese concessions on bilateral trade. Among other concessions, Chinese leaders agreed to

- allow full trading and distribution rights to U.S. firms doing business in China;
- reduce average tariffs on "priority" agricultural goods from 32 to 15 percent by 2004;
- phase out quotas on foreign versus domestically produced goods and suspend other non-tariff barriers;
- permit greater access to the Chinese market by U.S.-based automobile companies by 2006; and
- improve the treatment of foreign firms operating in China.[34]

The Chinese government had long acknowledged that reaching a trade accord with the United States was essential if its goal of obtaining WTO membership was to be accomplished. If China had joined the trade body without a positive U.S. vote, its ability to play a meaningful role would have been greatly limited, and chronic differences between China and the United States would have remained unresolved. Thus the WTO served a useful function for U.S. officials, whose efforts to gain Chinese cooperation on bilateral trade had previously been frustrated.

The Clinton administration came under attack immediately after the WTO agreement with China was reached. "The fevered rush to admit China to the WTO is a grave mistake," declared the AFL-CIO's Sweeney. "By continuing to persecute dissenters, to imprison labor leaders and worker activists, and to export goods produced by child and slave labor, China shows it has no interest in playing by even the most basic rules of the world community."[35] Non-profit NGOs made the same arguments in policy statements in major U.S. newspapers. Their views were more fully detailed on their Internet sites, which became a primary means of NGO communication, coordination, and mobilization.

While negotiating with the United States, Chinese officials were simultaneously engaged in trade talks with other industrialized countries in their drive for WTO accession. Of particular interest was the European Union, whose progress toward regional economic integration had taken a great leap forward in 1999 with the introduction of the euro as a common currency. Under the terms of the 1992 Maastricht Treaty, the major European states (except for the United Kingdom) agreed to coordinate all facets of their fiscal and monetary policies. Such coordination included the conduct of trade relations, which the union would pursue with one voice. A "bilateral" trade deal between the European Union and the PRC was within reach, although EU members demanded many of the same market-opening concessions that China had granted the United States. The China-EU accord was reached on May 19, 2000, when the union formally endorsed China's bid to join the WTO in return for promised reforms in the PRC's trade practices. Through this single agreement, Beijing garnered the blessing of France, Germany, Italy, and twelve other western European countries.

The EU-PRC pact added momentum to China's drive for permanent normalized trade relations with the United States, an issue soon to be before Congress. In this respect the shifting landscape of U.S. foreign policy was revealed: yet another non-state actor—the intergovernmental European Union—interjected itself in the Sino-American trade debate.

The PNTR Debate in Congress

Under U.S. law, Congress was not required to play a direct role in the bilateral negotiations on U.S. support for China's WTO membership. Congress was also not required to ratify the pact signed by President Clinton. This did not mean, however, that Congress was irrelevant to this process. To the contrary, given its other constitutional powers to regulate trade—specifically its authority to grant or deny "normal" status to U.S. trading partners—Congress effectively held the key to China's entry into the WTO. Furthermore, legislation passed during the cold war imposed explicit conditions on U.S. trade with communist states. These conditions would violate the basic principle of the WTO that terms of trade among all its members be maintained consistently and unconditionally. For this reason, a bilateral trade agreement between the U.S. and China approved by both houses of Congress was the last major hurdle in Chinese membership in the multilateral WTO. The Clinton administration, therefore, directed its efforts early in 2000 toward gaining Congress's approval for PNTR with Beijing, which would effectively end the annual debate over China's MFN status.

Clinton assigned lobbying duties to Secretary of Commerce William Daley and Deputy Chief of Staff Stephen Ricchetti. The president also recruited former presidents Gerald Ford, Jimmy Carter, and George Bush to endorse the bill, along with Federal Reserve Board chairman Alan Greenspan and leading foreign policy advisers in the State and Defense Departments. Clinton's sense of urgency owed much to the setbacks and frustrations that plagued his second term in office. His impeachment by the House of Representatives for the

Monica Lewinsky sex scandal had crippled Clinton domestically. In foreign policy, his goal of achieving a comprehensive Middle East peace treaty was proving beyond reach, and his conduct of the military intervention in Kosovo received more criticism than praise. Clinton, therefore, looked to the China trade pact to define his legacy in foreign affairs.

Fortunately for Clinton, the political winds in Congress were in his favor. Under the trade bill introduced on May 15 in the House of Representatives (H.R. 4444), the United States would extend PNTR status to China upon its accession to the WTO. In approving the bill on May 17, the House Ways and Means Committee included an "anti-import surge" amendment that protected U.S. firms in the event of sudden increases in Chinese imports of specific commodities. The House Rules Committee further amended the bill on May 23. Among other provisions of the amended bill, a commission would be established to monitor and report on the PRC's human rights and labor practices. In addition, the U.S. trade representative would annually evaluate China's compliance with WTO regulations, and a special task force would confirm that Chinese exporters were not shipping goods manufactured by prison laborers to the United States. Finally, the House bill called for increased technical assistance to the PRC's efforts to enact legal reforms, and it urged the WTO to consider Taiwan's application to join the trade body immediately after China's accession.

Lobbying efforts peaked as the bill awaited a final vote in the full House. On the day before the vote was taken, about 200 business lobbyists met on Capitol Hill to coordinate their strategy for swaying undecided members.[36] On May 24, the House approved H.R. 4444 by a vote of 237-197. Although a majority of the 224 Republicans in the House voted for the bill, most of the 211 Democrats voted against it. Opponents came largely from urban areas with large populations of industrial workers and a strong labor union presence. On both sides of the aisle, support was primarily from members representing suburban or rural districts. Approval in the Senate was virtually assured, although its timing was uncertain given the Senate's approaching summer recess, other legislation on its schedule, and the distraction of a presidential election campaign.

Many prominent senators opposed the measure although Senate approval was considered a given. Paul Wellstone, D-Minn., for example, spoke out against normal trade with China because of the PRC's continuing repression of human rights and religious freedoms. Republican critics included Fred Thompson, R-Tenn., who sought without success to include an amendment that would link PNTR with Chinese restraint on nuclear weapons proliferation. Jesse Helms, R-N.C., chairman of the Foreign Relations Committee, argued that PNTR status would reward Chinese leaders for maintaining the communist system he had long condemned. As in the House, supporters and opponents of PNTR crossed party lines to an extent otherwise unseen in the 106th Congress.

As the Senate vote approached in September 2000, the lobbying among NGOs on both sides of the China trade issue resumed, although at a lower level of intensity than that preceding the House vote. Among pro-PNTR interest groups was the American Electronics Association, one of the largest and most influential high-tech trade associations in the United States, which stepped up its lobbying campaign in early September. Representing small and medium-sized industrial firms, the National Association of Manufacturers met with Senate majority leader Trent Lott, R-Miss., and Sen. John Breaux, D-La., and received their assurances that the bill would be approved. Once their position was made known, other business groups relaxed their lobbying efforts.[37]

Critics of PNTR also revived their campaign as the Senate vote approached. Among the most prominent NGOs was American Renewal, a non-profit organization concerned with the promotion of "traditional" American values. "The communist government continues to crack down on Protestant and Catholic Christians, followers of the Falun Gong Buddhist meditation sect, and other religious believers," charged Richard Lessner, vice president of the group. "Before the Senate gives China an implicit pass on this latest assault on religion by handing the persecutors permanent trade status, it should adopt tough, enforceable sanctions linked to improvements in China's appalling human rights record."[38]

The Senate was under strong pressure from the Clinton administration and business groups to pass the legislation without amendments. Clinton warned senators that amendments to the bill would force a new round of negotiations—first with the Chinese government and then with the House of Representatives. The outcome of these talks would be highly uncertain and would put the legislation in the hands of a new Congress and presidential administration in 2001. The Senate soundly rejected a series of proposed amendments linking China's trade status to improvements in human rights, religious freedom, labor standards, and weapons proliferation. The final bill, identical to that passed by the House, moved quickly toward a vote on the Senate floor.

As expected, the Senate approved H.R. 4444 on September 19 in a 83-15 vote and sent it to the White House for Clinton's signature. Again, support and opposition to the bill had crossed party lines to an unusual extent, with seven Democrats joining with eight Republicans in opposing the legislation. Whereas the Democrats were primarily concerned with labor issues, Republican opponents most often cited the security threat posed by the PRC. Human rights concerns were raised by critics of China in both parties. Clinton signed the legislation on October 10, and normalized Sino-American trade relations became a reality.

Conclusion: The Privatization of Foreign Policy

As we have seen, Sino-American trade relations emerged as a central foreign policy issue in the aftermath of the cold war. The Clinton administration, upon taking office in 1993, shifted the focus of U.S. foreign policy from the security dilemmas of East-West relations to the geoeconomics of global commerce. Clinton introduced engagement as a means to maintain close economic relations with Beijing while encouraging greater respect for human rights in the PRC and cooperation from its government on global issues, including environmental quality and weapons proliferation.

The interest groups discussed above were intimately involved in the policy process long before the trade bill was debated in Congress. U.S. and foreign business groups that had previously found favor within the Clinton administration continued to lobby members of Congress on behalf of the trade bill. Their contributions to the campaigns of pro-engagement lawmakers were openly acknowledged. Meanwhile, a variety of non-profit interest groups— including labor, human rights groups, and environmental groups—continued to oppose the legislation. Through direct lobbying, information campaigns, and appeals to grassroots organizations at the state and local levels, these NGOs hoped to compensate for their lack of economic clout.

The debates over Sino-American trade relations serves as a microcosm of a larger phenomenon in the formulation of post–cold war U.S. foreign policy. With the end of the cold war, the containment doctrine was no longer the centerpiece of foreign policy. A variety of new issues, actors, and policy calculations emerged in the 1990s. Of particular concern to this study is the heightened stature of foreign economic relations on the policy agenda of the first post–cold war administration. With the easing of security concerns following the Soviet Union's collapse in 1991, U.S. leaders identified "competitiveness" in the rapidly integrating global economy as a pressing national interest. A related trend was the growing role of non-state actors, international and domestic, seeking to promote their interests in this more fluid, pluralistic environment. Their activism was facilitated by modern computer technologies, particularly the Internet, which allowed the interest groups on both sides of the debate to mobilize the public for their cause.

All these elements greatly complicated the policy-making environment, which had already been altered by the diffusion of foreign policy roles beyond the State Department and Defense Departments. As the foreign affairs bureaucracy grew to include economics-oriented executive branch agencies such as the Treasury and Commerce Departments, the opportunities for private interest groups to penetrate the policy making process greatly increased. This trend was replicated in Congress, whose committees engaged in foreign economic relations became a focus of interest-group lobbying and political pressure. The outcome of this legislative process reflected the more complex setting, in which "intermestic" issues, crossing foreign and domestic boundaries, dominated the agenda. In this respect, the debate over Sino-American trade relations typified the new era in U.S. foreign policy after the cold war.

Notes

1. Jeffrey E. Garten, *The Big Ten: The Big Emerging Markets and How They Will Change Our Lives* (New York: Basic Books, 1997).

2. White House, Office of the Press Secretary, press conference, May 26, 1994.

3. For an elaboration, see Steven W. Hook and John Spanier, *American Foreign Policy since World War II,* 15th ed. (Washington, D.C.: CQ Press, 2000), 68–79.

4. See Andrew Nathan, *China's Transition* (New York: Columbia University Press, 1997).

5. China's economic output grew by an average of 10 percent annually in the 1980s, with much of this growth based on foreign commerce. See Claude E. Barfield, "U.S.-China Trade and Investment in the 1990s," in *Beyond MFN: Trade with China and American Interests,* ed. James R. Lilley and Wendell L. Willkie II (Washington, D.C.: AEI Press, 1994), 63.

6. William R. Keylor, *The Twentieth Century World: An International History,* 3d ed. (New York: Oxford University Press, 1996), 479–480.

7. The figures in this section are derived from Wayne M. Morrison, "China-U.S. Trade Issues," Congressional Research Service, July 20, 2000, 2–5.

8. U.S. Census Bureau, Foreign Trade Division, *U.S. Trade Balance with China,* May 7, 2000, http://www.census.gov/foreign-trade/balance/c5700.html.

9. U.S. Department of Agriculture, Economic Research Service, "China's WTO Accession to Significantly Boost U.S. Agricultural Exports," press release, February 2000.

10. See Hook and Spanier, *American Foreign Policy,* 361–363.

11. John T. Rourke and Richard Clark, "Making U.S. Foreign Policy toward China in the Clinton Administration," in *After the End: Making U.S. Foreign Policy in the Post–Cold War World,* ed. James M. Scott (Durham, N.C.: Duke University Press, 1998), 203.

12. Ibid., 208.

13. During his November 1997 visit to the White House, Chinese leader Jiang Zemin agreed to halt the sharing of nuclear technology with Iran, among other concessions. A

similar concern among congressional critics involved the Clinton administration's support for sharing satellite-launch technology with China. White House officials certified in May 1999 that these technology exports to China would neither harm U.S. firms in this sector nor threaten U.S. strategic interests.

14. For a review of the shift in public opinion and its relationship to Sino-American relations, see "Support for NTR/MFN Status," *Americans on Globalization: A Study of Public Attitudes,* College Park, Md., Center on Policy Attitudes, University of Maryland, March 28, 2000, http://www.pipa.org/OnlineReports/Globalization/appendixa/appendixa.html.

15. Susan Schmidt, "Businesses Ante Up $30 Million," *Washington Post,* October 26, 2000, A26.

16. For links to the *China Insider,* see www.uschamber.org.

17. Ron Woodard, "Normal Trade with China—'Sooner' Rather than Later," speech delivered at "Opportunities in International Trade," Oklahoma City, Okla., May 5, 1998, http://www.boeing.com/news/speeches/current/woodard05-05.html.

18. "In 2000, 7 Percent of Urban Households in China Intend to Purchase Vehicles," *China Online,* January 27, 2000. As China's domestic auto industry began to grow in the 1990s, the government acted aggressively to prevent outside competition smothering its growth. Tariffs on automotive imports ranged between 80 and 100 percent, and by the time imports reached the consumer market, overall taxes nearly tripled the sticker price. China's entry into the WTO would reduce tariffs by 25 percent beginning in 2006, with additional reductions in subsequent years. "China to Protect Fledgling Auto Industry in the Short Term," *China Online,* February 9, 2000.

19. China Business World Online News Service, "Joint Venture Project with GM," February 25, 1997, http://www.cbw.com/business/quarter1/automoti.htm.

20. Zhonghua Gongshang Shibao, "Beijing Traffic Restrictions Decimate Jeep Sales, Cause Layoffs," *China Online,* February 4, 1999.

21. Richard Pastore, "Motorskills: Emerging Markets," *CIO Magazine Online,* September 15, 1998, http://www.cio.com/archive/enterprise/091598_ford.html.

22. Lester J. Gesteland, "Foreign Firms to Benefit from China Unicom US $16 Billion CDMA Market," *China Online,* December 13, 1999.

23. For more information regarding the impact of NGO pressure on government policies, see Margaret E. Keck and Kathryn Sikkink, *Activists beyond Borders* (Ithaca, N.Y.: Cornell University Press, 1998).

24. "Human Rights Watch Reports on China," February 22, 2000, http://www.hrw.org/research2/china.html.

25. Freedom House, *Freedom in the World, 1997–1998* (Piscataway, N.J.: Transaction Publishers, 1998), 190–191.

26. *Amnesty International Annual Report, 1999: China,* http://www.amnesty.org/ailib/aireport/ar99/asA17.htm.

27. Elizabeth Economy, "Painting China Green," *Foreign Affairs* 78 (March/April 1999): 16.

28. For examples of environmental NGOs' Internet lobbying activities, see http://www.greenpeace.org and http://www.sierraclub.org.

29. United Methodist Church, General Board of Church and Society, "An Appeal of Conscience by Religious Leaders to Members of the U.S. Congress," September 19, 2000, http://www.umc-gbcs.org/advocacy16_letter.htm.

30. While most religious groups opposed the engagement policy, some sided with the Clinton administration in arguing that toleration of faith would be more likely once the PRC became more integrated in the global economy. One example was a Quaker group, the Friends Committee on National Legislation, which became active during the 1990s on many aspects of Sino-American relations. "The Chinese government is much more likely to respect the rule of law and observe international norms of behavior if it is recognized by the U.S. government as an equal, responsible partner in the community of nations." Friends Committee on National Legislation, "Quaker Lobby Supports Permanent Normal Trade Relations with China," May 9, 2000, http://www.fcnl.org/issues/int/sup/chin_quaksup_rel.htm.

31. Federal News Service, "Prepared Testimony of John J. Sweeency before the Senate Finance Committee," March 23, 2000.

32. U.S. State Department, Bureau of Democracy, *Human Rights and Labor, 1999: Country Reports on Human Rights Practices,* February 25, 2000, www.state.gov.

33. See the Freedom House Web site, http://www.freedomhouse.org.

34. Wayne M. Morrison, "U.S.-China Trade Issues," National Council for Science and the Environment issue brief for Congress, January 3, 2001, http://cnie.org/nle/econ-35.html.

35. Statement by AFL-CIO president John Sweeney on China and the WTO, November 15, 1999, www.aflcio.org/publ/press1999/pr1115.htm.

36. Anne E. Kornblut, "House OK's Normalizing China Trade, Bipartisan Vote Praised and Assailed," *Boston Globe,* May 25, 2000, A1.

37. Edward Daniels, "Manufacturing Advocate Confident China Trade Bill Will Pass," States News Service, August 23, 2000.

38. PR Newswire, "As China Cracks Down on Religion, American Renewal Calls on Senate to Adopt Tough, Enforceable Human Rights Sanctions," September 5, 2000.

13 The Kyoto Protocol on Climate Change: A Balance of Interests

Uma Balakrishnan

Before You Begin

1. Who are the key players in this case and what are their competing interests? What are the possible coalitions of these interests?

2. How do debates in the scientific community affect debates in the political arena?

3. Did the party affiliation of the president have an impact on the outcome of the Kyoto Protocol debate? How would the outcome have differed if President George Bush had remained in office until 1996?

4. What options did the Clinton administration have going into the environmental meetings at Berlin and Geneva that set the stage for the Kyoto Protocol? Would building a Senate consensus prior to accepting the Geneva declaration have affected the outcome in the later acceptance of limitations on emissions in the Kyoto Protocol?

5. What impact did Senate opposition to the Kyoto Protocol have on the final deliberations of the parties to the Rio convention in 1997? Would the outcome have been different had the Senate been more conciliatory? Would the outcome have differed if the Byrd-Hagel bill had passed along largely partisan lines?

6. What are the prospects for U.S. leadership in the area of climate change? Did the Senate refusal to ratify the Kyoto Protocol hurt U.S. credibility in this area? What impact has President George W. Bush's decision to withdraw the United States' signature had on perceptions of U.S. foreign policy, especially among European Union countries?

7. What are the national interests of the United States in the area of climate change? Can the long-term and short-term interests of the United States be separated or are they necessarily intertwined?

8. How important is the perception of U.S. leadership of the world economy to the American people? Is it possible for the United States to lead in the world economy and in environmental politics?

Introduction: Is It Getting Warm in Here?

The issue of global warming begins, as most other environmental stories do, with a scientist wondering about human actions. In 1896, Swedish chemist Svante Arrhenius asked what happens when carbon dioxide (CO_2) is released into the atmosphere by the petroleum-based industries of the industrial revolution.[1] The natural properties of carbon dioxide should lead it to trap heat rising from the surface of Earth. Does the heat then dissipate into outer space or does it stay in the atmosphere and warm the surface of the planet? Little debate ensued at that time, but the issue remained just over the scientific horizon. Half a century later, the topic re-emerged during the International Geophysical Year (1957–1958),[2] an event coordinated by the International Council of Scientific Unions. As part of the observance, Charles Keeling of the Scripps Institution of Oceanography set up two stations to monitor levels of atmospheric carbon dioxide. The first of their kind, one station was placed at Mauna Loa in Hawaii and the other at the South Pole.[3]

In 1978, the U.S. government responded to growing scientific concerns that atmospheric carbon dioxide was affecting Earth's climate by passing the National Climate Program Act (PL 95-367), which established the National Climate Program for "research, collection, analysis, forecasting, modeling, and dissemination of data concerning climate and its variations, and for the assessment of the impact on human activities for climatic changes." It also established a federal agency to manage the program.[4] The debate over global warming assumed greater importance in the formulation of U.S. foreign policy as the United Nations Framework Convention on Climate Change drew near to signing as part of the so-called Earth Summit, the 1992 United Nations Conference on Environment and Development in Rio de Janeiro. The convention was a formal acknowledgment that global warming had international effects that unilateral action could not change.

The Earth Summit and related events culminated in the 1997 Kyoto Protocol, which contained provisions for binding limits and targets on greenhouse gas emissions believed responsible for global warming. This case study details the events and policy decisions leading up to the Kyoto Protocol and the subsequent attempts in the United States to limit the impact of President Bill Clinton's decision to sign it.

Background: Scientific and Political Debates

Global warming is the phenomenon whereby the temperature of Earth's atmosphere, and consequently the temperature on the surface of Earth, rises due to increased levels of so-called greenhouse gases—carbon dioxide, methane, nitrous oxide, chloroflourocarbons (CFCs), and hydroflourocarbons (HCFCs). While some portion of these first three gases occurs naturally, the last two are anthropogenic, that is, they result from man-made processes. The levels of carbon dioxide in the atmosphere rose from 280 parts per million around the 1750s to 350 in 1990, an increase said by some scientists to account for 61 percent of the rise in temperatures over the last one hundred years. Fifteen percent of the temperature increase during the same time period is believed the result of rising levels of methane.[5] The measurements of atmospheric carbon dioxide from the stations set up by Keeling have shown that the rise in the levels of the gas has been uninterrupted. This increase has been accompanied by higher global average temperatures. Studies of temperature variations, using ice-core data, indicate a strong positive correlation between the increase in greenhouse gases and the rise in temperature, yet there is a great deal of debate about whether global warming is really taking place.[6]

While there is still uncertainty about the rate of temperature change, most observers agree that some warming is taking place. The uncertainty stems partly from the lack of temperature statistics over a sufficient period of time and partly from the number of linkages among assorted elements, which make it impossible to accurately point to the effects of rising temperatures. The predictions for temperature increases by the end of the next century range from between 2 to 5 degrees centigrade, which will probably affect sea levels, agriculture, and forests and thus human and animal life. That different areas will be affected at different rates will only serve to further confound decision making.

At the forefront in the global warming debate are groups of scientists in epistemic communities, "transnational networks of knowledge-based communities that are both politically empowered through their claims to exercise authoritative knowledge and motivated by shared causal and principled beliefs."[7] The members of these communities not only share common beliefs in the causal structures of an issue area, but also possible technological solutions and policy applications of these technologies. They help in the four political processes that form a major part of environmental negotiation: "issue definition, fact finding, bargaining, and regime strengthening."[8] Ideally, epistemic communities provide a clear definition of a problem and choices for a solution.

By its very nature, the global warming issue demands a scientific basis for political decision making. Unfortunately, uncertainty among scientists studying the issue makes this bad situation worse.

The scientific literature on global warming is broad, yet the common thread underlying all the research is the acknowledgment that predictions about Earth's climate are not a hundred percent reliable. The most common criticism against theories of global warming focuses on accuracy. The critics claim that due to the relative inaccuracy of daily weather forecasts, there is no reason to believe that the long-term forecasts based on global circulation models are reliable. Global warming theorists counter that present-day global atmospheric circulation models are not fine-tuned to predict local or even regional weather patterns because they focus only on large areas covered by a particular grid. While they are inefficient as tools for daily weather forecasting, they are relatively sophisticated when dealing with longer-term climatic variations.

Another line of criticism has focused on an observed cooling in the middle of the twentieth century. Temperatures rose until the 1940s, and then they fell until the early 1970s, when warming began again. In addition, the observed temperature increase in this century has been about half of what the global circulation models (GCMs) predicted.[9] Such temperature fluctuations are considered proof against the warming theory. GCMs, however, have not been able to resolve whether there is a relation between clouds and warming. As Earth warms, more water will evaporate, leading to increased cloud formation. One school of thought argues that such an increase in clouds causes cooling due to higher humidity and precipitation levels.[10]

Other studies have reported that satellite information indicates that there has been no warming trend at all.[11] Most scientists agree, however, that global warming is a slow, evolutionary process, so satellite observations (even over the period of a decade) may not show a significant increase in temperature. If, however, these observations were carried out for three decades or more, they may very well detect a warming trend. Some uncertainty also arises from the current lack of understanding of the processes involved. For example, will the warming of the oceans lead to a massive discharge of carbon dioxide? Will the warming of the atmosphere lead to increased intake of carbon dioxide by plants, thereby reducing the net levels of this gas in the atmosphere? Questions like these do not have any firm answers, although the research into the global climate system continues. Ironically, the proposed curbs on greenhouse gases could further add to current uncertainties, since scientists are working on the assumption that such emissions continue to affect the climate. Limiting these emissions could change a major source of global warming, while reducing deforestation could perhaps enhance the trapping (or "sink") of such gases.

Although some critics argue that there is no conclusive proof for global warming and that more research must be conducted before policy responses are formulated,[12] most others involved believe that compelling evidence for warming exists. In their eyes, it does not seem unreasonable to prepare for warming now. According to the Intergovernmental Panel on Climate Change (IPCC), while increasing research may generate new evidence in the global warming debate, the "basic conclusions concerning the reality of the enhanced greenhouse effect and its potential to alter global climate are unlikely to change significantly."[13] Yet, uncertainty continues to fuel the debate, as do those scientists who maintain that there is sufficient doubt about this phenomenon to warrant further research before actions are taken. In the words of one, "very little risk" exists "in delaying policy responses to this century-old problem, since there is every expectation that scientific understanding will be substantially improved within a few years."[14] The primary concern here is that since the rate of change is unknown, any drastic action at this point in time could overcompensate and lead to needless controls on industrial development.

Although this criticism appears valid, the same lack of knowledge about the rate of change is used by others to counter this very argument. If there is a chance that Earth is warming slowly, there is about an equal chance that the warming could proceed more rapidly than predicted. In that case, curbing emissions now could only be beneficial. Further, no one has an idea when clear scientific "proof" of warming will be available; even conservative estimates have convincing proof as much as twenty years away. Thus, waiting for more undeniable evidence might make later solutions difficult.[15]

These uncertainties about the warming process itself make the continued effort of scientists to provide answers a vital factor in the formation and maintenance of a regime on global warming. Clearly, today's uncertainty could be used by some nations, as it has already been, to adopt a wait-and-see approach.[16] At the same time, there appears to be enough evidence to support the idea that once the process of warming begins, it will be very difficult to control.

Politically, global warming is a hot potato that no one wants to handle. It is difficult for most political decision makers to sell the idea that scarce resources must be allocated to help solve a problem that may never arise. The best political metaphor for the current situation is the tragedy of the commons.[17] This is the notion that resources held in common for everyone tend to suffer because, while everyone is willing to use them, no one wants to pay the costs associated

The Kyoto Protocol

1896 Swedish scientist Svante Arrhenius questions the effect of fossil fuel emissions on the atmosphere.

1957–1958 During the International Geophysical Year, Charles Keeling establishes stations at Mauna Loa and the South Pole to monitor changes in atmospheric carbon dioxide.

September 1978 Congress passes the National Climate Program Act, which calls for the collection of data on climatic changes.

June 1992 The United Nations Framework Convention on Climate Change is approved at the so-called Earth Summit, the 1992 United Nations Conference on Environment and Development in Rio de Janeiro. President George Bush signs the convention, which does little more than state that there is a problem of increasing global temperatures.

October 1992 The Senate ratifies the Rio framework convention.

March–April 1995 The Berlin Mandate is approved by the UN Preparatory Committee. It exempts developing countries from the emissions limitations target-setting process.

June 1996 Deputy Undersecretary of State Rafe Pomerance informs the Senate that the Clinton administration will not accept emissions limits during deliberations in Geneva as part of the second conference of parties to the Rio convention.

July 1996 In Geneva, Undersecretary of State for Global Affairs Tim Wirth commits the United States to setting emissions targets at the 1997 Kyoto summit.

September 1996 Sen. Jesse Helms, R-N.C., lambasts the Clinton administration, claiming that by signing on to agreements in Berlin and Geneva it is setting the stage for a treaty that will devastate U.S. economic and national interests.

July 1997 In a 95-0 vote, the Senate passes the Hagel-Byrd resolution opposing the signing of a global warming treaty in Kyoto that hurts the U.S. economy and exempts developing states from reducing emissions.

December 11, 1997 The Kyoto Protocol on global warming is adopted by more than 150 nations, including the United States.

December 12, 1997 Vice President Al Gore says that the Clinton administration will not send the Kyoto treaty to the Senate for ratification until key developing nations participate in the effort to slow down global warming.

November 1998   President Bill Clinton orders the U.S. signing of the Kyoto Protocol on global warming.

November 2000   During talks at The Hague, the European Union and the United States fail to reach a compromise on the level to which the United States must cut greenhouse gas emissions.

March 2001   President George W. Bush announces formal U.S. withdrawal from the Kyoto Protocol.

with their maintenance and use; each user feels that it is not solely his responsibility. Thus, developing states argue that they have little incentive to spend their scarce resources on curbing greenhouse gas emissions, as they are not the primary creators of these gases. Yet with their rapid attempts to industrialize, these states are the ones that pose the greatest threat for increasing emissions.[18] Given all the scientific uncertainties, the George W. Bush administration feels that any attempt to limit emissions, thereby possibly making U.S. products less competitive in the global market, would be bad policy. Scientific uncertainty continues to influence the debate and stymies effective policy responses.

Searching for a Policy: The Road to Rio and Beyond

The current debate over global warming began at the international level as early as 1979, when the first world climate conference was held and the issue began to be taken seriously. Various conferences were then held under UN auspices, including at Villach in 1985, Toronto and Ottawa in 1988 and 1989, respectively, and Cairo in 1989. In December 1990, the UN General Assembly passed a resolution to begin treaty negotiations that would, after five negotiating sessions in two years, lead to the United Nations Framework Convention on Climate Change.[19]

On May 7, 1992, Senator Al Gore, D-Tenn., introduced a bill to force President George Bush to take a more proactive stand on the issue of cutting greenhouse gas emissions.[20] Specifically it called for the enactment of regulations to stabilize carbon dioxide emissions by January 1, 2000.[21] Sen. Mitch McConnell, R-Ky., immediately derided the Gore effort:

Listening to them [the proponents of the Gore bill], you would think that carbon dioxide was equivalent to mustard gas. They fail to mention that the vast majority of carbon dioxide in our atmosphere is from natural sources.

> You would think that global warming is a scientific certainty equivalent to
> the law of gravity. In truth, it is more like trying to grab a fistful of water.[22]

McConnell was, in part, reflecting the lack of a scientific consensus about global warming at that point in time.

On May 12, 1992, Pete Dominick, R-Colo., one of the Senate observers to the climate change treaty negotiations, reported agreement on the final text of the treaty. A reading of the text in the Senate was warmly received by many members of the Republican Party, because it had been sufficiently watered down to their tastes. Along with numerous Republican senators like McConnell and Trent Lott, R-Miss., President Bush had not wanted compliance dates for greenhouse emissions established at Rio, and that was the outcome. The United Nations Framework Convention on Climate Change, which Bush signed, essentially did nothing more than state that there was a problem with the increase in planetary temperatures. It put off compliance dates for five years, until the next meeting, in Kyoto, Japan. In Rio, Bush was politically isolated from the other developed nations[23] in opposing the agreement. "It is never easy—it is never easy—to stand alone on principle," Bush said. "But sometimes leadership requires that you do. And now is such a time."[24]

In part, Bush's position was influenced by industry efforts to discredit the "science" behind global warming. Bush's vice president, Dan Quayle, headed the Council on Competitiveness, which focused on the economy to the exclusion of everything else. Former Bush chief of staff John Sununu earned the enmity of the environmentalists by claiming that there was a global cooling rather than warming. Sununu also argued that "attempts to impose prior restraints on the American economy were politically motivated by anti-capitalist forces."[25]

Major industries were well represented in Rio, and as Tia Armstrong, an environmental specialist for the U.S. Chamber of Commerce, stated, "Every time we see timetables and targets, we go berserk."[26] The groups represented in Rio included the National Coal Association and the Edison Electric Institute, representing the utilities. In addition to these groups, the Global Climate Coalition was formed, consisting of the Chamber of Commerce, eighteen major trade associations, and twenty-five corporations.[27] John Shlaes, the executive director of the coalition, was in Rio to "ensure that there was an equal playing field."[28] Another group, the Climate Council, represented by lobbyist Donald Pearlman, a former Reagan administration official, also lobbied U.S. delegates.

The biotechnology industry was also nervous about the U.S. position at Rio. As G. Kirk Raab, president of Genentech, said, "The vague language relating to 'technology transfer' and equitable sharing appear to be code words for compulsory licensing and other forms of property expropriation."[29] It is not particularly surprising that such firms objected to any possibility of being forced to turn over to others the products of their own research and development programs for cutting emissions. Some industry groups favored the middle ground. The Business Council for Sustainable Development, which was made up of chief executive officers and board chairs of forty-eight international corporations,[30] issued a report arguing in favor of pollution taxes paired with tax breaks for clean industries, that is, industries employing environmentally friendly and emissions-limiting technologies. Some corporations, like Dow Chemical, straddled the fence and were part of the Global Climate Coalition *and* the Business Council for Sustainable Development, in essence arguing that industries should favor efficiency as well as oppose regulation. Labor unions, fearing a loss of jobs and a major recession, opposed regulation. The auto industry, which was already having trouble competing with foreign cars, joined the other opponents in a blitz of publicity designed to draw attention to the uncertainties of the debate.

Proponents of regulations were equally represented in Rio by nongovernmental organizations (NGOs) like the Environmental Defense Fund, Greenpeace, and the World Wildlife Fund. Not surprisingly, these environmentally oriented groups favored a strong framework convention to reduce greenhouse gases and thereby slow global warming. When the summit produced a weak convention, opponents of an aggressive approach to global warming celebrated. Senator Tim Wirth, D-Colo., expressed the environmentalists' perspective on the convention that was adopted:

> A lost opportunity for the United States to lead; deferral of a vigorous U.S. role in a new world order; the loss of commitment by developing countries, who ask if the richest country will not stretch to change, why should we; a loss of market opportunities for the United States; the loss of a set of forest principles; a watered-down Earth charter; and, most alarming, the loss of precious time.[31]

Other critics also chimed in. "The most charitable thing you can say about it is the Administration believes in recycling," said Alden Meyer of the Union of Concerned Scientists. "It's another finger in the eye of international public opinion." For his part, Indian foreign secretary J. N. Dixit expressed sorrow that the Bush administration had not had greater "empathy for a collective approach."[32]

Such U.S. bashing after Rio led to a further erosion of relations in the Senate between the environmentalists and those advocating the wait-and-see approach on warming. There was also a great deal of senatorial resentment about the lack of support from traditional U.S. allies among developed nations.[33] Senator McConnell, in a speech in October 1992, said,

> Our European allies, appeasing their strong green lobbies back home, cynically cried alligator tears, with their pecuniary interests foremost in mind. Carbon dioxide targets and timetables would give these countries an enormous competitive advantage over the United States, which relies on its natural endowment of coal. The representatives of Third World countries wanted more aid with fewer strings attached. The emotionally charged pleas of environmental groups trying to pump up their membership rolls make great direct mail, but poor environmental policy. And the politically driven diatribes of liberal politicians in the United States now appear to be their best bet at getting off the political endangered species list.[34]

In voting for the weakened framework convention in 1992, Senator Lott took on the question of carbon taxes as a means of regulating emissions. He expressed serious reservations about the science involved and the impact of regulation on the economy. As he put it, "The approach to the issue of potential global climate change in the convention is responsible and realistic, considering the uncertainties of the science and the risk of tremendous adverse economic impacts from ill-advised policies . . . (even without obligating) the United States or any other country to achieve any particular target or timetable for limitation of greenhouse gas emissions."[35]

Another opponent of the treaty, Sen. Frank Murkowski, R-Ark., cited the scientific community's uncertainty about global warming, even as he accepted the need for science to "guide" policymakers.[36] Murkowski reflected the prevailing opinion that the cost of taking precautions against a nebulous problem could not be borne by the U.S. economy. The reasons for these concerns derived from two aspects of the framework convention, which set the tone for the U.S. foreign policy debate leading up to the Kyoto meeting. The first problem was Article 3 of the convention, commonly called the Precautionary Principle. Considered by most environmental lawyers to be revolutionary, it stated,

> The Parties should take precautionary measures to anticipate, prevent or minimize the causes of climate change and mitigate its adverse effects. Where there are threats of serious or irreversible damage, lack of full scientific

certainty should not be used as a reason for postponing such measures, taking into account that policies and measures to deal with climate change should be cost-effective so as to ensure global benefits at the lowest possible cost. To achieve this, such policies and measures should take into account different socio-economic contexts, be comprehensive, cover all relevant sources, sinks and reservoirs of greenhouse gases and adaptation and comprise all economic sectors.[37]

Having agreed to this principle, the United States could no longer use the issue of scientific uncertainty to block action on global warming. Even more disturbing to many U.S. foreign policy makers was the fact that the framework convention limited actions addressing the problem to developed countries. Only they would be required to implement regulations to mitigate climate change by reducing emissions of greenhouse gases and to protect and enhance greenhouse sinks and reservoirs.[38] Not only were developed countries called upon to change their behavior, the convention also called upon them to "provide new and additional financial resources to meet the agreed full costs incurred by developing country Parties in complying with their obligations." That is, the world's wealthiest countries were required to transfer to developing countries any technology they might require in meeting their obligations under the framework convention.[39]

The fact that developed countries were required to change their own behavior and pay for (and provide technology for) developing countries to change theirs was predictably controversial in the United States. Both these provisions immediately raised hackles in the Senate, and opposition to the framework convention grew. Opponents argued that not only were the developing countries being given a free pass in terms of limiting emissions, but the U.S. economy now also had to generate additional funding to pay for Third World development.

Getting to Kyoto

Although the Senate ratified the Rio framework convention in 1992, there remained anticipation of the battle to come. The November 1992 election of Bill Clinton as president, and perhaps even more important, of Al Gore as vice president, led to renewed hope in some quarters of more enthusiastic participation on the part of the United States in the global warming regime. Prior to the 1997 Kyoto summit, there were two meetings of the parties to the framework convention. The first meeting, in Berlin in 1995, generated the Berlin Mandate, which officially exempted developing countries (or the so-called non-Annex 1 countries) from the emissions limitations target-setting process. At the second meeting of the parties, in Geneva in 1996, Undersecretary of State for Global Affairs Tim Wirth committed the United States to setting emissions goals at the Kyoto summit. Among other things, the annex to the report of the parties meeting at Geneva stated that those represented in Geneva, meaning developed countries, were obligated to

- accelerate negotiations of a "legally binding protocol" so it could be addressed in Kyoto;
- follow the Berlin Mandate and commit to "policies and measures including, as appropriate, regarding energy, transport, industry, agriculture, forestry, waste management, economic instruments, institutions and mechanisms";
- commit to legally binding numerical targets for limiting emissions within specified time frames; and
- make commitments "to a global effort to speed up the development, application, diffusion and transfer of climate-friendly technologies, practices and processes; in this regard, further concrete action should be taken.[40]

By agreeing to these positions at the 1996 Geneva meeting, the Clinton administration incensed many members of the GOP majority in the Senate and House, who were headed into an election. In a speech on September 27, 1996, Sen. Jesse Helms, R-N.C., the chair of the Senate Foreign Relations Committee, lambasted the administration, claiming that it was setting the stage for a treaty that would be devastating for U.S. economic and national interests. Helms characterized the U.S. "capitulation": "In plain English this means that any new treaty commitments regarding greenhouse gas emissions will set forth legally binding emission levels that must be met by industrialized countries only. The U.S. position turns basic principles of sound economic policy on its head since it directs industrialized countries to subsidize developing countries by polluting less while incurring higher costs so that developing countries can pollute more without incurring costs."[41]

In fairness to Undersecretary Wirth, it should be noted that he actually negotiated a far better deal that he was given credit for, because it still left the United States a player in the global warming game. What the European states wanted in Geneva was an across-the-board 20 percent cut in emissions. In agreeing to set limits in Kyoto, Wirth had actually salvaged a bad situation. Congress, however, was not pleased because earlier, on June 19, 1996, Deputy

Undersecretary of State Rafe Pomerance had "assured jittery lawmakers that the administration would not accept any emissions limits during the Geneva deliberations."[42] Although Wirth had accepted no limits in Geneva, he had bound the United States to accept such limits in the near future.[43]

The anxiety generated by the U.S. position led to a strange coalition of interests that succeeded in creating a commanding consensus in the Senate against emission regulations. The process began with the introduction of Senate Resolution 98. In an unusual move, the bill was sponsored by a Republican freshman, Chuck Hagel of Nebraska, and by a senior Democratic veteran, Robert Byrd of West Virginia. The non-binding resolution said it was the sense of the Senate that at the December 1997 Kyoto meeting, the United States should not sign any agreement regarding the Rio framework treaty that put emissions limitations on developed countries, unless those same limitations were placed on developing countries as well, or that could cause serious harm to the U.S. economy. Further, the resolution said that any agreements reached in Kyoto needing Senate approval should be accompanied by a detailed explanation of the legislation or regulatory actions required. A report detailing the financial impact on the U.S. economy of any such agreement would also be mandatory. According to John Passacantando, director of the non-profit advocacy group Ozone Action, "From the day [the Byrd-Hagel resolution] was passed in July, its language has shaped both the negotiations over and the debate about the global warming treaty agreed to in December 1997. Now the Byrd-Hagel resolution is also likely to influence the coming Senate debate about ratification of the treaty."[44]

Senators were reacting to two different concerns. The first was that the Senate did not, and could not, approve of the perceived free ride given to the developing states by the Berlin Mandate. As Senator Byrd put it, the question was not whether legally mandated regulations were necessary but whether the entire international community, including the developing world, would participate. Byrd particularly did not like the "free rider" issue. He believed that it was wrong to allow "big carbon dioxide emitters" like Brazil, China, India, Indonesia, Mexico, and South Korea to continue or expand dirty, inefficient methods of fossil fuel combustion while calling only on developed countries to pay the costs of reducing emissions of greenhouse gases. In his view, if the developing countries that produced large quantities of greenhouse gases did not participate in the agreements, the global problem might not be solved. He also pointed out that significant reductions could be made in the carbon dioxide emissions of developing countries by the application of new technologies, and that the costs of doing so would not be unbearable if shared on a truly global basis. Finally, he feared that, if left unchanged, the situation created incentives for big polluters in developed countries to relocate to developing countries to avoid the costs of having to clean up their act. In short, Byrd felt that any pending agreement could actually be counterproductive at the global level and at the local level could lead to the loss of U.S. jobs.[45]

Sen. Larry Craig, R-Idaho, provided the second reason for the hard line taken by the Senate when he stated that this would be a "wake-up call" to the Clinton administration that had ignored the Senate in its formulation of policy on global warming. Craig said that he was "particularly concerned the administration did not consult with Congress prior to taking this new position, which I am told, was reached in the early morning hours of the last day of the Berlin negotiations. Subsequently, the administration has not sought, and certainly not received, consensus support from the Senate on its new approach."[46] Thus, the ramifications of Undersecretary Wirth's agreement in Geneva were becoming clear. In disregarding the Senate in accepting the Geneva agreement, the Clinton administration had postponed but not avoided an inevitable confrontation. Further, it had unwittingly created a coalition that would block every attempt at ratifying the Kyoto Protocol. The administration did not even have the flag of partisan politics to wave in this instance, as numerous Democrats went on record as opposing the tenor of the Kyoto Protocol.

In an address to the National Geographic Society on October 22, 1997, President Clinton tried to clarify his administration's policy on global warming:

Today we have a clear responsibility and a golden opportunity to conquer one of the most important challenges of the 21st century—the challenge of climate change—with an environmentally sound and economically strong strategy to achieve meaningful reductions in greenhouse gases in the United States and throughout the industrialized and the developing world. It is a strategy that, if properly implemented, will create a wealth of new opportunities for entrepreneurs at home, uphold our leadership abroad, and harness the power of free markets to free our planet from an unacceptable risk; a strategy as consistent with our commitment to reject false choices. America can stand up for our national interest and stand up for the common interest of the international community. America can build on prosperity today and ensure a healthy planet for our children tomorrow.[47]

Clinton's effort to garner support drew a storm of criticism from the opponents of the protocol. In an attempt to make the plan more concrete and realistic, Sen. Bob Kerrey, D-Neb., proposed six steps that he claimed "plays to our strengths—innovation, creativity, entrepreneurship. Our companies already are showing the way by developing tremendous environmental technologies and implementing commonsense conservation solutions":

- using up to $5 billion in tax cuts and research and development incentives to encourage the use of more efficient and cleaner energy sources;
- giving credit to companies that take "early actions" in the reduction of their own emissions;
- relying on a market-based system to reduce emissions inexpensively, such as was done with acid rain permit trading;
- reinventing how the federal government buys and uses energy, working to use new technologies (such as an initiative to have 20,000 solar roof projects on federal buildings by 2010), and relying more on public-private partnerships;
- creating more real competition in the electricity industry and reducing the waste heat typically lost in the generation of electricity; and
- helping private industry to create their own emissions reduction plans and removing barriers to efficient energy usage.

Kerrey called his plan "sensible and sound" and argued that with "a decade of experience, a decade of data, a decade of technological innovation, we will launch a broad emissions trading initiative to ensure that we hit our binding targets. At that time, if there are dislocations caused by the changing patterns of energy use in America, we have a moral obligation to respond to those to help the workers and the enterprises affected—no less than we do today by any change in our economy which affects people through no fault of their own."[48]

Kerrey, the Democrat from Nebraska, was challenged by the Republican senator from Nebraska, Chuck Hagel. Co-author of the Byrd-Hagel resolution, Hagel continued to argue that scientific support for the global warming was uncertain at best and dubious at worst and that the Kyoto proposals would spell economic ruin for the United States. Hagel's position was clear: "We shouldn't take any action until we know the consequences."[49]

Kyoto and Beyond

On December 11, 1997, the Kyoto Protocol was adopted by more than 150 nations, including the United States. Its adoption merely meant recognition of the achievement of a common draft. The United States would not sign the protocol for another year. While Vice President Gore claimed "history was made yesterday in Kyoto,"[50] others blasted the treaty. Both of Missouri's Republican senators vociferously opposed the protocol. Senator Christopher Bond called it a "turkey," claiming that it would drastically hurt the U.S. economy; Senator John Ashcroft claimed that the U.S. negotiators would have done better to "return empty-handed than to place America in a straitjacket."[51]

President Clinton did not authorize signing of the Kyoto Protocol until the last minute of the fourth meeting of the parties to the convention, held in Buenos Aires in November 1998. Despite signing the document, the administration decided to delay submitting the protocol for ratification by the Senate. As early as December 12, 1997, twenty-four hours after the international acceptance of the accord, Vice President Gore said that the administration would not send the treaty to the Senate for ratification "until key developing nations participate in this effort. This is a global problem that will require a global solution."[52] Sen. John Kerry, D-Mass., advised caution when he stated, "I would counsel the president to go very slowly as to ratification."[53] The final word on the Kyoto Protocol may have come from Senator Byrd when he offered that if the treaty was not altered, he would join others in "stabbing it in the heart."[54] Senator Murkowski went a step further, declaring the treaty "fundamentally flawed and dead on arrival."[55] Senator Hagel represented the attitude of the Senate toward the developing countries when he said, "There was tremendous anti-American, anti-West bias" in Kyoto and "the attitude of the officials of developing countries was that now it is their turn to prosper. It's a very unsettling prospect that 134 developing nations will be making decisions about America's future."[56]

In November 2000, there was yet another attempt to reconcile U.S. interests with those of the Kyoto Protocol. At a climate change conference at The Hague, the American delegation failed to arrive at a compromise with the members of the European Union on emissions limits. In fact, Australia, Canada, Japan, and the United States were all criticized by environmental groups for having let an opportunity to compromise vanish. The lame duck Clinton administration tried to convince the European Union that the United States should be allowed to reduce its costs of compliance with the protocol by purchasing cheap emissions cuts from other states. Further, the administration also wanted the conference participants to take into account that U.S. forests and farmlands serve as sinks or traps for greenhouse gases. With the exception of the British, the Europeans saw this as an attempt to find loopholes in the treaty.[57]

In 2001, what to do with the signed but unpopular and unratified protocol fell to the George W. Bush administration. Bush had been harshly criticized during the 2000 presidential campaign for having a poor environmental record as governor of Texas. Consequently, environmentalists were surprised and encouraged when during the campaign he acknowledged carbon dioxide as a pollutant and pledged to limit its emission. Bush's Environmental Protection Agency (EPA) director, former New Jersey governor Christine Todd Whitman, spent much of her first month in office speaking on behalf of an administration proposal to limit power plant emissions of carbon dioxide.[58]

The Bush initiative, however, upset some in Congress, including Senators Craig, Hagel, Helms, and Pat Roberts, R-Kan., who began complaining to the office of White House legislative liaison Nicholas Calio. The complaints seemed serious enough for the president's domestic policy advisers to raise them in a March 5 meeting with the president. At the meeting, Bush declared that he had been wrong to label carbon dioxide a pollutant, and he noted that the Clean Air Act seemed to omit it from the list of known pollutants. A working group led by John Bridgeland, White House deputy domestic policy adviser, was formed to poll the cabinet and other administration actors on the issue. Meetings were quickly held with representatives from the Departments of Commerce, Energy, Interior, State, and Transportation, the EPA, and the Office of Management and Budget. Also present at these meetings were Vice President Dick Cheney and White House economic adviser Lawrence Lindsey. With the exception of the EPA, all involved agreed that the carbon dioxide policy, such as it was, should be reversed.[59] Upon returning from a meeting in Italy with European environmental ministers on March 13, EPA director Todd Whitman was told by the president that he had changed his mind, he had been wrong to name carbon dioxide as a pollutant, and he was rescinding the proposal to reduce its emissions.[60] Moreover, Bush later explained that the United States would not abide by the Kyoto Protocol unless it was completely renegotiated.[61]

What changed his mind? Bush later said, "I was responding to reality. And the reality is the nation has got a real problem when it comes to energy." Any further limitation on carbon dioxide emissions, the president said, would force an increased reliance on natural gas for the generation of electricity, and that would drive up energy costs, since natural gas supplies were short in some areas.[62] The lack of reciprocity in commitments between the developed and the developing countries, coupled with a slowdown and possible recession in the global economy, gave Bush the perfect opportunity to torpedo a sinking treaty. The fact that he was pressing Congress for a controversial $1.6 trillion tax cut proposal at the same time may have also played a role, as he was going to need every Republican vote he could get for the tax cut.

Conclusion: Where Do We Go from Here?

The question of global warming, crossing myriad geographic and issue boundaries, highlights new trends in U.S. foreign policy making. No longer does the United States have the framework for decision making provided by the cold war. This has generated new problems for policy making. On the one hand, the United States is the sole superpower and therefore looked upon as an actor capable of financing global environmental change. Yet, the interdependence of a rapidly globalizing economy has weakened the U.S. position as hegemon. The United States can neither isolate itself from the problems facing the world nor can it afford to fix these problems unilaterally. What it can do is cooperate with the community of nations. This process places the United States in the unpalatable position of having to bargain with the world.

Domestically, bargaining does not sit well. The country that won the cold war is being asked to participate in environmental regimes that make it one actor, albeit an influential one, among many. Partisan debates on unilateral versus multilateral approaches to global problems further complicate the picture. The result has been varied responses and the generation of a whole new group of governmental and non-governmental actors becoming involved in policy making. Industry-affiliated and non-profit environmental organizations are trying to sway policy making. Scientists in each group argue their positions fervently, thereby adding to the policy-making dilemma. The debate continues.

Notes

1. Arrhenius's research was based on work done by Jean-Baptiste Fourier of France and John Tyndall of Great Britain, both of whom were fascinated by the idea of the absorption and transmission of heat and radiation. For a brief description of this research, see John Gribbin, *Hothouse Earth* (New York: Grove Weidenfeld, 1991), 30–33.

2. On the International Geophysical Year, see http://www.nationalacademies.org/history/igy/.

3. See Jim Falk and Andrew Brownlow, *The Greenhouse Challenge: What's to Be Done* (New York: Penguin Books, 1989), 17–18.

4. See H.R. 6669 at http://thomas.loc.gov/BSS/D095/D095laws.html

5. See Intergovernmental Panel on Climate Change, *Climate Change: The IPCC Scientific Assessment Report* (Cambridge: World Meteorological Organization and United Nations Environment Programme, 1991), 9, fig. 1.4, for the monthly average carbon dioxide concentration in parts per million of dry air, observed continuously at Mauna Loa. See also figure 7.6 (p. 207) for irregular increases in temperature from the late nineteenth century until 1990. The Intergovernmental Panel on Climate Change was created by the UN General Assembly. Also see the essay by V. Ramanathan, "Observed Increases in Greenhouse Gases and Predicted Climatic Changes," in *The Challenge of Global*

Warming, ed. D. E. Abrahamson (Washington, D.C.: Island Press, 1989), 239–247. Also see the essay by Gordon MacDonald, "Scientific Basis for the Greenhouse Effect," in ibid., 123–145; and M. I. Budyko, A. B. Ronov, and A. L. Yanshin, *History of the Earth's Atmosphere* (New York: Springer-Verlag, 1987).

6. For details on the possible causal relationship between greenhouse gases and global warming, see Stephen Schneider, *Global Warming: Are We Entering the Greenhouse Century?* (San Francisco: Sierra Club Books, 1989); and Ralph Cicerone, "Methane Linked to Warming," *Nature,* July 21, 1988, 198.

7. Peter M. Haas, "Obtaining International Environmental Protection through Epistemic Consensus," *Millennium: Journal of International Studies* 19 (fall 1990): 347–363.

8. Gareth Porter and Janet Welsh Brown, *Global Environmental Politics* (Boulder: Westview Press, 1991), 69.

9. A number of factors could explain this difference, including the ocean thermal delay, urban pollution, and the role of clouds in warming. The fact remains, however, that greenhouse gases do trap heat and that average global temperatures have risen in the last century.

10. See P. H. Abelson, "Uncertainties about Global Warming," *Science,* March 30, 1990, 1529.

11. See Mark K. Andersen, "What Warming?" *Times,* July 19, 1993, A4.

12. For example, Andrew Solow, a statistician at the Woods Hole Institute of Oceanography, says, "Some will say that if we wait until we are sure about climate change, it will be too late to do anything about it. This argument applies equally to an invasion of aliens from outer space. More seriously, this argument neglects the costs of overreaction now." "Pseudo Scientific Hot Air: The Data on Climate Are Inconclusive," *New York Times,* December 28, 1988, A15. See also S. Fred Singer, "Fact and Fancy on Greenhouse Earth," *Wall Street Journal,* August 30, 1988, 22; and P. Michaels, "The Greenhouse Climate of Fear," *Washington Post,* January 8, 1989, C3.

13. IPCC, *Climate Change: The IPCC Scientific Assessment,* xiii.

14. S. Fred Singer, *Global Warming: Do We Know Enough to Act?* Formal Publication 104 (New York: Center for the Study of American Business, 1991), 2.

15. Schneider, *Global Warming.*

16. This was evident in the Bush administration's approach to the problem in the period before the United Nations Conference at Rio de Janeiro in 1992.

17. Garrett Hardin, "The Tragedy of the Commons," *Science,* December 13, 1968, 1243–1248. See also Elinor Orstrom's idea of common pool resources, or CPR, which she characterizes as "self-financed contract enforcement." CPR allows for the apportionment of costs among players and tries to avoid the free rider issue. This approach also has some fundamental problems related to the idea of universal cooperation. See Elinor Ostrom, *Governing the Commons: The Evolution of Institutions for Collective Action* (Cambridge: Cambridge University Press, 1990), 13–18.

18. It sounds strange, but the greenhouse gas emissions from the United States and other developed states, while high, have reached a plateau and in some cases have even begun to decline. Emissions from the newly industrializing economies, partly due to the rapidity of the process of development and to the use of obsolete technology, have the potential to do great harm.

19. See Climate Change Information Kit: Climate Change Information Sheet 17, http://www.unfccc.org/resource/iuckit/fact17.html.

20. See "Global Climate Protection Act: A Bill to Stabilize Emissions of Carbon Dioxide to Protect the Global Climate and for Other Purposes," *Congressional Record,* May 7, 1992, S2668.

21. In addition to Senator Gore, other members of the Senate who supported the bill were George Mitchell, D-Maine; Tim Wirth, D-Colo.; John Kerry, D-Mass.; Brock Adams, D-Wash.; Daniel Akaka, D-Hawaii; Alan Cranston, D-Calif.; Christopher Dodd, D-Conn.; James Jeffords, R-Vt.; Bob Kerrey, D-Neb.; Frank Lautenberg, D-N.J.; Patrick Leahy, D-Vt.; Joe Lieberman, D-Conn.; Paul Wellstone, D-Minn.; Edward Kennedy, D-Mass.; Tom Harkin, D-Iowa; Tom Daschle, D-S.D.; and Claiborne Pell, D-R.I.

22. "The United States Must Take a Cautious Approach," *Congressional Record,* May 7, 1992, S6285.

23. It is interesting that the United States received a great deal of support from the Organization of Petroleum Exporting Countries (OPEC) and from key developing states. While OPEC nations could not afford to endorse limits on carbon dioxide emissions from fossil fuels, Brazil did not want further international pressure preventing it from deforestation, and India and China, fresh from the Montreal Protocol negotiations on the depletion of the ozone layer, were not interested in participating in any regime that would interfere with their development. U.S. movement away from the traditional alignment with the developed nations prevented a deadlock in negotiations between the developed and developing nations but served to weaken the basis of the climate regime, since the pressure to reform the structure of the international political economy was lessened. See K. Ramakrishna and O. R. Young, "International Organizations in a Warming World: Building a Global Climate Regime," in *Confronting Climate Change: Risks, Implications and Responses,* ed. I. M. Mintzer (Cambridge: Cambridge University Press, 1992), 253–264.

24. Douglas Jehl and Rudy Abramson, "Bush Defends U.S. Policy at Summit; Environment: President Refuses to 'Apologize,' Saying Leadership Sometimes Requires a Nation to Stand Alone. His Message Gets Lukewarm Response," *Los Angeles Times,* June 13, 1992, A1.

25. Peter Stothard, "Why the Greens Are Poison to President Bush," *Times,* May 28, 1992.

26. Maura Dolan, "U.S. Business Woos Delegates to Earth Summit," *Los Angeles Times,* May 30, 1992, A1.

27. Ibid.

28. Ibid.

29. Steven Greenhouse, "A Closer Look: Ecology, Economy and Bush," *New York Times,* June 14, 1992, sec. 4, 1.

30. Ibid.

31. *Congressional Record, The Earth Summit,* May 12, 1992, S6474.

32. Ibid.

33. "Saying that no country in the world is doing as much as the United States for the environment is simply not in concert with the facts," complained Hans Alders, head of the Dutch delegation to Rio. Gro Harlem Brundtland, prime minister of Norway, regretted that Bush offered "no new signals" of a willingness to assist poorer nations in coping with environmental challenges." Ibid.

34. "Framework Convention on Climate Change," *Congressional Record,* October 7, 1992, S17151.

35. Ibid.

36. "Global Climate Change," *Congressional Record*, May 7, 1992, S6300.

37. For the full text of the convention, see http://www.unfcc.org/resource/conv/conv-005.html.

38. Ibid.

39. Ibid.

40. Ibid.

41. "Global Climate Change," *Congressional Record*, September 27, 1996, S11490.

42. Tony Snow, "Clinton Reveals Self with Foreign Pact That Guts Economy," *Arizona Republic,* July 26, 1996, B7.

43. There is some evidence that the Clinton-Gore team was trying to gain public support for its environmental agenda while hoping for a change in the composition of Congress. Curtis Moore, "How Gore Lost His Balance in Kyoto," *Washington Post,* December 14, 1997, C1. Moore served as Republican counsel to the Senate Committee on the Environment and Public Works from 1978 to 1989.

44. Robert C. Byrd and Chuck Hagel, "Advice to Heed on the Kyoto Treaty," *Washington Post,* May 6, 1998, A19.

45. "Senate Resolution 98—Expressing the Sense of the Senate regarding the United Nations Framework Convention on Climate Change," *Congressional Record,* June 12, 1997, S5622.

46. Ibid., S5624.

47. "The Climate Change Treaty," *Congressional Record,* October 23, 1997, S11019.

48. Ibid.

49. C. David Kotok and Julie Anderson, "Hagel, Kerrey See Trouble in Global Warming Treaty: Differing Views on Global Warming," *Omaha World Herald,* October 27, 1998, 1.

50. Brian McGrory, "Negotiators on Warming Get Big Chill; Senate Demands Will Delay Submission of Treaty on Gases," *Boston Globe,* December 12, 1997, A1.

51. Richard Dudman, "Global Warming Treaty: What It Would Mean to St. Louis: Bond, Ashcroft Blast Accord's Economic Effect," *St. Louis Post-Dispatch,* December 12, 1997, A1.

52. "U.S. to Delay Global Warming Treaty; Till Third World Accepts Limits, Gore Says; Washington Won't Consider New Taxes, Vice President Says," *Baltimore Sun,* December 12, 1997, 26A.

53. "U.S. Agrees to Cut Fuel Emissions Below 1990 Levels: Global Warming Pact Gets Preliminary Approval; Senate Will Make Final Call," *St. Louis Post-Dispatch,* December 11, 1997, A16.

54. Jake Thompson, "Winning Friends, Influencing Senate Freshmen Sen. Chuck Hagel Crafts a Reputation as a Consensus Builder," *Omaha World Herald,* July 26, 1997, 1.

55. McGrory, "Negotiators on Warming Get Big Chill."

56. Kotok and Anderson, "Trouble in Global Warming."

57. Martin Wolf, "Hot Air about Global Warming: The World Has Every Reason Not to Worry about the Failure of Climate Change Talks to Impose Radical Restrictions on Emissions," *Financial Times,* November 29, 2000, sec. 1, 27; *Financial Times,* December 19, 2000, sec. 1, 23.

58. Amy Goldstein and Eric Pianin, "How Bush Changed His Stance on CO_2 Emissions: Flip-Flop Occurred as Conflict with Congress Became Apparent," *Dallas Morning News,* March 18, 2001, 13A.

59. Ibid.

60. Ibid.

61. Dan Bilefsky et al., "Bush Says Kyoto Deal Would Hit Jobs and Industry; President Is Unrepentant over U.S. Decision Not to Ratify the Treaty on Climate Change," *Financial Times*, March 30, 2001, 1.

62. Goldstein and Pianin, "How Bush Changed His Stance on CO_2 Emissions."

14 Funding the IMF: Congress versus the White House

Ralph G. Carter and James M. Scott

Before You Begin

1. Who were the key actors in the debate over increasing U.S. funding for the International Monetary Fund (IMF) because of the 1997–1998 Asian economic crisis? How did they characterize U.S. interests in the issue?

2. What were the main arguments for and against the IMF funding proposal advocated by the Clinton administration? Why did the proposal cause so much controversy?

3. What were the key factors leading to passage of the IMF funding proposal? Why did the proposal eventually succeed? What does the role played by Sen. Chuck Hagel indicate?

4. Why was passage of the funding proposal easier in the Senate than in the House of Representatives?

5. What do the interactions among the various actors in this case suggest about foreign policy decisions on issues involving funding for multinational financial institutions?

6. Do you think the United States should have provided additional funding to the IMF? Why or why not?

Introduction: The Long Road to IMF Funding

The 1997 Asian economic crisis produced an extended battle along the fault line thought to separate domestic from foreign policy. For a year, this battle was waged between a presidency weakened by scandal and a Congress controlled by the opposition party. At issue was the Clinton administration's request for additional U.S. funding for the International Monetary Fund (IMF), which provides short-term loans to countries experiencing sharp drops in the value of their currency. Although a number of Asian economies were in dire straits and the IMF could be called upon to make major loans at any time, this request was challenged by both the Left and Right in Congress. Between the time the administration proposed additional funding in November 1997 until Congress agreed on a funding bill in October 1998, the issue became a struggle between the White House and Congress, between the two houses of Congress, and between factions within each house of Congress. Although the Senate approved additional funding in March 1998, and again in early September, the House of Representatives delayed taking action. Ultimately, after considerable negotiation in Congress and between Congress and the White House, a bill was agreed to by both houses and signed by the president on October 21.

Background: The Asian Meltdown and the IMF Response

For years, a number of Asian countries had used an economic model in which commercial banks readily provided loans to businesses based on high debt-to-equity ratios. Because individuals put their money in banks, these institutions had lots of cash to loan. Thus businesses were able to acquire loans with generous terms, in some cases requiring only payment of the interest to keep the loans in force. Such easy access to large amounts of capital, so-called crony capitalism, helped fuel rapid growth in the Asian economy.[1]

The apparent weakness of this economic model was revealed when an economic meltdown began on July 2, 1997. Easy access to large amounts of credit had created speculative bubbles in the Thai property and stock markets. When investors drove these markets to unreasonable heights, these bubbles inevitably burst, and the markets plummeted in value. Trying to keep the situation from getting any worse, the government of Thailand was forced to devalue its currency to make Thai products more attractive to buyers. Not surprisingly, this devaluation scared foreign investors. Given the interrelation of regional Asian economies and similar business practices throughout the region, the Thai currency devaluation began a process of private capital flight. Currency values plunged not only in Thailand, but also in Indonesia, Malaysia, the Philippines, and South Korea. As their economies grew worse, banks were forced to demand repayment of loan principle and interest. Many businesses could not repay and were forced into bankruptcy, thereby making the situation even worse.[2] The IMF responded with huge, multilateral bailout packages for Indonesia ($40 billion), South Korea ($57 billion), and Thailand ($17 billion), to help stabilize their economies.[3]

These IMF allocations put great stress on the organization's resources, prompting the United States and other major donors to consider an increase in their contributions to the fund in order to help meet the challenges of the so-called Asian flu. Many countries waited to see what the United States—the architect of the IMF after World War II and its largest contributor (IMF contributions, or quotas, are determined by the relative economic size of its members)—would do. At issue was an IMF-approved plan to create an emergency fund, New Arrangements to Borrow, or NAB, of $24 billion, of which the U.S. share would be $3.4 billion, and expand quota funds to $90 billion, of which the U.S. share would be $14.5 billion. The NAB constituted a new contribution and was established specifically to stanch the rapidly spreading Asian financial crisis. The second was simply an expansion of the periodic quota contributions by the United States and other donors. These contributions were in keeping with more than fifty years of support for the IMF, but also designed to meet the demands on the institution raised by the Asian crisis and the general pressures of a globalizing economy. Contributions to the fund, the quotas, and emergency funds are liquid, interest-bearing monies that, over time, have returned profits to the U.S. Treasury; thus they are actually investments, not expenditures.

The IMF Funding Debate, 1997–1998

In November 1997, President Bill Clinton asked Congress for a foreign operations spending bill that included $3.4 billion for the IMF emergency rescue fund, and the Senate approved his request that same month. House conservatives, led by Christopher Smith, R-N.J., insisted on adding an anti-abortion provision to the bill, the so-called Mexico City policy of the Reagan era that barred federal funds to organizations providing abortions or abortion counseling overseas. The president threatened to veto such a bill, so House Speaker Newt Gingrich, R-Ga., agreed to remove the anti-abortion language if the $3.4 billion for the IMF, reauthorization of the State Department, and repayment of almost $1 billion in back dues to the United Nations were eliminated from the spending bill. Clinton reluctantly agreed.[4]

For Sen. Chuck Hagel, R-Neb., the deal was decidedly disappointing. In December 1997, following the House's refusal to take up the Senate-passed IMF funding legislation, Hagel convened a roundtable of eighteen Nebraska export business representatives. At this gathering, concern over the crashing Asian markets emerged as a major issue, and broad support for IMF stability packages to bolster these markets was expressed. According to Hagel, everyone at the roundtable discussed being negatively affected by the Asian crisis. Later reflecting on the meeting, Hagel told Treasury Secretary Robert Rubin, "I have some understanding of how real this problem is and how it is affecting our country. . . . I happen to support what you're trying to do [to secure additional

The IMF Funding Debate

July 1997   The currency of Thailand collapses, spurring the subsequent collapse of local currencies in Indonesia, Malaysia, the Philippines, and South Korea,. The International Monetary Fund responds with loans to Indonesia, Thailand, and South Korea totaling $114 billion.

November 1997   President Bill Clinton asks Congress to provide $3.4 billion in emergency funding for the IMF, and the Senate approves the funding.

December 1997   The House refuses to approve the IMF funds without adding anti-abortion restrictions to the accompanying bill.

January 27, 1998   In his State of the Union address, Clinton calls on Congress to authorize $17.9 billion for the IMF to address the growing Asian crisis and cover the U.S. share of its IMF quota.

January–February 1998   Administration officials testify before Congress on the need for IMF funding. Organized business interests press for the funds. Senator majority leader Trent Lott, R-Miss., asks Sen. Chuck Hagel, R-Neb., to spearhead the IMF funding issue.

March 4, 1998   The House Banking Committee passes an IMF funding bill with some conditions, and with administration support, but conservative Republicans vow to add conditions and anti-abortion language.

March 13, 1998   Hagel constructs a compromise bill with moderate conditions.

March 17, 1998   The Senate Appropriations Committee adds restrictions to Hagel's compromise bill and passes the revised version (S. 1769).

March 18, 1998   Hagel counters the Appropriations Committee by introducing the original bill (S. 1765) on the Senate floor.

March 24, 1998   Hagel offers an amendment to an emergency supplemental bill (S. 1768) that restores most of the original compromise language and removes most of the added restrictions.

March 26, 1998   IMF funding (S. 1768) passes by a 84-16 vote in the Senate.

April 23, 1998   The House passes an emergency funding bill omitting IMF funding.

June 1998   The financial crisis in Asia spreads to Russia.

July 13, 1998   The IMF offers Russia $22 billion in credits.

July 14, 1998   The House Appropriations Subcommittee on Foreign Operations passes $3.4 billion in new IMF funds.

July 22, 1998   The House Appropriations Committee takes the IMF funding bill off its agenda.

July 28, 1998   Hagel attaches an IMF funding amendment to the foreign operations appropriations bill (S. 2334).

September 2, 1998   Hagel's IMF funding amendment passes with a 90-3 vote in the Senate.

September 10, 1998   The House Appropriations Committee votes 30-22 for $3.4 billion in IMF funding, with anti-abortion restrictions.

September 17, 1998   The House of Representatives passes the foreign operations appropriations bill by a 255-161 vote, with $3.4 billion in IMF funding and anti-abortion restrictions.

September–October 1998   Conference committee and White House–Congress negotiations ensue over IMF funds and conditions.

October 7, 1998   The House leadership accepts the full funding, $17.9 billion, for the IMF without anti-abortion restrictions.

October 15, 1998   House leaders and the Clinton administration agree on a set of IMF reforms to attach to the $17.9 billion in funds.

October 20, 1998   The House approves full IMF funding by passing 333-95 the conference committee report for H.R. 4328.

October 21, 1998   The Senate passes the conference report with a 65-29 vote. Clinton signs the bill into law.

IMF funds]." Hagel also recognized the strength of those in Congress committed to reforming the way the IMF did its business: "But in one sense, this is a political issue. . . . [I]f we are to persuade enough of our colleagues to get this done, then the reform piece must be attached to whatever we do."[5]

The Battle Lines Form

Over the Christmas holiday, the administration proposed $17.9 billion in new IMF funding—the $3.4 billion previously requested and $14.5 billion in new capital reserves—as part of a fiscal 1998 emergency supplemental appropriations bill. With the Asian economic house afire, warnings that delays in IMF funding could harm U.S. interests came from Treasury Secretary Rubin,

UN ambassador Bill Richardson, and Defense Secretary William Cohen, among others.[6] In Congress, opponents included conservative Republicans who saw IMF actions as a form of international welfare and liberal Democrats who questioned whether IMF responses were good for the citizens of the target countries or workers in export-driven industries in the United States.[7] In January 1998, Rep. David Bonior, D-Mich., the number two Democrat in the House, said, "We all have a stake in Asia's financial stability. But this help should not be a bailout for bankers, speculators, or repressive dictators." The ranking Democrat on the House Banking Committee, John LaFalce, D-N.Y., added, "We have to tell the banks once and for all that they can't expect to be held harmless for their imprudent financial judgments."[8] Additionally, conservative representatives led by Representative Smith were adamant in their desire to link IMF funding to a provision barring the United States from supporting or promoting abortion overseas, a move that once again prompted the White House to threaten a veto.

President Clinton responded to these challenges by asserting that stabilizing Asian economies was in the "plain, brutal, short-term economic interest" of the United States, because devalued Asian currencies would erode Asian markets for U.S. exports and flood the U.S. market with cheap Asian goods. Rubin echoed Clinton's sentiments and began making phone calls to key members of Congress, including Sen. Mitch McConnell, R-Ky., chair of the Appropriations Foreign Operations Subcommittee handling IMF funding.[9] The Economic Policy Institute released a study suggesting that 1.1 million Americans would lose their jobs because of the Asian crisis. The states hit the hardest would be California, Illinois, Michigan, New York, North Carolina, Ohio, Pennsylvania, and Texas.[10]

In his State of the Union address on January 27, the president called for full funding of the IMF requests.[11] News of Clinton's affair with White House intern Monica Lewinsky hung over the address and complicated Clinton's relations with Treasury Secretary Rubin, a key player in the IMF debate.[12] Nonetheless, the administration put on an impressive full-court press. In remarks to the U.S.-China Business Council in Washington, U.S. Trade Representative Charlene Barshefsky called on Congress to fund the full $17.9 billion.[13] On January 30, Rubin and Federal Reserve Board chairman Alan Greenspan testified before the House Banking Committee on behalf of IMF funding. Rubin stressed that in the Korean bailout, banks were in fact penalized, being forced to honor their old loans and to accept market interest rates on new loans to South Korea.[14] Defense Secretary Cohen testified to the potential damage to U.S. national security interests by the Asian meltdown, particularly in the case of a weakened South Korea.[15]

Just a few days later, Lawrence Summers, deputy secretary of the Treasury, and Stuart Eizenstat, undersecretary of state for economics, business, and agriculture, appeared at a hearing before the Senate Finance Committee. Summers called the IMF issue "the key legislative choice before the Congress this year," and Eizenstat argued that IMF programs supported U.S. security, trade, prosperity, values, and credibility."[16] About a week later, before the Senate Foreign Relations Committee, Chairman Greenspan and Secretary Rubin again defended IMF funding. Senator Hagel registered his support (noted earlier), while others made clear that they were considerably more skeptical. Foreign Relations Committee chairman Jesse Helms, R-N.C., likened the IMF to a "worn out jalopy that should be traded in for the free market model."[17]

By February, organized interests began to make appearances on both sides of the debate. Representatives of Boeing and the American Farm Bureau Federation warned the House Banking Committee that the Asian crisis was threatening the U.S. economy and asked for full funding of the $17.9 billion request. IMF managing director Michel Camdessus made an urgent appeal for funding in a speech to the Council on Foreign Relations in New York.[18] The U.S. Chamber of Commerce formed a coalition of 300 members to press for full funding. The group included Fortune 500 companies and small businesses, local chambers of commerce, business and trade groups, and agricultural associations.[19] On February 11, 1998, the *New York Times* and the *Washington Post* ran a two-page "Open Letter to Congress," signed by former presidents Jimmy Carter and Gerald Ford and eighty-eight business leaders, calling for full funding of the IMF. Among the signatories were chief executives of American International Group, AT&T, Bloomberg News, Exxon, GM, IBM, Time-Warner, and major banks and brokerage houses. The National Association of Manufacturers also announced that it would immediately begin lobbying Congress on behalf of the IMF.[20] Further, the National Governors' Association unanimously endorsed IMF funding, and the U.S. Chamber of Commerce announced a letter-writing campaign to pressure members of Congress to vote for the funding.[21]

On the other hand, labor union representatives asked the House Banking Committee not to allot the funds without looking carefully at the need for reforms in IMF procedures and changes to improve labor conditions in target countries.[22] The *Wall Street Journal* opposed full funding of the request.[23] Administration officials continued to press, but their opponents were unbowed. Sen. Lauch Faircloth, R-N.C., chairman of the Financial Institutions and Regulatory Relief Subcommittee of the Senate Banking, Housing, and Urban Affairs Committee announced that the $3.4 billion request would probably be funded, but denounced the additional $14.5 billion as "a total folly, an absolute joke."[24] Financier George Soros and Harvard professor Jeffrey Sachs came out in opposition to the IMF's austerity programs in Asia, and Republican presidential hopeful Steve Forbes called for the IMF's demise.[25] Rep. Jim Saxton, R-N.J., chairman of the Joint Economic Committee, said there were "major problems with existing IMF lending practices . . . which cannot be ignored." These included lack of transparency, excessive protection for banks, and inadequate protection for taxpayers.[26]

On March 3, 1998, Clinton requested the $17.9 billion for the IMF in the fiscal 1998 supplemental spending bill.[27] Democratic House leader Richard Gephardt of Missouri announced his support of the funding package, and Representative Bonior announced that he was reconsidering his opposition to it.[28] Both Greenspan and Rubin appeared before the Senate Appropriations Committee's Subcommittee on Foreign Operations to ask for prompt approval of the funding.[29] Rubin again advocated fulfilling the full funding request, stressing the drain on existing IMF resources and the need for U.S. leadership—because U.S. action would encourage others to help replenish the funds—and he also warned against strapping the IMF with excessive reform requirements. He asserted that the United States should not overemphasize the importance of such conditions if it meant failing to deal with the severe financial instability in Asia. Although key Republicans signaled their reluctance, Rubin received some support from panel members, such as Ted Stevens, R-Alaska, who expressed his general support while acknowledging some need for reforms. Subcommittee chairman McConnell announced that although broad support among Senate Republicans existed for the new borrowing ($3.4 billion), he and Senate majority leader Trent Lott, R-Miss., had reservations about how recipients of recent IMF loans were complying with loan conditions and wanted to delay consideration of the $14.5 billion in new capital reserves until compliance could be reviewed.[30] McConnell warned, "Before action on the quota, I hope to achieve a consensus . . . toward real reform and not just more bland recommendations in order to assure our continued participation in these institutions."[31]

Hagel Joins the Fray

In late February, Senate majority leader Lott had approached Senator Hagel to spearhead an effort to craft a compromise bill that would provide IMF funding, but with conditions for IMF reform acceptable to a majority in the Senate (especially Republicans) and the White House.[32] According to Hagel, Lott gave this charge: "I want you to put together a package everybody can agree on."[33] Hagel went to work immediately, building what he later described as "inner and outer circles" made up of staff, senators from both political parties, administration officials, and business leaders.[34] In the Senate, Hagel's key allies were Sens. Rod Grams, R.-Minn., and Pat Roberts, R-Kan. From the administration, Hagel worked closely with Treasury Secretary Rubin. For Hagel, the challenge was substantial: provide the $17.9 billion while mending a split among his Republican colleagues, securing enough Democrats to ensure passage, and persuading the White House to accept conditions.

What ensued was a four-cornered bargaining and negotiating game. In one corner, Republican and Democratic senators strongly supporting IMF funding sought immediate passage of the administration's request with minimal conditions (for example, Pete Domenici, R-N.M., Paul Sarbanes, D-Md., Joe Biden, D-Del., Roberts, and Grams). In the next corner, a group of Republican senators preferred allocating IMF funds, but with stringent restrictions, including fundamental transparency and accountability, adoption of market principles, and conditions on borrowers before any funds are available (for example, Faircloth, Helms, Jon Kyl, R-Ariz.). In the next corner Democratic senators sought IMF reforms that would emphasize worker rights and the environment (for example, Patrick Leahy, D-Vt., Paul Wellstone, D Minn.). In the last corner, the Clinton administration pushed for IMF funds without restrictions or conditions. Exacerbating the situation were the general hostility of the House Republicans toward the funding request and the insistence of some House members that an anti-abortion provision be attached to the legislation, which, according to the White House, would trigger a presidential veto.

As Hagel worked, there were encouraging signs from Capitol Hill. On March 4, 1998, the administration agreed to a compromise that gained the support of liberals on the House Banking Committee. The bill, as introduced by committee chairman Jim Leach, R-Iowa, already included conditions on IMF funding that appealed to many conservatives, such as greater transparency and the creation of a business-labor advisory committee to monitor IMF reform. The changes were agreed to when the Treasury Department said it would use U.S. influence at the IMF to focus more attention on workers' rights and similar issues in countries receiving IMF loans. These changes earned the support of House minority whip Bonior and House Banking Committee member Barney Frank, D-Mass. The committee approved the compromise bill in a 40-9 vote.

With the support of GOP leaders, House conservatives proceeded with plans to add anti-abortion language to the amendment on the House floor.[35] Additionally, House majority leader Dick Armey, R-Texas, announced that he would back Representative Saxton's alternative bill that would include reforms in IMF operations but not endorsements of workers' rights, a move that would provoke many Democrats to abandon the bill. According to an Armey aide, "Republicans aren't going to vote for a bill that turns the IMF into a union organizing institution."[36] Thus, what had appeared to be a breakthrough in the House seemed likely to deteriorate into a stalemate.

In the Senate, Majority Leader Lott said he probably would not support the compromise bill approved by the House Banking Committee because it had included compromise language emphasizing labor rights and environmental issues.[37] Thereafter, House and Senate Republican leaders reached an agreement to separate IMF and UN funding from the president's supplemental spending bill.[38] Instead, the IMF and UN funding proposals were attached to the foreign operations appropriations bill that contained anti-abortion provisions championed by Representative Smith, who had also secured support from the House GOP leadership for his plan to add the restrictions to any IMF bill that reached the floor. Again, the White House threatened a veto if the anti-abortion language was kept in the bill.[39]

With the help of Senators Grams and Roberts, Senator Hagel worked for about three weeks on language acceptable to a majority in the Senate and to the White House. Hagel consulted with Rubin and Greenspan regularly, having more than a dozen discussions with each of them during this period to ensure that the compromise reform language would have administration support.[40] By mid-March, his efforts appeared to pay off. He carried his compromise to the Senate Appropriations Committee, in which the IMF bill was being considered, and prepared to see it reported out to the whole Senate and passed on the floor. At a March 16, 1998, news conference, Majority Leader Lott referenced the deal, noting,

> I understand there may have been a breakthrough late Friday afternoon on language that could be added to IMF in terms of conditions that might make it possible for the IMF matter to be brought up sooner than it looked like might have been possible. I do not have the details on that. I received just a very brief notification of it from Senator Chuck Hagel, who has been working with Senator Stevens, Senator McConnell, Secretary Rubin, Senator

Helms, and others to see if we could get an agreement on what the conditions would be that would be added to the IMF in order for the full complement to go forward.[41]

Senator Hagel was, unfortunately, in for a quick education in congressional politics. As the Senate Appropriations Committee took up the language, a number of Republican senators balked. In spite of Hagel's careful compromise, these senators, including Faircloth and Kyl on the committee and Phil Gramm, R-Texas, and Helms from outside the committee, demanded tougher reform measures. With Lott's blessing—he preferred tougher conditions as well—the Appropriations Committee rewrote Hagel's compromise by including stringent conditions, which threatened to kill the entire bill.[42] Since Hagel was not on the Appropriations Committee, he could not defend the compromise language he had crafted.[43] The new, tougher language—which included greater accountability in fund operations, the elimination of crony capitalism in recipient countries, equitable treatment of domestic and foreign creditors in recipient countries, and compliance with other international trade rules—was reported out of the committee on March 17 in the form of Senate bill 1769 (S. 1769).

Treasury Secretary Rubin immediately telephoned Hagel and told him that the new language was "not achievable" and that the administration would not support the conditions established by S. 1769.[44] Publicly, Rubin called the conditions "impractical . . . to the point of being genuinely unworkable."[45] Members of Hagel's bipartisan circle of support also rejected the new conditions. His hard work thus in jeopardy, Hagel "mounted a rescue operation," giving his opponents their own lesson in congressional politics. Shoring up support among his colleagues, he immediately began more discussions with Rubin and Greenspan and initiated talks with former members of the Bush administration, including former president George Bush himself.[46]

The following day, March 18, Hagel took advantage of a previously scheduled hearing before the Foreign Relations Committee's Subcommittee on International Economic Policy, Export, and Trade Promotion, which he chaired, to begin re-mobilizing his supporters. He introduced testimony from a number of officials from government and business—August Schumaker, undersecretary of agriculture; Errol Small, director of marketing for the Maryland Department of Agriculture; John Hardin, former president of the National Pork Producer's Council; Bryce Neidig, president of the Nebraska Farm Bureau; and John Campbell, vice president of AG Processing—to stress the importance to U.S. exporters of IMF support for countries in crisis, especially in Asia, and the critical need for the IMF funding.[47] Campbell called the IMF bill "the agriculture issue of the day," and Hagel summed up the hearing as a reinforcement of "the need for the economic security that the IMF can bring and has brought to Asia."[48] Hagel also took aim at the Appropriations Committee, noting,

> I must say that I was rather disappointed with the language that the appropriations committee reported out yesterday. I have put a lot of work in helping—with many of my colleagues—in bolting together achievable reform language. I don't think we did that yesterday. So, we have more chapters to read and write here and some of my colleagues and I will probably be doing something today or tomorrow regarding new language.[49]

Senator Hagel, who had been tapped by the Republican leadership to take the point on the IMF issue, was now clearly engaged in a struggle with members of that leadership, including Gramm, Helms, Lott, and McConnell. As Hagel had promised in the subcommittee hearing, on the Senate floor that same afternoon he introduced S. 1795—"To reform the International Monetary Fund and to authorize United States participation in a quota increase and the New Arrangements to Borrow of the International Monetary Fund, and for other purposes"—with his original compromise language. His core allies— John Chafee, R-R.I., Domenici, Grams, and Roberts—were co-signers.[50] Having made an end-run around his opponents in the Appropriations Committee, Hagel told his colleagues that "this legislation is the product of weeks of work and negotiation . . . to develop a package of very tough—but achievable—reforms for the IMF. . . . We are introducing this legislation so that all our colleagues can review the compromise language we have put together."[51]

Hagel next brought pressure to bear from a number of directions, bucking opposition from top Republican Party leaders, including the majority leader and the Senate Foreign Relations Committee chairman, as he attempted to salvage his bipartisan deal.[52] First, he enlisted his high-powered ally on the Appropriations Committee, Ted Stevens, the committee chairman, to endorse and advocate for the original deal.[53] Stevens provided key support to Hagel. From the Senate floor, Stevens explained,

> I am normally neutral on most of these subjects but I am not neutral on this. . . . The Asian flu is the El Niño of economics. Unless we understand that, unless we understand the fear that is coming in our country, we are liable to make a great mistake. I do not want to see games played with the IMF. . . . I am one who is going to vote for IMF. It may be that others want to delay it. Others want to handle it in different ways. I want to make sure that the first bill that goes to the President has IMF on it, and I hope the rest of the Senate will agree with me.[54]

Second, Hagel firmed up his core supporters, getting reaffirmations from Chafee, Domenici, Grams, and Roberts, and new or stronger endorsements from Biden and Sarbanes, among others. For example, as Hagel planned his counterattack, Sarbanes argued, "I don't mind trying to move the IMF in certain directions because I do think there's some practices of theirs that need to be changed and modernized. But if we put it in a context in which it is so conditioned that either we won't be able to meet the conditions or it will take a long time to meet the conditions, then we're not addressing the financial crisis which now exists."[55] The next day, Biden took to the floor of the Senate and expressed his concern "about some of the conditions put on the IMF funds in the Appropriation Committee on Tuesday," especially since Treasury Secretary Rubin "has called those conditions—and I quote—'impractical, to the point of being unworkable.'"[56] Biden went on to argue that

> we must act quickly and decisively to maintain the strength of the IMF. . . . We should not make demands of the IMF that could delay indefinitely the day when private financial markets regain the confidence that will mark the turning point in the current financial crisis. That is why I am pleased that my friend and colleague on the Foreign Relations Committee—chairman of the International Economic Policy Subcommittee—Senator Chuck Hagel, has taken the lead in introducing legislation authorizing funds for the IMF with workable, sensible reforms. Together with Senator Grams on our committee, and Senators Roberts, Chafee, and Domenici, Senator Hagel has provided us with an important point of reference when we consider IMF funding here on the Senate floor.[57]

Third, Hagel worked with others outside Congress, including the administration, to generate momentum and restore the original deal. He coordinated with Rubin and Greenspan to shore up their support for his compromise language and bring administration pressure to bear on other senators.[58] In conjunction with Hagel and his staff, the administration released a report showing that 30 percent of all U.S. exports went to Asia and breaking down the exports by state.[59] Additionally, Peter G. Peterson, former commerce secretary and chairman of the Council on Foreign Relations, and Maurice R. Greenberg, chairman of the Asia Society, organized a $400,000 newspaper ad campaign pressing for IMF funding. They also sent a letter to every member of Congress, signed by a number of top corporate executives and a bipartisan group of former cabinet secretaries. They highlighted the amount of international business in each state or congressional district at risk without IMF funding.[60]

Hagel generated support from members of the Bush administration, including the former president himself, who advocated for IMF funding.

A few days later, Hagel was called into Lott's office, where Lott, Gramm, and Helms complained that his formula was too weak. They threatened to block it from a floor vote unless he toughened it. According to Hagel, he told them "that'd be political suicide" and threatened to force a vote between the two proposals. Hagel then stressed to them that he had strong majority support for his language, as well as administration approval.[61] The tension was reduced only when they agreed to keep tinkering,[62] but no agreement appeared to be in sight. Lott commented to the media on March 23,

> Efforts are still under way to reach an agreement on the conditions that would be added to the IMF legislation to make it possible for the replenishment to be provided. I think it's very important that we take steps to try to protect American taxpayers' dollars at IMF, make sure we know how these funds are being spent by the IMF. I think we need to have transparency so that we can look at what's happening, how much of this money is going for bad loans or how much of it involves cronyism. . . . I just don't think we're going to be able to get IMF passed without some conditions that provide some protections or guarantees.[63]

As Lott was predicting another week's delay, however, a breakthrough occurred. The right language was found when a member of Hagel's staff suggested, simply, that recipient countries were to be expected to comply with all trade agreements and to end crony capitalism. Hagel, Lott, Gramm, and Rubin found it acceptable.[64] With the support of Senators Stevens and McConnell, Hagel's compromise language on IMF funding was added to the fiscal 1998 emergency supplemental bill (S. 1768) in the form of an amendment (no. 2100) and brought to the Senate floor on March 24. This amendment—authored by Hagel but co-sponsored by Gramm, McConnell, and Stevens—was introduced with the support of the leadership, Hagel's bipartisan group, and the administration.[65] After McConnell summarized the amendment, Hagel again emphasized the need for the bill, and other senators, including Grams and Domenici, offered their endorsements.

In spite of the broad consensus, some senators continued to oppose the language. Faircloth, for example, denounced the funding as "absolutely sinful," arguing that "the IMF is the problem, not the cure."[66] The next day, Majority Leader Lott carefully qualified his support, suggesting that "we should find a way to provide the funds, but only—only—if strong conditions are in place to make sure that the American people have confidence these funds are not being misused and we have a chance to see how they are being used."[67] Reflecting the concerns of liberal Democrats, Senator Wellstone offered four amendments to the compromise language that would have required conditionality for IMF loans based on worker rights, environmental protection, and other social concerns.[68] By voice vote, the Senate also approved an amendment by Robert Byrd, D-W. Va., to restrict the ability of recipients of IMF loans to subsidize steel producers. Ernest Hollings, D-S.C., broadened the amendment by adding prohibitions against subsidies for textile or automobile manufacturers. The bill already carried restrictions against subsidies for the semiconductor industry and included conditions requiring the IMF to allow U.S. General Accounting Office inspectors to review its books and to lend only to those recipients willing to develop Western-style financial and bankruptcy systems.[69] Finally, on March 26, after another round of debate—with Biden, Hagel, Roberts, and Sarbanes speaking for and Spencer Abraham, R-Mich., Connie Mack, R-Fla., and Wellstone speaking against—the legislation passed by a vote of 84-16. At this point, Hagel noted, "I honestly believe that we've gone too far in micromanaging the IMF. . . . But it was the best language I could get to keep everyone satisfied."[70] Lott, on the other hand, continued to express his reservations: "I did want tougher restrictions, and I made it clear. . . . I wanted more restrictions . . . and we're going to get more. We're going to toughen those conditions up."[71]

The House Delays

Despite its overwhelming support in the Senate, IMF funding was still in jeopardy. The House retained its version of the emergency spending bill that omitted IMF funding and instead included it in the fiscal 1999 foreign operations appropriations bill that also dealt with UN financing. The House version of this latter bill still included anti-abortion provisions.[72] On April 23, House Republicans approved their version of the emergency military operations and disaster relief bill, which did not include IMF funding. A Democratic floor effort to add the funding to the bill, as was done in the Senate, failed by a vote of 222-186. House Speaker Gingrich promised a vote on IMF funding later in the year. When the issue of including UN financing came up, Majority Leader Armey depicted the IMF as part of the problem in overseas economies, not part of the solution.[73]

The chances for House approval of IMF funding seemed to dim further in May. Former secretary of state George Shultz called for the abolition of the IMF, saying it had exceeded its mandate.[74] House minority leader Gephardt and five other Democrats sent Secretary Rubin a letter stating that they would withdraw their support of IMF funding if he did not stop supporting the IMF's plan for unrestricted capital movement in and out of recipient countries. Others signing the letter included Democratic Representatives Bonior and Frank and Nancy Pelosi, Esteban Torres, and Maxine Waters of California. They wanted capital movement linked to protection of the environment and workers' rights.[75] Within days, however, Gephardt retreated, saying House Democrats would not jeopardize IMF funding despite their concern about the IMF's attempts to open up capital markets.[76]

The delay in the House proved frustrating for Hagel and his Senate colleagues. GOP leaders, anti-abortion proponents, and those advocating IMF reforms and restrictions had effectively bottled up the issue. Efforts to persuade their counterparts to act were to no avail. Senator Grams' pleas for action in support of U.S. leadership and interests in a hearing before the Joint Economic Committee on May 5 produced no movement.[77] In fact, Representative Jim Saxton, R-N.J., the chairman of the committee, used the hearing to air arguments against the IMF. Hagel took to the floor of the Senate in early June to put pressure on the House, expressing his great concern "that this Congress is not paying enough attention to what is going on around the world." Reviewing the economic crises in Southeast Asia and China, Japan, Russia, and South Korea, Hagel warned that

> the longer we lock up important decisions on IMF . . . that we should be tending to and focusing on, the more dangerous this world becomes. I hope my friends in the House are going to unlock this debate on IMF and allow this IMF debate to come to the floor of the House for an honest, open debate, and a vote. . . . I hope we get very serious about this, Mr. President, and understand the consequences of what is happening around the world.[78]

Hagel ally Pat Roberts echoed his colleague's concerns just a few days later, expressing his hope that "the House of Representatives would somehow see its way clear to simply address that legislation."[79] Finally, Hagel held another hearing in his subcommittee on the Asian financial crisis, from which additional endorsements of IMF funding emerged.[80] In spite of these and other efforts to prod the House into action, the IMF legislation continued to languish.

By June, the escalating financial crisis in Asia had spread to Russia. According to House Banking Committee chairman Leach, "The IMF has had enough money in the till to handle the Asian crisis if the crisis did not deepen and did not widen. It now appears that Indonesia is deepening it and Russia is widening it. These are issues that Congress ignores at the peril of international economic stability." Majority Leader Armey responded in a letter to his colleagues, "The International Monetary Fund bears much responsibility for Russia's current financial straits. The ever present hope of an IMF bailout—reinforced by the enormous international bailouts of Mexico in 1995 and Asia now—has until recently diluted Russia's willingness to embrace the financial reforms necessary to save herself."[81] When on July 13 the IMF approved a package of $22 billion in credits to Russia, the IMF's ready cash reserve dropped to less than $10 billion, a level considered dangerously low by experts.[82]

The next day, the House Appropriations Subcommittee on Foreign Operations approved the $3.4 billion request for new emergencies but not the rest of the $17.9 billion request. Representative Pelosi's attempt to add the additional $14.5 billion was defeated by voice vote.[83] Six days later, Majority Leader Armey vowed to hold IMF financing to the $3.4 billion approved. He asked, "Why should we spend taxpayers' money on an agency that seems to have a mania for raising taxes?"[84] House Speaker Gingrich said that without significant operational reforms, IMF funding would not be approved.[85] The anti-abortion coalition again announced plans to attach an anti-abortion amendment to any bill reaching the floor.

On July 22, the House Appropriations Committee took the bill containing IMF funding off its agenda, thereby delaying a vote until the fall. The reason for the action was the evolving behind-the-scenes battle over succeeding Newt Gingrich as speaker. Vying for the post were Appropriations Committee chairman Bob Livingston, R-La., and Majority Leader Armey. Livingston supported IMF funding, while Armey was courting conservative support and opposed full funding.[86]

The Final Push

The House agenda revision triggered action in the Senate. With the supplemental appropriations bill dead, on July 28 Hagel, McConnell, and Stevens attached the IMF section of S. 1768 to the foreign operations appropriations bill (S. 2334) in another effort to force action. Reflecting the Senate's broad support for this measure, Senator Biden took to the floor on July 30 to commend Hagel for his leadership and to chastise the House for playing "a dangerous game of chicken with international financial markets" and for holding "the IMF, and by extension global financial stability, hostage to increase their bargaining leverage on unrelated issues at the end of the legislative session this fall." According to

Biden, House Republicans were "playing with fire," so he called on them to "cease this recklessness."[87]

The foreign operations bill came up on the Senate floor on September 2, at which point IMF opponents made one last attempt to scuttle it. Republican senator Kyl offered an amendment (no. 3522) to replace the Hagel compromise with the more restrictive measures the Senate Appropriations Committee had passed on March 17, arguing that the Hagel compromise "does not go far enough to move the IMF toward reform."[88] Hagel and his allies reacted immediately. One after another, the key players in the bipartisan agreement took to the floor to defend the compromise language. Insisting that "it would be absolutely irresponsible for Congress to shrug off the IMF as economies around the globe falter," Hagel rejected the Kyl amendment as "a mechanism that we considered but abandoned on the Senate floor early in our negotiations 6 months ago." He also defended his compromise as a "strong IMF package" with "strong and achievable IMF reforms and the full $17.9 billion funding."[89] Hagel was joined in his aggressive defense by Biden, Grams, Roberts, and Sarbanes, all of whom offered strong endorsements of the compromise.[90] The Kyl amendment was defeated by a vote of 74-19. A short time later that same day, the Senate again passed the entire $17.9 billion in IMF funding by a 90-3 vote.[91]

In the House, Republicans met with a group of international advisers who endorsed the view that the IMF needed serious reforms. Dick Armey noted, "I felt particularly gratified, personally validated by the clear consensus of this group, all of whom are internationalists, that we ought not throw more good money after bad."[92] On September 10, the House Appropriations Committee voted 30-22 to only provide $3.4 billion to the IMF in the fiscal 1999 foreign operations bill, not the full $17.9 billion.[93] In addition, the committee approved by voice vote an amendment offered by Mississippi Republican Roger Wicker adding anti-abortion restrictions to international family planning assistance.[94]

The pro-IMF forces launched yet another counterattack. On September 14, President Clinton—in his first public appearance following the publication of the Starr report detailing his affair with White House intern Monica Lewinsky—addressed the Council on Foreign Relations in New York and urged passage of the $17.9 billion IMF request.[95] The next day, George Soros testified before the House Banking Committee. Although Soros had opposed some of the specifics of the IMF bailouts in Asia, he called support of a reformed IMF essential to the prosperity of the U.S. economy.[96] Speaking in Charlotte, North Carolina, Secretary Rubin called on Congress to approve the full financing of the IMF "to protect our national interests."[97] Senator Hagel used several public forums to cajole his "silly colleagues"[98] in the House to abandon their "demagogic rhetoric."[99] At a September 23 Senate Budget Committee hearing on the global economy, Domenici devoted much of the time to the IMF, giving Deputy Treasury Secretary Summers and Chairman Greenspan another chance to endorse IMF funding, while also providing another opportunity for Senators Gramm, Lautenberg, and Grams to press for action.[100]

Since numerous departmental budgets had not yet been approved for FY 1999, on September 17 Congress passed the first of several stopgap funding measures to keep the government operating into the new fiscal year beginning October 1. The House also approved by a vote of 255-161 the bill funding the $3.4 billion in IMF funding. By a procedural vote of 229-188, the House prevented Democrats from trying to add the remaining $14.5 billion on the House floor. Again, however, the House version included the prohibitions on aid to family planning groups that perform or counsel on abortion that the Wicker amendment had added in the Appropriations Committee. House Democrats opted not to challenge the provision on the floor, because the GOP leadership had promised Representative Smith an opportunity to reattach the restrictions if they should fall to such a challenge. Instead the Democrats left it to the House-Senate conference committee to work out, since the Senate version did not include such a provision.[101]

With the new fiscal year under way and congressional elections in November drawing near, continuous budget negotiations were held between the White House and the Republican leadership of Congress. House Speaker Gingrich feared that the IMF issue might cause another government shutdown and that the Republicans would be blamed. A breakthrough occurred on October 7, when the House Republican leadership finally agreed to fund the full $17.9 billion for the IMF, remove the anti-abortion language, and attach the IMF funding measure to a bill providing for the payment of nearly $1 billion in U.S. debts to the United Nations. During this period, there was continuing pressure from business and farm groups for IMF funding, as well as efforts by Senators Helms, Biden, and Tom Daschle, D.-S.D., to drop the anti-abortion restrictions.[102] The only remaining issue was the extent of reforms to be required of the IMF. A number of conservative House members were angry that a "disgraced" Democratic president, staring impeachment in the face, could still dictate spending priorities to a Republican-controlled Congress. According to one Republican aide, "We've got some angry members, but we're trying to get out of here so people can get home to campaign."[103]

On October 15 House Republicans, led by Majority Leader Armey, and the Clinton administration agreed on a set of reforms for the IMF. The final obstacle to the agreement was removed when the Republicans relinquished their demand that the IMF enact the reform package before receiving additional U.S. funds.[104] On October 20, the House approved the conference committee report on H.R. 4328, which included the IMF funding, by a 333-95 vote. The Senate approved the bill by a 65-29 vote on October 21, and President Clinton signed the bill that day.[105] The IMF would receive full funding.

While the administration got the full $17.9 billion it had requested, the final IMF bill contained more reforms than it would have preferred. For one, countries facing currency runs due to balance-of-payment problems or loss of market confidence would no longer have access to loans at below-market interest rates and for periods of up to ten years. Instead, loans would be at a rate of 3 percent above the average market rates in the five major industrialized countries and for periods of no longer than two and a half years.[106] Thus such recipients would have to repay loans sooner and at higher rates of interest. Regarding transparency, the Treasury Department would have to certify to Congress that the G-7 states—the seven major industrialized countries: Canada, France, Germany, Italy, Japan, the United Kingdom, and the United States— would vote for publication of the agreements that the IMF makes with recipients. Also, the G-7 countries would need to endorse disclosure of IMF board discussions, prior loan performance measures, and annual economic reviews of member countries. Such disclosures should take place within ninety days of the decisions.[107] Independent monitoring of the IMF was also included, as both Congress and the Treasury Department would be required to create their own advisory committees to review IMF operations.[108] The Treasury Department would also have to certify that IMF loans were not subsidizing industries in direct competition with those in the United States, such as South Korea's semiconductor, steel, textile, and automobile industries. Also, recipients of loans would be required to liberalize their agricultural trade restrictions and treat foreign lenders on an equal basis with domestic creditors.[109] The concerns of congressional liberals were not ignored, as the reforms required the U.S. representatives on the IMF board to use their "voice and vote" to study the impact of IMF loans on the poor, working classes, and on environmental and labor standards in recipient countries.[110]

Thus, the year-long debate was over. The White House's request for $17.9 billion was fully funded. However, the bill included more conditions than the administration liked. Majority Leader Armey claimed a major victory for those committed to changing the IMF restrictions, while other observers noted that most of the conditions imposed by the bill would require the IMF to do things it was already doing.[111] More than a year after the beginning of the Asian financial collapse, the United States finally took steps to strengthen the IMF's ability to respond to regional economic crises.

Conclusion: The Complex Politics of Foreign Economic Policy Making

President Clinton hailed the passage of the IMF legislation as an important step toward addressing global economic problems and U.S. economic interests. While Clinton may have accurately characterized this result, the preceding account also highlights the increasingly complex and divided domestic political environment in which U.S. foreign policy decisions must be made. In this instance, the political environment proved highly contentious, with multiple actors and interests pressing hard for their preferences.

The IMF policy was not the result of a "preeminent president," able to unilaterally make important decisions and have Congress follow, but the consequence of a complicated negotiation (and confrontation) among a variety of players from the executive branch, the House and Senate, and nongovernmental actors. Each faction had a different set of interests and a different interpretation of the problem. Notably, for some players, participation in the IMF issue was driven by fundamentally domestic, seemingly unrelated political issues (for example, the anti-abortion faction). With labor, business, agriculture, human rights, and ideological interests weighing in, this case reflects the complexities of so-called intermestic policies, which many observers believe to be increasingly prominent in the foreign policy arena. This, of course, suggests the likelihood of similar contests on other issues in the future.

The axis of politics and policy making in the IMF case was Congress. Not only does the IMF case suggest a Congress less deferential to presidential leadership and less concerned with the potential costs of challenging presidential foreign policy initiatives, it also illustrates a highly fragmented and partisan environment in which domestic politics and foreign policy overlap. As this case suggests, members of Congress had many opportunities and channels through which to influence policy making, ranging from formal legislative avenues to more informal and indirect paths by which to shape, condition, and influence it. Indeed, the IMF funding debate reveals how individual members of Congress have ample opportunity to engage in personalized policy making.

Although President Clinton was able to get what he wanted, it required more than a year of bargaining and wrangling and a unique constellation of allies within and outside government, across two branches of government, within the two houses of Congress, and between the two major parties. As much as the process resulted in a presidential victory, it also signaled the diffusion of policy influence with which all presidents must deal. This more open, pluralistic, and partisan environment is indicative of further serious challenges for presidential leadership.

Notes

1. See Robert Wade, "The Asian Crisis and the Global Economy: Causes, Consequences, and Cure," *Current History* 97 (November 1998): 361–373; and *Los Angeles Times*, April 15, 1998, D1.

2. See Wade, "The Asian Crisis and the Global Economy."

3. *Independent* (London), April 12, 1998, 2.

4. *New York Times*, November 14, 1997, A1.

5. Senate Foreign Relations Committee, *The IMF and the Asian Financial Crisis*, hearing, February 12, 1998, 15, electronic version obtained via CIS Congressional Universe.

6. *Washington Post*, January 13, 1998, A5.

7. Ibid.

8. *Washington Post*, January 16, 1998, G1.

9. *Washington Post*, January 22, 1998, E1.

10. *Journal of Commerce*, January 26, 1998, 3A.

11. *Congressional Quarterly Almanac*, 1998, D-5.

12. *Business Times* (Singapore), January 30, 1998, 3.

13. *Business Times* (Singapore), January 31, 1998, 3.

14. *Washington Post*, January 31, 1998, A4.

15. *Los Angeles Times*, January 31, 1998, D1.

16. Senate Finance Committee, *Consequences of the Asian Financial Crisis*, hearing, February 4, 1998, 6 and 8, electronic version obtained via CIS Congressional Universe.

17. Senate Finance Committee, *The IMF and the Asian Financial Crisis*.

18. *Guardian* (London), February 9, 1998, 16.

19. *New York Times*, April 5, 1998, 10.

20. *Ottawa Citizen*, February 12, 1998, D6; *Omaha World-Herald*, February 12, 1998, 13.

21. *Journal of Commerce*, February 26, 1998, 2A.

22. *Straits Times* (Singapore), February 5, 1998, 42.

23. *Guardian* (London), February 9, 1998, 16.

24. *Journal of Commerce*, February 13, 1998, 4A.

25. *South China Morning Post*, February 16, 1998, 10.

26. *Journal of Commerce*, February 26, 1998, 2A.

27. *Congressional Quarterly Almanac*, 1998, 2-121.

28. *New York Times*, March 4, 1998, A15.

29. Senate Appropriations Committee, Subcommittee on Foreign Operations, *Foreign Operations, Export Financing, and Related Programs,* hearing March 3, 1998, 5, electronic version obtained via CIS Congressional Universe.

30. *Financial Times,* March 4, 1998, 7.

31. Senate Appropriations Committee, *Foreign Operations, Export Financing, and Related Programs.*

32. *Omaha World Herald,* March 27, 1998; *Washington Post,* April 21, 1998; *New York Times,* June 7, 1998; *Omaha World Herald,* March 12, 1998.

33. *Omaha World Herald,* March 27, 1998, 1.

34. Ibid.

35. *Washington Post,* March 5, 1998, A11.

36. *Washington Post,* March 6, 1998, A32.

37. *Houston Chronicle,* March 7, 1998, 2.

38. *Washington Post,* March 12, 1998, A5.

39. Ibid.

40. *Omaha World Herald,* March 27, 1998, 1.

41. News conference with Senate majority leader Trent Lott, March 16, 1998, 4–5, electronic version obtained via CIS Congressional Universe.

42. *Washington Post,* April 21, 1998, A1.

43. *New York Times,* June 7, 1998, sec. 1, 14.

44. *Omaha World Herald,* March 27, 1998, 1.

45. *Washington Post,* March 18, 1998, A5.

46. *Washington Post,* April 21, 1998, A1; *Omaha World Herald,* March 27, 1998, 1.

47. Senate Foreign Relations Committee, Subcommittee on International Economic Policy, Export, and Trade Promotion, *Role of IMF in Promoting U.S. Agriculture,* hearing, March 18, 1998, electronic version obtained via CIS Congressional Universe

48. Ibid.

49. Ibid.

50. *Congressional Record,* March 18, 1998, S2214.

51. Ibid., S2216-2217.

52. *Washington Post,* April 21, 1998, A1.

53. *New York Times,* June 7, 1998, sec. 1, 14.

54. *Congressional Record,* March 25, 1998, S2506.

55. Senate Foreign Relations Committee, *Role of IMF in Promoting U.S. Agriculture.*

56. *Congressional Record,* March 19, 1998, S2347.

57. Ibid., S2348.

58. *Omaha World Herald,* March 27, 1998, 1.

59. *Journal of Commerce,* March 25, 1998, 2A.

60. *New York Times,* April 5, 1998, 10.

61. *Washington Post,* April 21, 1998, A1.

62. *Omaha World Herald,* April 18, 1998, 1.

63. News briefing with Senate majority leader Trent Lott, March 23, 1998, 2, electronic version obtained via CIA Congressional Universe.

64. *Omaha World Herald,* March 27, 1998, 1.

65. *Congressional Record,* March 24, 1998, S2463.

66. Ibid., S2465.

67. *Congressional Record,* March 25, 1998, S2505.

68. Ibid., S2525–2526; see also Wellstone's comments, S2554–2556.

69. *Congressional Quarterly Almanac,* 1998, 2-126.

70. *Omaha World Herald*, March 27, 1998, 1.

71. *Omaha World Herald*, April 18, 1998, 1.

72. *New York Times*, March 27, 1998, A8.

73. *New York Times*, April 24, 1998, A9.

74. *San Diego Union-Tribune*, May 6, 1998, A17.

75. *New York Times*, May 2, 1998, A7.

76. *Washington Post*, May 6, 1998, A5.

77. See U.S. Congress, Joint Economic Committee, *The International Monetary Fund and International Economic Policy,* hearing, May 5, 1998 (Washington, D.C.: GPO, 1998).

78. *Congressional Record,* June 12, 1998, S6291.

79. *Congressional Record,* June 16, 1998, S6362. About this time, Hagel and Max Baucus, D-Mont., formed a bipartisan group of senators "to focus more energy seeking constructive solutions to American foreign policy problems . . . [and] to help reduce the rancor that partisan bickering tends to produce." *Congressional Record,* June 23, 1998, S6863.

80. See Senate Foreign Relations Committee, Subcommittee on International Economic Policy, Export, and Trade Promotion, *The Financial Crisis in East Asia,* hearing, June 24, 1998, electronic version obtained via CIS Congressional Universe.

81. *Washington Post,* June 4, 1998, E1.

82. *Washington Post,* July 14, 1998, A1.

83. *Washington Post,* July 16, 1998, A5.

84. *Washington Post,* July 21, 1998, A4.

85. *Journal of Commerce,* July 21, 1998, 3A.

86. *New York Times,* July 23, 1998, A7.

87. *Congressional Record,* July 30, 1998, S9423–9424.

88. *Congressional Record,* September 2, 1998, S9826.

89. *Congressional Record,* September 2, 1998, S9828.

90. See *Congressional Record,* September 2, 1998, S9829–9831.

91. *Houston Chronicle,* September 3, 1998, 3.

92. Ibid.

93. *New York Times,* September 11, 1998, A12.

94. *Congressional Quarterly Almanac,* 1998, 2-51; Miles A. Pomper, "Panel Approves Foreign Aid Bill Despite Threat of Veto," *CQ Weekly,* September 12, 1998, 2416.

95. *New York Times,* September 15, 1998, A1.

96. *Star Tribune* (Minneapolis), September 16, 1998, 5D.

97. *Journal of Commerce,* September 16, 1998, 2A.

98. *Omaha World Herald,* October 18, 1998, 16A, referring to a speech at the University of Nebraska at Omaha.

99. *Omaha World Herald,* September 30, 1998, 1, referring to comments at the John F. Kennedy School of Government.

100. See Senate Budget Committee, *The Global Economy,* hearing, September 23, 1998, electronic version obtained via CIS Congressional Universe.

101. *Washington Post,* September 18, 1998, A4; Miles A Pomper, "Foreign Aid Bill Fails to Resolve Deep Divisions over IMF Funding," *CQ Weekly,* September 19, 1998, 2505.

102. Miles A. Pomper, "Deal Gives Clinton IMF Credit; GOP Wins Conditions on Loan," *CQ Weekly,* October 17, 1998, 2833.

103. *Houston Chronicle,* October 8, 1998, A1.

104. *New York Times,* October 16, 1998, A8.

105. *Congressional Quarterly Almanac,* 1998, 2-45.

106. Ibid.

107. *New York Times,* October 16, 1998, A8; *Financial Times,* October 16, 1998, 8.

108. *New York Times,* October 16, 1998, A8.

109. Ibid.; *Congressional Quarterly Almanac,* 1998, 2-54.

110. *New York Times,* October 16, 1998, A8; *Journal of Commerce,* October 22, 1998, 1A.

111. Pomper, "Deal Gives Clinton IMF Credit," 2833.

15 The International Criminal Court: Present at the Creation?

Ralph G. Carter and Donald W. Jackson

Before You Begin

1. What is the International Criminal Court (ICC)? Why do many international observers feel it is needed?

2. Who were the key American players trying to shape the creation of the ICC? What were their motivations or concerns? How much influence over shaping the ICC did they wield in comparison to their foreign counterparts?

3. Why was the position of the United States so contrary to positions taken by its allies? Why did the American participants find the principle of complementarity insufficient to satisfy their concerns?

4. U.S. politicians and citizens pride themselves on living under "the rule of law and not of men." To what extent is there a contradiction between that assertion and the U.S. position that its military personnel should not be tried before international tribunals without U.S. consent?

5. What might be the justification for holding that the United States should not be bound by laws applicable to other, less powerful nations?

6. Are there principles of universal human rights that should be enforced wherever these principles are violated? If so, what might be some prominent examples? If not, do you believe that international law simply represents the means by which the strong impose their judgment on the weak?

7. Do you think that the history of U.S. involvement in world politics justifies the conclusion that the United States as a country has been unusually moral or altruistic in the commitments it has made and in the wars in which it has fought?

8. Compare the position of the United States in international politics today with that of other nations involved in the creation of the ICC. Does the United States act like an imperial power? If so, does this bother you? If not, why not?

9. Will the twenty-first century be the century in which significant political, legal, and military authority and power pass from nation-states to international institutions such as the United Nations or the International Criminal Court? Do you think such a transition will ever occur?

Introduction: The Rise of International Law

From 1989 to 1991, a remarkable change occurred in international politics. A process of disintegration began that led to the dissolution of the Soviet empire and ultimately of the Soviet Union itself. Some of the early beneficiaries of this change seemed to be international institutions and international law, as was illustrated by Soviet-U.S. cooperation during the 1990–1991 Persian Gulf crisis and war. With the apparent end of the cold war, the U.S.-led international coalition that drove Iraqi forces from Kuwait justified and coordinated its actions through the United Nations and the application of international law. Events in the late 1980s and early 1990s led President George Bush to declare that an increasingly democratic "new world order" had arrived, a time when "the international system would be based on international law and would rely on international organizations such as the United Nations to settle international conflicts."[1]

An illustration of this trend toward international institutions—though perhaps not of the new world order envisioned by Bush—occurred on July 17, 1998, when 120 states voted at a UN diplomatic conference in Rome to create the International Criminal Court (ICC) with powers to try perpetrators of genocide, crimes against humanity, and war crimes. Only seven states voted against creating the ICC: China, Iraq, Israel, Libya, Qatar, Yemen, and the United States. How did the United States suddenly find itself on "the other side" of international law?

Background: The Rise of International Tribunals

International courts are not unique to the twenty-first century. The Hague Peace Conference of 1899, convened for the primary purpose of promoting peace and stability by limiting or reducing armaments, also created the Hague Convention for the Pacific Settlement of International Disputes and the Permanent Court of Arbitration.[2] With the League of Nations in 1920 came the Permanent Court of International Justice, which rendered thirty judgments and issued twenty-seven advisory opinions from 1922 to 1946.[3] After World War II, the United Nations created the International Court of Justice (or World Court), but two exceptions to this previous international court's jurisdiction remained: the court's decisions generally applied only to states, not individuals, and, moreover, it was possible for states, through reservations, to avoid the court's obligatory jurisdiction.[4] The idea for the International Criminal Court did not arise in a political vacuum and was not a dream of idealistic abstractions; rather, it followed a series of precedent-setting tribunals. Between 1919 and 1994, five ad hoc international commissions, four ad hoc international criminal tribunals, and three international or national prosecutions of "crimes" arising during World Wars I and II were convened. The first commission sought to prosecute German and Turkish officials and military officers for war crimes and crimes against humanity during World War I. Crimes against humanity generally consisted of the abusive or murderous treatment of civilians by military personnel. This commission's efforts resulted in a few token convictions in the German supreme court.[5]

After the ineffective United Nations War Crimes Commission was created in 1942, the Allies signed the London Charter for the Prosecution and Punishment of the Major War Criminals of the European Axis in August 1945. The principles contained in the 1945 agreement were later recognized as binding precedents in international law by UN General Assembly Resolution 95 of December 11, 1946. The London Charter created the International Military Tribunal (IMT), consisting of four judges (one from each of the four powers). The jurisdiction of the IMT included the following crimes:

- crimes against peace—Article 6[a] of the London Charter: planning, preparation, initiation or waging a war of aggression or a war in violation of international treaties or agreements;
- war crimes—Article 6[b] of the London Charter, though the most definitive statement appears in the Charter of the International Military Tribunal (annexed to the London Charter): violations of the laws or customs of war, to include murder, ill-treatment, or deportation to slave labor of civilian populations in occupied territory, murder or ill-treatment of prisoners of war or persons on the seas, killing of hostages, plunder of public or private property, wanton destruction of cities, or devastation not justified by military necessity;
- crimes against humanity—Article 6[c] of the London Charter: murder, extermination, enslavement, deportation, and other inhumane acts committed against any civilian population, or persecutions on political, racial or religious grounds in execution of or in connection with any crime within the jurisdiction of the tribunal.[6]

The IMT's role concluded with the Nuremberg trials in 1946. The tribunal found eighteen of twenty-one prominent Nazi defendants guilty; twelve of these eighteen were given the death penalty, and the other six were imprisoned for terms ranging from ten years to life.[7]

With the occupation of Japan, the International Military Tribunal for the Far East (IMTFE) was created in Tokyo in 1946. Its list of punishable crimes was essentially the same as that for the IMT in Germany.[8] The results were generally similar as well; all twenty-five defendants were found guilty, seven were executed, sixteen were given life imprisonment, and two were given lesser prison terms.[9]

The London Charter and the Nuremberg precedent were affirmed in 1946 by the UN General Assembly in Resolution 95 (I). In December 1946 the assembly unanimously adopted Resolution 96 (I), which expressly made genocide—derived from the London Charter's definition of crimes against humanity—a crime under international law. Two years later the General Assembly adopted the Convention on the Prevention and Punishment of the Crime of Genocide.[10] In the United States the genocide convention was submitted to the Senate for ratification in 1949, but U.S. ratification (with reservations) came almost forty years later, in 1988.

Much of the substantive international criminal law as applied by the IMT at Nuremberg was expanded and codified in the Geneva Conventions of 1949. In 1948 the UN General Assembly invited the International Law Commission to study the possibility of creating an international criminal court with jurisdiction over the crime of genocide and of crimes that might be defined by international conventions. Because of the cold war, however, it was not until 1989 that the idea of an international criminal court was again brought before the General Assembly.[11]

U.S. Concerns

The protection of U.S. sovereignty vis-à-vis international law has been a long-standing issue. In 1945, it took presidential reassurance to the Senate that Article 43 of the UN Charter, which obligated members to make available to the Security Council "armed forces, assistance, and facilities," would not rob Congress of its right to declare war. In 1946, it took two amendments to ensure Senate support for U.S. acceptance of the jurisdiction of the World Court. The Vandenberg Amendment specified that the court's jurisdiction would not apply to "disputes arising under a multilateral treaty, unless (1) all parties to the treaty affected by the decision are also parties to the case before the court, or (2) the United States specially agrees to jurisdiction."[12] The more famous reservation was the Connally Amendment, which drew the line of the ICJ's obligatory jurisdiction at "disputes with regard to matters which are essentially within the domestic jurisdiction of the United States of America as determined by the United States of America."[13] In the eyes of its critics, this amendment essentially said that the United States would obey the World Court when the U.S. government happened to agree with it. In 1959, the Connally Amendment was revisited, when the American Bar Association's Committee on World Peace Through Law tried to repeal it. That effort died when the Senate Foreign Relations Committee voted to postpone the matter indefinitely.[14]

These were not the only instances of U.S. unwillingness to be bound by international law. For example, in 1977 the United States and Panama reached agreement on two treaties that returned sovereignty of the Panama Canal and the canal zone to Panama and guaranteed neutral operation of the waterway. In approving the treaties, however, the Senate added the DeConcini Amendment, which reserved the right of the United States to intervene militarily in Panama to keep the canal open if the United States (not Panama) decided that such a step was necessary.[15] Not surprisingly, the Panamanians were outraged by this infringement on their national sovereignty, and it nearly scuttled the treaties. More recently, in 1984, when the World Court ruled that the United States was illegally trying to overthrow the government of Nicaragua, the United States announced its rejection of the court's jurisdiction, for a period of two years, regarding any of its actions in Central America. Like most countries, the United States has continued to reject the obligatory jurisdiction of the World Court, and many states that have accepted obligatory jurisdiction have attached reservations to their acceptance.[16]

Creation of the ICC

Unlike the Nuremberg and Tokyo trials, the idea for the permanent International Criminal Court was not something victors in a war imposed on the vanquished. Instead, the genesis of the ICC came from smaller powers in the international system. In 1989, sixteen Caribbean and Latin American nations suggested international criminal prosecutions for narco-traffickers.[17] In 1990, a committee of non-governmental organization (NGOs) prepared a draft statute for an international court and submitted it to the Eighth United Nations Congress on the Prevention of Crime and the Treatment of Offenders. In 1991, the International Law Commission prepared a draft code of international crimes. These events culminated in November 1994, when the commission produced its draft statute for an international criminal court.[18]

Creation of the International Criminal Court

1946 The UN General Assembly passes Resolution 95, recognizing the principles contained in the 1945 London Charter as binding precedents in international law. It also passes Resolution 96 (I), making genocide a crime under international law. Trials are held in Nuremberg and Tokyo of Germans and Japanese accused of crimes against peace, war crimes, and crimes against humanity. In the U.S. Senate, the Vandenberg and Connally Amendments (resolutions of U.S. reservations) are approved, which ensure congressional support for U.S. acceptance of the jurisdiction of the new International Court of Justice (or World Court).

1989 Sixteen Caribbean and Latin American nations propose a permanent International Criminal Court (ICC) for the prosecution of narco-traffickers.

1991 The International Law Commission prepares a draft code of international crimes.

1993 The UN Security Council passes Resolution 808, providing for the establishment of an International Criminal Tribunal for the Former Yugoslavia.

1994 The UN Security Council passes Resolution 955, creating the International Criminal Tribunal for Rwanda. The International Law Commission prepares a draft statute for an international criminal court.

1995 The UN General Assembly creates the Preparatory Committee for the Establishment of an International Criminal Court.

March 26, 1998 Sen. Jesse Helms, R-N.C., sends a letter to Secretary of State Madeleine Albright vowing that any agreement that might bring a U.S. citizen under the jurisdiction of a UN criminal court would be "dead on arrival" in the Senate.

March 31–April 1, 1998 Defense Department leaders meet in Washington with military attaches of more than 100 countries to warn them of the possible jurisdiction of the ICC over their soldiers.

June–July 1998 At a conference in Rome, delegates discuss and then vote 120-7 to establish the International Criminal Court.

June 14, 2000 Helms introduces the American Service Members Protection Act (S. 2726), which would prohibit U.S. officials from cooperating with the proposed ICC. Majority Whip Tom DeLay, R-Texas, introduces the same measure in the House of Representatives (H.R. 4654).

continued on the next page

continued from the previous page

December 31, 2000 The Clinton administration unexpectedly signs on to the ICC treaty, so the United States can participate in decisions about implementation of the new tribunal.

At this time, the international legal community was reacting to allegations of horrendous human rights violations in civil wars in Yugoslavia and Rwanda. In 1993 UN Security Council Resolution 808 provided for the establishment of the International Criminal Tribunal for the Former Yugoslavia to "prosecute persons responsible for serious violations of international humanitarian law committed in the territory of the former Yugoslavia since 1991."[19] The International Criminal Tribunal for Rwanda was established by UN Security Council Resolution 955, with jurisdiction starting January 1, 1994. The mandate of the Rwanda tribunal was to prosecute genocide and crimes against humanity.[20] These tribunals were temporary, however, and dealt only with specific conflicts.

In December 1995 the UN General Assembly created a Preparatory Committee for the Establishment of an International Criminal Court. The committee, PrepCom, first met in March 1996. Its membership was open to all the member states of the United Nations, UN specialized agencies, and the International Atomic Energy Agency.[21] The Clinton administration was a strong supporter of the temporary tribunals for Yugoslavia and Rwanda and had pushed the general issue of criminal prosecution for persons accused of war crimes. In 1997 it created the position of ambassador at-large for war crimes in the State Department and named David Scheffer to the post. In September 1997, President Clinton, in his address to the UN General Assembly, endorsed the establishment of a permanent international criminal court "to prosecute the most serious violations of international humanitarian law."[22]

By April 1998, six PrepCom sessions had been held. The aim of the last meeting was to prepare for an international conference in Rome in 1998 to conclude a treaty that would establish the permanent court.[23] The working draft at the last PrepCom meeting was the Zutphen Text, which had been produced during a January 1998 meeting in the Netherlands. The document called for a court that would complement national criminal courts. The crimes within the proposed jurisdiction of the international court were not yet determined, but the proposals included genocide, aggression, war crimes, and crimes against humanity. The definition of these crimes varied in different proposals. The draft statute included bracketed language wherever PrepCom had been unable to reach consensus.

Near the completion of the last PrepCom meeting, the 175-page draft statute contained 99 articles and about 1,700 bracketed words or provisions.[24]

The proposals included a listing of sexual offenses under war crimes, including rape, sexual slavery, enforced prostitution, enforced pregnancy, and enforced sterilization. One proposal included war crimes against children, for example, forcing children under the age of fifteen to take part in hostilities, recruiting children under the age of fifteen into the armed forces, or allowing them to take part in hostilities. Another proposed the inclusion of terrorist actions, while another would have included narco-trafficking as well. A further issue discussed was criminalizing the use of certain weapons likely to cause "superfluous injury or unnecessary suffering," a list that might include expanding bullets, chemical and biological weapons, land mines, and nuclear weapons.[25]

The most difficult issues touched on in Rome involved delimiting domestic criminal jurisdiction relative to the criminal jurisdiction of the international court and the means by which cases would reach the ICC. The domestic–international jurisdictional issue involved complementarity, the idea that international prosecution ought to occur only when a state had failed to take responsibility for its own good faith investigation and prosecution of crimes defined by the statute. The statute provided that a case would be admissible before the ICC only when a domestic judicial system was "unwilling or unable" to conduct the proper investigation or prosecution. In addition, a U.S. proposal on complementarity required the prosecutor for the international court to notify state parties and to make a public announcement when a case had been referred. A state could then step forward and inform the prosecutor that it was taking responsibility for prosecution. In the U.S. proposal, the assertion of domestic responsibility for prosecution would delay international criminal jurisdiction for a period of six months to one year, thus giving home governments more time to try accused individuals. One of the concerns expressed before the PrepCom was the length of this delay.[26] Other issues over the means by which cases might come to the court were more vexing.

The draft statute provided that the ICC prosecutor initiate an investigation only when the UN Security Council referred a case or when a state party that had accepted the jurisdiction of the ICC filed a complaint with the prosecutor. Those favoring a strong ICC wanted the prosecutor to have independent authority to investigate and file charges. At the other end of the controversy were those who, like the United States, preferred that the Security Council determine the agenda of the prosecutor and the ICC. That, of course, would give the United States and the other permanent members of the Security Council a veto over the ICC's jurisdiction. As former president Jimmy Carter noted, "Such a move rightly would be seen by many nations as a means for serving only the interests of the permanent members of the Security Council rather than as an independent arbiter of justice."[27]

The U.S. Reaction

In February 1998 Ambassador Scheffer, who was acting as chief negotiator for the United States on the creation of an international court, identified three issues involving the relationship between a court and the UN Security Council that needed to be addressed. The first was the need for the two institutions to operate compatibly, with neither undermining the legitimate pursuits of the other. The second issue involved the council's power to refer situations to the ICC, and the third was the council's role in assisting the court with the enforcement of its orders. Scheffer also made note of the unique position of the United States in the world. Either alone or in concert with NATO and the United Nations, the U.S. military often "shoulders the burden of international security." As he put it, "It is in our collective interest that the personnel of our militaries and civilian commands be able to fulfill their many legitimate responsibilities without unjustified exposure to criminal legal proceedings."[28] State Department spokesman James Rubin followed up on Scheffer's view, adding, "We need to ensure that, in pursuit of justice, a permanent court does not handcuff governments that take risks to promote international peace and security and to save lives."[29]

In August 1997, Singapore had presented a compromise proposal requiring the Security Council to take an affirmative vote to delay ICC proceedings, so the United States, for example, would have to have the consent of the rest of the council to delay a case. The United Kingdom accepted Singapore's proposal, and for a while it appeared that the United States might be moving in that direction as well.[30] Sen. Jesse Helms, R-N.C., chairman of the Foreign Relations Committee, stopped any such momentum. In a March 26, 1998, letter to Secretary of State Madeleine Albright, he vowed that any compromise that might bring an American citizen under the jurisdiction of a UN criminal court would be "dead on arrival" in the Senate. He declared that there should be no flexibility with respect to a U.S. veto over the court's power to prosecute U.S. citizens.[31] A week later, Helms again publicly encouraged the State Department to take aggressive actions to block the establishment of the ICC.

Helms's letter and public statements were the first warning shots. On March 31 and April 1, 1998, in Washington, Defense Department leaders held meetings with military attaches of more than 100 countries. Their message was that an international criminal court could "target their own soldiers—particularly when acting as peace keepers—and subject them to frivolous or politically motivated investigations by a rogue prosecutor or an overzealous tribunal." It was by all accounts quite an unusual briefing for Pentagon officials. According to Frederick Smith, deputy assistant secretary of defense for International Security Affairs, "It was not lobbying; there was no arm-twisting—it was awareness raising."[32]

A contrasting take on the court's ability to prosecute appeared in the *Times of India*. Having read the State Department's comment that "the permanent court must not handcuff governments that take risks to promote peace and security," an Indian columnist considered the conduct of U.S. forces in the My Lai massacre in Vietnam and in an alleged massacre of 1,000 civilians by U.S. Rangers in Mogadishu, Somalia: "Shouldn't the ICC be allowed to prosecute those involved in such crimes? . . . Or, like the Security Council, will it become a victim of double standards?"[33] Going into Rome, those countries favoring a stronger and more independent international court and prosecutor, consisted at this point of about forty-two so-called like-minded countries, including Canada and most of Europe and many countries in Africa, Asia, and Latin America.[34] According to the *Economist,*

> After nearly four years of intense negotiations among some 120 countries, the effort to set up the world criminal court has run smack into the ambivalence that has always been felt by the world's biggest powers about international law: they are keen to have it applied to others in the name of world order, but loath to submit to restrictions on their own sovereignty.[35]

The Rome Conference

In June 1998, representatives from 162 nations gathered in Rome to see whether they could agree on the creation of a permanent international criminal court.[36] The five-week conference opened with four days of speeches, during which U.S. ambassador to the United Nations Bill Richardson reiterated the U.S. position that the Security Council should control the work of the ICC by referring critical situations for investigation and by instructing countries to cooperate. The ultimate goal, he said, is to create a court that "focuses on recognized atrocities of significant magnitude and thus enjoys near universal support."[37] At that time, the U.S. position put it in the company of China, France, and Russia, three other permanent members of the Security Council. Among the permanent members, only the United Kingdom had come out in favor of a stronger and more independent court. On the other side of the most critical issues, the group of like-minded countries had by then grown to about sixty members. They were especially intent on creating an independent prosecutor and a court with sufficient jurisdiction and authority to actually bring those who committed human rights crimes to account. The conference was monitored by more than 200 accredited non-governmental organizations. Most prominent among these were Amnesty International, Human Rights Watch, and the European Law Students Association. A coalition of NGOs had been working in the interest of creating a permanent court for several years.

During the conference, an enormous amount of time was spent pursuing the elusive goal of consensus among the 162 nations. In part, consensus was sought because each nation had a single vote in the conference, which meant a simple majority vote would not take into account the relative size, power, or influence of individual countries. Hours were sometimes spent on one clause of one section of one article, with delegates from country after country making statements that usually were repetitive and often only seemed to serve the purpose of giving that delegate the chance to claim a few minutes at the microphone. The U.S. delegation worked hard to persuade its traditional allies to accept U.S. conditions for the treaty, especially during the final week of the conference. Indeed, the behind-the-scenes "buzz" was that the United States was actually threatening poor states with the loss of foreign aid and its NATO allies with a reduction of U.S. military support, including the withdrawal of troops.[38]

Motivated by Senator Helm's "dead on arrival" letter, throughout the conference the "U.S. delegation seemed increasingly gripped by a single overriding concern"—that no American could be tried before the court without the consent of the U.S. government.[39] Philippe Kirsch of Canada, chairman of the Committee of the Whole of the conference, noted about the U.S. delegation,

> It was amazing. Nothing could assuage them. . . . They seemed completely fixated on that Helms/Pentagon imperative—that there be explicit language in the Treaty guaranteeing that no Americans could ever fall under the Court's sway, even if the only way to accomplish that was going to be by the U.S. not joining the treaty. . . . Clearly, they had their instructions from back home—and very little room to maneuver.[40]

Most of the world's countries were, however, more willing than the United States to be subject to the international rule of law. Even the United States' most powerful European allies, who had also participated in military "humanitarian" interventions, were far more friendly to the idea of the court than was the United States. The reasons for such differences were no doubt complex, but among them was the fact that since World War II European countries had been moving from the tradition of individual sovereignty toward "European" institutions transcending nationhood. One example of this was the adoption of the European Convention on Human Rights (1950) and the subsequent empowerment of a European Court of Human Rights. Ambassador Scheffer issued a public plea on July 15:

> [W]e stand on the eve of the conference's conclusion without having found a solution. We fear that governments whose citizens make up at least two-thirds of the world's population [chiefly China and the U.S.] will find the emerging text of the treaty unacceptable. The world desperately needs this mechanism for international justice, but it must be a community, not a club.[41]

The final draft document for an international criminal court was distributed early on July 17 by Chairman Kirsch. It appeared to offer more to the sixty or so like-minded countries that favored a strong court than it did to the United States. The draft provided for obligatory jurisdiction of the court upon ratification of the treaty by a country for the crime of genocide, crimes against humanity, war crimes, and the crime of aggression. The United States was willing to accept obligatory jurisdiction only for the crime of genocide. Jurisdiction over war crimes was limited by a new draft article allowing states that signed the Rome statute to opt out of the court's jurisdiction over war crimes for a period of seven years following the creation of the court. Consistent with its objective of blocking the creation of an institution that it could not control, or whose jurisdiction it could not veto, the United States sought a comprehensive opt-out provision that would allow it to be permanently exempt from the court's jurisdiction over war crimes. France agreed to support the draft proposal when the seven-year opt-out provision was added. The United Kingdom also supported the draft.

The United States again voiced its opposition to a criminal tribunal in essence beyond its control in the Committee of the Whole on July 17, when it offered an amendment to the proposal. India offered amendments that would have made use of nuclear weapons a war crime and limited the power of the Security Council over the court. Norway, however, moved to table the proposed amendments, and its motions were adopted. The vote against taking up the U.S. amendment was 113-17. The United States could not even muster the support of its closest allies. In the final conference plenary session, the United

States demanded a vote on the draft treaty. The Russian federation joined France and the United Kingdom in voting for the statute, leaving China and the United States as the only permanent Security Council members in opposition. Israel also voted against the draft, in part because it made the relocation of a civilian population in an occupied territory a war crime, a provision too close for its comfort. Iraq, Libya, Qatar, and Yemen also voted against.

The conference came to an end just before its scheduled deadline of midnight. The United States was clearly the big loser. The final vote was 120 countries for the treaty, with 7 against. As approved, the court would exercise its jurisdiction over individuals suspected of treaty crimes if the country where the alleged violation occurred or the country of which the accused was a national was a party to the treaty (Article 12). States would accept the jurisdiction of the court on a case-by-case basis. The United States strongly opposed these provisions because it might—as the United States had feared all along—subject American troops to prosecution for alleged crimes committed in countries that had accepted the jurisdiction of the court, without first requiring the consent of the U.S. government.

Most countries felt that there were sufficient safeguards in the treaty to address U.S. concerns. The new court would only take cases involving major human rights violations carried out as part of a plan, policy, or widespread practice, not actions by individuals acting on their own. The court would act only when the appropriate domestic jurisdictions were unable or unwilling to deal with alleged crimes themselves.

Early on, the United States had favored a proposal that would have charged the Security Council with referring cases to the court, in part so the U.S. veto in the council could be used to protect U.S. citizens from prosecution. Most countries, however, eventually supported the compromise initially put forth by Singapore that would allow the Security Council to defer a case for a period of twelve months, with the possibility of extension. The United States eventually accepted this proposal, a version of which was included in the final draft.

The draft called for a prosecutor with independent power to investigate and initiate prosecutions, as well as for the initiation of cases by a state party or by referral of the Security Council. The United States had fought hard against an independent prosecutor, but a strong and independent prosecutor was one of the fundamental requirements of the sixty or so like-minded countries. The draft statute did call for a court review panel that would have the power to reject cases arising from an abuse of prosecutorial power, but that safeguard was not enough to satisfy the United States.

The draft provided for jurisdiction over internal armed conflicts, such as in Bosnia, which most delegations, including the United States, believed to be absolutely essential for a credible international court. It also included among war crimes and crimes against humanity the crimes of rape, sexual slavery, enforced prostitution, forced pregnancy, and enforced sterilization. Aggression was made a treaty crime, but it was left to be defined at later preparatory meetings. This decision was a concession to the members of the Non-Aligned Movement, but the draft did not include the prohibition of nuclear weapons, which the movement also strongly supported. The draft left out chemical and biological weapons, as a concession to several Arab countries.

If the Rome statute is ratified by at least sixty nations, the new International Criminal Court will be located at The Hague in the Netherlands, where the ad hoc tribunal for the former Yugoslavia is located. The treaty was opened for signatures July 18, 1998, through December 31, 2000. As of July 4, 2001, 139 countries had signed it, and 36 had ratified it.[42]

The rift between the United States and its major European allies over the creation of the court widened and deepened after the Rome conference. Current signatories to the statute include Austria, Belgium, Canada, Denmark, France, Germany, Italy, the Netherlands, Norway, Spain, Sweden, and the United Kingdom. Completed ratifications include Austria, Belgium, Canada, Denmark, Finland, France, Germany, Italy, New Zealand, Norway, South Africa, Spain, and Sweden (of the thirty-six ratifications to date). The United Kingdom began its process for ratification in December, and by late March 2001 it appeared that all fifteen members of the European Community would soon ratify the treaty.

Although Europeans, like the Americans, put their troops in harm's way as peacekeepers in global hot spots, the general consensus among Europeans seems to be that the principle of complementarity protects them from unwanted or unwarranted international prosecution. U.S. government officials have been unwilling to put their trust in this principle thus far. If this pattern continues, the ICC will be added to a growing list of issues on which the United States and its European friends significantly disagree, among them U.S. dominance of NATO, U.S. exports to Europe, capital punishment, and U.S. attempts to revise the 1972 Anti-Ballistic Missile Treaty so it can develop a national missile defense system. The most recent differences have been over the efforts of EU members to create a rapid-reaction military force independent of NATO.

In June 2000 the PrepCom sought to finish work on the rules of evidence and procedure that would be used by the international court and to complete specifications for the elements of the crimes recognized by the Rome statute. The U.S. representatives at the June PrepCom sought to exempt from prosecution service personnel from countries that do not ratify the treaty. When a December PrepCom meeting ended, the United States still had not prevailed, but it left a proposal on the table that would require a "rigorous review of the admissibility of a case before any individual is in fact surrendered to the court."[43] The United States had until December 31 to sign the Rome statute, otherwise it would have been barred from further participation in PrepCom meetings.[44] The United States signed the treaty on December 31, 2000.

The ICC at the Turn of the Century

UN secretary-general Kofi Annan hailed the adoption of the Rome statute as a "giant step forward."[45] One of the proponents of U.S. participation in the court has argued that

> America does not commit genocide, war crimes, or crimes against humanity. Nor do our NATO allies… We thus have nothing to fear from the prosecution of these offenses, nothing to make us hesitate when the pleas of the victims of mass slaughter fill our television screens and their plight hounds our conscience.[46]

Further, should American troops cross the line, the principle of complementarity would protect them from international prosecution so long as the United States took action against them.[47] Nonetheless, others disagreed. One opponent called the treaty "a pernicious and debilitating agreement, harmful to the national interests of the United States."[48] On July 23, 1998, Ambassador Scheffer spoke at a hearing before the Senate Foreign Relations Committee and outlined the U.S. objections to the Rome statute. The four main concerns of the United States were as follows:

- that U.S. military personnel could be brought before the ICC prosecutor;
- the degree of Security Council control over prosecutions initiated by the ICC prosecutor;
- the ambiguity of the crimes over which the ICC would exercise jurisdiction, particularly the crime of aggression, which could conceivably extend to some U.S. troop deployments, and the alleged crime of settlement in an occupied territory, which would arguably implicate Israeli leaders for activities in the West Bank and the Gaza Strip;
- the relationship between the ICC and national judicial processes.[49]

Not only did Republican senators Helms and Rod Grams of Minnesota praise Scheffer's remarks, but so did Democratic senators Joseph Biden of Delaware and Dianne Feinstein of California. Republicans and Democrats alike on the committee congratulated Scheffer's resolve to protect U.S. interests in Rome and expressed their contempt for the ICC as created by the Rome statute.[50] At the hearing, Senator Helms made his position clear: the United States should block any organization in which it is a member from providing funding to the ICC; renegotiate its status of forces agreements and extradition treaties to prohibit treaty partners from surrendering U.S. nationals to the ICC; refuse to provide U.S. soldiers to regional and international peacekeeping operations when there is any possibility that they will come under the jurisdiction of the ICC; and never vote in the Security Council to refer a matter to the ICC.[51]

These concerns about protecting individual members of the U.S. armed forces may have been a stalking horse for another, broader concern. At the end of the hearing, "Helms picked off the examples defiantly, he was going to be damned if any so-called International Court was ever going to be reviewing the legality of the U.S. invasions of Panama or Grenada or of the bombing of Tripoli and to be holding any American presidents, defense secretaries, or generals to account."[52] Still by early August 1998, more than twenty editorials and op-eds had run in U.S. newspapers broadly supporting the creation of the ICC. One of the treaty's defenders argued that the United States had managed to have powerful national security safeguards added to the treaty:

First, Rome provides for "complementarity," the idea that the primary responsibility for enforcing the law of war must remain with each nation-state and with national military justice systems. . . . On another point of concern, the Rome Statute provides complete protection for sensitive national security information. . . . Isolated incidents of military misconduct that occur in wartime will not be prosecuted by the court. Rather, the tribunal is charged to focus on war crimes committed "as part of a plan or policy" or as part of "a large-scale commission of such crimes." . . . The Rome Statute also respects our bilateral treaty agreements protecting American troops stationed abroad against any attempted exercise of foreign criminal jurisdiction—the so-called Status of Forces Agreements.[53]

Countering the pro-ICC forces, on the op-ed page of the *Financial Times* Senator Helms wrote, "We must slay this monster. Voting against the International Criminal Court is not enough. The US should try to bring it down."[54] Another opponent suggested the treaty's wording would have found the United States guilty of war crimes for the bombing campaigns against Germany and

Japan during World War II.[55] Others raised the possibility of international prosecution for air strikes such as those against Libya in 1986 and Sudan in 1998.[56]

Controversy continued over who was to receive blame for genocide and other war crimes, and what to do after such crimes had occurred. On June 14, 2000, Senator Helms introduced the American Service Members Protection Act (S. 2726), which would prohibit U.S. officials from cooperating with the ICC. That same day, Majority Whip Tom DeLay, R-Texas, introduced the measure in the House of Representatives (H.R. 4654). It mandated that the president ensure that any Security Council resolution authorizing a peacekeeping operation exempt U.S. personnel from prosecution before the ICC. Additionally, it required the president to certify to Congress that U.S. personnel are immunized by each country participating in the operation. The bill proposed that no U.S. military assistance be provided to governments party to the ICC (with the exception of the United States' NATO allies and Israel), though this provision could be waived by the president. With these "big sticks," Senator Helms denounced "the ICC's bogus claim of jurisdiction over American citizens."[57]

In July 2000, a seven-member panel created by the Organization of African States issued a report blaming Belgium, France, the United States, the Catholic Church, and the UN Security Council for the 1994 slaughter of more than 500,000 Tutsis and moderate Hutus by more radical, xenophobic Hutus during the Rwandan civil war. Canadian panel member Stephen Lewis said the United States knew what was going on in Rwanda but prevented the Security Council from deploying an effective force to stop it, because of the political fallout that ensued after eighteen Americans were killed in the Somalia intervention in October 1993. As Lewis said, "It's simply beyond belief that because of Somalia hundreds of thousands of Rwandans needlessly lost their lives. I don't know how Madeleine Albright lives with it."[58]

Also in July 2000, U.S. military personnel figured prominently in two criminal trials. In the murder trial of three Serbs accused of killing two ethnic Albanians in Kosovo, the U.S. Army requested the Yugoslavian court to drop the charges against the Serbs. The army said it had discovered that the two Kosovars had been killed by U.S. troops. In the case of one of the deceased, the army said U.S. troops fired back in self-defense after first being fired upon, which was permitted under their rules of engagement. In the case of the other decedent, however, justification for U.S. actions was far less clear-cut. It was reported that the second Kosovar fled the scene and was killed by a pursuing U.S. soldier, who fired multiple shots through the door of the shed where the man was trying to hide.[59]

In the second case, involving the death of an ethnic Albanian girl in Kosovo, a U.S. soldier formerly assigned to peacekeeping duty in Kosovo pled guilty to charges of murder, forcible sodomy, and three counts of indecent acts with a child before a U.S. military court in Germany.[60] The event played into the hands of those who argued that U.S. troops are just as likely to commit such crimes as are the troops of other states. Because of complementarity, however, this case would not have fallen under the jurisdiction of the ICC if the court had been in operation, because it was prosecuted by U.S. authorities. In fact, for a case to be tried by the ICC over the wishes of the United States,

> the United States would have to be so biased that it could not evaluate the question of international crime, had no intention of investigating the claim, or was investigating only to protect an individual. The seriousness with which the modern U.S. military justice system treats international humanitarian law makes this a virtual impossibility in the case of a military investigation.[61]

Despite the protection complementarity offered the United States and other nations, Senator Helms wanted to leave nothing to chance. On November 29, 2000, his spokesman held a press conference at UN headquarters in New York. There he said Helms would make passage of the American Service Members Protection Act a top priority in the Congress convening in January 2001. On that same day, a letter signed by a dozen former U.S. foreign policy officials was released, supporting Helms's bill; it claimed that U.S. world leadership "could be the first casualty" of the new ICC.[62] Among the signatories were former secretaries of state James Baker, Henry Kissinger, and George Shultz and former U.S. ambassador to the UN Jeanne Kirkpatrick. As writer James Carroll concluded in the *Boston Globe*, "That James Baker is a party to the Helms campaign signals that an incoming [George W.] Bush administration would prefer to be shackled by a xenophobic Congress than to be constrained by multilateral and equitable agreements with other nations."[63] About a month after the letter was published, another of its signatories, Donald Rumsfeld, was named President-elect Bush's nominee for secretary of defense. With Rumsfeld's nomination, the Defense Department's opposition to U.S. involvement with the ICC could be expected to continue.

December 31, 2000, was the last day for states to become signatories of the original treaty. President Clinton instructed Ambassador Scheffer to sign it on behalf of the United States. In a press release, Clinton noted that he still had concerns about "significant flaws" in the treaty, but he hoped that they could be overcome in subsequent negotiations prior to the court becoming a reality.

He said it was important to sign it to "reaffirm our strong support for international accountability. . . . With signature, we will be in a position to influence the evolution of the court. Without signature, we will not."[64] Reaction to the U.S. signing was swift. Human rights groups praised it. Richard Dicker, associate counsel of Human Rights Watch, said Clinton's action had "offered the hope of justice to millions and millions of people around the world by signaling United States' support for the most important international court since the Nuremberg tribunal." On the other hand, Senator Helms warned that the president's "decision will not stand."[65]

While the United States continues to negotiate its preferences into the ICC treaty, the United Nations has convened ad hoc tribunals to deal with recent conflicts. In 2000, it began organizing courts to try former Khmer Rouge leaders for war crimes in Cambodia in the 1970s and to try those responsible for crimes committed against civilians in the nine-year-old civil war in Sierra Leone.[66] Until the ICC treaty is ratified by sixty states and goes into operation, ad hoc tribunals will remain the international forums for trying war criminals.

Conclusion: Americans and International Law

Israeli diplomat Abba Eban once said international law was "the law which the wicked do not obey and the righteous do not enforce." Whether the United States has lined up on the side of the wicked or of the righteous in this case probably lies in the eye of the beholder.

There is no question that U.S. political culture values the rule of law; Presidents Bush and Clinton saw reliance on international law as a mainstay of the post–cold war era. Clinton wanted to use international law to punish war criminals and those guilty of genocide and crimes against humanity, and he said so when he endorsed the creation of the ICC in his UN General Assembly address in September 1997. Yet by the time of the Rome conference the following summer, U.S. diplomats were swimming against the international tide by trying to ensure some degree of U.S. control over the ICC or its prosecutor. The inability to prevail on this issue produced the final vote that placed the United States in the somewhat unusual company of China, Iraq, Israel, Libya, Qatar, and Yemen. What accounts for this seeming about-face? The U.S. Congress.

In 1946, prominent senators ensured that the World Court would not act contrary to U.S. interests, as defined by the United States. Congressional emphasis on U.S. national sovereignty at the expense of international law, the United Nations, and a host of NGOs reappeared in the ICC case. Once powerful legislators staked out the priority of preserving U.S. sovereignty, the nature of policy making on the issue changed for the Clinton administration. The question was no longer whether the United States could agree with its friends and allies on an important issue in international law, but whether any set of procedures could be found that could assure Senate ratification of the treaty. Only time will tell, but the prospects for U.S. support of the ICC arguably worsened in 2001 with the inauguration of George W. Bush, who opposes the ICC. Still, the prospects of international criminal tribunals continue to be enhanced by events on the ground. In June 2001, former Yugoslav president Slobodan Milosevic was extradited to The Hague for trial before the International Criminal Tribunal for the Former Yugoslavia for war crimes and crimes against humanity. Days later the Bosnian Serb government expressed its willingness to surrender to that same tribunal Radovan Karadzic and Ratko Mladic, the most notorious Bosnian Serb leaders, who have been indicted on charges of genocide.

Notes

1. John T. Rourke, Ralph G. Carter, and Mark A. Boyer, *Making American Foreign Policy*, 2d ed. (Guilford, Conn.: Brown and Benchmark, 1996), 87.

2. Sir Arnold Duncan McNair, *The Development of International Justice* (New York: New York University Press, 1954), 4.

3. George Schwarzenberger, *International Law, as Applied by International Courts and Tribunals* (London: Stevens and Sons, 1986), 4:138.

4. Ian Brownlie, *Basic Documents in International Law*, 4th ed. (Oxford: Clarendon Press, 1995), 446. Reservations are legal statements of the conditions under which parties will agree to a treaty. Often during a debate over the ratification of a treaty, states will declare in advance certain circumstances under which they say a treaty will not apply to them or their actions. Accepting these conditions is the political cost of getting that state to agree to the treaty. Obligatory jurisdiction means that states are "obliged" to obey a court's jurisdiction. With obligatory jurisdiction, the states cannot deny that a court has jurisdiction in a case or matter. Through reservations, states can set the terms and conditions under which they will accept a court's jurisdiction.

5. M. Cherif Bassiouni, "From Versailles to Rwanda in Seventy-Five Years: The Need to Establish a Permanent International Criminal Court," *Harvard Human Rights Journal* 10 (1997): 11–62; Gerhard von Glahn, *Law among Nations: An Introduction to Public International Law* (New York: Macmillan, 1992), 878.

6. Von Glahn, *Law among Nations*, 880.

7. John E. Findling, ed., *Dictionary of American Diplomatic History*, 2d ed. (New York: Greenwood Press, 1989), 260.

8. Bassiouni, "From Versailles to Rwanda," 34.

9. Findling, *Dictionary of American Diplomatic History*, 259.

10. Von Glahn, *Law among Nations*, 354–357.

11. Michael P. Scharf, *Balkan Justice: The Story behind the First International War Crimes Trial since Nuremberg* (Durham, N.C.: Carolina Academic Press, 1997), 13–15.

12. *Congressional Record*, August 1, 1946, 10618.

13. Von Glahn, *Law among Nations*, 615–616.

14. *Congress and the Nation*, vol. 1, *1945–1964* (Washington, D.C.: Congressional Quarterly, 1965).

15. John T. Rourke, Ralph G. Carter, and Mark A. Boyer, *Making American Foreign Policy* (Guilford, Conn.: Dushkin Publishing Group, 1994), 209–210.

16. Von Glahn, *Law among Nations*, 192.

17. Scharf, *Balkan Justice*, 15.

18. Bassiouni, "From Versailles to Rwanda," 55–56.

19. Ibid., 43.

20. Ibid., 46–47.

21. "ABCs of ICC," 1998, http://www.iccnow.org.

22. Anne-Marie Slaughter, "Memorandum to the President," in *Toward an International Criminal Court?* ed. Alton Frye (New York: Council on Foreign Relations, 1999), 7.

23. "ABCs of ICC," 1998.

24. James Bone, "U.S. Seeks to Limit War Crimes Court," *Times*, March 30, 1998.

25. More information on these issues can be found at the Web site of the NGO Coalition for an International Criminal Court, http://www.iccnow.org.

26. Human Rights Watch, "Establishing an Effective International Criminal Court," 1998, http://www.iccnow.org.

27. Jimmy Carter, "For an International Criminal Court," *New Perspectives Quarterly* 10 (1997): 52–53.

28. David Scheffer, "An International Criminal Court: The Challenge of Enforcing International Humanitarian Law," address to the Southern California Working Group on the International Criminal Court, February 26, 1998, http://www.iccnow.org.

29. Agence France-Presse, "Paris, Washington in Agreement on UN Genocide Court," April 4, 1998.

30. John R. Bolton, "Why an International Court Won't Work," *Wall Street Journal*, March 30, 1998; John M. Goshko, "A Shift on Role of UN Court? Envoy Suggests U.S. May Alter Demands on Proposed Tribunal," *Washington Post*, March 18, 1998; Barbara Crossette, "U.S. Budges at U.N. Talks on a Permanent War-Crimes Court," *New York Times*, March 18, 1998.

31. Senate Committee on Foreign Relations, "Helms Declares UN Criminal Court 'Dead on Arrival' without U.S. Veto," press release, March 26, 1998.

32. Eric Schmitt, "Pentagon Battles Plans for International War Crimes," *New York Times*, April 14, 1998.

33. Siddharth Varadarajan, "Imperial Impunity: US Hampers World Criminal Court Plan," *Times of India*, April 23, 1998.

34. *New York Times*, June 15, 1998, A1.

35. "A New World Court," *Economist*, June 13–19, 1998, 16.

36. Bertram S. Brown, "The Statute of the ICC: Past, Present, and Future," in *The United States and the International Criminal Court: National Security and International Law*, ed. Sarah B. Sewall and Carl Kaysen (Lanham, Md.: Rowman and Littlefield, 2000),

62. Donald Jackson was an accredited correspondent at the Rome conference. Statements not otherwise attributed in this section are based either on direct observation or on contemporaneous conversations with conference participants, NGO representatives, or journalists.

37. UN press release, L/ROM/11, June 17, 1998.

38. Alessandra Stanley, "U.S. Presses Allies to Rein in Proposed War Crimes Court," *New York Times,* July 15, 1998, http://www.nytimes.com.

39. Lawrence Weschler, "Exceptional Cases in Rome: The United States and the Struggle for an ICC," in Sewall and Kaysen, *The United States and the International Criminal Court,* 91.

40. Ibid., 105.

41. David Scheffer, press release distributed at the conference, July 15, 1998.

42. "U.S. Signs Treaty for World Court to Try Atrocities," *New York Times,* January 1, 2001, http://www.nytimes.com. See also http://www.iccnow.org/rome/html/ratify.html, for state parties to the Rome statute.

43. NGO Coalition for an ICC listserv, December 12, 2000, http://www.iccnow.org; listserv: icc-info@egroups.com.

44. "U.S. Gains a Compromise on War Crimes Tribunal," *New York Times,* June 29, 2000, http://www.nytimes.com.

45. "Permanent War Crimes Court Approved," *New York Times,* July 18, 1998, http://www.nytimes.com.

46. Kenneth Roth, "Speech One: Endorse the International Criminal Court," in Frye, *Toward an International Criminal Court?* 31–32.

47. Ibid., 31.

48. John Bolton, "Speech Two: Reject and Oppose the International Criminal Court," in Frye, *Toward an International Criminal Court?* 37.

49. Slaughter, "Memorandum to the President," 8.

50. Weschler, "Exceptional Cases in Rome," 110.

51. Michael Scharf, "Rome Diplomatic Conference for an International Criminal Court," *ASIL Insight,* June 1998, http://www.asil.org.

52. Weschler, "Exceptional Cases in Rome," 111.

53. Ruth Wedgwood, "Speech Three: Improve the International Criminal Court," in Frye, *Toward an International Criminal Court?* 63–64.

54. "Personal View: Jesse Helms," *Financial Times,* July 31, 1998.

55. Bolton, "Speech Two: Reject and Oppose the International Criminal Court," 39–40.

56. William L. Nash, "The ICC and the Deployment of U.S. Armed Forces," in Sewall and Kaysen, *The United States and the International Criminal Court,* 156.

57. NGO Coalition for an ICC, August 29, 2000, http://www.cicclegal@iccnow.org; United Nations Association—USA, June 20, 2000, http://www.unausa.org/dc/info/dc062000.

58. "U.S., Others Blamed for Not Halting Slaughter in Rwanda," *Dallas Morning News,* July 8, 2000, 21A.

59. "Judge: U.S. Troops Admitted Killings," *Dallas Morning News,* July 22, 2000, 19A.

60. "Soldier Pleads Guilty in Albanian Girl's Death," *Dallas Morning News,* July 30, 2000, 28A.

61. Sarah B. Sewall, Carl Kaysen, and Michael P. Scharf, "The United States and the International Criminal Court: An Overview," in Sewall and Kaysen, *The United States and the International Criminal Court*, 10–11.

62. *New York Times*, January 1, 2001, http://www.nytimes.com/2001/01/01/world/01COUR.html.

63. James Carroll, "How Helms Is Sparking a Real Crisis," *Boston Globe*, December 5, 2000, A23.

64. "U.S. Signs Treaty for World Court to Try Atrocities," *New York Times*, January 1, 2001, http://www.nytimes.com.

65. "War Crime Pact OK'd by Clinton," *Dallas Morning News*, January 1, 2001, 10A.

66. "U.N. Compromises on Prosecutor," *Dallas Morning News*, May 25, 2000, 20A; and "U.N. to Create Special Court for Sierra Leone War Crimes," *Dallas Morning News*, August 12, 2000, 26A.

Conclusion

Ralph G. Carter

The case studies here illustrate the array of external challenges and opportunities, substantive issues, internal political situations, and policy-making dynamics likely to confront U.S. foreign policy makers in the post–cold war world. While each of these fifteen cases offers a unique perspective on policy making, patterns can be discerned in the internal and external policy-making environments.

On the Outside: Shifts in External Challenges

Foreign policy is made by those who act in the name of the state, and they do so in relation to the external and internal environments faced by a government. Although the idea of viewing "the state as an actor in a situation" may be a forty-year-old idea, it continues to be a helpful one.[1] The external environment could be an opportunity to seize upon a situation or to solve a problem. How foreign policy makers react to external situations often depends on the internal environment. Different policy makers bring different perspectives to the situation. Why they get involved in a situation makes a difference, and how their preferences correspond to those of the people, opinion makers, and the media plays a major role in decision making.

The cold war era was dominated by the politics of national security. To U.S. policy makers, the Soviet threat overrode all other foreign policy issues. Persistent images of a relentless enemy and the potentially catastrophic costs of a policy mistake typically led administration officials to neither seek nor encourage input from others who might know less about the external situation.[2] While some perceived that presidential policy-making preeminence ended with the Vietnam War,[3] there seemed little question that the situation changed at the end of the cold war. Without the threat of nuclear annihilation looming over policy discussions, reasonable people could disagree about what the United States should do in foreign affairs.[4] So in the post–cold war period, the external situation neither stifles foreign policy debate nor deters the participation of potential policy-making actors. While during the cold war many "realists" seemed to think that only the external environment mattered, there now seems little question that the external and internal political situations significantly influence U.S. policy makers.

In the post–cold war era, new, less traditional external challenges and opportunities confront U.S. foreign policy makers. Nuclear proliferation in Asia, genocidal civil wars in the Balkans and Africa, the violent suppression of nationalist movements in the Middle East and Asia, financial crises in East Asia, terrorism against U.S. citizens at home and abroad, drug smuggling from Latin America, and global environmental degradation are a few such examples. Other situations are more positive, like the structuring of beneficial trade relations, helping people and states through multilateral assistance, and creating new cooperative international institutions to handle complex problems. For U.S. policy makers, the difficult questions are whether the United States should respond to a given situation, and if so, how?

On the Inside: The New Foreign Policy Challenges

The answers to such questions are usually found in the internal political situations facing U.S. policy makers. As James Scott summed it up, "A changing agenda and increasing interdependence and transnational ties make foreign policy making more like domestic policy making: subject to conflict, bargaining, and persuasion among competing groups within and outside the government."[5] This statement echoes a remark by President Bill Clinton: "The more time I spend on foreign policy . . . the more I become convinced that there is no longer a clear distinction between what is foreign and domestic."[6] During the cold war, the president and his advisers directed foreign policy, but in the post–cold war era members of Congress and other powerful groups have become highly visible actors in the process. There are now numerous actors clamoring to act in the name and best interest of the United States.

Interbranch Leadership: Presidential-Congressional Interactions

In the post–cold war period, some actions remain clearly presidential, such as ordering missile strikes on targets associated with Usama Bin Laden. In other instances, Congress seems to be calling the tune, such as in establishing Cuba policy through the Helms-Burton Act, funding the V-22 Osprey, rejecting the Comprehensive Test Ban Treaty, and telling the president not to consider sending the Kyoto Protocol or the International Criminal Court treaty to the Senate for ratification.

Today it seems that presidents and members of Congress openly vie for influence over policy issues, with each branch doing its best to shape the outcome. The possible results of this so-called interbranch leadership include cooperation, constructive compromise, institutional competition, and confrontation and stalemate.[7] All four of these variants are illustrated by the cases in this volume. For example, the Colombian drug case reflects institutional cooperation, the International Monetary Fund case illustrates constructive compromise, the V-22 case shows institutional competition, and the Comprehensive Test Ban Treaty illustrates confrontation and stalemate.

Each branch of government uses direct and indirect tactics to accomplish its goals. Direct tactics reflected here include members of Congress introducing legislation to change U.S. policy (as in the Bosnia and Helms-Burton cases), presidents using the military (as in the Kosovo and Bin Laden cases), and initiating diplomatic negotiations (as in the India-Pakistan and International Criminal Court cases). Sometimes, when both branches want to "frame" issues in a favorable way, indirect tactics are chosen. Thus from President Clinton's point of view, Plan Colombia was not about getting the United States into another Vietnam War, but protecting Americans from the ravages of illegal drugs. Similarly, from Sen. Jesse Helms's point of view, the Comprehensive Test Ban Treaty and the International Criminal Court were not about the United States being a responsible member of the international community, but about threats to U.S. sovereignty. Once issues are framed in the negative, as in the latter case, no one wants to be seen as supporting them. The executive and legislative branches try to anticipate the reaction of the other, whether it is an administration trying to gauge Senate tolerance of a treaty (such as the Comprehensive Test Ban Treaty and Kyoto Protocol) or Congress testing how far it can diverge from an administration's policy preference without prompting a presidential veto (as in the cases of the Arms Control and Disarmament Agency and the International Monetary Fund).

New Influences: The Societal Actors

Government officials do not act in a political vacuum. They are the targets of interest group representatives, who usually believe that their interests are identical to those of the collective nation (as in the cases of the V-22 and hormone-injected beef exports to Europe). The media reports on politics, and how the news is reported can sway public opinion (for example, in the cases of

East Timor and Bosnia). The public's opinion is then used to impress a policy preference on policy makers (as with Bosnia and the Comprehensive Test Ban Treaty). Opinion leaders try to have their desired policy enacted (as regarding funding of the IMF and acceptance of the Kyoto Protocol). Even within an administration, experts will at times work against the policy preferences of the president, like the military officers who balked at going into Bosnia or the directors of nuclear weapons labs who wanted to keep conventional nuclear testing as an option in the Comprehensive Test Ban case.

Different Stimuli: Underlying Causal Factors

Governmental and non-governmental actors often disagree on foreign policy issues because they respond to different stimuli. Issues are often framed differently.[8] One person's "new Vietnam in Colombia" is another person's "war on drugs." At other times agreement can be reached on the definition of an issue but not on the policy solution. For example, nuclear proliferation concerns virtually everyone. Key foreign policy makers in the Clinton administration thought the Comprehensive Test Ban Treaty was a good policy for combating the spread of nuclear weapons. Many senators, however, thought the treaty was too risky, so the votes necessary for ratification could not be found. As the product of a political process, foreign policy is influenced by what government officials think they should do—enact good policy or garner institutional prestige and stature—and what they think they must do—address the potential preferences of citizens and voters.[9]

Sometimes these differences are simply the products of partisanship and ideology. In the late 1940s and early 1950s, politics stopped "at the water's edge."[10] The last two decades, however, have brought increasingly ideological partisanship to foreign affairs.[11] The 1998 IMF funding crisis provides a stark example. The issue in the House of Representatives came down to whether the IMF was part of the problem—a conservative Republican view—or part of the solution—the view of liberal Democrats. This ideological divide shows no signs of narrowing anytime soon.

Looking to the Future

Each case in this collection touches on the unifying theme that the U.S. foreign policy–making process is becoming more open, pluralistic, and partisan. More and more governmental and non-governmental actors are getting involved for various reasons. As foreign policy becomes increasingly "intermestic" and more like domestic policy, reasonable people can be expected to disagree and try to shape policy based on their own values and attitudes. Without the overriding fear of global annihilation, there seem to be few reasons for congressional and other societal actors to defer to the president or other officials of the executive branch. These other actors bring their ideas, attitudes, passions, ideological beliefs, and partisanship with them as they try to affect policy making. The short-term trends do not look promising as the foreign policy process continues to become more political.

The internal situation that President George W. Bush faced in 2001 provides an interesting illustration of the challenges likely to face U.S. presidents into the near future. Like other former governors elected to the presidency, Bush came into office with little foreign policy experience, as did his predecessor, Bill Clinton. The comparison of the two stops there, however. Clinton was widely acknowledged as a "policy wonk," someone who immersed himself in the details of policy. With the exception of relying at times on Vice President Al Gore, Clinton was not known for policy delegation. He wanted to make decisions and initially sought appointees who would follow his lead, such as Anthony Lake as national security adviser, William Cohen as defense secretary, and William Christopher as secretary of state.

During his campaign for the presidency, Bush promised to run the administration like the chief executive officer of a major corporation. As CEO, he promised to set broad strategies and then delegate to others the job of actualizing the goals established. Thus he sought "experts" who would be loyal to him but who, within the administration, would press for their preferred policies. Many of those chosen to serve in top positions were veterans from prior Republican administrations.[12] According to one close observer, "There has been a special effort to get really good people who sometimes disagree with each other. They are strong-willed people who might well create sparks in the inner circle."[13]

With a more open and pluralistic foreign policy–making process, those who oppose the president's policy preferences will seek to exploit any internal divisions within the administration. Members of Congress, interest groups, nongovernmental organizations, and media pundits will seek to find policy allies in the Bush administration. It will be interesting to see to what degree officials' loyalties to the president outweigh their occasional differences with his policy preferences. President Bush will have to find policy positions that feel right to him, and then he will have to convince the country that his policy prescriptions are best for the nation.

Bush's relations with Congress will be more difficult than for most new presidents. The November 2000 elections produced a slim Republican majority in the House of only eleven seats, and a tenuous 50-50 partisan split in the Senate allowed Republican control of the chamber only by virtue of the tie-breaking vote of the vice president.[14] When Vermont senator James Jeffords defected from the Republican Party to become an Independent in June 2001, the Republicans' narrow margin in the Senate disappeared, as Democrats regained control of that chamber for the first time since January 1995.[15] Democratic leaders gained control of the Senate's policy agenda, and as important, if not more so, Republicans lost their chairmanships. The Democrats took control of the agendas and activities of committees, the most influential being Foreign Relations, Appropriations, Armed Services, and Select Intelligence. The change in Senate control will put pressure on the Bush administration to shift its foreign policy agenda toward a more centrist position on issues like national missile defense, global environmental challenges, and working with international organizations. If the White House adopts a more centrist position, House Republican leaders will be in a bind. They will have to decide whether to support their president or to seek ideological consistency with past, more conservative policy preferences.

In general, post–cold war presidents can be expected under the best of circumstances to have difficulties with Congress regarding foreign policy. As a noted congressional scholar argues,

> The Constitution establishes a fluid decision process that cannot ensure a creative governmental response to issues that confront the country. The system of separation of powers, with its checks and balances, works to constrain the enactment of public programs. Partisanship (embodied in divided or unified government), the responsiveness of government to electoral considerations, the character of congressional organization, and the quality and commitment of presidential leadership conspire in distinctive ways to create a policy process prone to delay and deadlock.[16]

In such an environment, anything controversial will complicate policy making and lessen the president's ability by weakening his credibility. The multiple scandals that plagued the Clinton administration undermined Clinton's ability to act by diverting his energy to managing the scandals. As illustrated by a number of the cases in this volume, at times the attention of the president and other top officials in his administration was distracted from policy making. Scandals not only disrupted the normal policy-making process, they also gave

Clinton's opponents additional ammunition in opposing administration initiatives by discrediting his leadership.

George W. Bush will not be immune to controversy. His presidency is the product of a controversial election. His opponent, Al Gore, won the popular vote, while Bush won the electoral college vote. When a president wins fewer popular votes than his opponent, there are bound to be questions about the legitimacy of the victory. Some observers feel that electoral irregularities in Florida and a hotly contested Supreme Court decision allowed the Republicans to "steal" the election. Bush narrowly prevailed in a contest marked by allegations of improprieties involving vote counts, recounts, and the denial of voting rights. In the words of Congressional Black Caucus chair Eddie Bernice Johnson, D-Texas, "There is overwhelming evidence that George W. Bush did not win this election."[17] To dramatize her point, she led the members of the caucus in walking out of the joint session of Congress when Florida's electoral votes were certified. The controversy surrounding Bush's declared victory hampered his ability to work with congressional Democrats early in his administration.

Another point of controversy for the incoming administration was its corporate ties. Liberals, populists, and others perceived the administration as a tool of big business. When critics reflected on the oil industry backgrounds of President Bush and Vice President Dick Cheney and they saw former heads of major corporations like Alcoa (Secretary of the Treasury Paul O'Neill) and Searle (Secretary of Defense Donald Rumsfeld) in the cabinet, they questioned whose interests the administration would represent. Such concerns were voiced when the president announced his national energy policy. Initially, it was widely reported that the focus would be on producing energy, not on conserving it. Consequently, the oil industry backgrounds of both the president and vice president were widely rehashed in the media.[18]

As the twenty-first century dawns, U.S. foreign policy making continues to grow more pluralistic, partisan, and political. The good news is that U.S. foreign policy is becoming representative of more organized interests and points of view and more democratic. The bad news for policy makers is that the road to foreign policy enactment and successful implementation shows signs of becoming an increasingly bumpy ride. To paraphrase Winston Churchill's seafaring analogy, democracies are like rafts—they are virtually unsinkable, but they proceed slowly and one's feet always get wet. In this more open process, post–cold war foreign policy making will almost always be slower in the making but hopefully surer in its outcomes.

Notes

1. See Richard C. Snyder, H. W. Bruck, and Burton Sapin, "The Decision-Making Approach to the Study of International Politics," in *International Politics and Foreign Policy*, ed. James N. Rosenau, rev. ed. (New York: Free Press, 1969), 199–206.

2. See Richard Melanson, *American Foreign Policy since the Vietnam War*, 2d ed. (Armonk, N.Y.: M. E. Sharpe, 1996).

3. See Thomas Franck and Edward Weisband, *Foreign Policy by Congress* (New York: Oxford University Press, 1979); and Ralph G. Carter, "Congressional Foreign Policy Behavior: Persistent Patterns of the Postwar Period," *Presidential Studies Quarterly* 16, no. 2 (spring 1986): 329–359.

4. See James M. Scott and A. Lane Crothers, "Out of the Cold: The Post-Cold War Context of U.S. Foreign Policy," in *After the End: Making U.S. Foreign Policy in the Post–Cold War World*, ed. James M. Scott (Durham, N.C.: Duke University Press, 1998), 1–25.

5. James M. Scott, "Interbranch Policy Making after the End," in Scott, *After the End*, 401.

6. In Ralph G. Carter, "Congress and Post–Cold War U.S. Foreign Policy," in Scott, *After the End*, 129–130.

7. Scott and Crothers, "Out of the Cold," 11.

8. James M. Lindsay, *Congress and the Politics of U.S. Foreign Policy* (Baltimore: Johns Hopkins University Press, 1994).

9. For more on congressional policy motivations, see R. Douglas Arnold, *The Logic of Congressional Action* (New Haven: Yale University Press, 1990); Aage Clausen, *How Congressmen Decide* (New York: St. Martin's Press, 1973); Richard F. Fenno, *Congressmen in Committees* (Boston: Little, Brown, 1973); and John W. Kingdon, *Congressmen's Voting Decisions*, 3d ed. (Ann Arbor: University of Michigan Press, 1989).

10. See Carter, "Congressional Foreign Policy Behavior."

11. Carter, "Congress and Post–Cold War U.S. Foreign Policy," 128.

12. For more information on Bush's nominees, see the collection of stories available through the *New York Times* at http://www.nytimes.com.

13. Bruce Buchanan, University of Texas at Austin political science professor, quoted in the *Financial Times*, January 8, 2001, 22.

14. The congressional partisan breakdown can be found at http://clerkweb.house.gov/mbrcmtee/stats.htm.

15. *New York Times*, May 24, 2001, http://www.nytimes.com; CNN, May 24, 2001, http://www.cnn.com.

16. Leroy N. Rieselbach, "It's the Constitution, Stupid! Congress, the President, Divided Government, and Policymaking," in *Divided Government: Change, Uncertainty, and the Constitutional Order*, ed. Peter F. Galderisi (Lanham, Md.: Rowman and Littlefield Publishers, 1996), 129.

17. *Dallas Morning News*, January 14, 2001, 11A.

18. For example, see *Washington Post*, May 20, 2001, A3; *Newsday*, May 20, 2001, B1; and *U.S. News & World Report*, May 21, 2001, 29.

Appendix

Key Actors

Chapter 1   East Timor: Reluctant Support for Self-Determination

Carlos Belo   Roman Catholic bishop of East Timor and human rights advocate, co-recipient of the 1996 Nobel Peace Prize

Bill Clinton   President, supporter of close U.S.-Indonesian ties

East Timor Action Network (ETAN)   The New York–based grassroots network of activists and principal lobby supporting East Timorese self-determination

Russell Feingold   Senator, D-Wis., leading congressional advocate of restricting U.S. military ties to Indonesia

Amy Goodman   Freelance American reporter and human rights activist, survived the 1991 Dili massacre

B. J. Habibie   Indonesian president Suharto's handpicked successor (1998–1999), allowed East Timor's 1999 referendum for independence

Allan Nairn   Freelance American reporter and human rights activist, survived the 1991 Dili massacre

Jose Ramos-Horta   De facto East Timorese foreign minister and chief pro-independence spokesman, co-recipient of the 1996 Nobel Peace Prize

Suharto   Authoritarian president of Indonesia from 1965 to 1998, ordered the 1975 invasion of East Timor

United States–Indonesia Society   Principal pro-Indonesia lobby, backed by Indonesian and U.S. business interests

Chapter 2   Public Opinion and Bosnia: Anticipating Disaster

Madeleine Albright   U.S. ambassador to the United Nations, favored a multilateral interventionist policy on Bosnia to address internal conflicts

Warren Christopher   Secretary of state, wanted to keep foreign policy from interfering with Clinton's domestic agenda

Bill Clinton   President, desired a stop to the killing in Bosnia but felt the constraints of public opinion and allied governments

Anthony Lake   National security adviser, favored U.S. action on Bosnia to stem ethnic cleansing

Dick Morris   Political consultant, favored resolving the Bosnia problem before the 1996 presidential election campaign went into high gear

Colin Powell   Chairman of the Joint Chiefs of Staff, opposed extensive intervention in Bosnia for fear that it would become a quagmire

Chapter 3   The War in Kosovo: Coercive Diplomacy

Madeleine Albright   Secretary of state, favored the immediate threat of significant military force to compel Serbian president Slobodan Milosevic to agree to end repression of ethnic Albanian Kosovars

Samuel Berger   National security adviser, sought to protect the domestic and international interests of President Bill Clinton and consequently opposed immediate threats to use force in Kosovo

Bill Clinton   President, sought a policy solution to the situation in Kosovo that would prevent a humanitarian catastrophe and domestic political costs

William Cohen   Secretary of defense, reluctant to use military force in Kosovo unless U.S. policy had clear and limited objectives supported by the American public

Richard Holbrooke   Ambassador, believed that both the threat of air strikes and the deployment of U.S. troops as peacekeepers would be necessary to end the conflict in Kosovo

Slobodan Milosevic   Serbian president, sought to use events in Kosovo to protect and enhance his control over Serbia

Henry Shelton   Chairman of the Joint Chiefs of Staff, opposed the use of U.S. troops in the Balkans and believed that air strikes were not likely to be effective against Serbian actions in Kosovo, supported the continued use of economic sanctions and diplomacy to constrain Milosevic

Chapter 4   The Colombian Drug Trade: National Security and Congressional Politics

Dan Burton   Representative, R-Ind., wanted Colombia to receive a national security waiver in 1996 and 1997 to allow U.S. assistance to be disbursed despite Colombia's being denied certification as a partner in the war on drugs, supported more aid to the Colombian national police

Bill Clinton   President, wanted to shift drug policy to make it more balanced between demand and interdiction

Ben Gilman   Representative, R-N.Y., supported more aid to the Colombian national police

Dennis Hastert   Speaker of the House, R-Ill., strong proponent of additional military aid to Colombia

Jesse Helms   Senator, R-N.C., critic of aid to Colombia because of corruption in the Colombian government

Patrick Leahy   Senator, D-Vt., advocate of including human rights provisions in foreign aid bills

Barry McCaffrey   Retired U.S. Army general, head of the White House Office of National Drug Control Policy, advocate for a supply-side approach to combat drug smuggling

Andrés Pastrana   Colombian president, struggled to regain confidence of the United States, devised the Plan Colombia to deal with Colombia's drug and guerrilla problems

Ernesto Samper Pizano   Colombian president, plagued by allegations of ties to drug traffickers through Cali cartel contributions to his electoral campaign

Paul Wellstone   Senator, D-Minn., advocate of human rights in Colombia

Chapter 5   The Demise of the Arms Control and Disarmament Agency: Arms Control Politics

Madeleine Albright   Second secretary of state in the Clinton administration, managed the process of merging the Arms Control and Disarmament Agency (ACDA) into the State Department

Warren Christopher   First secretary of state in the Clinton administration, originated the post–cold war plan to merge the ACDA into the State Department, but later disavowed the idea

Bill Clinton   President, 1993–2001, oversaw the ACDA's merger into the State Department, argued for Senate consent to the Chemical Weapons Convention

Tom Daschle   Senate minority leader, D-S.D., participated in finalizing the agreement to merge ACDA into the State Department

Dwight Eisenhower   President, 1953–1961, initiated the institutionalization of arms control, although with limited success

Jesse Helms   Senator, R-N.C., chairman of the Foreign Relations Committee, ardently supported merging the ACDA into the State Department

John Holum   Last director of ACDA, 1993–1999, opposed merging the ACDA into the State Department

Hubert Humphrey   Senator, D-Minn., "father of the ACDA"

John Kennedy   President, 1961–1963, supported and signed the ACD Act creating the ACDA in 1961

John Kerry   Senator, D-Mass., handled on behalf of the Clinton administration the negotiations with Senator Helms that led to the merger of the ACDA with the State Department

Trent Lott   Senate majority leader, R-Miss., participated in finalizing the agreement to merge the ACDA into the State Department

Chapter 6   India and Pakistan: Newest Members of the Nuclear Club

Bill Clinton   President, condemned the testing in May 1988 of nuclear devices by India and Pakistan, approved the imposition of U.S. economic sanctions against these two countries and encouraged other countries to also impose sanctions

George Fernandes   Indian defense minister, caused an international and domestic uproar by identifying China as the primary threat to India

Jesse Helms   Senator, R-N.C., chairman of the Foreign Relations Committee, strongly condemned the Indian government for testing nuclear devices in May 1998, supported the imposition of economic sanctions

Gohar Ayub Khan Pakistani foreign minister, criticized the international community for ignoring the nuclear aspirations of India

Nawaz Sharif Pakistani prime minister, approved the testing of nuclear devices a few weeks after India had done so

George Tenet Director of the Central Intelligence Agency, asked retired admiral David Jeremiah, former vice chairman of the Joint Chiefs of Staff, to oversee a review panel investigating the failure of the intelligence community to warn of India's plans to test nuclear devices

Atal Bihari Vajpayee Indian prime minister, approved the testing of nuclear devices in May 1998

Chapter 7 Rejection of the Comprehensive Test Ban Treaty: The Politics of Ratification

Joseph Biden Senator, D-Del., ranking Democrat on the Foreign Relations Committee and a passionate advocate of the Comprehensive Test Ban Treaty, chastised and taunted Sens. Trent Lott, R-Miss., and Jesse Helms, R-N.C., for blocking consideration of the treaty

Bill Clinton President, the first world leader to sign the CTBT, push for the Senate to ratify the treaty fell nineteen votes short

Tom Daschle Senate minority leader, D-S.D., pushed for consideration of the CTBT in the summer of 1999 and scrambled to avoid a final vote the following fall

Byron Dorgan Senator, D-N.D., strong supporter of the CTBT, threatened to bring Senate business to a standstill unless the treaty was placed on the agenda

Jesse Helms Senator, R-N.C., used his power as chairman of the Foreign Relations Committee to block formal consideration of the CTBT for almost two years

Jon Kyl Senator, R-Ariz., worked quietly behind the scenes with Sen. Paul Coverdell, R-Ga., to line up enough Republican votes to defeat ratification of the CTBT

Trent Lott Senate majority leader, R-Miss., used his control over the Senate agenda to block consideration of the CTBT for almost two years and then forced Democrats to accept a truncated schedule for hearings, a floor debate, and a final vote

Arlen Specter Senator, R-Pa., one of four Republican senators who voted in favor of ratification, joined forces with Senator Biden on several occasions to promote the CTBT

John Warner Senator, R-Va., chairman of the Armed Services Committee and opponent of the CTBT, joined forces with Sen. Daniel Patrick Moynihan, D-N.Y., in an effort to delay consideration of the treaty until 2001

Chapter 8   The Clinton Administration's Strikes on Usama Bin Laden: Limits to Power

Samuel Berger National security adviser, the principal adviser to Clinton regarding the strikes on Bin Laden

Usama Bin Laden Islamist believed to have orchestrated the bombings of the U.S. embassies in Nairobi, Kenya, and Dar es Salaam, Tanzania

Bill Clinton President, principal decision maker for the missile strikes on Bin Laden

James Risen Reporter for the *New York Times*, raised questions about the legitimacy of the strikes on the al-Shifa plant in Sudan

George Tenet Director of the Central Intelligence Agency, delivered key intelligence to the White House linking Bin Laden to the attacks on U.S. embassies

Tim Weiner Reporter for the *New York Times*, raised questions about the legitimacy of the strikes on the al-Shifa plant in Sudan

Chapter 9   The V-22 Osprey: Pure Pork or Cutting-Edge Technology?

Richard Cheney Secretary of defense, opposed the Osprey for four years on the basis of affordability

David S. C. Chu Head of the Pentagon Office of Program Analysis and Evaluation, proposed the cancellation of the V-22 to Cheney

Pete Geren Representative, D-Texas, a staunch advocate of the Osprey, elected from the district that is home to Bell Helicopter's V-22 plant

Curt Weldon Representative, R-Pa., the fiercest proponent of the Osprey, elected from the district that is home to Boeing's V-22 plant

Chapter 10   The U.S.-EC Beef Hormone Dispute and U.S. Trade Strategy

Charlene Barshefsky   U.S. trade representative, committed to balancing the goals of U.S. access to European Community markets with good U.S.-EC relations

Leon Brittan   EC trade commissioner, EC counterpart to the U.S. trade representative, committed to balancing European interests with good U.S.-EC relations

Bill Clinton   President, tried to balance U.S. trade interests with larger U.S.-EC relations

Dan Glickman   Agriculture secretary, committed to opening the EC market to U.S. beef exports

National Cattlemen's Beef Association   Producers interest group that supported the use of growth-promoting hormones in beef and advocated the opening of the EC market to beef exports

Office of the United States Trade Representative   Administrative body charged with enforcing fair trade laws and negotiating with trading partners

U.S. Meat Export Federation   Interest group that supported a retaliatory strategy against the European Community

Chapter 11   The Helms-Burton Act: Congress and Cuba Policy

Brothers to the Rescue   Group that sponsored two planes shot down by the Cuban air force over the Florida Straits, an incident that changed the fortunes of the Helms-Burton Act

Dan Burton   Representative, R-Ind., co-sponsor of the Helms-Burton Act

Bill Clinton   President, initially opposed Helms-Burton but agreed to sign the bill after the downing of the Brothers to the Rescue planes

Cuban American National Foundation   Interest group that strongly supported the U.S. embargo against Cuba and lobbied for Helms-Burton

Lincoln Diaz-Balart   Representative, R-Fla., Cuban American sponsor of Helms-Burton and one of the leaders of the move to codify the U.S. embargo against Cuba

Bob Graham   Senator, D-Fla., supporter of Helms-Burton and sponsor of the Cuban Democracy Act of 1992

Jesse Helms   Senator, R-N.C., co-sponsor of Helms-Burton and initiator of the legislation

Ileana Ros-Lehtinen   Representative, R-Fla., Cuban American supporter of Helms-Burton

Robert Torricelli   Representative, D-N.J., supporter of Helms-Burton and sponsor of the Cuban Democracy Act of 1992

Chapter 12   Sino-American Trade Relations: Privatizing Foreign Policy

Amnesty International   Non-governmental organization, opposed the Clinton administration policy of engagement with China based on Beijing's ongoing political repression of dissidents

Bill Clinton   President, an advocate of engagement and normalized trade relations with China

General Motors Corporation   The largest U.S.-based automaker, proponent of normalized trade relations with China, involved since 1997 in a joint venture with Shanghai Automotive Industry Corporation

Human Rights Watch   Non-governmental organization whose annual reports highlighted ongoing political repression in China despite closer economic relations with the United States

Jiang Zemin   Chinese president, an economic reformer who sought closer economic relations with the United States

Qualcomm Corporation   A San Diego–based business, proponent of normalized trade relations with China, partnered with two Chinese companies to modernize the country's telecommunications network

John Sweeney   AFL-CIO president, an outspoken opponent of normalized trade relations on the basis of Chinese trade restrictions, the country's human rights record, and the potential loss of jobs in the United States

United Methodist Church   Issued a report condemning the Chinese government's crackdown on religious freedom and opposing closer Sino-American trade relations

U.S.-China Business Council   An industry-based group strongly in favor of engagement

Chapter 13   The Kyoto Protocol on Climate Change: A Balance of Interests

George Bush   President (1989–1993), successful in ensuring that the Rio Earth Summit did not include binding limits on the reduction of greenhouse gases

George W. Bush   President (2001–), campaigned on the promise of reducing carbon dioxide emissions but later reversed his stance, proclaimed that the United States would not abide by the Kyoto Protocol

Business Council for Sustainable Development   A group of forty-eight major corporations calling for pollution taxes as well as tax credits for clean industries

Robert Byrd   Senator, D-W. Va., helped lead the opposition to limits on U.S. emissions of greenhouse gases, co-sponsored the Byrd-Hagel resolution expressing Senate opposition to any agreement at Kyoto that would place limitations on developed countries without similar limitations on developing countries

Bill Clinton   President (1993–2001), supported the Kyoto Protocol, which called for binding limits on the reduction of greenhouse gases

Environmental Defense Fund   Supported the Kyoto Protocol

Global Climate Coalition   A coalition of twenty-five corporations and eighteen major trade associations opposed to the Kyoto Protocol

Chuck Hagel   Senator, R-Neb., helped lead the opposition to limits on U.S. emissions of greenhouse gases and co-sponsored the Byrd-Hagel resolution

Bob Kerrey   Senator, D-Neb., tried to fashion a compromise between the Clinton administration and opponents of Kyoto in the Senate

U.S. Chamber of Commerce   Opposed the Kyoto Protocol

World Wildlife Fund   Supported the Kyoto Protocol

Chapter 14   Funding the IMF: Congress versus the White House

Dick Armey   House majority leader, R-Texas, favored limiting International Monetary Fund allocations and attaching conditions

Joseph Biden   Senator, D-Del., supported the Clinton administration's request for IMF funding without conditions and worked with Sen. Charles Hagel, R-Neb., to craft a compromise for funding with limited conditions

Alan Greenspan   Chairman of the Federal Reserve Board, advocated the IMF funding package proposed by the Clinton administration

Chuck Hagel   Senator, R-Neb., supported IMF funding and crafted a compromise to provide the full administration package with limited conditions

Jon Kyl   Senator, R-Ariz., offered an amendment to limit IMF funding and impose strong conditions

Trent Lott   Senate majority leader, R-Miss., favored limiting IMF funding and attaching strong conditions

Robert Rubin   Secretary of the Treasury, the administration's chief advocate and spokesperson for IMF funding without conditions

Christopher Smith   Representative, R-N.J., sought to attach anti-abortion restrictions to IMF funding

Chapter 15   The International Criminal Court: Present at the Creation?

Bill Clinton   President, unexpectedly ordered Ambassador David Scheffer to sign the International Criminal Court treaty on the last day to be considered an original signatory

Jesse Helms   Senator, R-N.C., chairman of the Foreign Relations Committee, an early and active opponent of U.S. participation in the ICC

International Law Commission   Produced the first draft statute for an international criminal court

Like-minded countries   A group of about sixty countries, including Canada, most of Europe, and many countries in Africa, Asia, and Latin America, that at the Rome conference argued for a stronger international court and an independent prosecutor

PrepCom   The preparatory committee established by the United Nations in 1996 to work out the details of an international criminal court

David Scheffer   Ambassador at-large for war crimes, led the U.S. effort to modify the ICC treaty so the United States would have some control over the Court's future actions

Index